D1524091

OXFORD STUDIES IN AFRICAN AFFAIRS

General Editors
JOHN D. HARGREAVES *and* GEORGE SHEPPERSON

AN ECONOMIC HISTORY OF
CENTRAL NIGER

AN
ECONOMIC HISTORY
OF
CENTRAL NIGER

BY
STEPHEN BAIER

WITHDRAWN

CLARENDON PRESS · OXFORD
1980

Oxford University Press, Walton Street, Oxford OX2 6DP
OXFORD LONDON GLASGOW
NEW YORK TORONTO MELBOURNE WELLINGTON
KUALA LUMPUR SINGAPORE JAKARTA HONG KONG TOKYO
DELHI BOMBAY CALCUTTA MADRAS KARACHI
NAIROBI DAR ES SALAAM CAPE TOWN

© *Stephen Baier 1980*

Published in the United States by Oxford University Press, New York

British Library Cataloguing in Publication Data

Baier, Stephen
An economic history of central Niger.
– (Oxford studies in African affairs).
1. Niger – Economic conditions
I. Title II. Series
330.9'66'2601   HC547.N5   79-41134

ISBN 0-19-822717-5

*Typeset by Oxprint Ltd, Oxford
Printed in Great Britain by J. W. Arrowsmith Ltd, Bristol*

Contents

FOR JANE

Acknowledgements

I WOULD like to express my gratitude to all those who helped in the completion of this study. First mention must go to the people of Damagaram, whose patience, co-operation, and hospitality made it possible. Most of those who gave their time so willingly are listed in the bibliography, and many of them took an active interest in historical research. Muhamman Kane, the eldest of the Zinder traders in 1972, was especially helpful, as was Lawan Sidi. Mato Sarki, who accompanied me on most of the interviews and introduced me to many people, provided invaluable assistance. An expression of gratitude is also due to the numerous Nigérien government officials whose warm welcome was much appreciated. Dioulde Laya and Insa Garba of the *Centre Nigérien des Recherches en Science Humaines* and Issaka Dankousou of the *Centre Régional de Documentation pour la Tradition Orale* gave me much valuable assistance in Niamey. André Salifou kindly provided drafts of some of his unpublished material. I would also like to thank Professor Abdullahi Smith of the Department of History at Ahmadu Bello University for his help during my stay in Nigeria, and John Collins of the Department of Politics for his hospitality.

This work was completed in two stages, first as a doctoral thesis at the University of Wisconsin–Madison in 1974. Many people gave me much in the way of valuable advice and criticism which helped in the completion of the thesis. Jane Baier devoted a good deal of time to early drafts, and her assistance in archival research was also very much appreciated. I am grateful to Dennis Cordell for his reading of parts of the thesis and for our many interesting conversations on the history of Sahelian Africa. Ann Dunbar, whose research on nineteenth-century Damagaram prepared the way for this study, offered useful suggestions on material related to the thesis. Steven Feierman and Peter Lindert made many helpful suggestions for revision. I am especially indebted to Philip Curtin, whose advice and encouragement on countless occasions had a profound influence on the course of my work.

The expansion and revision of my work after the completion of the thesis owe much to the encouragement and advice of others. A. G. Hopkins read the manuscript and made many helpful and constructive suggestions. I am also indebted to Paul Lovejoy, Ralph Austen, David Northrup, Kristin Mann, and Fred Cooper who read and commented on my work. I learned much from Paul Lovejoy and David J. King in collaborative writing projects, and material in the first chapter of this book draws upon articles which Paul Lovejoy and I co-authored. I would like to thank my colleagues at Boston University, especially Sara Berry, John R. Harris, and Allan Hoben, who read and critiqued early drafts, related material, or chapters of the manuscript.

Finally I owe a debt of gratitude to numerous archivists and librarians in London, Paris, Dakar, Niamey, Kaduna, Madison, and Boston, and to Martha Older and Ronnie Conner, who typed the final manuscript.

A generous grant from the Fulbright-Hays programme made overseas research possible, and funds from the Ford Foundation supported me when the thesis was being written. A grant from the Boston University graduate school helped pay for the costs of typing the final manuscript.

List of Tables

List of Maps

List of Abbreviations

ADZ	Archives du Département de Zinder
AMS	Archives Militaires de Zinder
ANF-AE	Archives Nationales de France, Ministère des Affaires Étrangères, Paris
ANF-OM	Archives Nationales de France, Ministère d'Outre-Mer, Paris
ANN	Archives Nationales du Niger, Niamey
ANS	Archives Nationales du Sénégal, Dakar
ASTa	Archives de la Subdivision de Tanout
ASTe	Archives de la Subdivision de Tessaoua
BCEHSAOF	*Bulletin du Comité d'Études Historiques et Scientifiques de l'Afrique Occidentale Française*
Bull. IFAN	*Bulletin de l'Institut Fondamentale de l'Afrique Noire*
CNRSH	Centre Nigérien des Recherches en Sciences Humaines
NNAK	Nigerian National Archives, Kaduna
PRO	Public Record Office, London
SEDES	Société d'Études pour le Développement Economique et Sociale
SEVPEN	Service d'Edition et de Vente des Publications de l'Education Nationale
USNA	United States National Archives, Washington

Tape citations refer to interviews recorded in Hausa (except for three recorded in French) in the Baier Collection, on deposit at the African Studies Association Center for African Oral Data, Archives of Traditional Music, Indiana University, Bloomington, Indiana, and at the Centre Régional de Documentation pour la Tradition Orale, Niamey, Niger.

Introduction

A THEME of general importance in the economic history of West Africa is a shift in the direction of contact with the world economy, from trans-Saharan trade, which came into existence more than a millenium ago, to southern routes of access connecting to Atlantic seaborne trade. This process of transition began with the arrival of the Portuguese in the late fifteenth century, but at first maritime trade affected only a small area near the coast. As time passed coastal trade drew larger regions into the Atlantic economy, principally as suppliers of slaves for distant plantations. Contact with the international economy began again on a new basis in the nineteenth century and accelerated with the colonial occupation. For a time the old desert trade coexisted with maritime trade, and caravan trade lasted longest along the Sahel, the southern shore of the desert, in the Central and Eastern Sudan — the area best protected from the competition of cheap maritime freight rates.[1]

The drought of 1969–73 in the West African Sahel has underscored the need to understand the impact of intensifying contact between arid regions and the outside, especially because of the suspicion prevalent among planners and administrators that the quickening pace of change has upset a precarious balance between nature and human activities. The economic history of the Sahel is an indispensable element in grasping these problems, and modern history must begin with the transition from desert to maritime routes of access. For centuries North African merchants living in expatriate communities south of the desert had sold trans-Saharan imports and assembled local products and slaves for export to North Africa and Europe. Operating in networks which sometimes joined and sometimes remained separate from external trade, local long-distance traders channelled salt, dates, and animals from the desert and returned grain, gold, cloth, and articles manufactured from wood and leather. At the end of the nineteenth century these interregional and intercontinental commercial systems linked the Central Sudan, a term used here to refer to the area which is now central and eastern Niger and northern Nigeria, with areas as far away as Tripoli in the north, Lagos in the south, the middle Volta basin to the west, and Borno (Bornu) to the east. But the nature and direction of contact with the outside changed radically with colonial rule, especially when the railway to Kano was completed in 1911.

The purpose of this book is to trace the economic history of central Niger, a portion of a larger desert-edge region, over a period when the railway displaced desert caravans and the shift from northern to southern routes of access intensified; when trade of live-stock for internal West African markets increased rapidly; and when a peasant export economy took root. It will follow the inter-play of the local economy and outside forces beginning about 1850, though some previous history will be included as background material, and it will trace economic change until the end of the colonial period.

This book is intended to fill a number of gaps in the existing litera-ture, the first of which is a lack of treatment of the impact of trans-Saharan trade on the Sahel. Trans-Saharan trade has attracted the attention of many historians who have been able to mine an exten-sive array of travellers' accounts and other contemporary documents reflecting the interest of European nations and North African states in desert trade and the economic potential of the Sudan. An early and by now classic study by E. W. Bovill first appeared in 1933, was revised extensively in 1958, and was updated by Robin Hallett a decade later.[2] A. Adu Boahen examined British exploration of the desert, efforts to end trans-Saharan slave trade, and attempts to promote trade with the Sudan, and he presented much useful information on the conditions of commerce in the early and middle nineteenth century.[3] A major study of Morocco by J.-L. Miège included a thorough treatment of trans-Saharan trade on the western routes.[4] Boahen's belief that the volume of trade was in decline in the nineteenth century came under close scrutiny in an article by C. W. Newbury, and Newbury's general conclusion about the decline of trans-Saharan trade has been further revised by Marion Johnson with new information on Tripoli–Kano trade.[5]

Yet these major studies fail to cover the impact on sub-Saharan Africa of trans-Saharan trade and its ending. In fact, histories of trans-Saharan trade in the nineteenth century skirt this issue almost completely, except to echo the truism first voiced by nineteenth-century abolitionists that the slave trade was damaging to Sudanic Africa. One exception is an article by Louis Brenner on the role of the North African community in the Central Sudan, but he concentrates on the middle nineteenth century when European travellers' accounts were plentiful.[6] Another exception is an excellent paper by Marion Johnson on caravans between Tripoli and Kano in the final decades of trade; but the wealth of materials for this study from the northern terminus contrasts with the relative paucity of sources from the southern end. This touches upon the first of two reasons why historians have been preoccupied with the European and North African side of trans-Saharan trade, namely the wealth of written European sources and the dearth of material on the involvement of African societies in trans-Saharan trade.[7]

The second reason for the imbalance is the lack of full-scale economic study of a region of the West African Sahel in the nineteenth century which would provide the background necessary for an understanding of the role of external trade in African economies, and would also establish a base line from which change in the colonial period could be measured. Philip Curtin has written a major economic history of the Senegambia in the three centuries which preceded colonial rule, but his interests and findings differ from those of the present study in several important ways.[8] Although he examines relations between internal and external trade, he does so for an earlier period than will be considered here, and his study is mainly concerned with the effects of involvement in the Atlantic slave trade. While he wrote on an area which faced both Atlantic and desert outlets, coastal influences became predominant early in the period he studied, and hence he concentrated on coastal rather than desert-edge history.

The neglect of Sahelian history has precluded comprehensive treatment of the climatic history of the area. What is needed is not merely chronologies of famine and prosperity, but a history of human adaptation to climatic change. Local socio-economic systems and indigenous response to drought must be understood as a basis for rational development planning. At the time of writing donor agencies from many industrial nations were preparing to spend vast sums of money on a variety of projects. While efforts have been made to discover how cultural and social factors affect economic life in the Sahel, most such studies would benefit from an added historical dimension. Certain key economic structures become apparent only after examining historical change as related to climatic fluctuations. In addition economic history demonstrates that considerable growth and change have taken place and that economic progress can be defined in broad enough terms to include a role for indigenous institutions.

Perhaps the most serious omission in the modern economic history of West Africa is the lack of treatment of commerce in the goods of internal demand in the twentieth century. A. G. Hopkins has called attention to the importance of studying relations between external commerce and production and trade for domestic markets. The only extensive treatment of internal commerce to date is found in a thesis by Paul Lovejoy on kola trade between the Hausa states and the upper Volta basin. Lovejoy's pioneer study provided much useful information on the subject, as did his article on trade between the Sokoto Caliphate and Yorubaland; but he was primarily interested in the pre-colonial period. Jan Hogendorn has described the initiative and resourcefulness of Hausa traders engaged in the production and trade of groundnuts for export in the early twentieth century, but he defined the scope of his study to exclude detailed treatment of domestic commerce.[9]

Although this study touches on events as early as about 1800 and as late as 1960, it concentrates on the decades before the colonial occupation in 1899 and in particular on the early colonial period. The main consideration in the choice of the period for study was the constraint of available source material as discussed below. Within these limits, a focus on the period between 1870 and 1940 has an advantage in that it is possible to follow several shifts in the relative importance of production for internal and external markets, as the volume of trade destined for overseas markets first increased, then declined, and increased once again. These changes in production affected local merchants, cultivators, and ruling élites, and this study follows the responses of these groups through the colonial period. The juxtaposition of pre-colonial and colonial history is an essential element in the approach of this study. Pre-colonial history provides a knowledge of social, political, and economic adaptation to the constraints of the desert-edge environment. This approach makes it possible to understand the persistent features of the environment and their impact on society and economy, and to view change during the colonial period as an overlay which either ran counter to or accentuated deeper, long-term processes of change. Furthermore, colonial economic history has an importance of its

own, especially in light of frequently repeated yet inaccurate statements in general histories about the economic impact of colonial
rule in Africa. And finally the juxtaposition of colonial and pre-
colonial history serves a crucial historiographical purpose. Any
information about a society inevitably affects the historian's
approach to the past, since new questions can be asked of historical
data and new concepts can be framed. Hence it is possible to work
backwards and to allow knowledge about the recent past to inform
the study of more remote eras.

The choice of a geographical area for the study was partially
determined by my own experience in Niger but also by other considerations. Trans-Saharan trade to the Central Sudan lasted longer
than desert trade on routes farther west, so that sources of all kinds
are relatively plentiful. In addition the volume of trade crossing the
ecological frontier at the desert edge was high, and this large flow of
trade made it possible to collect a wealth of oral data which revealed
shifts in trade and production for both domestic and external
markets.

This study focuses on central Niger and in particular on
Damagaram, a pre-colonial state with its capital in the walled city of
Zinder, and also on Damergu, a region of the Sahelian fringe north
of Damagaram. But the intention is to understand events and processes in Damagaram and Damergu in the context of the larger
region to which they belonged as well as in the perspective of more
general themes of the long-term history of the area. For the sake of
convenience this study uses the term Central Sudan to designate an
economic region between the Chad Basin and the Niger with an
agricultural and manufacturing centre in Kano, Katsina, and Zaria
and a desert extension northward toward the Aïr Mountains, and
a secondary centre in the Sokoto-Rima valley with its northern
adjunct in the steppe of Adar. This was in short the area which
became the Sokoto Caliphate, along with adjacent steppe and
desert to the north.

There are two main justifications for seeking a wider geographical context for the history of central Niger. First, as this study
demonstrates, the volume of trade in animals, foodstuffs, raw and
finished products, minerals, labour, and enterpreneurial talent
within the region and especially across the ecological frontier was
great enought to draw most areas of the Central Sudan into this
regional economy. Second, because the environmental determinants of Sahelian history are broadly similar from Senegal to Wadai,

and because relations between pastoral and sedentary people had a determining impact on many Sahelian regions, the main themes of Damagaram's history, though not its detail, are shared elsewhere. In keeping with the interest in desert-edge history, this study will concentrate on the northern sector of the Central Sudan. By the end of the nineteenth century areas of Borgu, Nupe, and northern Yorubaland had important economic links with the Sokoto Caliphate, but the southern side of the Central Sudan economy will remain beyond the scope of this study.

The third and final reason for seeking a larger geographical context is that the history of central Niger has to take account of events in a north—south corridor which cuts across the African continent, extending from Tripoli in the north to Lagos on the Atlantic coast. Tripoli and Lagos, the two end-points for different kinds of economic and cultural contact, symbolize two main themes in the history of the Nigérien Sahel. The Mediterranean port stands for trans-Saharan trade, which remained for centuries the main avenue of access to the world beyond Africa. These commercial contacts fed slaves, gold, ivory, and more mundane products north across the desert in return for cloth, luxury products, hardware, and a variety of European manufacturers; but they also brought a world religion and the chance to participate in Islamic civilization. Lagos, on the other hand, was the end point of trade in animals and potash from Damagaram for a brief period before the turn of the century, and it stands for the integration of Damagaram into a wide variety of domestic West African markets and trading systems.

In the search for historical sources an effort has been made to balance oral and archival information. One particularly satisfying aspect of historical research in Africa is the possibility of developing an interplay between oral and archival sources, so that each informs the other. Early colonial French archives for the Zinder *cercle* and some territorial correspondence are located in Zinder, and the result of finding decentralized archives was that the interaction of these two different types of sources was possible on a daily basis. For example, an archival report might mention a name in passing, in itself a nearly useless piece of information. But the mere mention of a name often jogged the memory of certain informants and provoked a lengthy discourse on the person, his activities, and related events. Similarly information from oral testimony might otherwise remain obscure without background from archival reports, which were useful because they often revealed a radically different point of view.

During field research oral evidence was subjected to the same kind of critical scrutiny that historians normally apply to documentary sources. This involved cross-checking, testing informants to see if they knew what I already knew, looking for synchronisms between written and oral information, and a critical examination of informants' motives and the social context of their testimony.

For reasons which I only partially understand, the sources for an economic history of Damagaram are far better for the early colonial period than for more recent times. For the period of about 1903 to 1922, when the territorial capital was at Zinder, substantial parts of the total correspondence have survived and are to be found in the Zinder archives, while later records, especially those of the Zinder *cercle*, which are especially useful sources for economic history, have largely been lost. The volume and quality of oral data is also skewed towards the early twentieth century. The reluctance of younger merchants to be interviewed accounts for this, and their attitude is explained by current jealousies and rivalries and by the possibility that some of their activities may be deemed illegal should the central government learn of them. Merchants active in the early twentieth century, on the other hand, were for all intents and purposes retired when I spoke to them. They had time to talk and as elderly persons a perspective far different from their younger counterparts, and a genuine interest in telling the stories of their lives and having them recorded.

In an attempt to write a comprehensive economic history of an area for which sources are limited, it is necessary to use existing material creatively. The emphasis on commerce in the following pages stems not from a superficial capitalist ideology − a position which would value the exploits of merchants as innovators and heroes of private enterprise − but from an assessment of the type of economy found in the Sahel. In a desert-edge region the distinction between the trading economy and the total economy seems less valid than for other areas of Africa. Because trade based on the complementary production of different ecological zones was common, the trading economy involved most segments of the population, rural and urban, and all ethnic groups. The emphasis of this study was thus a conscious choice, and it also turned out to be a practical necessity when conducting field research. What little archival information was available reflected the preoccupation of the colonial government with production for overseas export and with the collection of taxes, and it left untouched vast areas of activity on the part of Africans. Without doubt oral data could be generated for many of these activities, but interviewing is not an ideal way of learning about gradual change in the past, since often informants are not clear about the time a gradual process began or ended. But in the case of migration or travel for trade this was not the case, because movement from one place to another or journeys to exotic new places were remembered. And finally commerce provided a good index of historical change in other sectors. Shifts in trade for local, regional, West African, or overseas markets mirrored changes in productive activity in agriculture, stock breeding, and local craft industries. I decided that intensive studies of any of these sectors were not likely to change the over-all picture to any great extent.

This study concentrates on the market sector of the economy because this approach permits an understanding of large-scale historical change—a summary of the principal trends. But the use of oral histories of merchants has another advantage in that it permits historical analysis at the level of the African firm. Once again the commercial sector has been chosen for detailed study, this time because commerce was the only activity in which profits were great enough to allow enterprises to expand to include people outside the immediate families of producers. This focus on indigenous enterprises, aside from balancing the history of larger trends and forces, permits a study of how African firms increased the scale of their undertakings. It also provides an entirely new perspective on the plight of African entrepreneurs under colonial rule, the degree to which certain opportunities and activities were blocked to them, and their response to the colonial situation. The history of the firm, and the use of oral data in general, has the advantage of placing colonial policy in its proper perspective; what colonial rulers said was often far different from what they did. The only sure way of unravelling these differences is to take account of the point of view of the people being ruled.

Interviews conducted in Niger in 1972 were recorded on tape and placed on deposit at the *Centre Régional de Documentation en Tradition Orale*, Niamey, and the Archives of Traditional Music, Indiana University, Bloomington. Access is open to the public, and it is hoped that in the future researchers can make use of these sources. I conducted these open-ended interviews in Hausa, except in three cases, when French was spoken. Tapes have been left untranslated because researchers working in the area would have to know French and Hausa in any case. I worked with Mato Sarki, an assistant who was present during interviews to correct my Hausa and was also present when I took notes on taped conversations to provide background information and to translate answers which I could not understand.

CHAPTER I

Central Sudan Society and Economy

THIS chapter provides background material on the Central Sudan and its people and seeks to develop a framework of analysis for the history of a desert-edge region. The presentation attempts to strike a balance between information on the desert and the savannah. But particular emphasis is given to the role of the desert because until now it has been studied less thoroughly than the savannah. The economic history of the region must take account of both sectors, the influence of one on the other, and modes of interaction between the two.

The theoretical work of Frederik Barth on relations between pastoral and sedentary people serves as a point of departure.[1] Barth argues that the initial emphasis should be placed on types of production rather than on groups of people, and that both productive regimes, the pastoral and the sedentary, should be analysed within a common perspective in much the same way an economist examines the component sectors of an economy. This approach permits an analysis of the impact of productive regimes on relations of dependence, dominance, and stratification. Barth also emphasizes differences in capital formation in the two regimes, taking the point of view of persons or groups making management decisions. In pastoral production savings and investment are necessary, since herd capital is perishable and must be replaced. In addition, such investment is automatic unless herders decide to slaughter animals, and it takes place in the absence of public economic institutions. In contrast, in agricultural regimes, land cannot be increased by the reinvestment of its products except through elaborate institutions functioning to make the conversion from the product of the land to more land. For example, crops may be used to attract warriors or buy slaves, and in turn more land and the labourers to work it can be taken by conquest or brought under cultivation peacefully. Provided the marketing system is elaborate enough, crops can be sold and converted into more land. But the central point is that in agricultural societies conversions depend upon institutions outside the firm, whereas pastoral accumulation does not. Thus the potential for growth in the two regimes is strikingly different. Enterprise in the pastoral sector always faces the possibility of rapid growth, or conversely precipitious decline, whereas agricultural production may stagnate in the absence of channels for the conversion of the surplus product of the land. The tendency, therefore, is for the pastoral sector to be volatile in comparison to the agricultural sector, even though the contrast need not apply in every real-life situation.

Barth's framework represents an ideal type, a generalization of empirical data derived from observations of pastoral nomadism in the Middle East. While it is only a model, it has the virtue of focusing attention on a series of important issues: differences in the pastoral and sedentary sectors with respect to the potential for growth and reinvestment, migration between the two sectors, and social stratification within and across ethnic and ecological boundaries. The plan of attack in this chapter is to describe pastoral and sedentary production in the Central Sudan and to examine mechanisms of interaction between the two sectors—first regional trade and then climatic cycles. The final section will return to Barth's analytical framework and use it and other material presented in the chapter to give a brief account of pre-colonial economic history in the northern sector of the Central Sudan.

THE CENTRAL SUDAN AND ITS PEOPLE

The influence of the physical environment in Hausa and Tuareg country reinforced the contrast between pastoral and sedentary production indicated by Barth. In West Africa rainfall is largely determined by the movement of the inter-tropical convergence zone, a weather boundary characterized by the interaction of moisture-laden air from the coast with a warm, dry continental air mass.[2] The convergence zone sweeps inland roughly parallel to the coast, reaching the desert fringe in June, July, and August. At the northernmost limit of the convergence zone, the rainy season is shortest, and rainfall more highly variable than nearer the coast. Patterns of rainfall are characterized by great variations from place to place within each season in one place, from year to year, and over the long run. In addition, during drought in the Sahel, rainfall remains far below long-term averages, whereas the deficit is less pronounced farther south. With distance south of the desert, annual average rainfall increases and becomes much less variable in space and time. The steppe gradually merges into open savannah, which in turn shades off imperceptibly into more heavily wooded areas, and finally into tropical rain forest in a narrow belt at the southern extreme of the area influenced by the inter-tropical convergence zone, near the Atlantic coast.

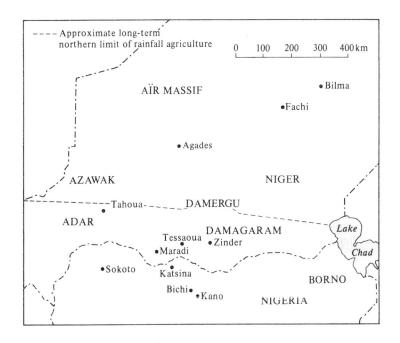

As a result of this pattern of climatic zones, with rainfall scattered and spotty at the northernmost limit of the coverage of the weather system, vast areas of the southern Sahara and Sahelian steppe received some precipitation but not enough to support the culti- vation of millet and sorghum, the staple crops of the savannah. In arid regions animals could graze a variety of perennial and annual grasses and shrubs, and so these areas supported nomadic pastoral- ists. Because of the great spatial, seasonal, and long-term variation in rainfall, herdsmen could only survive by taking their animals from place to place in search of pasture. In the dry season nomads had to move toward the fertile savannah or to other areas where pasture and water from either wells or surface pools was available. And even during the short rainy season herdsmen had to move quickly and cover long distances to take advantage of areas where rain squalls had passed.

This northern, nomadic sector was the province of noble Tuareg, Berber-speaking camel nomads with traditions of migration from the central Sahara. From these traditions it is clear that a southward migration had begun by about AD 1000, and it continued over the centuries, especially during periods of bad climate, as during the middle eighteenth century. The result was that it placed the majority of Tuareg population along the southern fringe of the desert. The attraction of the south was better pasture, proximity to the fertile savannah, and opportunities to raid or to conduct peaceful relations and to trade. In the desert the Aïr Mountains receive more rainfall than the surrounding desert because the elevated land lifts moist air, and in rising columns of air the dew-point drops and precipitation forms. Over the centuries the Aïr functioned like a magnet, attracting Tuareg to its fertile valleys. It was the site of several protracted struggles for supremacy between warring Tuareg factions which ended with the defeated group leaving for the south.[3]

Political power in this desert society was fragmented. At the lowest level was the camp, which consisted of not more than five or six individual families of four or five members each, along with their servile dependants, who were rarely as numerous as the free population of the camp. The next largest groupings was the section or *tauchit*, which might include as few as two or three or as many as ten or twenty camps. Male household heads of the noble clan of the section chose chiefs from the members of their own clan, but the election was usually confirmed by all the component clans of the section, since the tenure of chiefship depended on the willingness of all free members of the section to pay a small tribute to the chief each year.[4] At the next highest level was the drum group or confederation, a grouping of sections recognizing a common leader. The drum group derived its name from the *ettebel*, a drum symbolizing the authority of the drum chief. At the turn of the century confederations numbered as many as 10,000 people in the case of the Kel Ewey (Kel Oui in French souces), or as few as 2,000 or 3,000 in the case of the Kel Fadai.[5] Together the noble clans of the drum groups of the Aïr Tuareg elected the sultan or *amenokal* of Agadez, who was chosen from people of servile ancestry. He had little control over the people nominally under his command, except in the case of an external threat. His chief function was to conduct peaceful relations with outsiders or to lead expeditions against enemies, and in this respect his position resembled that of the drum chiefs and section chiefs.[6] As in other segmentary societies, no leader had power over his followers solely by virtue of his position in the political hierarchy. But wealth was enough to guarantee influence. Nobles (Tamashek, *amajer*, pl. *imajeren*) in effect acted as managers of large firms and controlled most resources even though they constituted less than 10 per cent of the nomadic population. They alone decided on war and peace; from their ranks came political leaders; and they were patrons of Muslim clerics (*inislimen*). They owned animals and especially camels, the principal productive resource of the desert and the main instrument of raiding and warfare as well. They monopolized the supply of arms. Scholarly lineages of *inislimen* though of noble origin themselves, were subordinate to warrior overlords and generally identified themselves as having renounced warfare. While *inislimen* relinquished temporal authority to warriors, their knowledge of Islamic jurisprudence and mysticism proved to be highly practical skills in the context of a segmentary social system, for it permitted them to serve as mediators.[7] Below the aristocracy were people in a range of categories including employees, craftsmen and blacksmiths, tenant farmers, herders who worked on contract or as servants, and slaves. The status of each individual or group depended on their position in the larger desert-edge system, and each was attached to a specific noble or noble section. They had varying degrees of freedom and geographical mobility; they could be directly attached to a noble camp, or they could trade, farm, or nomadize on their own.[8]

At the bottom of the status hierarchy were slaves called *iklan* (sing. *akli*) who were newly purchased or captured people. Some served their master directly and accompanied him on his travels; some were semi-sedentary; others' farmed the estates of the Sahel and savannah. Those living separate owed the master a fixed annual payment in millet or a portion of the harvest, as well as a proportion of the increase in their own herds. Those directly attached to their master's camp were integrated into Tuareg society at the level of the family. Slaves were fictive children, used kinship terms to address members of the master's real family, and were enmeshed into quasi-kinship relationships with the master's more distant kin.[9]

But kinship analogies should not gloss over the fact that *iklan* were different from real kin–they did most of the hard work around the campsite. Male slaves tended animals and drew water from wells, while female slaves cooked, brought firewood to the campsite, and fetched water.

While some workers on agricultural estates at the northern fringe of permanent settlement were *iklan*, most residents of Tuareg-owned estates farther south were apparently *irewelen*, or people of servile ancestry.[10] Since they were freed slaves, their status was higher, but their daily life differed only slightly from that of *iklan* living independently. Like *iklan*, these people owed a portion of their harvest to Tuareg nobles, but their only other obligation was to lodge their masters during the dry season or during drought. In a separate category were nomadic *irewelen* who enjoyed higher status than their sedentary counterparts because they engaged in herding and trade, work involving higher prestige. They were attached to their former master's camp, but herding and running caravans might take them away for extended periods of time.

Another category of Tuareg dependants, the *imrad,* can roughly be described as 'clients'. Most *imrad* lived in independent nomadic sections, and while their exact origins are not clear, it can be hypothesized that they were Tuareg or other nomads who had sub-mitted to noble sections after losing their herds or suffering defeat in battle.[11] Unlike other dependants, *imrad* participated in political life, since they had the right to confirm the election of the drum chief, but they did not have the full range of political rights reserved to the nobles.

To the outsider, the Tuareg seemed to make little distinction between their various types of dependants and most seemed well treated. Most, for instance, shared the same basic diet, and all but those of the lowest status wore similar clothing. Status was fluid and social distinctions were not always apparent to outsiders. Hausa-speaking people, for example, referred to all Tuareg of low status as *bugaje* (sing. *buzu*), thus lumping together people of most dependent categories, slave and free, nomadic and sedentary. While this shows an unfamiliarity with the status hierarchy, it accurately reflects the fact that Tuareg treated most dependants alike.

In addition, status was flexible. The existence of many free and servile categories may seem to suggest that the society was rigidly stratified, but in practice the status of individuals and groups could and did change over time to reflect changing political and economic relations. *Iklan* underwent a gradual upward evolution in status, with length of service, reliability, initiative, and other personal qualities playing a critical role in the process. Dependants tended to rise in status almost as soon as they entered the service of a Tuareg family, in part because they increasingly shared common interests. Intermarriage also affected status. In theory, the offspring of marriage between free and servile Tuareg inherited the status of their mother, but in practice children of free men and servile women were also free. Offspring of persons from different servile categories were known as *ibureliten* (sg. *abureli*). *Abureli* referred not only to a person's personal status, but might also denote membership in a collectivity. *Ibureliten* sections were transitional groups evolving toward the status of free Tuareg. Sometimes a servile section, for example, might be granted freedom as a reward for services performed.[12]

Two other nomadic groups, the Tubu and the Ful'be, used pastures in the Central Sudan. Although both groups kept slaves in pre-colonial times, neither had a social system as highly stratified as the Tuareg. Like the Tuareg, the Tubu were desert nomads with a segmentary political system, a mode of social organization suited to opposing needs for dispersal in search of pasture and unification in the face of an outside threat. But unlike the Tuareg, Tubu spoke a Nilo-Saharan language closely related to Kanuri and very distant indeed from Tamashek, the Berber lanugage of the Tuareg.[13] This linguistic evidence suggests that Tubu originated south of their present distribution in the Tibesti Mountains and north and northwest of Lake Chad. The Tubu once transported salt from Fachi and Bilma to Borno, but by the early nineteenth century most Tubu salt trade had already shifted to the Tuareg, who used their military strength to assure access to desert salt. This westward shift in the salt trade at the expense of the Tubu corresponded with economic and demographic growth in the Hausa states and the eclipse of Borno.[14]

A third group of pastoralists, the Ful'be (sing. Pullo) spoke a language of the West Atlantic sub-group of the Niger—Congo family. Unlike the Tuareg and Tubu, Ful'be lived in the savannah, where they concentrated on herding cattle as well as goats and sheep. The original Ful'be migrants began to arrive in the Central Sudan before 1400 and were periodically joined by new arrivals from the west.[15] Ful'be nomads traded with sedentary Hausa farmers, exchanging animals and animal products for grain, cloth, articles manufactured from wood and leather, and iron tools and weapons. Ful'be often made arrangements with Hausa farmers to graze their herds on crop residues after the harvest; the presence of animals in fields was desirable because of the manure they left behind. Most Ful'be retained a strong commitment to animal husbandry, although some divided the labour of their families between farming and stock-breeding.[16] Over the centuries others who had accumulated wealth settled in towns; among these settled Ful'be prominent Muslim clerics emerged. But most nomadic Ful'be seem to have been only partially Islamized, even after the Ful'be religious revolution of 1804–20. Today many nomadic Ful'be retain non-Muslim beliefs and practices despite nominal adherence to the religion of the prophet. And again in contrast to their settled kinsmen, who took control of a centralized state, nomadic Ful'be have retained an egalitarian political system. Lineages were the largest groups to come together in times of danger, for long-distance migration, or when rich pasture permitted. Although these lineages were defined in terms of descent, in fact genealogies were in constant flux – ancestors being appropriated and discarded according to ephemeral needs. The real reason for the formation of these 'lineages' was the necessity of coming together in larger groups in order to migrate to new grazing areas or because of proximity to other groups after having arrived in new territory.[17]

Most sedentary farmers in the Central Sudan spoke Hausa, though Kanuri-speaking people lived in Borno and on the frontiers of Borno, in Mangari, Muniyo, and eastern Damagaram, and to the north in the Sahelian fringe areas of Damergu, Alakos, and Koutous. In addition, many areas of predominantly Hausa settlements had histories of Kanuri immigration of two types. First, over the centuries Kanuri warriors established principalities in a band of territory north of the original Hausa states extending as far west as Arewa and the area which became Gobir. After subduing or being accepted by local people, these pioneer warriors founded dynasties and applied to Borno for recognition; but in the west they were to all intents and purposes independent, while Damagaram, for example, owed tribute to its suzerain. The second pattern of Kanuri immigration was a gradual movement of Kanuri-speakers of low status, some of whom were war captives, while others were free farmers.[18] Most descendants of all groups—warrior aristocrats, slaves, and farmers—spoke Hausa. Along the threshold of the desert Hausa-speaking farmers and hunters lived under the control of noble Tuareg, sharing this ecological niche with sedentary Tuareg slaves and descendants of slaves. Apparently in most areas of Hausa settlement, farmers once lived in clan villages, but this primordial settlement pattern began to break down with Islamization and increasing intercommunication within the region.

Among free Hausa peasants the basic economic unit was an exogamous residential group living in an enclosed area (Hausa, *gida*) and working land held in common. This unit consisted of a male household head (*mai gida*) and his wife or wives, sometimes one or more of his brothers and their wives and children, and often one or more adult sons and their wives and children.[19] Mutual rights and obligations among senior and junior males within this farming enterprise took the form of an institution, the paternal *gandu*, which Hill describes as a 'voluntary, mutually advantageous agreement between father and married son under which the son works in a subordinate capacity in return for a great variety of benefits including a share of the food supplies'.[20] The details of *gandu* arrangements varied from place to place and presumably changed over time, but in general sons were obliged to work *gandu* land a certain number of days per week but were free to work private plots (*gayauna*) evenings and on the remaining days of the week. In return they received food, lodging, tax payments, marriage expenses, and a portion of the land to which the *gandu* unit held rights—should the son leave the gandu before the death of his father. If the father died while the unit was still intact, sons inherited the principle resource, namely land, according to customary rules for the division of estates. Islamic law, which stipulated that daughters of the deceased receive half shares, was usually disregarded, even among Muslims.[21] Since land was abundant, it was usually possible to acquire it by clearing forest after obtaining permission from the district clief or the fief-holder in the area. *Jigawa* or upland farms could be acquired in this way, but low-lying, fertile land in areas where the water-table was near the surface was scarce because it could be cultivated throughout the year; hence rights in this *fadama* land were more clearly defined. In pre-colonial times many free peasants owned slaves who cultivated *gandu* land alongside sons and therefore took part in the system of prestation of labour and redistribution of the product of labour by the household head. Sons were usually, however, treated more leniently.[22]

Division between the nomadic and sedentary way of life should be viewed along a continuum rather than as two entirely distinct categories, [23] but nevertheless the occupations of most people in the Central Sudan fell at one end of the spectrum or the other. In the first place, in the northern, desert sector, cultivation was impossible except in oases, so there most enterprises devoted labour exclusively to pastoral production. And second, even in the savannah, where both kinds of activities were possible, a number of factors tended to encourage the division of labour. Sedentary people could not keep large herds of animals near villages because they interfered with cultivation by damaging standing crops. Farmers sometimes kept small herds despite these problems, or they entrusted their animals to Ful'be herders for several months of the year or longer. This arrangement was less than ideal because farmers often suspected the herders of cheating them. A more extensive commitment to animal husbandry would have required a nomadic life.[24] Only in fringe areas such as Damergu or Adar did sedentary people keep large herds, for there it was possible to pasture animals fairly near villages for most of the year because population was sparce.[25] Conversely nomads could and did farm, especially after severe losses in the herds. But transhumance in search of pasture meant that semi-nomadic people had to lessen their commitment to farming, and neglect of fields always resulted in crop yields lower than would have been the case if more labour had been invested. In short, at any given time most producers tended to devote their labour either to pastoral or sedentary production, except in the case of semi-sedentary Ful'be or of farmers living at the northernmost limit of rainfall agriculture. But these exceptional cases accounted for a tiny proportion of the population of the region as a whole.

Up to this point the presentation has ignored historical change in choices between sedentary or nomadic occupations, and this static description needs to be modified. For example, most sedentary Ful'be have a tradition of herding at some point in their past; conversely most pastoral Ful'be have had to take up agriculture when drought, animal disease, or raids by hostile neighbours reduced the size of their herds.[26] Similarly the history of nearly all low-status Tuareg shows that they have had to shift emphasis from one form of activity to another, and these historical adjustments will be taken up in a later section. The point which should be emphasized here, however, is that both physical environment and the prevailing technology were such that a division between pastoral and sedentary activity has some empirical validity. And at another level, the usefulness of theoretical division between the two regimes worked out by Barth is at least partially independent of the situation in the Central Sudan. An analytical scheme must always be judged by its ability to raise useful questions which then can be answered with reference to empirical data.

SEDENTARY STATES

In the savannah the basic wealth was the production of an agricultural surplus and proximity to the desert, with its strong demand for grain, other foodstuffs, and manufactured articles. Farmers cultivated cereal grains, principally sorghum and pennisetum millet, as well as peppers, groundnuts, and indigo on light upland soils called *jigawa,* and they irrigated crops in low-lying *fadama* or swamps. Some principal *fadama* crops were manioc, sugar cane, onions, tomatoes, sweet potatoes, and rice. Some cotton was grown north of the Sokoto Caliphate, but heavier soils and higher rainfall in the southern savannah were more favourable for growing most varieties of *gossypium.*[27] As a result, Sahelian regions imported a large proportion of the raw cotton used by local spinners and weavers from areas which specialized in cotton production, such as Zaria, Kano, and the Sokoto river valley.

The ability to produce an agricultural surplus permitted sedentary areas to support complex administrative structures and to evolve elaborate military institutions. As in the desert warfare and the accumulation of booty were, as Smaldone has observed, 'integral parts in the entire economic process'.[28] Sudanic armies were composed of contingents of infantry who fought with bow and arrow, light cavalry, and smaller groups of heavy cavalry wearing quilted armour. Although military technique and the organization of armies changed in the course of the nineteenth century, cavalry remained the key to success up to 1900 because of the advantage of speed and mobility which it conferred on those who used it.[29] Cavalry was a powerful tool of slave-raiding and state-building, and by its very nature a weapon of the upper classes. Horses were expensive to buy and maintain, as was quilted armour.[30] Although the political systems of the sedentary states differed from each other with respect to size, emphasis on revenue from trade or agricultural production, the place of religion in the state structure, and the internal organization of administrative offices and constitutional structures, they also shared basic common features which reflected the paramount importance of warfare in shaping the political economy. In the Central Sudan a hereditary warrior aristocracy (*sarakuna* in Hausa) ruled over commoners (*talakawa*) and slaves. One function of the aristocracy was to defend the frontiers of the state, and for this the rewards were slaves and other wealth taken as booty. Another function was to collect taxes, and for these administrative and military purposes a system of fiefdoms and sub-chieftaincies linked free farmers and slaves with the ruler (*sarki*), though often a large proportion of the ruling class lived near the palace. Defensive fortification also buttressed the power of the élite, since only capitals or *birane* (Hausa, sing. *birni*), with their massive earthwork fortifications, enjoyed any degree of immunity to attack by a large, mobile army, since these capitals alone were capable of withstanding siege for any length of time.[31] These walled towns combined commercial with administrative functions, for they were the dwelling places of not only the ruling family, title-holders, and clients of the ruling class, but of influential merchants as well.

The *jihad* of 1804–20, which drastically altered the political structure of a large area of the Central Sudan, fitted into a long-term process in the spread of Islam in West Africa.[32] The religion had arrived in Hausaland many centuries earlier, carried by Muslim Mande merchants from the west or by Muslim merchants and clerics from North Africa.[33] After the conversion of rulers, Islam spread slowly from its urban, commercial base to rural areas and to other segments of the population. Some converts acquired a religious education equal to the best obtainable at the time, but the instruction of all but this small minority remained imperfect, and consequently most who called themselves Muslim saw nothing wrong in mixing Islamic and non-Islamic practice. In addition many rural people remained loyal to chiefs who had the religious function of mediating between human society and local spirits. Governing Muslims, partial converts, and resistors remained an exercise in the art of the possible, with the need for compromise limiting the strict application of Muslim law. At the same time a literate urban minority clamoured for reform to bring government up to the standards of the *shariᶜa*, since they clearly perceived the gap between local reality and the standards of learned Muslims regarding both public administration and private religious practice.

In Hausaland in the late eighteenth and early nineteenth century, the religious motivation of a learned, devout minority coincided with a range of economic and political issues. Usuman 'dan Fodio, a Ful'be cleric, declared a *jihad* or holy war against the rulers of the Hausa kingdom of Gobir in 1804 because of the lax Islamic practice condoned by them. Usuman formed a coalition of nomadic Ful'be with grievances against settled rulers, Hausa converts, settled Ful'be clerics and other Muslims from towns, and Tuareg allies. Within a few years the movement had engulfed most of Hausaland in a revolution which was successful nearly everwhere because of its broad appeal and because Ful'be commanders developed military organization and tactics to take full advantage of the use of light cavalry.[34] The victorious Ful'be aristocracy replaced Hausa emirs, but the new élite ruled in much the same manner as had their predecessors and often governed the same territorial entities. Ful'be emirs formed a loose confederation, owed allegiance to Usuman and his successors in Sokoto, and looked to Sokoto for guidance in legal and spiritual matters and for legitimacy.

The present boundary between Niger and Nigeria corresponds approximately to the northern limit of the Caliphate. In the area to the north were states which Ful'be were unable to conquer — Gobir and Damagaram — and Maradi, a state formed by Hausa who fled after the Ful'be takeover in Katsina.[35] The wars which led to the formation of the Caliphate produced a wave of migration to all these areas to the north, since disturbances in the savannah happened to coincide with a period of good climate in Hausa–Tuareg country.

After the victory of the Ful'be and their allies, relatively peaceful conditions returned in the centre of the Caliphate, a situation which favoured economic growth, as did a period of good climate beginning in the early nineteenth century. But the most important economic effect of the *jihad* was the forced relocation of agricultural population toward the prosperous central regions. Although the details of this process will have to await the publication of research by Paul Lovejoy and Jan Hogendorn, the main historical outlines of the slave economy of the area are now clear.[36] First, slave raiding in peripheral areas provided the mechanism for the capture and displacement of population. Second, the influx of servile population was so great that in some areas slaves outnumbered free peasants, though it appears that the rate of absorption of slaves into the free population was rapid compared to other instances of heavy reliance on slave labour elsewhere in the world. But the ready availability of slaves, good soil, markets for agricultural produce, and a developing textile industry encouraged large-scale commercial production by slaves living on estates and working in supervised gangs. And finally, while the timing of these events remains unclear, plantation agriculture appears to have been in full swing by mid-century in the textile belt of Kano, northern Zaria, southern Katsina, and Zamfara.[37]

Viewed from a wider perspective than that of socio-economic change within the Caliphate, the Ful'be *jihad* assumes the character of just one event in a larger process in which Islamization, economic growth, and increasing centralization of state structures were inter-related. Nicolas has called attention to an essential duality in Hausa society, and his analysis aids greatly in understanding these long-term forces.[38] The original inhabitants of Hausaland, called *anna*, *azna*, *arne*, or *asna* depending on their location, once lived in clan villages which were largely self-sufficient, though long-distance trade in some commodities, notably salt and iron weapons and implements, was undoubtedly of great antiquity. Opposed to these non-Muslim villagers were what Nicolas calls the dynastic segment of Hausa society — the builders of Hausa states who ruled villages from their fortified *birane*. Nicolas correctly points out that to adopt current usage and to call the two segments 'Muslim' and 'pagan' is to follow too closely the categories of thought of the segment which eventually prevailed, and to ignore an important historical process. Over the centuries the dynastic segment grew at the expense of the *anna*, aided by the growth of towns, increasing regional trade, and an expanding system of administration controlled by the ruling warrior aristocracy. The *jihad* of Usuman 'dan Fodio greatly speeded up the process of Islamization within the dynastic segment, providing rulers with a blueprint for strong central government according to Islamic law. With economic growth in the nineteenth century, Islam spread from its dynastic base to other segments of the population. Non-Muslims constituted reservoirs of population which were raided for slaves, and the re-location of population towards the centre of the region, in the textile-producing regions of Kano, Katsina, Zaria, and Zamfara, ultimately promoted Islamization among those removed by force from the periphery to the centre through the mechanism of emancipation and conversion. Although the *jihad* marked a turning-point in the establishment of Islamic law and religion in the urban, commercial sector, pre-Islamic practices persisted in rural areas, and especially on the periphery of the growing economic region in the Hausa heartland.

Nevertheless it is possible to discern similar though less dramatic turning points north of the Caliphate. When and if they occurred, they came later. In addition, the progress of Islam in Gobir, Maradi, and Damagaram appears to be correlated with economic growth and the degree to which the northern regions were tied into the economy of the Caliphate. It is significant that the turning-point came first in Damagaram, the state with an economy most closely tied − with links of trans-Saharan and regional trade − to growth at the centre of the region. The official establishment of Islam came more gradually than in the Caliphate, and it occurred peacefully as a result of the initiative of Sarki Tanimu in the 1870s.[39] In Maradi and Gobir dualistic systems of government permitted autochthonous *anna* and immigrant Muslims to live side by side in peace. In these states sizeable proportions of the population remained non-Muslim at the turn of the century, but conversions have proceeded rapidly under colonial rule.[40]

THE REGIONAL ECONOMY

Religious heterogeneity, the diversity of political institutions, ethnicity, and a wide range of adaptations to the physical environment may seem to have separated the people of the Central Sudan from each other, and in a sense this was true. But at another level operated powerful forces for economic integration. Specialization in agricultural or pastoral activities and within each of the productive regimes necessitated large-scale economic interactions. And even ethnicity, while to a certain extent reflecting occupational specialization in one of the many possible niches in the regional economy, also helped to organize and regulate interaction.

Both ethnicity and specialization, for example, helped to shape the character and organization of the Tuareg economic network. The Sahelian ecological frontier functioned as a dividing line in a figurative sense only, for strong currents of trade linked the two sub-regions. The Tuareg gained a living from the arid environment of the desert edge by concentrating on pastoral activities, by providing armed escorts and transport animals for trans-Saharan caravans, and by trading. Desert people could live on milk from the herds for extended periods, but they also needed grain. Consequently they traded animals, salt, dates, and hides for grain, clothing, articles made from wood and leather, kola nuts, and tobacco. The constant search for pasture and the need to follow the seasonal rhythm of rainfall prevented the Tuareg from settling down in one place. The yearly cycle of transhumance which resulted provided a framework not only for animal husbandry, but for trade contacts with the savannah as well.[41] During the short rainy season the desert supported a large population, and the pastures of the Aïr massif, where rainfall was greater than the surrounding desert, were sufficient for a large contingent of the Aïr Tuareg, as well as others from the south and west, to make the trek across the arid Tenere in late October and early November. At Fachi and Bilma they traded grain obtained in the south for salt and dates. With the return of the salt caravan in December, most Aïr Tuareg left for the south, selling salt, dates, and animals along the way, and pasturing the animals they were breeding. Many moved as far south as Sokoto, Katsina, and Kano during the dry season, while others used pastures farther north, within the territory of the sedentary states of the Sahelian fringe. With the beginning of the rains in May or June, they left for the north, since the excessive dampness of the savannah at this time of year endangered the health of the camels, and the return of the land to cultivation hindered the free movement of herds. In addition Tuareg were attracted to the vast areas of rainy season pasture in the Sahel and southern desert.[42]

At the end of the nineteenth century the principal north–south corridor of trade and transhumance extended from Agadez through Damergu, Damagaram, and terminated at Kano. The Kel Ewey confederation dominated this route, while the Kel Gress controlled a more easterly route through Adar and Gobir Tudu ending in the western Hausa cities. But not all Tuareg of the Aïr and Azawak were fully or directly involved in the economy of the savannah. The Kel Ferwan and Kel Fadai, for example, seem to have concentrated almost entirely on animal husbandry and had few direct contacts with their sedentary neighbours. These people traded for grain and other goods at Agadez and other northern market towns, but their animals were often exported south by livestock dealers from the savannah or Sahel. Purely nomadic Tuareg with an almost complete specialization in animal husbandry were less numerous than the Kel Ewey and Kel Gress, and they were less wealthy and powerful.[43]

To support their trade with the savannah, the Tuareg maintained a network which included farming estates located along trans-humance routes and near dry season grazing sites, and urban communities of brokers, landlords, traders, and craftsmen.[44] These diaspora communities and rural estates permitted Tuareg of most status categories to move freely throughout the savannah. In fact, a large proportion of Tuareg trade was handled by servile *irewelen*, who were usually people of rural or nomadic origin travelling from place to place to trade for their masters, or less frequently, on their own account. Tuareg residing on rural estates were slaves or people of servile descent who owed a portion of the harvest to their master, had to feed and lodge noble Tuareg when they arrived in the savannah during the dry season, and sometimes helped herd animals belonging to their masters.[45] Another sub-category of low-status Tuareg were permanent residents of towns and provided ancillary services to Tuareg traders. These northern immigrants remained subject to their nomadic masters, although they usually had a great degree of freedon of action and ample chance to accumulate wealth and advance in status. They provided accom-modation, brokerage and banking services, and storage facilities for travelling merchants. Diaspora communities in towns also included craftsmen, since noble Tuareg invested heavily in craft production in savannah towns. For example, they financed such activities as weaving and dyeing in Kano and Kura, a town south of Kano, and tanning and leather-work in Zinder.[46]

This brief description shows that the Tuareg economy was in fact a multi-ethnic system and that ethnicity was related to various occupations within the network. In the north pastoral specialists spoke a Berber tongue, possessed a distinctive culture, and occupied the top rank in a multi-tiered social system. Most, even those recruited into the pastoral system as slaves, and who con-tinued to occupy independent positions, aspired to the topmost positions as long as they practised nomadic pastoralism. But the Tuareg network also included Hausa and Kanuri at lower levels occupying positions as slaves or resembling tenant farmers or serfs, and as craftsmen and trade specialists in savannah towns. Within the network language and ethnicity tended to mark the division between pastoral and sedentary occupations, although lags could occur when people were brought into the system or if they changed occupations. Aristocratic nomads dominated both sectors by virtue of their wealth and experience in warfare, and also because some possessed the political and entrepreneurial skill needed to run large, diverse, and geographically dispersed enterprises.

Specialized production along the desert edge and trade from the desert sector fit into a wider pattern in West African interregional trade. Most desert salt and a large proportion of the dates traded from the oases went no farther south than Borno or the Hausa states, but animals entered trade networks which extended beyond, to Nupe and Yoruba country. Once again the basis for trade was the complementary production of different ecological zones. Because of tsetse fly infestation, the southern savannah and forest could not produce as much meat as it consumed, with the result that slaughter animals from the Sahel and savannah brought good prices on southern markets. The forest earned foreign exchange for animal protein and beasts of burden by exporting a range of products in demand in the savannah and Sahel. Chief among these was the kola nut, a mild stimulant consumed over a wide area of West Africa and grown only in the forest.[47] The southern savannah and forest were also net exporters of raw cotton and finished garments, products which were also in short supply in the north. Other exports from the south included relays of European coastal imports such as tobacco, cowries, and European-made cloth.[48]

Saline and other mineral deposits also determined the direction of flow of interregional trade. Desert oases, principally Fachi and the oases in the Kawar (Bilma) group, supplied salt-cones and tablets made by evaporating salt-bearing water. A much smaller volume of salt made by a similar process came from Tegidda-n-tesemt to the west of Aïr.[49] From the Aïr massif itself came a low-grade salt suitable for feeding to animals. In the Dallol Fogha, one of the dry river beds extending southward from the Azawak to the Niger, a high quality salt could be made by processing salt-bearing earth and grasses. In the Manga country to the east of Damagaram another form of high quality salt was obtained by evaporating salty water over fires. Perhaps the most significant sources of salt were potash deposits found in the area extending eastward from Damagaram toward the Lake Chad basin. Potash was consumed over a wide area for medicinal purposes, as a thickener in cooking, as an additive to flavour chewing tobacco, as a fixing agent for dyes, but most importantly as a salt substitute for animals. Potash from Muniyo and Borno reached markets in the Sokoto Caliphate and far beyond. Hausa traders from Kano took potash to Gonja, far to the west, where they exchanged it for kola from Asante. Together potash and animals represented the most important exports of the

Sahel and savannah in trade toward Nupe and Yoruba states. Finally, trade in iron ore and other minerals from the Bauchi plateau should be mentioned.[50]

Regional or local specialization in processing or craft industries, which took place throughout the region but was concentrated in the cities and towns of the Caliphate, also helped to shape patterns of trade. For example, during the nineteenth century Kano and neighbouring towns such as Kura developed extensive textile industries, so that a very large area of the Sahel and savannah came to depend on Kano and secondary centres for clothing.[51] The ready supply of slave labour to produce raw cotton or foodstuffs during the farming season, and to weave cloth during the dry season, stimulated the development of this industry. Wealthy merchants, Ful'be noblemen, and Tuareg aristocrats as well as others invested in agricultural production for the market, in weaving, dyeing, or related activities.[52] Although Kano and its surrounding region were net exporters of cloth, they also imported the specialized products of other areas. For example, Kano and Nupe exchanged locally manufactured cloth, and by the end of the nineteenth century both areas imported European textiles as well.

Just as the Tuareg network dominated long-distance trade in the northern part of the region, Hausa trading networks carried the lion's share of trade in minerals, agricultural products, and manufactured goods to the south and south-west. As in the case of the Tuareg network ethnicity served as an organizing principle in the movement of trade beyond the borders of Hausaland, but it worked independently of social stratification. Hausa diaspora communities in the upper Volta basin, Borgu, Nupe, Yorubaland, and areas east of the Caliphate welcomed newcomers, lodged traders, provided brokerage and banking services, and guaranteed credit transactions. Often commercial reference groups, whose members were descendants of immigrants to Hausaland, and as such formed ethnic sub-groups, served as a focus for the formation of specialized groups of traders within which skills, knowledge of routes and market conditions beyond Hausaland, and trading capital passed from father to son. Two such groups were the Agalawa and Tokarawa, descendants of low-status Tuareg who migrated to the savannah and were able to take advantage of the general commercial expansion of the Caliphate in the nineteenth century.[53]

DROUGHT

The Tuareg economic network, which dominated regional trade in
the northern part of the Central Sudan, provided a framework for
the interaction of desert people with their southern neighbours
along a series of frontiers including not only the Sahelian border,
but also savannah cities, rural estates, and areas near transhumance
routes. This spatial pattern provides the first important backdrop
for desert-edge history, but a second, temporal pattern must also be
considered. Water was the critical scarce resource in a wide area of
the desert and Sahelian fringe. Just as production by pastoralists
followed the rhythm of rainfall and the distribution of surface and
well water, so also did the lives of farmers. Crops needed rainfall;
surface water permitted *fadama* cultivation; and villages needed
year-round supplies of drinking-water. It is necessary to examine
long-term fluctuations in climate because variation in rainfall, a
critical resource, introduced a strong cyclical tendency in the desert-
edge economy.

   Over the centuries the Central Sudan, along with the entire
Sudanic belt of West and Central Africa, has been affected by a
series of severe droughts. Although the climatic history of the
Central Sudan has not yet been worked out in detail, information
from several sources provides a good general outline. First, Paul
Lovejoy has drawn up a list of major droughts in the last five
centuries mentioned in the political chronicles of Kano, Agadez,
and Borno and in accounts of nineteenth-century European travellers. The results of this research have been presented elsewhere
in greater detail, but the findings for the last several centuries can be
summarized briefly.[54] A seven-year drought hit Borno between
1690 and 1720, but it was not recorded in Hausa country; it might
have coincided with a famine among the Tuareg in the late 1690s.
The major development of the eighteenth century was the drought
of the 1740s and 1750s, which struck the entire Sudano-Sahelian
belt in West Africa, and was more severe than any drought until
1969–73. Another occurred in the 1790s but was not as devastating
as the great drought of mid-century. The nineteenth century was
remarkable for the absence of prolonged drought, and only one of a
single year's duration, in 1855, is reported in travellers' accounts.
Years of localized shortages or inadequate rainfall are reported
occasionally in the period 1860–90, and worsening climate after
the turn of the century culminated in the severe drought of

1911–14.[55]

Partial confirmation of this chronology comes from another, entirely independent source. Jean Maley has attempted to reconstruct the climate of the area in the past by using the level of Lake Chad as an indicator, along with pollen counts from sedimentation in the lake bed.[56] Although dendrochronology lacks the precision of the Central Sudan chronicles, it does provide over-all corroboration for them, with the exception of the early nineteenth century. Maley's data indicate lower than average rainfall in the mid-eighteenth century, the early nineteenth, and the early twentieth.

These two sources apparently contradict each other on the early nineteenth century, but in fact the experience of the Lake Chad basin, especially the area east of the lake, differed markedly from the situation to the west. Data assembled by Nicholson for a general climatic chronology of Africa north of the equator include a variety of travellers' reports and other sources indicating severe, recurring drought in the eastern Chad basin between about 1810 and 1840. In this area bad climate corresponded with a period of lower-than-average rainfall in a wider area. But at the same time the climate was relatively good to the west of the lake, especially in Hausaland and Tuareg country, and this good climate stands out as an exceptional case in that for once Central Sudan climate did not fit into a wider pattern. During most other periods of exceptionally poor rainfall – the late seventeenth century, the mid-eighteenth, the late eighteenth, and the early twentieth – climate in the Central Sudan corresponded with general climatic patterns in the rest of Africa.[57]

Differences in climate east and west of Lake Chad in the early nineteenth century bring up an issue which cannot be decided on the basis of existing evidence, but which should nevertheless be considered. Better rainfall in Hausa–Tuareg country may have set up an east–west gradient which combined with political factors to encourage Kanuri migration to the west. This shows up in early nineteenth-century Damergu, though here the size of this immigration was insignificant in terms of the total population of the Central Sudan.[58] In any case bad climate in the east and good climate in the Sokoto Caliphate may have contributed to a process of economic growth in the west at the expense of Borno, though of course the process was under way long before the early nineteenth century, as indicated by the westward shift of desert salt trade and a gradual, long-term westward drift of Kanuri-speaking farmers. In the early nineteenth century, the military success of the Caliphate and political integration over a wide area also played a role in attracting population and forcibly relocating enslaved easterners.

Cyclical climatic change had a major impact on Tuareg society, since during drought social stratification came into play as a mechanism whereby nobles enforced their claims to scarce resources and passed on most risk associated with life in the desert to lower strata. Most low-status Tuareg enjoyed considerable freedom of movement, but they lacked permanent claims on the productive resources with which they supported themselves. Nobles sometimes gave animals to *irewelen* or *imrad* groups to allow them to nomadize on their own;[59] nobles also provided trade capital and transport animals and allowed *irewelen* to trade on their own account, as long as they handled some of their master's business as well.[60] But when resources became scarce, nobles began to call in animals loaned to people of low status; the enforcement of claims of ownership rested ultimately on the monopoly of force held by nobles as a warrior class. Those in the lowest status category left first. They left as soon as their herds were no longer large enough to support them; once in the savannah, where the effects of drought were less pronounced, they took up farming. If the drought was prolonged, they were soon followed by people of higher status, as the nobles continued to call in animals in the herds of *irewelen* and *imrad*. In the long run even nobles might be unable to return to the desert because of herd losses, but they were able to rely on income from savannah estates while they attempted to gather sufficient resources to return to extended transhumance.[61] When climate improved, this process worked in reverse, and the desert economy expanded to take up population just as it had sloughed people off during the climatic downturn. Nobles returned first, and as their herds grew in size they recalled more and more of their former dependants.[62] As the size of herds continued to grow, the desert economy needed the services of even larger numbers of people to take care of herds, to participate in trade, and to lead pack animals. Some low-status Tuareg returned of their own free will, while others were brought into Tuareg networks through enslavement.

By setting limits on the economic and demographic growth of the desert sector, climatic cycles had far-reaching ramifications in the wider region as well. Just as economic specialization necessitated trading contacts between the two sub-regions, drought reinforced this need for close ties. In bad times the resources of the desert – water and pasture – were insufficient to support the population, and so many had to leave in order to save themselves and a part of the herd. Drought therefore acted as a kind of demographic pump which repeatedly drove people from the arid lands. Refugees had to be accepted in receiving areas, and therefore the Tuareg had a strong incentive to maintain close economic, political, and military ties in the savannah. These contacts with the south permitted desert people to conserve their resources as best they could in bad times, so that life in the desert and steppe could resume after interludes of drought.

This model of reactions to drought permits an understanding of Tuareg social stratification in an entirely new light. Thus far ethnographers have viewed this social system solely as it operated in the desert, have ignored the Tuareg network in the savannah, and have failed to take account of cyclical historical change.[63] Consequently they have been unable to interpret it properly. Seen in its entirety and with its dynamic dimension, Tuareg stratification assumes the character of a clearly delineated blueprint of the order of precedence in access to resources. Distinctions between different kinds of dependants had little meaning except at the lowest levels of the system and during drought, when they provided a pattern for sloughing off excess population and allowing the social system to replicate itself when climate returned to normal. The freedom granted to all but newly acquired slaves can be seen in terms of an environmental adaptation which permitted the delegation of responsibility for certain economic activities and allowed the movement of large numbers of people over long distances in response to opportunities to trade and as a means of survival in case of drought.

Drought had a differential impact on sedentary and pastoral production, and contrasting patterns of growth and differing possibilities for reinvestment can best be understood by returning to the framework advanced by Barth. First, the physical environment accentuated risk in pastoral activities, since drought was always more severe in the steppe and desert than in savannah farmland. Second, the impact of drought on the productive base was greatest in the pastoral sector. Barth has called attention to the possibility of rapid growth and sharp decline in pastoral production, and at this point it is necessary to enlarge upon this consideration. Research by Dahl and Hjort demonstrates the extent to which drought undermined the productive capacity of pastoral enterprise.[64] Based on information about typical patterns in age and sex structures of African herds, Dahl and Hjort constructed a demographic model and introduced a two- and three-year drought, assuming effects reported from the field. They found that drought creates irregularities in the age structure of the herd which have a long-term impact on the production of calves and milk. Some of the effects can still be seen eighteen years after the drought, and herds are vulnerable to further reduction in productive capacity if another drought strikes, especially about four years after the end of the first. In the Sahel reported growth rates for cattle have been about 5 per cent per year and somewhat less for camels, while greater for sheep and goats. Once the herd has been reduced by drought, therefore, even under the best conditions recovery takes time. Whereas pastoral output is constrained by these factors, production in the settled agricultural sector is comparatively quick to recover. Even if the farming population were to be reduced by famine, survivors can bring land back into production and produce a surplus relatively quickly. Empirical evidence on the desert economy in the early twentieth century tends to support this notion of differential recovery, and this will be discussed in Chapter VI.

Tuareg nobles had two main strategies for dealing with the risk inherent in pastoral production. The first was to use the lower echelons of society as a buffer by forcing them to shoulder the burden of herd losses and to take up farming if necessary during periods of minor climatic trouble. The second was to seek protection for accumulated wealth by diversification — by investing in agricultural production on estates in the savannah, by building an infrastructure for trade, and by sponsoring craft production in savannah towns. In short, the possibility of investing in relatively stable and riskless economic activities in the savannah, together with the need for seasonal transhumance, a refuge in case of drought, and an outlet for the sale of pastoral products, helps explain the development of a far-flung and economically diverse network extending far to the south of Tuareg pasture lands in the desert and steppe.

CONCLUSION

At the same time as the Tuareg network expanded from its northern base, a series of factors permitted the growth of an agricultural economy centred on the area of exceptionally fertile soil in Hausaland. This good agricultural base encouraged early population growth and increased specialization of craft production. As the savannah economy prospered, larger numbers of pastoralists arrived in the southern desert fringe to trade with sedentary farmers, and periodic drought between 1500 and 1800 gave added impetus to this southward migration. Between 1750 and 1900 the savannah economy grew rapidly, with only one major interruption in the late eighteenth century because of drought. Political unity and peaceful conditions in the Sokoto Caliphate after about 1820 favoured economic growth, as did favourable climate in the Caliphate and in Tuareg country, in contrast to repeated drought and famine in the eastern Chad basin. Concomitant with increased trade, urbanization, and the relocation of population in the centre of the Caliphate was the progress of Islam. The religion of the prophet also made gains in sedentary states north of the Caliphate to the extent that the northern, peripheral states participated in economic and demographic change at the centre of the region. In the middle and late nineteenth century, both Hausa and Tuareg trading networks expanded to handle an increased volume of trade or to cover new territory. By the end of the century, complex trading systems linked settled agriculture, animal husbandry, craft production, mining, and the exploitation of salt deposits over a wide area.

CHAPTER II

Damagaram and Damergu
in the Nineteenth Century

THE preceding chapter included material intended to place the history of Damagaram in the wider geographical context of the regional economy to which it belonged and to provide background on the nature of relations between pastoral and sedentary people in this area. It is now possible to turn to the narrower focus of this study, Damergu and Damagaram, with a full appreciation of the influence of the physical environment and wider historical patterns.

Two predominant influences in the nineteenth-century history of both Damagaram and Damergu were the expanding economy of the desert-edge and trans-Saharan trade. As the climate improved after the major drought of the middle eighteenth century and the minor setback in the decade 1790–1800, hunters and farmers moved north towards the desert fringe in response to opportunities to use land which was once again productive. In Damergu these settlers grouped themselves into villages and submitted to Tuareg control, paying an annual tax in millet in return for protection.[1] Many immigrants to Damergu during the period of resettlement came from the Caliphate, and without doubt unsettled conditions produced by the *jihad* of 1804–20 encouraged emigration. Although oral tradition concerning the founding of these villages is not entirely clear on the religious motives of the original settlers, it is possible that non-Muslim or partially Islamized people found it preferable to live under the control of nomads than in the new theocratic states being formed by Ful'be aristocracy. Oral tradition also obscures the social status of the immigrants. It is entirely possible that warfare in the Caliphate produced a supply of slaves who were captured by Tuareg allies of warring parties, or bought by Tuareg, and forcibly resettled in the desert fringe. Regardless of the original status of the immigrants, the conditions of Damergu were such that slave villages quickly assumed a quasi-independent tributary relation with their masters; by the second generation slaves worked

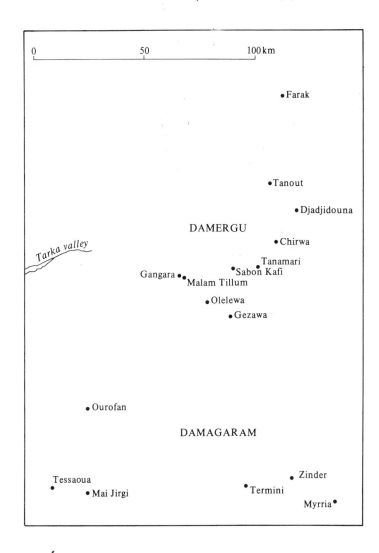

without supervision from day to day and were free to travel for the purposes of trade during the dry season.[2]

Growth in Damagaram as in Damergu should be viewed in the context of a wider pattern of resettlement in the Sahel, but the process assumed a far different form in the south. In the first place, while the Tuareg ruled Damergu, in Damagaram a sedentary aristocracy owing allegiance to Borno (Bornu) was in power. The ruling dynasty traced its origins back to the middle of the eighteenth century, when, according to traditions recorded by Dunbar, raids from the Tuareg were frequent and the small chieftaincy was only one among many in the area. Then with the accession of Sulayman to the throne (c.1812), the dynasty gained strength and built a permanent capital at Zinder.[3] Pressure from Tuareg during the mid-eighteenth century probably reflected unsettled conditions in the desert and steppe during the great drought which affected the entire Sudano-Sahelian zone at that time.

Another similarity between the two neighbouring areas was that both, especially Damagaram, owed their development in the nineteenth century to trans-Saharan trade. Zinder was little more than a village in the eary decades of the century, but it grew to be an important trade city with the eastward shift of the major caravan route to Tripoli. Until the *jihad* Katsina had been the principal southern terminus of this trans-Saharan route, but warfare undermined Katsina's position of leadership. The Hausa dynasty of Katsina retreated northward and entrenched itself at Maradi, a position from which it was able to wage a protracted campaign against the new Ful'be rulers of Katsina. The conflict soon became a stalemate, but it dealt a severe blow to trade and production. The economy of Kano grew as Katsina declined, with the result that Kano displaced its rivals as the entrepôt for trans-Saharan trade.[4] Since the more easterly route to Kano passed through Damagaram and Damergu, the local economy benefited from its position on a major caravan route.

THE LOCAL EFFECTS OF TRANS-SAHARAN TRADE

The organization of trans-Saharan trade will be treated in detail in the following chapter, but for the present it is necessary to examine late nineteenth-century changes in the volume and composition of trans-Saharan exports and the effects of these shifts on the economy of the Sudan. British consuls in Tripoli recorded estimates of the value of Sudan products passing through the port for export to Europe and America, and these figures represent an important though neglected source of information for the history of the late nineteenth-century Central Sudan. Although these estimates do not have the accuracy of official statistics, the general picture of the export trade they provide is corroborated by a wide variety of published sources from both the northern and southern ends of the Tripoli–Kano trade route, as an article by Marion Johnson has shown.[5] In addition, archival and oral sources in central Niger also support the accuracy of these estimates and the image of ebb and flow they impart.[6]

Briefly, British consular reports show the familiar increase in the value of Sudan trade in the 1870s led by a boom in exports of ostrich feathers, a sharp drop from a peak in the early 1880s to a low in 1886–9, followed by a strong recovery based on the exports of tanned goat skins. The value of exports slumped during the trade depression of the late 1880s, but it recovered to a sustained level averaging over £110,000 per annum in the 1890s. While this was only half the level of the 1880s, it was well over twice the value of trade before the trade boom of the 1870s. (See Table 1.)

Trans-Saharan trade from the Central Sudan grew even more rapidly than the Tripoli consular series would seem to indicate for the simple reason that an increasing proportion of the trade reported in Tripoli estimates came from the Central Sudan, as first Timbuktu trade and then traffic from Borno dropped from the figures. In the 1860s trade from Timbuktu may have accounted for as much as a quarter of the Tripoli totals, but this trade disappeared before 1880, having been diverted either to Mogador or to river and ocean routes pivoting on St.-Louis and the lower Senegal. In 1893 Borno trade suffered a severe blow with the attack and capture of the Borno capital by Rabih b. Fadallah, who seized property belonging to locally-based North Africans. They never again trusted Rabih enough to return to the former level of commercial activity; but even beforehand Borno trade had been much less significant than trade from Kano, which had surpassed Borno traffic by 1880 at least and probably earlier. In any case trade between Borno and Tripoli was insignificant by the late 1890s; the British consul estimated that 84 per cent of Tripoli exports toward the Sudan in 1897 was destined for the route which ended at Kano.[7]

One indirect conclusion which emerges from an examination of the Tripoli consular series is that the proportional share of slave exports in the trade totals decreased after mid-century. Unfortunately the relatively good estimates of volume in the new staple exports cannot be matched for slave trade. Traffic on the Tripoli–Kano route may have been as high as 1,000 slaves per year in the 1850s before the trade was outlawed in the Ottoman sultanate, but it was probably insignificant twenty or thirty years later.[8] After painstaking investigations in 1876, an abolitionist American consul estimated Tripoli slave exports at about 150 per year.[9] In the absence of good data on contraband trade, about all that can be said is that the traffic probably declined slowly. But whatever the case, new exports assumed an increasingly important share of the trade totals after the trade booms of the 1870s and 1890s, and it is certain that the composition of exports from the Cental Sudan changed drastically.

Without doubt this transition to non-slave exports was the most significant event in African economic history during the period 1800−70. Economic historians have begun to work out a framework for classifying responses throughout African to this change in external demand, focusing on differences in the degree of original involvement in slave exports, the availability of non-slave exports, and the reactions of slave-traders and slave-raiding societies to declining overseas demand for slave labour. Hopkins and others have described coastal areas where the shift in external demand was relatively rapid, although slave and legitimate exports co-existed for some time.[10] As long as slaves could be sold, the ruling class maintained its power because economies of scale continued to come into play; slave-raiding was an activity that rewarded those who could assemble and arm large armies. But as slave exports declined and palm-oil exports rose, the influence of economies of scale decreased. Anyone, no matter how humble in status, could gather palm product for sale or cultivate trees, and large producers did not enjoy an advantage because of the lack of increasing returns to scale. Trade, however, tended to remain in the hands of those with relatively large-scale operations.

This framework is not completely transferable to the Sahel, where transit trade in slaves probably always overshadowed local slave-gathering operations. Yet it does point to interesting questions about changes in the position of the ruling class when external demand permitted a dramatic increase in small-scale production for export. As on the coast the rising importance of new forms of trade might be expected to require a reaction from the ruling élite because of the absence of economies of scale in these new activities. In the case of ostrich feathers, large-scale production enjoyed an advantage over small operations only to the extent that hunting wild birds was more productive when the people of a village co-operated with each other. Revenue from tanned goat skins went less automatically to the bottom of the social ladder because tanning had to be paid for, and those who accumulated the necessary capital therefore had an advantage. Both these activities were inherently different from slave-raiding, where the necessity of large scale armed operations and the ease with which a state monopoly on trade could be enforced combined to favor the ruling classes.[11]

This analysis focuses attention on Damergu, where the rise of new opportunities for farmers to earn private, dry-season earnings had a dramatic effect. In the late 1870s and early 1880s North African merchants from Ghadames set up a community in Djadjidouna, a small village on the main caravan route four days march north of Zinder. Operating from their compounds these merchants broke bulk in the importing trade and collected feathers for export, dealing directly with village heads, the organizers of hunting expeditions.[12] Ostriches could also be raised in captivity, but the feathers of wild birds brought better prices. Since wild ostriches were numerous in Damergu, sedentary farmers concentrated on hunting during the off season, while raising caged birds was more common farther south.

By providing a new source of income for villagers, the rapid growth in ostrich feather trade upset the balance of power between the two dominant Tuareg groups in Damergu. Sections of the Kel Ewey confederation controlled villages and estates in western Damergu, but agricultural production in this area was only part of a larger Kel Ewey network which included homes in the Aïr, estates throughout the Sahel and savannah, and a large-scale commitment to animal husbandry and long-distance trade, with revenue from desert−savannah trade in salt, dates, grain, and animals supplementing the income they earned by providing transport animals, guides, and escorts for trans Saharan caravans. The chief rivals of the Kel Ewey were the Imezureg, who controlled villages and estates in central and eastern Damergu. In contrast to the Kel Ewey, Imezureg concentrated on the taxation of agricultural production at the expense of trade and animal husbandry. Hence they were less nomadic and their sources of wealth were more localized than in the case of the Kel Ewey. They were also in a better position to profit when the rise of the ostrich feather trade altered the structure of income opportunities for sedentary farmers to earn extra dry-season income. Imezureg simply levied a heavy export tax − possibly as much as half the catch − payable in feathers of the choicest grade. Growing wealth enabled the Imezureg to mount a successful challenge to their Kel Ewey rivals. The ensuing conflict remained indeterminate until the French arrived in

Damergu at the turn of the century and sided with the Kel Ewey. The French correctly perceived that an alliance with the Kel Ewey served their own interests, since the extensive Kel Ewey commitment to long-distance trade and their widespread and diverse economic activities seemed to indicate that they would be able to keep the caravan routes open.[13]

While the composition of Sudan exports shifted over a period of time, the proportional share of imported goods in the total remained relatively constant in the final three or four decades of trans-Saharan trade, except near the end of the period. According to the British consul, English 'T' cloths (a variety of Lancashire cotton cloth made especially for the export market), white long cloths, other assorted cotton goods and yarns, silks and silk thread, and a small quantity of woollens consistently accounted for over 70 per cent of the yearly totals of value between 1870 and 1900. The remainder was composed of a wide variety of imports including Venetian beads, French loaf sugar, green tea, mirrors, knives, swords, sword blades, paper, razors, perfume, jewellery, soap, spices, wooden clocks, rosaries, smuggled arms, gunpowder, garments made in Europe and North Africa, and assorted hardware.[14] In 1851 Barth estimated that imported silks dyed in Tripoli accounted for about a third of the total value, but the importance of this item seems to have declined in the following years at the expense of Manchester cottons. But otherwise the general pattern of trade remained unchanged, even after the turn of the century, when most imports consisted of printed and embroidered cotton, poor quality striped or printed cotton goods, bales of white cotton cloth, some of which was good quality, North American garments, silk and cotton thread, and assorted cloth such as handkerchiefs.[15]

In 1879 and 1880 the American consul in Tripoli spearheaded a drive to attract American cloth manufacturers to the Sudan trade, an effort which proved unsuccessful. But in doing so he investigated the cloth trade at the time and reported on it. He estimated the total annual value of imports at over £200,000, most of which went into the Sudan trade. Imports consisted of cotton piece goods and skeins of cotton yarn packed in 10-lb bundles; much imported yarn was retained in North Africa, where it was woven into garments worn only by Sudanese women. The most popular cotton piece goods were 'T' cloths, long cloths, mandapollams, and bright coloured calicoes. A large proportion of the grey 'T' cloths were dyed indigo in Tripoli before being shipped to the Sudan.[16] Indigo for dyeing came from the Sudan, as did some woven cloth.[17] The consul sent to the State Department a sample of cloth woven and dyed in the Sudan, probably in Kano; it consisted of thin strips of unequal length sewn together, and the process by which it had been dyed was unknown in Tripoli.[18]

It should be emphasized that the market for trans-Saharan imports in the Central Sudan had a broad social base. While the evidence for this is indirect, it is impossible to believe that cheap prints and grey bafts, the main imports, went totally or even in large part to the ruling class. Other items in the import list – mirrors, needles, knives, and hardware – must have been destined for a wide market as well. While luxury items continued to be imported, the characterization of trans-Saharan trade after 1870 as solely or principally an exchange of luxury goods for Sahelian products is inaccurate. In the Sahel the rapid growth of exports of feathers generated new income; although ruling groups were able to skim off a portion of this income to spend on luxury items, they were unable to take it all. Hence villagers traded feathers and skins for imported cloth and other items.

ECONOMIC GROWTH IN DAMAGARAM

Trans-Saharan exports were also available to the south in Damagaram. Wild ostriches were not as numerous as in Damergu, but the birds could be raised in captivity, although the plumage of caged animals was not as rich and had a lower market value than that of wild ostriches. Tanned goat skins were the speciality export of Damagaram, so that expanded trade in the 1890s was accompanied by intensified activity on the part of tanners and leather workers. For the first time local processing and manufacturing was connected with long-distance trade in a major way, though craft industries had served local and regional needs to a lesser extent for some time.

Exports of ostrich feathers and tanned goat skins stimulated local production, and growing trans-Saharan exports had important indirect effects as well. Agricultural production grew in response to an increase in urban population, increased specialization of production, and small-scale trans-Saharan exports of condiments such as okra, peppers, and groundnuts, as well as other items such as indigo, henna, and small amounts of potash for special uses. In addition, trans-Saharan trade had the seemingly paradoxical effect of stimulating cloth production in the Central Sudan, since Kano cloth was taken to Ghat, where some was taken to North Africa, and the rest was returned to markets in the Western Sudan via the trans-Saharan route to Timbuktu.[19] Undoubtedly the principal bene-ficiary of this export trade was the textile-producing region in the heartland of the Caliphate, and indirect effects in Damagaram were probably slight. Agricultural products and Kano cloth served the needs of Sudanese slaves and their dependants in North Africa, as well as the wider North African market, and in the case of indigo and potash, the North African cloth dyeing industry.

Economic growth in response to the expansion of trans-Saharan trade in the last three decades of the century continued a process begun earlier. Both Dunbar and Salifou stress the degree to which the people of Damagaram honour the memory of the second reign of Tanimu (1854–84).[20] Tanimu came to power because military success enabled him to attract a following early in life, and through-out his reign repeated triumph on the battlefield continued to strengthen the position of the state he ruled. Trans-Saharan trade contributed to the military advantage which Tanimu and his suc-cessors gained over neighbours to the south and west. Smaldone has described what he calls an incipient revolution in warfare because of fire-arms imports in the late-nineteenth-century Central Sudan.[21] Although trade in guns from both the Mediterranean and the Atlantic coast was prohibited by European powers, in the case of the northern route with the co-operation of the Ottoman sultanate in Tripoli and Cyrenaica, some muskets and even modern, rapid-firing rifles inevitably slipped through the arms embargo.[22] During the last quarter of the century the Sanūsīyya brotherhood, which controlled trade on the Benghazi–Wadai route, stepped up the flow of contraband arms trade, most of which went to the eastern Chad basin.[23] The result was that the area where either muskets or modern fire-arms were in use began to expand. The leakage of guns into the pre-colonial Central Sudan was never great enough, and the fire-arms which did arrive were not of good enough quality, to break the hold of old weapons and tactics. Consequently the revolution in warfare which might have occurred did not in fact take place, and Central Sudanic armies fought European conquerors with cavalry and archers.

But the gradual expansion of the gun frontier favoured states which had access to the limited supply which did arrive. In Damagaram, for example, Tanimu tapped the contraband trade to acquire perhaps as many as 6,000 muskets and 40 muzzle-loading cannon. Sulphur for gunpowder was imported from Tripoli, while saltpetre and carbon were obtained locally.[24] Muzzle-loading weapons, even in large quantities, did not necessarily tip the balance on the battlefield because they could not be reloaded and fired rapidly. But Tanimu went to a great deal of trouble to obtain them, organizing his own caravans to Tripoli and Egypt. Furthermore, Damagaram successfully blocked the flow of fire-arms from the north into the Sokoto Caliphate. Fire-arms, therefore, doubtlessly had some military value, and the supply of guns must have contributed to the ability of Damagaram to take Muniyo, Machena, and Nguru from Borno and to raid successfully into the territory of Kano, Kazaure, Daura, Hadeija, and Gumel.

As Dunbar notes, however, the military strength of Damagaram was built on trade, which oral tradition correctly recognizes as the true contribution of Tanimu.[25] The *sarki* invested personally in trade and was rewarded for his effort by personal wealth and the ability to purchase fire-arms. A growing volume of trade attracted North African merchants in larger numbers than before and promoted an increased interest in Damagaram on the part of Tuareg. Military success ensured peace and security, in contrast to unsettled conditions elsewhere, so that migration on a large scale took place, especially from the Caliphate. Pastoral Ful'be, who rarely ventured into Damagaram earlier, now arrived in numbers for the first time. Most important perhaps was the construction of the city walls: '. . . Zinder, a populous town under Ibrahim, became a *birni* or walled city under Tanimu. The construction of that wall remains an important symbol of the Sarki's wealth in material, of his administrative organization that could command a labour force sufficient to undertake such a project, and of his independence from Bornu.'[26] In addition Tanimu attracted to Zinder a prominent Muslim clerical scholar, Malam Sulayman, who assisted in the establishment of law and administration according to the *shariᶜa*.

Tanimu also set up a number of plantations east and south of the city. These plantations, worked by slaves under the supervision of a *sarkin gandu*, produced *fadama* crops of various kinds as well as dates and barley. Although neither Salifou nor Dunbar were able to assign precise dates to the establishment of these plantations, their founding may represent a response to increased local demand for foodstuffs during the period of rapid growth in trans-Saharan exports which took place in the 1870s and later. Certainly from this

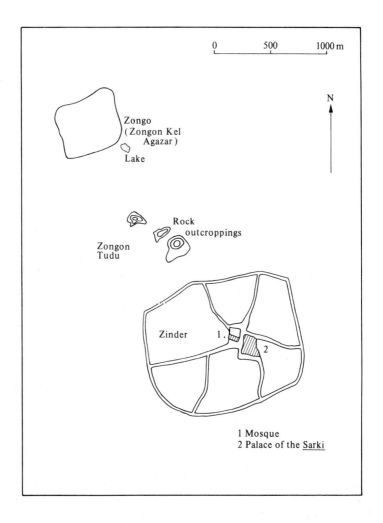

1 Mosque
2 Palace of the Sarki

period on large numbers of war captives were available; the ready supply of slave labour, at a time when trans-Saharan slave exports were dwindling, doubtless encouraged plantation agriculture, whatever its connection to regional or trans-Saharan exports may have been.[27] At the turn of the century Malam Yaro, a prominent merchant who exported from Zinder to North Africa on his own account, owned at least one plantation worked by slaves and supervised by his *sarkin gandu.* Along with the more usual exports −

tanned skins, ostrich feathers, and ivory — Malam Yaro also exported produce from plantations, and presumably from his own, such as indigo and hot peppers.[28] This produce, however, probably never accounted for more than a small fraction of the total exports of Damagaram. Unfortunately the evidence on slave plantations is too scanty to permit statements about the proportion of slaves in the rural population, changes in the ratio of slave to freeman over a period, or the rate at which slaves were absorbed into the free population.

Another direct result of economic growth was increased involvement in desert-side networks. Tuareg settlement in Zinder began when sections of the Kel Ewey confederation shifted the southern segment of their transhumance cycle eastward in response to the reorientation of trans-Saharan trade. The first section to arrive, the Kel Agazar, set up camp north of Zinder in the first reign of Sarki Ibrahim, between 1822 and 1846.[29] The Kel Tafidet, another Kel Ewey section, established a camp at Zongon Tudu, less than a kilometre north of where the city walls were to be located. (See Map 3.) By the end of the century these campsites had become permanent dry-season homes for many Tuareg of all social strata from a dozen sections, most belonging to the Kel Ewey confederation. Among nobles a common pattern was to maintain two households — one in Damagaram and another in Aïr, each near the extreme northern or southern limit of the transhumance cycle.[30] After arriving in the south nobles gave some servants the task of taking animals to dry-season pasture, and these servants returned from time to time if grazing lands were not too far from the main *zongo,* or campsite.

Nobles also used homes in Damagaram as bases from which to sell salt and dates and buy grain during the dry season, and they employed several methods for delegating responsibility for this trade. First, they entrusted goods to servants working under agents called *wakilai* (sing. *wakili*) who either sold from the noble's house, advertised around town, or travelled to periodic markets in the countryside nearby. Individual Tuareg sections also kept *wakilai,* who were people of servile origin, as commercial representatives in other Hausa cities.[31] A second method was for nobles to leave women of servile origin in charge of their houses and possessions after they returned to the north during the rainy season. Most dependent Tuareg left with the master, but these women stayed behind and continued to sell salt and dates from the caravan of the previous year on the master's account. Since they were by themselves for about half of each year, they were able to accumulate resources of their own by trading with their master's capital, and Tuareg nobles saw nothing wrong in this. Several women from the *zongo* near Zinder became landlady-brokers for stranger Tuareg belonging to sections which did not maintain dry-season camps near Zinder. They lodged guests, helped them sell merchandise, and provided storage facilities. They played a social role at least as important as their economic function, since they often found marriage partners for the servile Tuareg men who did most of the travelling necessary for salt trade.[32]

One of the principal attractions of the south was the market for salt from the desert. This was an extremely important current of trade, with up to 1,500 metric tons of salt passing through Damagaram each year near the end of the century. The value of this trade was about £60,000 or about half the value of trans-Saharan exports in an average year in the 1890s.[33] In 1903 an observer estimated that five-sixths of the salt entering Damagaram continued on to Kano; hence a rough estimate of local salt trade, excluding this transit trade, would be £10,000.[34] Although Kano and other areas of the Sokoto Caliphate overshadowed Zinder as a market, the Tuareg none the less had a considerable interest in the sale of salt in Damagaram, as their well-developed marketing system attests.

Growing involvement in the Tuareg network brought resources and trained personnel to Damagaram. Most Tuareg had experience and skill in commerce for the simple reason that long-distance trade played such a prominent role in their economy. Tuareg had access to transport animals and could therefore take advantage of opportunities to profit by transporting commodities from place to place. In addition, Tuareg nobles sometimes channelled resources into activities such as cloth dyeing and leather-working, forms of production only indirectly connected with the desert-side sector. In Zinder, for example, most tanners were *bugaje* or Hausa who lived in the Tuareg encampment. These craftsmen lacked resources of their own, so that Tuareg or North African financiers gave them raw skins to work and paid them in kind when the finished product was delivered. Immigrants of northern origins were also involved in fashioning finished products such as sandals.[35]

Tuareg nobles also invested in grain production on rural estates south and south-west of the city. The largest wave of Tuareg settlement in Damagaram dates from a later period and was the result of troubles associated with the drought of 1911 – 14 and the revolt of 1916 – 18.[36] But a nucleus of sedentary Tuareg activity south-west of Zinder existed as early as 1851, when Barth passed through on his way from Kukawa to Sokoto. The residents of these estates were either slaves or the descendants of slaves. Their principal obligations were to pay an annual tax in millet, to provide food and lodging for their masters when nomads passed through on transhumance, to help with dry-season herding, and to give gifts to their masters at important ceremonial occasions such as weddings. Servile Tuareg living on these estates saw their masters only rarely; if the noble or noble section to whom they belonged spent the dry season in the Zinder *zongo,* they might see nobles several times each year. But in case the owners of the estate spent the dry season farther south, servile Tuareg saw them only when they passed through on the way to and from rainy-season pasture in the desert.[37]

Tuareg investment in craft production, grain-producing estates, and a trading and marketing infrastructure for desert products led to political, administrative, and military involvement in the affairs of Damagaram. In effect two entirely separate systems of government coexisted side by side and met only at the highest level. Servile Tuareg paid tax to their masters, who in turn settled disputes and listened to grievances. On the other hand peasants at the bottom of the sedentary hierarchy, whose economic and social position was roughly similar to that of low-status Tuareg, paid tax to territorial chiefs and fiefholders, and ultimately to the *sarki.*

The mechanism for regulating relations between Damagaram and the Tuareg at this level centred on the office of the Tuareg *manzo.* This official was appointed by the *anastafidet* of the Kel Ewey, and his duty was to represent the interests of the Tuareg to the court in Zinder.[38] Apparently unsettled disputes between low-status Tuareg and their Hausa and Kanuri counterparts were always resolved at the level of the *sarki* and the *manzo.* Little detail on this process is known except that those in the upper levels of both systems dealt harshly with infringements on the part of commoners; both ruling groups realized that solidarity was in their own best interests.[39]

Not only did the rulers of Damagaram forgo rights of sovereignty in certain enclaves within the state where Tuareg held sway, but they also forfeited revenue by exempting Tuareg settlers from certain taxes. Tuareg who settled in Zinder paid no tribute to the *sarki* other than transit taxes on salt and dates which entered or

passed through.[40] The forfeiture of revenue in order to encourage
transit trade was probably wise in a narrow fiscal sense — in that it
was offset by transit taxes — and in the sense that the Tuareg
presence benefited the growth of a number of sectors which
depended on desert-side contacts or trans-Saharan trade. In
addition, Tuareg were useful allies in campaigns against eastern and
southern neighbours of Damagaram, and they would have made
dangerous enemies had their involvement in the local economy and
co-operation in military matters not been carefully cultivated.

Thus it appears that the growth of the state, which owed much to
trans-Saharan trade, was accompanied by far-reaching internal
change; the institutionalization of Islamic law within the state
structure; important work on the defensive fortification of the
capital; increasing involvement of Tuareg, with their estates and a
commercial infrastructure extending outward from the camps at
Zongo and Zongon Tudu; and possibly, though the evidence is less
clear, a shift to large-scale production on estates owned by the ruler,
title-holders, or rich merchants.

Internal change naturally affected external relations, and an
important long-term result of economic growth, the availability of
fire-arms, and the use of Tuareg allies was an increasingly autono-
mous relation between Damagaram and its suzerain state, Borno.
From the origins of the dynasty the *sarakuna* of Damagaram had
paid tribute to Kukawa, the Borno capital. When Richardson
passed through Zinder in the early 1850s, the ruler in Kukawa kept
a close watch over the actions of the local *sarki*; his agent, a wealthy
and influential merchant of Moroccan origin named Sharif Kebir
al-Fasi, reported back to Borno on all matters of importance.[41] But
a few years later the Zinder ruler Tanimu had begun to act
independently, as he brought Damagaram's new military and
economic power to bear on his neighbours to the west, south, and
east, often with the Tuareg as allies. Borno made an effort to keep
peace between Damagaram and its other western vassals, but it was
powerless to oppose the annexation by Damagaram of Myrria in the
late 1850s and Muniyo in 1876.[42] By 1892, when Monteil visited
Kukawa, Damagaram had not paid tribute for some time.[43] The
next year Rabih b. Fadallah, a military adventurer from the Sudan
who had conquered Bagirmi and part of the Shari Logon region,
attacked Borno from the east. In Zinder Sarki Ahmadu Maje
Rumji ignored a desperate plea from his former suzerain for
military assistance, and Borno soon fell to Rabih. Damagaram

continued to expand eastward in order to keep Rabih at a comfortable distance, and Zinder even mounted a partially successful
military challenge to Kano in the late 1890s.[44]

SOUTHERN NETWORKS

Perhaps the best index of the local effects of the late nineteenth-
century growth of trans-Saharan trade is the record of immigration
of long-distance traders to Damagaram late in the second reign of
Tanimu, and their subsequent activities, which can be documented
in some detail. One example is the local tradition of migration from
Tessaoua, a town west of Zinder on the trade route to Katsina which
lost its position at Zinder's expense. About 1880 'Dan Bade and
'Dan Maleka, two important traders, joined the movement to
Zinder. 'Dan Bade, who settled at Zongon Tudu just north of the
city wall, had a monopoly on the supply of water skins to caravans
setting out for the desert, and he also traded in slaves sold for
internal use. 'Dan Maleka did some local trading and employed
labourers during the dry season to weave cloth for sale, paying them
with a share of the output. Both served as landlord-brokers for
traders from Katsina and nearby villages who brought kola and
tobacco to Damagaram to exchange for salt, potash, and animals.
They lodged and provided meals for these traders, helped them
buy and sell merchandise, and guaranteed transactions and credit
exchanges – all in return for a fee paid by the guest trader.[45]
    Another migration to Damagaram was an influx of Kanuri-
speaking people which took place some time between 1860 and 1885
and was associated with the Tuareg attack on the town of Kulumfardo. While the date of the event is uncertain, the immigrants
arrived in the second reign of Tanimu. One immigrant was a trader
who operated from a base in Zinder, but a far more common
pattern was dry-season trade by people from small villages whose
principal occupation was farming. They formed expeditions to take
grain east to Muniyo to trade for potash which they then took to
Kano where they traded it for cloth. Most of the cloth they obtained
was for their own needs rather than for resale.[46]
    The practice of joining caravans heading south for Kano and
other areas in the Caliphate must have been as old as agricultural
settlement in Damagaram, but the importance of these dry-season
trading expeditions increased in the 1870s and 1880s. For the first
time the far northern fringe of Hausa settlement participated in a

surge of commercial growth which had begun earlier. By the early
nineteenth century good climate, political unity in the Caliphate,
the strength of the Central Sudan economy, and the collapse of Oyo
in Yoruba country combined to allow Hausa traders to assume a
larger and larger share of long-range trade in an area extending
from the middle Volta basin to Adamawa in the east and south as
far as the coast. The first Hausa traders known to have reached the
coast arrived early in the nineteenth century, and by the 1880s and
1890s they travelled to Lagos in large numbers.[47]

The general commercial expansion of the nineteenth century
formed a backdrop, but desert-edge economic growth led by trans-
Saharan exports was a prerequisite for local participation. The
principal evidence for greater integration of Damagaram into larger
Hausa trading networks consists of oral data on the immigration
and subsequent activities of two men who were to become the two
most important caravan leaders (Hausa, *madugai,* sing. *madugu*) in
the area.

The story of the career of one of these men, Madugu Isa, illustrates how the economy of Damagaram was linked to markets and
resources far to the south. Isa was born to Hausa-speaking parents
of Kanuri origin in the village of Mai Jirgi near Tessaoua. After
establishing himself as a successful farmer, he moved into the potash
trade to Nupe. He set himself up as a landlord-broker for northern
traders in Bida, where he lived permanently for seven years, trading
as well as offering brokerage services in partnership with three of
his brothers. He decided to move to Zinder because of a prior
friendship with Malam Sulayman, whom Sarki Tanimu had
appointed his principal counsellor and given the task of setting up
the rule of Muslim law in Damagaram. Isa joined Sulayman at
Zongon Tudu, just north of the city walls, but Malam Sulayman
thought it best for Isa to set up his household farther from Zinder
where more land was available. Isa agreed because he had many
dependants to feed, and he founded the vllage known locally as
Kwarin Bakwai.[48]

Madugu Isa led the annual caravan from Damagaram to Nupe
and later as far as Ilorin. He was at the top of a hierarchy in local
maduganci (leading caravans), so that lesser *madugai* from near and
far joined him for the departure from Damagaram. Both the other
caravan leaders in Damagaram of any importance in the late
nineteenth century, Madugu Sharubutu and Madugu Ilias, married
Isa's daughters. These alliances were expressions of Isa's accept-

ance of the two junior caravan leaders and their recognition of his seniority.[49] Isa and his caravan may have joined forces with a *madugu* of higher rank once they reached Kano, but so far no information is available to either confirm or refute this. The first leg of the trip was the journey east the the natron lakes of Muniyo, where Madugu Isa led the bargaining for potash. He gave gifts to whoever held rights over the potash deposits, then bargained for the price of a donkey-load of the salt in terms of millet. Once established, the exchange rate held for all traders in the caravan.[50]

The organization of the caravan as it headed south for Zaria followed a pattern common in most pre-colonial Hausa trade. As the caravan leader, Isa made all important decisions about matters affecting the caravan: where it was to stop each day, when to load up in the morning, who would keep watch at night, and how to divide up the load of an animal that died or was too weak to continue. The *jagaba*, or principal assistant of the *madugu*, led the march with a party of armed men mounted on horseback. Next followed the donkeys and their drovers, and then another party of armed men followed by the *madugu,* who travelled last.[51]

Caravans in the potash trade were similar to the kola caravans which plied routes between Hausaland and the Volta basin, though more loosely organized.[52] Kola caravans had to be run like war parties in order to be able to defend themselves against large bands of raiders. The principal dangers in the potash trade, on the other hand were wild animals and thieves in relatively small groups. Conseqently potash caravans were smaller, and the power of the *madugu* was not as great as in the case of the kola trade. In potash caravans the influence of the *madugu* derived more from his power and prestige as an important trader in his own right than from his position at the head of a quasi-military expedition.

Return merchandise could be of several varieties. Some traders stopped at Kano; usually there were farmers who traded for cloth for their own use rather than for resale. Another section, probably larger than the former, stopped at Zaria and pastured their animals, bought raw cotton, engaged in some local relocation trade, and awaited the return of the main body of the caravan from Nupe.[53] In Nupe traders exchanged potash and animals for locally made garments, beads, ironwork, and swords. As the century drew to a close, imports from the coast had a progressively greater importance; these were Manchester cottons, kola imported by sea from Accra, and imported salt. In the 1890s Ilorin replaced markets in

Nupe as the southern terminus of the trade, and soon afterwards traders from Damagaram went as far as Lagos.[54]

When the caravan returned to Damagaram, traders disposed of their merchandise in local markets or through house trade. They gave out raw cotton on loan to women who spun it into thread and repaid traders after having sold spun thread. Merchants took some merchandise on tour of a number of rural markets in the area, selling small quantities whenever they were able to command a satisfactory price. Another approach was to give merchandise to a *dilali* or commission seller in Zinder, who received a commission for the merchandise he could sell.[55]

Still another approach was to take goods to Myrria, the site of a large periodic market located about 20 km east of Zinder. Myrria was one of two principal geographical focuses for interregional trade in pre-colonial Damagaram. The first was Zinder; here the physical layout of the city, with Tuareg settlements close to the walled *birni*, reflected the close ties between sedentary rulers and the northern Tuareg network. Zinder was the central place in its region for trans-Saharan trade and for commercial circuits which distributed salt and dates and collected grain and other staples for provisioning caravans.

While interregional trade from Zinder was primarily connected to northern, nomadic networks, Myrria handled trade from the south and east which was carried principally by traders of sedentary origin. The market at Myrria grew steadily in the last quarter of the nineteenth century, and by 1900 it met three days each week — Saturday, Sunday, and Monday — and overshadowed the Thursday market at Zinder.[56] Underlying the growth of Myrria was an environmental factor. In contrast to Zinder, Myrria had plentiful surface water. Zinder was hindered by its location on a granite plateau, a site only slightly above surrounding country on three sides, but well above land to the north. At Zinder wells were deep, and the water supply was not only limited in quantity but poor in quality.[57] These limitations were not serious in the case of trade carried by camels, which could be taken to pasture and wells in the countryside. But abundant water was a necessity for a market which handled large quantities of staple trade. Grain, salt, potash, and kola were all high weight, low value products, and the result was that moving them from place to place required many transport animals, all of which had to be watered at or near the market. Large numbers of cattle, sheep, goats, and camels also changed hands at the market each week, and these animals also had to be watered. Myrria grew at Zinder's expense because surface water was available all year long from spring-fed surface lakes.

In part because of this abundance of water, the functions of the market at Myrria differed from those performed in Zinder. First, staples entering and leaving the region from the south or from the east were distributed or bulked at Myrria, and were passed from Myrria to smaller periodic markets which met only one day. Second and most importantly, Myrria was a transit market; Kanuri traders brought animals and potash from the east and north-east, while Hausa from the south brought cloth made in Kano or in Kura, a town which like Kano had a large spinning, weaving, and dyeing industry. Traders coming from either direction found landlord-brokers who specialized in certain kinds of products and dealt primarily with traders of a certain ethnic background or area of origin.[58] While these landlord-brokers were not often from the same area of origin as their clients, they did learn to cater to the tastes and needs of traders of a particular region or background.

CONCLUSION

To summarize, growth in the trading economy of Damagaram and its northern neighbour, Damergu, had far-reaching ramifications in the lives of merchants, cultivators, herdsmen, craftsmen, and ruling élites. Zinder, the central place for both regions, had a dual orient-ation. The city was not only a stopping-place for caravans plying the Tripoli–Kano route, but it was also a point of contact between the desert-side sector and the economy of the savannah. The rulers of Damagaram taxed the production of fertile agricultural land and reinvested their wealth in military conquest and slave-labour. Tuareg involvement in Damagaram led to closer ties between nomadic nobles and the local ruling élite, and it resulted in the formation of a state within a state, one territorially defined and relying on revenue from agriculture, and the other with a wider geographical scope, a marked seasonal fluctuation in the size of population, and a greater diversity of economic activities. These two systems came together in the context of the regional economy, and from the second quarter of the nineteenth century growth in the two sectors was mutually reinforcing. Both benefited from trans-Saharan trade, especially after the volume of legitimate exports increased rapidly in the 1870s. Trans-Saharan trade allowed

Damagaram to attract farmers and craftsmen and to wage war successfully on its eastern and southern neighbours. Prosperity also served as an indirect stimulus for greater involvement from desert-side networks, as Tuareg reacted to opportunities to sell services and desert products and to invest in the savannah. For the first time Hausa-speaking traders from Damagaram were able to participate fully in the process of Hausa commercial expansion which had begun a century earlier or more, but which had affected principally the central area of Hausa settlement until the 1870s. To the north in Damergu, the growth of legitimate exports created new possibilities for dry-season earnings among villagers subject to Tuareg. Economic growth, and in particular the rise of opportunities for cultivators to earn extra income, required a response from the rulers of Damergu, whose reaction was to tax the new trade. In Damagaram the response of the ruling group was to attempt to expand the area they ruled by continued military pressure on their neighbours to the south and east.

CHAPTER III

Trans-Saharan Trade

WHILE prosperous trans-Saharan trade presented opportunities to the merchants of Damagaram, it also tied them to forces beyond their control, and in particular to a dependence on North Africa for commercial capital. When trade between Tripoli and the Sudan ended abruptly, merchants in the Central Sudan faced unprecedented problems of adjustment. The purpose of this and the following chapter is to describe the organization and finance of the desert trade in its final decades, to analyse the causes of its collapse, to reinterpret the timing of the collapse, to show how Sahelian merchants functioned in this larger system, and to trace their reactions when Saharan trade ended. The use of a wide variety of historical sources, including archival material from both the northern and southern end of the Tripoli–Kano route and oral data, makes it possible to avoid distortions inherent in local accounts and to gain a much more complete picture of the trade than would otherwise be possible. In addition, an analysis of the finance of trade aids in assessing the impact of trans-Saharan trade on the economy of the Central Sudan and in understanding changes in local trade and production which took place in the period 1870–1920.

THE GHADAMASI TRADE DIASPORA

The principal agents of trans-Saharan commerce in Zinder were the merchants of Ghadames, an oasis in the desert about 450 km southwest of Tripoli. Early French sources refer to all North Africans in the Sudan as Arab, but in fact Ghadamasi spoke a Berber language closely related to Tamashek, the language of the Tuareg.[1] To the British consul Thomas Jago, the location of Ghadames and the linguistic abilities of its inhabitants went a long way in explaining their success:

The monopoly of the Tripoli–Western Sudan trade enjoyed by the Ghadamseen merchants residing in the town of Tripoli is due, apart from their superior intelligence and business habits, to the geographical position of their birth-place, an oasis in Tuareg territory, giving them a knowledge of the Arabic, Hausa, and Tuareg languages, in addition to their own language, a dialect of the Berber.[2]

The exact extent of Ghadamasi dominance in Tripoli–Kano trade over the centuries is unknown, but their prominence may date to the fourteenth century or earlier.[3] By the second half of the nineteenth century their ethnic monopoly on this trade route was nearly complete. In 1851 Barth remarked that most North African inhabitants of Dala quarter in Kano were Ghadamasi, and a decade later Duveyrier visited Ghadames and noted the widespread commercial contacts of Ghadamasi firms 'which have branches at Kano and Katsina in the Sudan, in Timbuktu on the Niger, in Ghat and in Sallah in the central Sahara, and in Tripoli and Tunis on the mediterranean shore'.[4] El-Hachaichi, who travelled through the oases in the late 1890s, supplied an extensive list of Ghadamasi living in Wadai, Kanem, Borno, Adamawa, and Nupe, in the Hausa cities of Kano, Zaria, and Sokoto; at Ghat, Ghadames, and Murzuk in the desert; in Zinder and at Djadjidouna, a small village four days north of Zinder. Ghadamasi merchants also lived in Tripoli and Tunis and traded between these two cities by sea.[5]

   The process of dispersal for the purposes of cross-cultural trade is best viewed in the framework of the 'trade diaspora', a concept put forward by Lloyd Fallers and elaborated by Abner Cohen and Philip Curtin.[6] A trade diaspora can be defined as dispersed communities of traders living as minorities in a foreign culture. Their purpose is to facilitate cross-cultural trade under conditions found in pre-industrial societies. Given slow communication and transportation and the absence of centralized banking and credit institutions, merchants often found it necessary to travel from place to place in order to conduct their business. Pioneer merchants established homes in foreign trading centres, forming minorities of trade specialists within the host culture. Travelling merchants moved freely along the trade network because they shared a common culture and similar occupational interests with the pioneer merchants. More important, established merchants provided essential services for newcomers: temporary lodging, storage facilities, advice on local conditions, credit guarantees, and brokerage services. The function of the established merchants was to interpret, both literally and figuratively, the local culture to their travelling associates. Defined in this way, trade diasporas occur in a wide variety of situations in world history – settings ranging from European overseas trade before the nineteenth century to the Hausa kola and cattle trade of the present day. Widespread distribution simply reflects the broadly similar way pre-industrial societies have solved problems involved in moving goods from place to place and exchanging them with foreigners.

In the Central Sudan landlord-brokers in Hausa-Kanuri trading networks and landlady-brokers in the Tuareg network are examples of variations on this theme.[7] In this case their purpose was not to translate for their guests or to interpret a foreign culture and unfamiliar business practices. Hausa was the language of trade in the Central Sudan, even in the desert-side sector; as far away as Fachi and Bilma, Hausa was the common second language among Tuareg salt traders and their Kanuri suppliers. In addition, the commercial culture of the Central Sudan was relatively uniform over a wide area. But landlord-brokers and landlady-brokers provided services equally as important. They lodged their guests, gave them a place to keep their animals, provided servants to draw water and search for fodder. They also provided brokerage and banking services. Sometimes travelling merchants had to accept delayed payment for their goods, and in this case they needed credit guarantees, which the landlord-broker provided. Or if credit went in the opposite direction, the landlord-broker guaranteed the trustworthiness of his guest. Travelling merchants could also leave money with their landlords for safe keeping, and this service provided travellers with an important safeguard against theft in an unfamiliar urban environment. While these examples are drawn from the commercial history of the Central Sudan, they help to illustrate the pivotal role of those who performed similar functions in other trade diasporas.

The development of the Ghadamasi trade diaspora also fits into a broader pattern in the history of desert-edge people. At Ghadames, as in other oases, crops must be irrigated, with the result that growing wheat is labour-intensive. Maintaining date-palms, on the other hand, requires relatively little labour, so dates are abundant.[8] But as a result of the desire to vary their diet, the inhabitants of Ghadames, like those of other North African oases, developed trade contacts with areas near the coast where rainfall agriculture made large grain surpluses possible. Intensive exchange of dates for grain fostered trade in other items. Cloth, in particular, lent itself to exchange across the ecological frontier because cotton cannot be grown cheaply over a wide area of desert and desert edge. Once a group specialized in trade of cloth and staples, it readily adapted to trade on trans-Saharan routes. Since they lived in proximity to the Tuareg, the merchants of Ghadames were able to form alliances with noble lineages, without whose co-operation trade in the desert would have been impossible. This sequence,

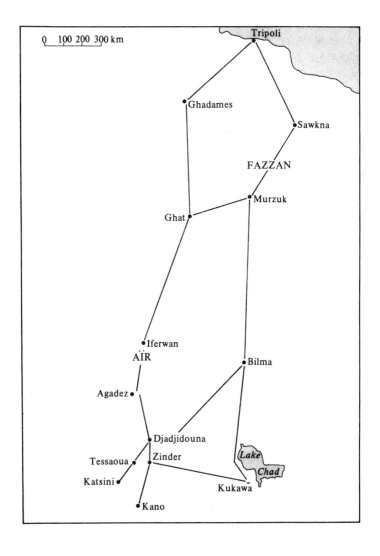

while it is a process model rather than events which can be documented, nevertheless helps to explain the prominence of traders from the northern oases on so many trans-Saharan routes. West of Ghadames, the Bani-Mzab dominated trade with the south until Algerian segments of trans-Saharan commerce declined in the mid-nineteenth century. To the east the merchants of Sawkna were the principal carriers between the Fazzan and the Mediterranean coast. The Mujabra and the Zuwaya, nomads who carried trade in dates and grain in Cyrenaica, pioneered the route from Benghazi to Wadai.[9] The southern desert edge also provides many examples of peoples whose historical development was similar. The history of the Sahelian Tuareg, to take an obvious case, illustrates the process by which wealth in interregional trade formed the basis for a broad range of other investments.

A central feature of the Ghadamasi trade diaspora was the common commercial culture which extended the length of the Tripoli–Kano route. Acceptance of Islam, literacy in Arabic, and participation in the cosmopolitan outlook of a world religion and Mediterranean culture formed the background in the social sphere. As the nineteenth century progressed membership in the Sanūsīyya, a Sufi order, which affected many aspects of merchants' lives, became increasingly common. At the heart of the economic life of the diaspora were institutions which permitted the flow of a large volume of trade and allowed agents to transact business at a distance on behalf of their associates. The practical basis of the system was an inventory list which accompanied each package and was reproduced in an over-all, comprehensive list, or waybill, for each consignment. The waybill gave an accounting of all goods and included the terms of credit or a contract for the division of profits.[10] Étiévant, who learned about Tripoli—Kano trade from a prominent Ghadamsi merchant in Zinder in 1908, reported an accounting arrangement used by merchants corresponding with one another. A merchant based in Tripoli would send cloth and other imports to an agent in the Sudan, listing prices well above Tripoli market prices. The agent exchanged these goods for Sudan products equivalent to the elevated value and returned them to his northern correspondent. This arrangement, according to Étiévant's informant, assured both merchants of a reasonable profit. Although Ghadamasi sometimes paid agents with a specified share of the profit, just as often as not they simply exchanged small commercial favours with one another.[11]

Another key institution was a transport system which allowed merchants to send shipments unaccompanied across the desert. At Ghat, one of the principal relay points, merchants or their agents contracted with Ajjer Tuareg who provided transport animals and armed escorts for caravans.[12] At Iferwan in the northern Aïr Mountains, another relay point, Ajjer Tuareg left the caravan and merchants or their agents made contracts with Kel Ewey, who provided similar services on the leg of the journey between Iferwan and Kano and other Hausa cities. An important aspect of the mutual trust and understanding underlying these contracts were customary alliances between merchants and Tuareg lineages, so that Ghadamasi often sought out Tuareg with whom they had had dealings. Tuareg transporters accepted full responsibility for the goods they carried. When a caravan arrived at a relay station or an end point, Tuareg in charge of the caravan delivered the merchandise to its owner or his agent.[13] Sometimes the principal investor in a caravan paid an agent or caravan leader, who was Ghadamasi in most cases, to accompany the caravan, but this was not always the case.

The commercial organization of the trade diaspora permitted the operation of small firms, but merchants could form enterprises larger than simple partnerships in several ways. One possibility was to use family members as subordinates. Examples of several Ghadamasi family firms have come to light. El-Hachaichi, who travelled in the desert in the early 1890s, mentioned the El-Tseni family of Ghadames, which had widespread commercial connections in Hausaland, Timbuktu, in North Africa, and in the oases.[14] Méry, who provided a detailed account of trade between Tripoli and the Sudan in 1892, described a family firm headed by El Haj Mohammed, who resided in Ghat. One son handled the family's business in Tripoli while another acted as its agent in Ghadames; seven others bought and sold in the Sudan.[15]

The Guenaba family of Zinder and Kano operated in a similar fashion. The Guenabas were descendants of an undistinguished Ghadamasi merchant who migrated to Zinder and had two sons by a Hausa woman, Dodo and Ahamed. Dodo stayed in Zinder, but his brother went to Tripoli to join another half brother, and both handled the family import–export business there. Ahamed and Dodo moved to Kano about 1905, but Dodo maintained a residence in Zinder for his brief yearly visits until he died in the late 1920s. Another example was a family firm oprated by Hassan and Abba Doma, immigrants from Sawkna, an oasis north of the Fazzan.

Hassan lived in Zinder, while Abba traded from Kukawa until the city fell to Rabih and Abba rejoined his brother in Zinder.[16]

Another way of enlarging the scale of operations of the firm was to use slave employees. Several agents named in El-Hachaichi's extensive list of Ghadamasi in the Sudan were listed as freed slaves.[17] In Damergu and Damagaram former slaves were known as black North Africans (Hausa, *bakin larabawa*) or by the Berber equivalent, *ikawaren*, a term originally applied to the dark-skinned inhabitants of the central Saharan oases but later extended to include merchants of servile origin. One of the Zinder *ikawaren*, a man named Bedari Zumut, was a former slave who became a wealthy and prominent member of the North African expatriate community. His master was very probably Mustapha Zammit, a prominent Ghadamasi merchant named in Bettoli's detailed description of the Tripoli trade.[18] Bedari was given his freedom on the condition that he and his descendants affix his master's name − Zumut in the Hausa version − to their own. Méry's description of the sons of El Haj Mohammed, which ends with the comment that 'they are all black', raises the possibility that some 'sons' were in fact freed slaves.[19] But this comment may also be simply a reflection of the fact that Ghadamasi men frequently married Sudanese women.

Although Zinder attracted North African merchants almost as soon as the city began to play a role in trans-Saharan trade, it was not until the last quarter of the century that Ghadamasi were the dominant group. The first North African to arrive was a man of unknown origin named Awali who lived alone east of Zinder in the 1830s. At mid-century the most important merchant in Zinder was the rich and influential Moroccan, Sharif Kabir al-Fasi, who also served as the chief agent of the Borno ruler. Most merchants of this era, however, were from the Fazzan, and they had been drawn to Zinder by the transit trade between Zinder and Borno. Fazzani had previously traded between Borno and North Africa, but the direct route north of Borno was much less safe for caravan traffic than the road north of Zinder. By making a western detour through Zinder, then north to Ghat and then to Murzuk, the Fazzani bypassed the dangerous section of the route between Borno and Bilma.[20]

North Africans came to Zinder in response to commercial opportunities, but events in North Africa also had an influence on migration. An example is the case of Sawkna, an oasis 450 km southeast of Tripoli. The conflict between the Awlad Sulayman and the Ottoman Turks led to reprisals by the Awlad Sulayman against the people of Sawkna. In 1841 Sawkna lost a large part of its productive capacity when the Awlad Sulayman cut down most of the date-palms in the oasis. Richardson, who passed through Sawkna in 1846, reported that it would be thirty to fifty years before new trees would be in full production and harvests could reach their former levels.[21] This severe blow to the economy of the oasis occurred during the heyday of the Fazzani commercial settlement in Zinder, and taken together these factors influenced further immigration. Between 1860 and 1880 a religious scholar and skilled artisan from Sawkna named Hassan Doma migrated to Zinder. His original intention was to be a scribe for Sarki Tanimu, but Tanimu was more interested in his skills as a leather-worker. He invited Hassan to set up a household near the palace and to encourage other artisans from Sawkna to come as well. The community founded by Hassan grew, and most of the new arrivals were skilled craftsmen. A few traders also came; for example, one of Hassan's cousins, who was a merchant trading between Borno and North Africa, established a permanent residence in Zinder.[22]

The growth of the Ghadamasi community in Zinder dates to the 1870s and 1880s and was a direct result of rapid growth in exports of tanned goat skins and ostrich feathers. From their houses Ghadamasi distributed cloth and other imports, financing much of the trade taking place in distribution networks radiating outward from the city. Newcomers already spoke Hausa, a consequence of interaction with the large Hausa-speaking population of servile origin living in the Saharan oases.[23] While new arrivals had some previous contact with sub-Saharan culture, they none the less relied on the services they found in Zinder. Merchants who were already established performed the functions characteristic of all trade diasporas, bridging the gap between local custom and the commercial culture of the Ghadamasi.

Despite its important role in Zinder's economic life, the Ghadamasi community was small. In 1899 when the *Mission Saharienne* passed through Zinder, Foureau reported that twelve North Africans lived in the city, most of them from Ghadames. Reibell, another member of the *Mission Saharienne*, visited the North African ward within the city walls, and reported seeing a few traders living alongside artisans from Sawkna. The most prominent of the group was Sharif Dodo of the Guenaba family. But most merchants lived in the Tuareg settlements north of the city walls, where about ten Ghadamasi maintained permanent residences.[24]

About a dozen Ghadamasi lived in Djadjidouna, a small village in Damergu which was a stopping-place on the trans-Saharan route. They traded from their houses, exchanging trans-Saharan imports for feathers and skins. Some of the merchants gave out goods on loan to Hausa or Kanuri traders who visited the periodic markets of the area and also traded at villages and encampments as they passed through. Other Ghadamasi dealt directly with Kanuri village heads who acted as entrepreneurs in the ostrich feather trade. For example, Kelzumi, the head of the village at Djadjidouna, financed small expeditions of hunters who went out during the dry season to hunt ostriches and bring back feathers and ostrich skins, a subsidiary export. At another village called Malam Tilum, the village head was also an intermediary between the Ghadamasi and villagers who collected exports.[25]

At the turn of the century all North Africans in Damagaram and Djadjidouna belonged to the Sanūsīyya, a Muslim *tarīqa* (brotherhood) which originated in Cyrenaica in 1843 when Muhammad al-Sanusi, its founder, established the first Sanūsī *zawīya* or lodge.[26] The order spread quickly among the Beduin people of Cyrenaica in the next decade because it was able to involve itself in useful religious and commercial functions and to fill a political vacuum in an area beyond the reach of effective Ottoman government. One particularly important service provided by the *tarīqa* was that of mediation. In the absence of central political authority, the arbitration and settlement of disputes between peoples, between hostile factions, or between lineage segments took on a special significance. In addition, Sanūsī lodges, built by local oases peoples but with technical aid from the brotherhood, provided a place for education and religious instruction.

The *tarīqa* also had an important commercial dimension, and its expansion southward into the interior was closely linked with the growth of trans-Saharan trade between Benghazi and Wadai. The order promoted trade both directly and indirectly. As Cordell points out, '. . . the founding of a loosely unified network of Sanūsī *zawīyas* along the main and secondary paths of commerce enabled the rapid exchange of information concerning commercial conditions'.[27] Sanūsī lodges served as resting places for travelling merchants, and legal scholars and courts associated with the lodges enforced commercial contracts. The brotherhood maintained wells along trade routes, and many of the leaders of the order engaged in trade themselves. The Sanūsīyya helped keep the peace and established common commercial culture along the entire length of the Benghazi—Wadai route, thereby greatly encouraging investment in commerce.

The Sanūsīyya also spread quickly along the Tripoli—Kano route, but it was unable to play the all-important role it attained farther east. By 1856 the order had established a *zawīya* in Ghadames, where it had a large following. It is likely that the Ghadamasi immigrants of the 1870s and 1880s belonged to the Sanūsīyya, and by the 1890s the entire Ghadamasi community at Djadjidouna were members of the order. The position of the brotherhood in Damagaram and Damergu was given formal expression by the visit of the Sanūsī missionary Shaikh Muhammad al-Sunni. While in Djadjidouna on the way to Zinder in 1897 or 1898, al-Sunni appointed a leader for the local Sanūsī mosque, the 166th such mosque officially consecrated by the leaders of the brotherhood. In Zinder al-Sunni encountered the opposition of Sarki Ahmadu Kuren Daga, who viewed the Sanūsīyya with suspicion because he believed it to be a threat to his authority. The *sarki* forbade the founding of a *zawīya* of the kind found in North Africa and in the oases, complete with lodgings and tax-exempt farmland. Nevertheless he permitted al-Sunni to establish a mosque, the 167th Sanūsī mosque, and appoint a leader for the members of the sect in Zinder.[28]

The second purpose of al-Sunni's visit to Damagaram and Damergu was to attempt to end hostilities which threatened to disrupt Tripoli—Kano trade. The leaders of the brotherhood made a concerted effort to reconcile warring factions of Tuareg and Tubu Reshada. In 1897, and again in 1900, al-Sunni himself went on missions to the Awlad Sulayman, whose raids threatened Benghazi—Wadai trade and prevented the revival of trade between Borno and the Fazzan. While in Zinder al-Sunni attempted to mediate a quarrel between Zinder and Kano which disrupted the smooth flow of trans-Saharan trade, but to no avail. It is interesting to speculate about what would have happened had the Sanūsīyya been as successful in keeping peace on the Tripoli—Kano route as it was between Benghazi and Wadai; undoubtedly Tripoli—Kano trade would have lasted longer than it actually did, but it would also have ended even more abruptly.[29]

Membership in the Sanūsīyya provided a means for North Africans to assert their separateness from local people. None of the Hausa, Tuareg, Tubu, or Kanuri of Damagaram belonged to the brotherhood. Sanūsī ceremonies, held twice each year in Zinder, were closed to local people, who attended only the opening of the ceremony in order to obtain the blessing of the founder of the sect.[30]

Although North Africans successfully retained a separate religious identity, assimilation in all other respects occurred rapidly. Some North Africans spent only a few years in the communities of the trade diaspora in the Sudan before returning home, and for these people the influence of Sudanese culture was slight indeed. But those who married and lived out their lives in Zinder were different. Most but not all immigrants were men, and the sexual imbalance of the community meant that most merchants' wives were local women. At least one North African woman migrated to Zinder in the nineteenth century, but this was exceptional. The descendants of the original immigrants tended to marry outside the community, and consequently successive generations moved farther and farther from the culture of their fathers. Except for membership in the Sanūsīyya, the descendants of early North African immigrants to Zinder are today completely acculturated.

Although Ghadamasi formed the dominant group in the trade diaspora, they were not its only members, for diaspora communities were open to outsiders. Employees and agents of Ghadamasi were not necessarily from Ghadames themselves. A case in point is Bedari Zumut, the slave-employee mentioned above. After being freed Bedari broke off relations with his former master, but another prominent Ghadamasi set Bedari up in business as his personal agent in Zinder. This merchant – unnamed in the account of Bedari's son – travelled occasionally between Ghat and Zinder and regularly sent consignments of goods to Zinder.[31]

At the end of the century most independent merchants trading between Zinder and North Africa were Ghadamasi, as were all of those stationed in Djadjidouna. But other North Africans worked side by side with them. One Mujabra Arab and one Gwaida Arab, for example, lived in the Zinder community.[32] For these people, acculturation to the norms of the dominant group was sufficient to win acceptance. Membership in the Sanūsīyya brotherhood, common occupational interests, and a sense of expatriate solidarity united all North Africans.

LOCAL MERCHANTS IN TRANS-SAHARAN TRADE

Just as the Ghadamasi trade diaspora accepted non-Ghadamasi

North Africans, it also served as a framework for the operations of local merchants. As long as local merchants accepted the dominant culture, namely literacy in Arabic, Islam, and North African commercial customs, they could work alongside Ghadamasi, Gwaida, and Mujabra. Unlike North Africans, traders from the Sudan were not backed by the capital of associates in North African and Tripoli mercantile firms, nor did they have a strong tradition of trans-Saharan commerce. These were severe handicaps, but some merchants overcame the odds against them.

One such merchant did a thriving business from his home in Zinder. Musa Abdallah, known locally and in French sources as Malam Yaro, was the wealthiest merchant of local origin in Zinder at the turn of the century. Sources conflict on his ethnic background, but the best evidence is from his descendants and other Zinder merchants. Malam Yaro's father was a Muslim cleric from the Kanuri town of Kulumfardo who migrated to Zinder and married Karu, the servant of a prominent noblewoman belonging to the Kel Tafidet section of the Kel Ewey.[33] He earned a reputation as a religious scholar, but he also made a comfortable living through trade, and Malam Yaro followed in his footsteps. Malam Yaro is said to have begun trading almost immediately after the completion of his religious studies. He gave millet to Tuareg traders in Zinder who took it to Bilma to exchange for salt; upon their return, they divided the profit from the transaction with him.

Soon Malam Yaro was doing business regularly with Ghadamasi merchants, and he used these contacts to build up an import and export business on his own.[34] Malam Yaro sent caravans north with an employee named Turare, who later married Malam Yaro's sister Cillum. To North Africa went tanned goat skins, untanned hides and skins, feathers, clothing made in Kano, indigo and indigo-dyed cloth, henna, and small quantities of condiments – baobab leaves, groundnuts, okra, and potash. Imports included cotton cloth, silk, perfume, jewellery, and other articles from Europe, as well as woollen garments from North Africa.

But this import–export business was small in comparison with Malam Yaro's activity in local markets. This was essentially the bulking of produce for export and the distribution of imports, and it benefited North Africans as well as his own trans-Saharan business. Malam Yaro bought ostrich feathers in Damergu, competing with the Ghadamasi of Djadjidouna. Since the head of the Damergu village of Malam Tilum agreed to supply him with feathers for export, Malam Yaro made the five-day trip to Damergu several times.[35] He also financed the collection and tanning of goat skins in Zinder. Tanners, most of whom were servile Tuareg, did not have resources of their own, so they accepted goods on loan with which to buy skins, and after tanning these skins they handed over the finished product to Malam Yaro. North African merchants also financed this kind of operation.[36]

Malam Yaro disposed of trans-Saharan imports by loaning them out to procure export products, through direct sale from his compound in Zongon Tudu, or through his agent in Kano. Malam Abdu, one of Malam Yaro's half brothers, lived in Kano and handled Malam Yaro's transactions there. Both maintained close relations with the head of the Ghadamasi community of Kano, Al-Hajj Abande, and used marriage alliances to reaffirm their ties. Nana, Malam Yaro's second wife, was the daughter of Al-Hajj Abande, who in turn married Balkissu, Malam Abdu's daughter. In addition, Malam Yaro and his brother were on close terms with Aliyu, the *sarki* of Kano, who was probably an important customer.[37]

Perhaps the most interesting aspect of Malam Yaro's business was a banking system which allowed transfers from one branch of the firm to another. North Africans who did business with his firm could sell in Zinder and buy return goods in Kano by taking advantage of an institution for the delegation of credit. A North African or Tuareg merchant could sell goods to Malam Yaro in Zinder, but receive in lieu of payment a letter instructing Malam Abdu to give the travelling merchant goods worth the amount deposited in Zinder. The balance was regulated by transfers of the same kind in the opposite direction, or by transfers of money or merchandise within the firm.[38] This delegation of credit, called *hawāla* in Arabic, was common practice among North Africans; it was mentioned by European travellers, who sometimes took advantage of it to deposit money in North Africa and receive goods or money in the Sudan.[39] The arrangements used by Malam Yaro and Malam Abdu were undoubtedly a borrowing from North African commercial culture. The only other instance of the use of delegation of credit by local merchants in Zinder was a case in which a Tubu landlord exchanged transfers of credit with a Kano landlord of unknown origin.[40] Since the Tubu trade diaspora developed in close association with the activities of Fazzani merchants, this is probably another case of borrowing from North African commercial culture. Unfortunately no information about the use of delegation of credit among North Africans living in the Sudan has come to light.

Sarki Tanimu and his successors are said to have traded to North Africa on their own account, but it is difficult to determine the scale of these royal ventures. His interests seem to have centred mainly on the procurement of contraband fire-arms, endeavours in which he enjoyed considerable success. He maintained a local arsenal of dated muskets and gave several hundred of the weapons to his suzerain, the *mai* of Borno, along with cannon to serve as models for Bornoan blacksmiths.[41] Although guns obtained from North Africa were of some military importance, the value of trade run by the rulers of Damagaram probably did not compare with that which passed through the hands of the merchants, whose regular trade contrasted with the intermittent dealings of the *sarki*.

The Tubu also participated in trans-Saharan trade as an extension of the salt trade they carried from Bilma to Zinder. They took cloth and grain to Bilma, and merchants who had more trade capital than was needed for salt trade bought feathers and skins to take to the Fazzan. Tubu living in Zinder did not make the trip to the Fazzan each year, but when they did they left their own camels with shepherds in the oases near Bilma and changed to fresh mounts to continue their journey. Upon arriving in the Fazzan, Tubu merchants bought English cloth, woollen garments, perfume, and fire-arms through a landlord-broker. It is unlikely that they received any of this merchandise on loan, because they did not make the trip regularly.[42]

The Tubu trade diaspora of Zinder was small, but it played a unique role. One important reason for the Tubu presence in Zinder was the need to bypass the dangerous trade route between Borno and the Fazzan. The search for a safe route to Borno had also brought Fazzani merchants to Zinder, but by the end of the nineteenth century Tubu had replaced them as the main agents of contact with Borno and the east. The Tubu had an important advantage because they were able to use the direct route between Zinder and Bilma. This was also a dangerous route, but Tubu could travel it by using kinship and ethnic ties with Tubu nomads to keep informed about conditions in the desert.[43] Much of the territory crossed by this route nominally belonged to Tubu, but the mobility of Tuareg raiders in the west and Awlad Sulayman in the east allowed them to prey on unlucky or unprotected caravans.

While the Tubu who migrated to Zinder were merchants with a tradition of living in towns, Tuareg immigrants were nomads whose principal contribution to trans-Saharan trade consisted of supplying transport animals and armed escorts. Nevertheless they also traded trans-Saharan imports and return goods on a small scale. Most of the Kano cloth they bought was for their own use, but some of it reached Iferwan and Ghat after changing hands. This Kano cloth being taken north crossed English cotton imports going south, the result of demand for various kinds of cloth over the length of the area served by the Tripoli–Kano route. According to Zinder oral tradition, Tuareg merchants and others from Zinder obtained credit at the large market for trans-Saharan goods in Ghat. The Ahaggar Tuareg, who began arriving in the Sahel in 1896, also traded trans-Saharan products between Ghat and Zinder, though this kind of exchange was much less important than the Ahaggar salt trade. Over-all the Tuareg share of trans-Saharan trade was undoubtedly very small in comparison with that of the North African merchants.[44]

FINANCE

Much of the capital necessary for trans-Saharan trade was received through North Africa, but it originated in a complex structure of credit extending back to Europe. European capital entered the trans-Saharan system through wholesale firms based in Tripoli and owned by two groups of outsiders, Jews of Italian origin and Maltese. Italian Jews had been in Tripoli for centuries, but the Maltese were latecomers in comparison and controlled a smaller share of the wholesale trade.[45] Tripoli wholesale firms received goods from European companies and advanced them to Ghadamasi in return for a promise to pay the debt with products from the Sudan. Tripoli wholesalers also prepared Sudanese products for export; ostrich feathers in particular required grading and extensive processing, and wholesalers employed a large proportion of the Jewish ghetto of Tripoli in this industry. Since Tripoli merchants provided important services for Europeans, they were under the protection of various European consuls, and they therefore enjoyed a privileged legal status under the Ottoman government of Tripoli.[46]

Like the Ghadamasi, Tripoli wholesalers were cross-cultural middlemen. They bridged the gap between local merchants and

Europeans, few of whom spoke Arabic or were familiar with North African commercial customs. The Maltese spoke a language closely related to Arabic in structure, though it borrowed vocabulary from a variety of European languages. As a result they had no difficulty learning the form of Arabic spoken in the interior, and many already spoke European languages. Italian Jews also knew European languages, and most spoke Arabic, a consequence of a long history of residence in Tripoli.

Although available sources do not treat the organization of these firms in detail, apparently family ties were important. At the end of the nineteenth century the Nahum, Arbib, and Hassan families – all Jewish – had representatives in England to facilitate trans-actions with suppliers. In Tripoli members of the Hassan family owned three separate firms, and the Arbib family also held three. The Nahum family, large and influential in Tripoli, formed a single firm. The Tayor family was also an important mercantile family, but the number of firms they controlled is unknown. Besides the commercial houses belonging to prominent families, there were also about twenty others of lesser importance.[47]

American consular archives represent an important though neglected source of information on the structure of commerce in Tripoli. One reason for the value of observations by American consuls is that Americans stood outside the commercial mainstream of the port. Although Americans bought the bulk of tanned hides and skins exports after 1890, American exporters never gained a foothold in the Tripoli market for cotton yarns and cotton piece goods. The American consul Cuthbert Jones tried without success to introduce American-made cotton cloth and yarns, and in 1878 he explained the failure with the following observation:

Large and extended credit is given by English banks who act at the same time as brokers, selling the cargoes of esparto grass and other articles sent from here, and returning cotton goods and other articles in payment. Buy-ing for cash is unknown to the Tripoli merchant, but where there is barter, he is willing and not unfrequently obliged to give very advantageous bargains, in order to be able to continue his floating business.[48]

A year later Jones complained of the lack of 'honest competition' in Tripoli trade and added, 'There is not one European house in this city, and only one Christian, that of G. and F. Galea, carrying on a whole-sale business.' These charges, which he later made public in an article in the *American Exporter* of February 1880, drew a strongly worded letter of protest from Tripoli Jewish merchants which Jones had translated from the Italian and transmitted with his dispatch to the State Department. The letter written by an organization calling itself the Delegates of Commerce of Tripoli and signed by most Jewish merchants, called attention to the solid reputation of the Tripoli firms and to the fact that they received substantial amounts of credit from European, and in particular English mercantile houses. They argued that their advantage stemmed not from dishonest practices, but from a knowledge of local customs, languages, and business practices, all of which were 'necessary to the merchant here to be able to do business with peoples so different from Europeans'.[49]

The American Congress discontinued the Tripoli consulate in 1882, but decided to reinstate it in 1908, two full decades after American firms had first involved themselves in a major way in buying Tripoli exports. The new consul found substantially the same lack of prospects for marketing cotton cloth as had his predecessor. He wrote that American firms could hope to export cotton piece goods to Tripoli only if they were willing to match the terms on which European firms allowed for payment, for: 'No Tripoli merchant, in order to meet the requirements of American exporters would either stand out of his money until he got his goods from the United States or pay the interest on a bank's letter of credit. It would eat up all his profits'.[50] At this time Tripoli wholesalers could take up to three months to pay and still receive a discount of 2½ per cent, and they received much merchandise on credit for longer periods of time.

The finance of the desert trade was a co-operative effort between Tripoli and Ghadamasi merchants, with the relative importance of the contribution from each group shifting over a period of time. Before the 1870s Tripoli merchants gave goods on credit to Ghadamasi for periods of from six months to a year, asking for payment in Sudanese goods.[51] Ghadamasi arranged for transport of the merchandise to Ghat, where a large market for trans-Saharan goods met twice yearly, in June or July and again in December or January. Ghat was the real starting-point for trade to the Sudan. Since the routes between Tripoli and Ghat were relatively safe, caravans were smaller and camels carried heavier loads than on the routes south of Ghat. Consequently loads had to be remade and caravans reformed.[52]

At Ghat Ghadamasi merchants either put out on credit the goods they had received in Tripoli, gave them to employees or agents, or sold them. Ghadamasi could not make the trade run on European and Tripoli capital alone. The round trip to the Sudan took between a year and a half and three years, but the Ghadamasi had credit in Tripoli for about half of this length of time on the average. Consequently Ghadamasi operating between Tripoli and Ghat had to have financial resources of their own if they wished to send merchandise on to the Sudan. If they had none, they could simply sell their merchandise in Ghat and return to Tripoli to pay off the debt.[53]

Another way of looking at the trans-Saharan finance is to conceive of the commerce in spatial segments. Tripoli merchants financed most of the trade between Tripoli and Ghat, whereas commerce south of Ghat ran largely on Ghadamasi capital. The contribution of the Ghadamasi was greater than it may seem at first glance, since they paid for the transport of merchandise on the two main segments, paid tolls, gave gifts to political authorities along the way, and extended credit to local merchants in the Sudan.[54]

While this description applies in a general way to the organization of trade before 1870, the relative importance of Tripoli and Ghadamasi finance shifted several times in the 1870s and 1880s. European capital played an even larger role than normal when market conditions were good. The trade boom of the 1870s occurred when rising prices for ostrich feathers on European markets drew increased investment in Sudanese trade from English, French, German, and Austrian mercantile firms. In the boom years of 1870 to 1883, the value of ostrich feathers arriving in Tripoli increased fifteenfold. (See Table 1.) This was partially the result of price increases, but the volume of feathers arriving from the Sudan also increased abruptly. (See Table 2.) In 1873, soon after the volume began to increase, Tripoli merchants began to work out new financial arrangement with the Ghadamasi. With more European capital in the network than before, Tripoli middlemen were willing to extend credit for up to three years, the net result of which was that they financed trade all the way to the Sudan and back, leaving only transport, tolls, and other incidentals to the Ghadamasi.[55] The British consul Thomas Moore gave the following description of the contract for the joint venture under the new system:

The contract, called "sened," stating the amount of the merchandise sent, is generally made on the basis of an equal division of profits. As a rule the merchant furnishes only the goods, the Arab [Ghadamasi] undertaking to buy or hire camels and his own supplies for the journey. Guarantees are frequently given, sometimes in the form of mortgages on property, or the personal undertaking of a resident merchant, when, however, the conditions are somewhat modified in favor of the Arab. . . . on the arrival of the caravan, if the price, as estimated by the receiver of the produce brought back, be not considered fair, the goods are put up to public auction, and the amount realized, after deducting the value of the goods originally sent, is equally divided between the merchant and the Arab.[56]

A report on the Tripoli trade by d'Attonoux also mentions that caravan traders guaranteed their debts to Tripoli merchants by mortgaging real estate and refers to the equal division of profits as well.[57]

Bettoli's detailed account of the Tripoli trade written in the early 1880s gives a more complete account of these co-operative financial arrangements. Bettoli noted that Jewish and Maltese merchants never travelled into the interior, which was the province of Muslim merchants he called caravan leaders. Bettoli listed the names of these caravan leaders, the most prominent of whom was Mustapha Zammit, identified in other sources as Ghadamasi. From this it is possible to infer that most of Bettoli's Muslims were in fact Ghadamasi. Bettoli explained that Muslim merchants were entitled to half the profit on capital supplied by their Jewish or Maltese backers. But they were also responsible for half the loss should the venture show a deficit, regardless of the reason. Before leaving Tripoli, Muslim merchants drew up two sets of contracts, the first specifying the exact amount of the contribution of each of the backers of the joint venture, in order to facilitate the division of profit when the caravan returned. In the second set the Muslims constituted themselves as debtors to their partners to serve as a guide in case the caravan was unsuccessful. A copy of this record of debt was left with the backers and served as a receipt for the merchandise supplied.[58]

Little detail is available on the profit margins of merchants engaged in Tripoli–Kano trade, but various records provide some indication. The first source is a detailed description given Étiévant by a Zinder-based merchant in 1909.[59] This appears to be an illustrative example rather than the reporting of actual transactions. According to Étiévant it was possible to buy cloth worth 800 francs in Tripoli, pay for transport and tolls to the Sudan, buy return merchandise worth 4,000 francs in Kano, which when returned to Tripoli sold for 16,000 francs. Total costs including the original purchase price amounted to a little over 6,000 francs, so that the profit (about 10,000 francs) was 160 per cent of the investment. This estimate evidently includes many categories of operating expenses under the label 'profit', and it may have been optimistic. Actual rates of return must have been lower, and of course the annual rates of return were cut to half or a third if caravans took two or three years to return to Tripoli. The second source is Newbury's report of similar illustrative examples given Colonel Mircher in 1862, showing a profit of from 36 to 40 per cent on caravans from Tripoli to Kano or Timbuktu.[60] Finally Méhier de Mathuisieulx, who interviewed Tripoli merchants, reported profits of as much as 35 to 40 per cent on outlays at best − during the period of greatest prosperity between 1870 and 1885.[61]

The infusion of trade capital in the form of European merchandise ended abruptly in the early 1880s when the price of ostrich feathers dropped precipitously to less than half its former level. (See Table 2.) The immediate cause was the low point in a European business cycle and the accompanying drop in demand for decorative feathers. Tripoli middlemen received no credit from European sources between 1884 and 1888, when the finance of the trade was left entirely in the hands of the Ghadamasi. In 1889 the prices paid in Tripoli for feathers rebounded from their depression levels, a movement not reflected in the price series in Table 2, which is from the London market for ostrich feathers. But the jump in prices in 1889 at Tripoli was enough to draw European capital once again into trans-Saharan trade. The Ghadamasi, who had a backlog of goods in storage throughout the network, had been waiting for a rise in prices. Those who had been in the Sudan during the trade depression were reluctant to return, fearing the loss of houses they had mortgaged for commercial capital. When prices rose they returned to Tripoli with the assurance that they could clear enough profit to be able to cover their debts. As a result, the volume of the trade rose rapidly after 1889.[62] (See Table 2.)

CONCLUSION

The concept of the trade diaspora focuses attention on the flow of capital from the most central places to the periphery. It would of course be unfortunate if an ideal type, which can serve as a useful framework of analysis, determined the nature of the empirical evidence brought to bear on an historical problem. A survey of the information available shows that trade capital came primarily from

Europe and Tripoli – centres of a higher order in terms of geo-graphical centrality than the Central Sudan. Although this was the dominant pattern, it was not the only possibility, and some trade capital came from sub-Saharan Africa as well. The trans-Saharan component of Tubu operations is a case in point; Tubu financed their own operations between Zinder and Bilma or between Zinder and the Fazzan, and to the extent that they did so their commerce represented a movement of capital against the main flow. Another source of sub-Saharan capital were successful merchants such as Malam Yaro, who operated in conjunction with North African net-works but financed operations from the Sudan. In addition, Kel Ewey merchants financed some trade between Zinder and Ghat, but they also received credit from North Africans in Ghat.[63] In any case Kel Ewey trans-Saharan trade was clearly much less important than participation in regional desert-side trade and trans-Saharan transport business. In separate accounts the rulers of Zinder and Wadai are said to have financed caravans in the late nineteenth century, and this form of trade – backed by the resources of sub-Saharan states – was by far the most important of all forms of finance which ran against the main flow. The rulers of Sudanic states were eager to trade for fire-arms in order to better their own military positions, and sometimes the best way to do so was to mount their own expeditions.[64] But far more often rulers merely had to let North Africans come to them with imported merchandise, thereby allowing the merchants to bear the risk of loss.[65]

Another departure from the common pattern was for merchants to attempt to bypass intermediaries. Transactions descending the hierarchy of central places, from European suppliers to Tripoli wholesalers and then to Ghadamasi, were most common, but there were other ways of doing business. In the early 1890s at least one foreign firm, the American- or British-based Wardel Riley and Co., operated in Tripoli and was said to have the largest import–export business, a description which suggests that it bypassed Tripoli wholesalers.[66] This firm did not exist in 1880, when the American consul complained of a lack of European businesses in Tripoli; nor was there any mention of Wardel Riley and Co. in detailed accounts of Tripoli trade written after the turn of the century.[67] Hence it is likely that the firm had a short existence; and it is possible that its presence represented a reaction to opportunities to export tanned skins to the New York market in the 1890s and for some reason the structure of commerce changed shortly after it set up operations in

Tripoli.[68]

Just as this company attempted to bypass Tripoli wholesalers, Tripoli merchants also tried to circumvent their suppliers by establishing direct contact with European firms. Both the American and French consuls reported one such effort in 1879, but it is unclear whether or not it was successful, and if so just how long business contacts which were established this way lasted.[69]

In short, despite exceptions, all available evidence points to the conclusion that most trade capital on the Tripoli–Kano route in its final years came from Europe, Tripoli, and the Ghadamasi. The participation of outsiders in this finance increased with the expansion of trade in the 1870s and again in the 1890s. While merchants sometimes attempted to bypass intermediaries, trans-Saharan commerce can be visualized correctly as a chain extending from European firms through Tripoli wholesalers to Ghadamasi, their associates in the Sudan, local distributors, and finally to consumers and producers in the Sudan.

CHAPTER IV

The End of Tripoli–Kano Trade

A PRECEDING chapter demonstrated that estimates of Sudan exports passing through Tripoli made by British consuls provide valuable information on trade from the Central Sudan in the late nineteenth century. These figures have far-reaching implications not only for the area of sub-Saharan Africa affected by changes in export trade, but for the history of trans-Saharan trade as well. Until recently it was thought, following Newbury, that the volume of trade on the three western routes declined after 1875.[1] While this was almost certainly true for the extreme western route to Morocco, the Tripoli consular series show that Tripoli–Kano trade lasted longer. As Marion Johnson has demonstrated, the consular series are corroborated by contemporary published accounts from both ends of the trade route and by data on the decreasing volume of British cloth exports to Tripoli, which were offset by increasing cloth trade to southern Nigeria as the new southern route replaced caravan trade to Tripoli. An important turning-point in the series on cloth exports occurred in 1905–7.[2] In addition evidence from the Central Sudan and Tripoli shows that trans-Saharan trade declined rapidly after 1900, not before, and that the major period of readjustment for North African merchants in the Sudan was after the colonial occupation. Farther east the Benghazi–Wadai route lasted longer still, with some trade continuing up to 1913.[3] In short, trans-Saharan trade from the Western Sudan was diverted initially, but trade from the Central and Eastern Sudan was better protected from the competition of coastal trade and hence lasted longer. The purpose of this chapter is to examine in detail decline on the Tripoli–Kano route, to describe some effects of the reorientation of import–export trade from the Central Sudan, and to trace the reactions of North African merchants in the Sudan as desert trade ended.

The first major cause of the diversion of caravan trade was increasing insecurity in the desert and growing risk of loss to raiders.

Normally caravans travelled in long files with as many as six or eight of these files abreast, but in times of danger a huge square formation was drawn up.[4] Even so, large caravans were vulnerable to well-armed bandits, who often waited in ambush for caravans to pass. The British consul Thomas Jago wrote that attacks began in 1895; but real trouble seems to have started in 1898, when Tubu pillaged two caravans south of Ghat, one outbound and the other returning from the Sudan.[5] 'Apart from the serious losses now sustained', wrote Jago, '. . . great consternation prevails among the merchants of Tripoli as to the future of their hitherto important trade with the Western Soudan, . . . on which their prosperity wholly depends.'[6] In the winter of 1899/1900 Shaamba Arabs attacked a caravan between Ghat and Ghadames, killing nine men, including the head slave of Malam Yaro, the wealthiest of the Zinder merchants.[7]

Increased risk failed to have an immediate effect on the volume of trade passing through Tripoli. According to the estimates of the British consul, the volume of Sudan products passing through Tripoli in 1899 and 1900 was only slightly below that of 1898, and also above average for the decade 1891–1900. (See Table 1.) The value of ivory traded to Tripoli was higher than usual, probably because the British levied a stiff export duty on ivory shipped south to the Nigerian coast.[8] Increased risk must have had an effect on decisions to invest, but what is known about the finance of Tripoli–Kano trade suggests that declining volume should have lagged several years behind bad news about insecurity in the desert. Tripoli wholesalers and their Ghadamasi associates invested in trade by sending Manchester cloth and other imports south and awaiting future delivery of Sudan products. Decisions to invest before the beginning of trouble in 1898 continued to bring feathers, skins, and ivory through Tripoli as much as two or three years later, the maximum time for the round trip. Trade figures after 1900 dropped steeply, reflecting cautious investment in 1899 and later years.

Uncertainty must have had a cumulative effect on the volume of trade, since the investment of each individual merchant became more exposed to loss as the average size of caravans decreased. As caravans became smaller, the costs of adequate defence had to be borne by a smaller group of merchants, or with each individual merchant running a smaller volume of trade than before. In addition, capital costs must have risen as potential lenders took a hard look at the safety of investment in the Sudan trade. Insecurity along the route also caused excessive and costly delays, since merchandise often had to wait at relay points or in the Sudan until caravaneers could be sure of safe conditions along the route. One caravan which left Tripoli in 1901 arrived in Kano two and a half years later, after exceptional delays; but in 1904 conditions had improved to the extent that this same caravan made the return trip in only four months.[9] It is difficult to imagine that trade capital tied up for this length of time could have made a profit for Tripoli investors, given the rates of return which seem to have been typical. In addition, insecurity may have made Tuareg camel-owners and escorts less willing to participate than they usually were; it was reported that excessive delays in 1901–4 resulted from difficulties encountered in assembling sufficient numbers of camels at relay points.[10]

Another serious threat to trade was the situation which the French found when they arrived in Zinder in the summer of 1899, namely a quarrel between the Kel Ewey confederation and the Imezureg, a quasi-territorial group whose wealth was based on the taxation of sedentary dependants – slaves, the descendants of slaves, and Hausa and Kanuri immigrants to the Sahelian fringe.[11] The Kel Ewey also controlled sedentary farmers in Damergu, but they also had an extensive commitment to ecologically-based trade and to providing services for trans-Saharan caravans between Kano and the relay point at Iferwan. The Imezureg profited from the ostrich-feather trade by levying a heavy tax, and with this wealth they were able to mount a successful military challenge to the Kel Ewey. The conflict remained indeterminate, but the arrival of the French provided the Kel Ewey with a unique opportunity. The French needed transport animals to continue the march east to do battle with Rabih, and the Kel Ewey offered 200 camels in return for French support against the Imezureg. The French sided with the Kel Ewey because they needed revenue for their newly created colony, and they intended to tax trans-Saharan trade. The French correctly judged that the Kel Ewey, with their widespread trade contacts, would be better able to keep the routes open than would the Imezureg. In addition the Kel Ewey represented the *status quo* whereas the Imezureg were upstarts and were likely to continue to make trouble in Damergu. Consequently the French sent a force against Musa Mai Damergu, the Imezureg leader, at his capital Tanamari. Taken by surprise, Musa was killed and the Imezureg survivors put to flight. Other Tuareg, though not Kel Ewey, and sedentary people joined forces with Imezureg and rallied under

Denda, Musa's half brother, and attacked and pillaged a caravan approaching the Farak well north of Damargu on the night of 16/17 July 1901.[12] The Kel Ewey were said to have lost 12,000 camels carrying millet north to provision the Aïr and for the salt trade, as well as 1000 camels carrying trans-Saharan merchandise belonging to Ghadamasi merchants. The Kel Ewey recovered some camels and loads of millet, but the entire trans-Saharan caravan was lost, and six Ghadamasi merchants travelling with the caravan were killed. The loss of the trans-Saharan caravan dealt a severe blow to Tripoli merchants, and it meant that Sudan imports to Tripoli for 1901, which would have entered the statistics for 1902, were completely cut off.[13] These and other incidents led the French to devote most available resources to the occupation of Damergu in 1901 and 1902, the Aïr in 1904, and Bilma in 1906.

Meanwhile, the route north of Aïr had become increasingly unsafe. In 1901 Shaamba Arabs attacked the Tuareg near Ghadames, an event which produced apprehension among merchants in Tripoli. About the same time Ahaggar Tuareg plundered a caravan farther south but took only merchandise belonging to Zinder-based merchants and left goods belonging to those based in Tripoli and Kano untouched.[14] Since Zinder alone was in the hands of a colonial power, contemporary observers interpreted the Ahaggar action as an expression of hostility to the French. In 1903 a large caravan, which normally would have been safe from attack by virtue of its size, fell prey to raiders between Ghat and Ghadames.[15] The situation improved in 1904, but by this time desert trade was beginning to fall victim to cheap transport south toward the coast.[16]

The exact cause of the increase in raids on caravans between 1898 and 1904 is unknown, but disruption resulting from the French occupation of the central Sahara was probably a factor. In 1881 Ahaggar Tuareg had massacred most members of the second Flatters expedition and had won a temporary respite from further French pressure. Since the Ahaggar had earned a reputation as irreducible foes of the French, they attracted small groups of other dissidents to their remote homeland, as for example the Djeramna, who had fallen foul of the French military in the region of Géryville, far to the north-west. The French reasoned that the easiest and cheapest way to subdue the Ahaggar was to deprive them of vital resources they needed from the oasis of Tuat. In 1899 the Flamand-Pein expedition occupied In Salah, Tidikelt, Tuat, and

Guerara, and the French presence in these oases posed a real threat to the Ahaggar, who relied on trade and the taxation of agricultural production in the oases. A few years earlier the Ahaggar had reacted to pressure from the north by initiating caravan trade to Damergu. In 1899 the response was to raid nomadic groups and oasis dwellers under French control. Attacks on Tripoli–Kano caravans should be seen in light of the encirclement of the Ahaggar and their growing desperation, for raiding a caravan with Ajjer camels and guides entailed a very real risk of inflaming old animosities between the Ajjer and Ahaggar confederations at a time when internal fighting would only hasten the victory of the French. At any rate the French won decisively in 1902 and Ahaggar resistance ceased.[17]

Another important cause of trouble on the caravan routes arose as a result of the spread of modern repeating rifles among desert people, which added fire-power to the tactical advantages of surprise already enjoyed by raiders. Smaldone has pointed out that despite a ban on fire-arms trade with the interior, Greek sponge-fishers were able to land considerable quantities of contraband weapons in smaller Mediterranean ports and even in Benghazi and Tripoli. While most smuggled fire-arms followed the Sanūsī-controlled route to Wadai, some weapons certainly reached the central desert as well.[18] In 1882 Bettoli reported that 18-shot Winchester rifles were being smuggled through Tripoli and that most were used by caravan escorts.[19] But some of these modern weapons must have reached Tubu, Tuareg, Shaamba, and Awlad Sulayman as well, allowing them to mount successful raids against well-defended caravans. Smaldone has assembled evidence which indicates that a turning-point in the spread of the gun frontier may have occurred among Ahaggar and other Algerian Tuareg in the 1890s.[20] If this was true and if other desert people began to use modern rifles at about the same time, then the increasing incidence of caravan raids before the turn of the century represents an example of a change in military technology which shifted the balance of power from caravan defenders to attackers. The growing power of raiders at this time was also a continuation of a process begun over a half a century earlier with the arrival in the northern Chad basin of the Awlad Sulayman, a group which had originally nomadized in the Syrte and the Fazzan but had been defeated in their homeland by a coalition of local enemies with Ottoman forces seeking to extend the influence of the Porte in the Fazzan and

Cyrenaica.[21]

The second major cause of the diversion of trans-Saharan trade was the decreasing cost of transportation on the southern route. The history of the decline of Tripoli–Kano trade presents the historian with a unique opportunity for the study of transport costs in a pre-industrial society. For a time a very old system of transport existed alongside a new one, and both French and British colonial officials took an interest in the situation and commented on it at length. The French in particular investigated trade and the prospects for its survival because they needed revenue from import and export duties and had to plan alternatives as this source of income failed.

Trans-Saharan freight rates were considerably lower than comparable rates within the savannah. As Curtin has noted, transport costs cannot be calculated by figuring differentials in the prices of goods between two points because this calculation yields the total cost of doing business over the distance involved, including the payment of tolls, capital costs, profits, and miscellaneous business expenses. The difficulty with many contemporary sources is that they fail to make this kind of distinction, so that the historian is almost never certain if he is dealing with an inclusive transport cost, and if so what it includes.[22] One rare trustworthy account is provided by Étiévant in 1909; he interviewed a prominent Ghadamasi merchant in Zinder and obtained a detailed breakdown of transport costs, tolls, and average profit on a typical transaction.[23] Transport costs on goods being shipped from Tripoli to Kano was from 670 to 930 francs per ton, with most of the variation coming from freight rates between Ghat and Kano, which apparently fluctuated greatly, depending on local conditions. Unfortunately Étiévant fails to specify the causes of these fluctuations. Including tolls, which were charged at different rates for different goods, the cost of transportation on desert routes was from 1,460 to 1,875 francs per ton for European-made cloth, and between 1,305 and 1,540 francs per ton for imported sugar and paper. Dividing these figures by the 2,500 km distance between Tripoli and Kano gives figures of between 0.25 and 0.50 francs per ton-kilometre excluding tolls, and something like 0.75 francs per ton-kilometre with tolls included. Reports of the going rate between Kano and Zinder show that freight costs in the savannah were 50 to 100 per cent higher than those in the desert.[24]

Freight rates were cheaper in the desert than in the savannah for two main reasons. First, camels are efficient and labour-saving beasts of burden. As Curtin has noted for the Senegambian Sahel, camels could travel farther in a day than donkeys and pack oxen, they carried heavier loads, and they required fewer drivers.[25] But camels could be used in the savannah only during the dry season because excessive moisture was injurious to their health. Second, nomads had to travel from place to place in search of pasture, and hence they carried freight cheaply because, in some cases at least, they planned to travel whether or not they were paid for it. For example, Kel Ewey Tuareg made the journey from Kano to Aïr in part because they carried trans-Saharan goods on this route and in part because they had to move in search of pasture.

Comparisons of the cost of transport on the two competing routes become available in 1903, when the French had been in Zinder long enough to familiarize themselves with local commerce, and the British had just begun to do so in Kano. In just a few years after the arrival of the French, the cost of shipment to Lagos and then north overland and by river had fallen within the range of trans-Saharan costs. Furthermore, the French calculated that if river transport linked Zunguru to the coast, the southern route would be significantly cheaper than the desert route.[26]

An important aspect of decreasing transport costs from nothern Nigeria to the coast was the government transport service set up by Lugard. In order to replace carriers and pack animals on the Zunguru–Zaria road, Lugard organized a service of over 200 ox-carts and hired Indian drivers to train local people how to use them.[27] The new method proved to be about as costly as old ones, but government transport services on the river fared better. Lugard inaugurated service by government steamers primarily to carry government freight, but he also had an interest in breaking the Niger Company monopoly on river freight. Accordingly he allowed European commercial firms and small traders to use free space on government steamers, which was usually available on the down-stream run. In the beginning rates were set at an artificially low level, but at a conference in December of 1906 representatives of the Niger Company and the Colonial Office agreed to revise the government rates upward and those of the Niger Company down-ward.[28] Although no data on the volume of goods carried are available, the establishment of the competing services and the intervention of the government to lower fares must have brought an increased flow of European imports to Kano. In 1908 a representative of the Niger Company reported that Kano received the majority of its European imports from the south, although desert caravans continued to carry an unspecified proportion.[29]

But the railway was of course a far more serious threat to desert trade. As the Baro–Kano line neared completion, new French estimates placed the cost of transport on the southern route at 230 francs per ton to Kano and 350 to Zinder, or about half or a third of the cost of transport across the desert. A difference of this magnitude, combined with the disruption of trade routes in the northern desert during the Italo-Turk war in Tripolitania, was enough to end trans-Saharan trade to the Central Sudan. By 1912 one variety of European cloth imported to Kano by sea and rail cost less than it did in Tripoli.[30]

Although North African merchants and their associates in the Sudan continued to use the desert route until 1912, apparently the volume of trade decreased rapidly after 1900. British estimates of the value of Sudan products in transit through Tripoli are not available after 1904, but in this year the Sudan trade had already declined to about half the value of an average year in the decade 1890–1900. (See Table 1.) In 1909 Étiévant estimated that about 1,500 camel loads of Sudan products – hides and skins for the most part, but also a very small quantity of ostrich feathers, leather goods, Kano cloth, saddles, and ivory – left for North Africa. Since the bulk of these shipments were hides and skins, the value of exports can be roughly estimated at £12,000, or one-tenth of the average yearly figures of the 1890s.[31] The figure of £12,000 is inexact, but it is corroborated by a comparison of Méry's estimate of 12,000 loads of Sudan products arriving in Tripoli in the early 1890s and Étiévant's figure of 1,500 loads – again roughtly one-tenth of the level for the 1890s.[32] Export data from the Zinder archives indicate that exports in 1908 and 1909 were greater than at any other time between 1905 and 1912. (See Table 3.) The British also reported that 1908 promised to be an exceptionally busy year for the caravan trade, and so it is possible to conclude that a minor revival was under way.[33] But the volume of trade must have declined very sharply indeed between 1900 and about 1906.

The continuing use of the desert route after 1905 represents an apparent failure on the part of merchants to heed the cost advantage of the alternative route. But the decision to continue to use the trans-Saharan route was rational in view of the fact that Tripoli held its position at the apex of a hierarchy of central places in the import–export trade even as the transition was under way. Merchants in Tripoli performed a number of specialized functions, including finance, sorting and grading of produce, and processing ostrich feathers. In addition, Tripoli merchants had an extensive knowledge of the market in the Central Sudan for European imports. Cloth accounted for about 70 per cent of the value of trade, and African consumers were known to have very specific preferences, so that considerable expertise was required. The role of Tripoli wholesalers in exporting tanned hides and skins was less crucial than it was in the case of ostrich feathers, and consequently some functions associated with the export of this product shifted to Manchester, Liverpool, and London. But many merchants had not transferred operations to England by 1912, and they preferred to have hides arriving in England from Lagos shipped back to Tripoli for grading and sorting before re-exporting them to New York or London. Consequently a portion of the hides and skins and all ostrich feathers arriving in England from Lagos were trans-shipped back to Tripoli.[34]

Goods followed the circuitous route from Lagos to England because Lagos and Tripoli were not directly connected to each other on steamship routes. The relevant calculation for the transport cost during the period of transition, therefore, included the cost of sending goods from Lagos to Tripoli by sea, and not directly to their final destination. Given the roundabout way ocean transport linked Tripoli to its commercial hinterland, much of the advantage of the maritime route was illusory.

One of the strangest aspects of the Kano–Tripoli trade route in its final years was that it functioned in part as a one-way road, with southbound traffic greater than northbound. When the French set up a customs post at Djadjidouna, a small village about 100 km north of Zinder, they were puzzled by a chronic trade imbalance. During a twelve month period in 1903–4, both the volume and the value of imports exceeded exports by a factor of three.[35] From July 1908 to June 1909, 925 loads of cloth and sugar arrived in Zinder, and apparently about as many loads of tanned skins left for Tripoli, although export figures are not completely compatible because they are only available for the calendar year. But the value of imports was roughly four times the value of exports. Since exports peaked in 1908, the normal trade imbalance must have been even greater than it was then.[36] In 1912 caravans from the north arrived with merchandise valued at 60,000 francs but returned nothing at all.[37]

The attraction of the new route was greater in the case of ostrich feathers, a product of extremely high value in relation to its weight. Soon after the British arrived in Kano in 1903, they initiated a parcel post service, using the government carts and river steamers to carry mail, so that Kano was tied into the postal systems of the wider world. By 1907 North African merchants in Kano shipped the top three grades of ostrich feathers to Tripoli by parcel post, but they continued to send the lowest grade across the desert. Parcel post rates were higher per unit of weight for ostrich feathers than for tanned skins, but the decreased risk of shipping packages of high value by the new route offset the higher rates.[38] Another important consideration was speed, since parcel post shipments arrived in Tripoli and could take advantage of cheap southbound transport, shipment time reduced the amount of capital tied up in exporting feathers and allowed merchants in Tripoli to respond much more quickly to price changes in the highly volatile market for this product. Merchants in Zinder began using the Nigerian parcel post soon after their counterparts in Kano. After about 1907 most shipments on the old route consisted of tanned skins, along with very small quantities of ivory and feathers. Most hides and skins from Kano went south, as did an increasing percentage of the exports of this product from Zinder.[39]

Apparently it made little difference to Tripoli wholesalers whether or not trade returned from the Sudan by the same route as it arrived. Tripoli merchants shipped imports to Zinder and Kano across the desert, but they had more than a proportional share of exports shipped out through Lagos. Some received deliveries of Manchester cottons in Liverpool, but most continued to take deliveries in Tripoli. As long as they received merchandise in Tripoli and could take advantage of cheap southbound transport, they continued to use the desert route even though maritime transport was better for return goods. Some North African merchants did use the southern route to import European cloth and other items, but the portion of the old trade route which had been financed from the north was slow to adjust to the change.

A third and final factor, the taxation of trans-Saharan trade by the British and the French, doubtless contributed to the decline of Tripoli–Kano trade, but its exact impact is difficult to assess. In 1903 the French levied a 5 per cent *ad valorem* export tax on hides and skins leaving their territory, and later they raised the tax to 10 per cent on hides and skins in transit from Kano. They taxed imports on a sliding scale, charging 5 per cent on small shipments but less on shipments of greater value. In addition the British levied caravan tolls on goods moving in northern Nigeria and later an export tax at the border.[40] The French found themselves in the awkward position of watching their own transit tax help divert trade to the south, but they refused to lower it until 1912, when it was already too late. One reason the French retained high transit taxes had to do with their futile efforts to protect local tanners, whom the French had encouraged to migrate from Kano to Zinder. It was felt that competition from the Kano tanning industry would be too great without transit taxes on exports of tanned skins from Nigeria.[41] In addition the French intended that transit taxes contribute to the revenue of a territory which had to support costly military operations in the desert in the first several decades of its existence.

Just how much these taxes contributed to the decline of trade depends on the level of taxation on the competing southern route, and because of faulty evidence on the complex structure of duties in Nigeria, this comparison is difficult to make.[42] But after 1903, when both the British and French charged import and export duties, the difference in taxation on the two routes must have been extensive, especially in the case of goods originating from, or being imported to, northern Nigeria. Tanned goat skins and ostrich feathers from Kano had to pay export duties at the Nigerian border, the transit tax of 10 per cent in Niger, and also a 10 per cent duty in Ottoman controlled Tripolitania. Taken together this was undoubtedly greater than export duties through southern Nigeria. But in the case of products collected in Niger, it was probably still advantageous to ship them north – until transport costs tipped the balance. Favourable taxation of ostrich feathers on the Nigerian route may have been the principal cause of the diversion of the top grades of this product. But once again freight rates entered the picture.

REACTIONS OF DIASPORA MERCHANTS

Caravan trade came to an end in 1912 as a result of the arrival of the railway in Kano, disruption in Tripolitania caused by the Italo–Turkish war, and other contributory causes discussed above. The sudden reorientation of the export economy of the Central Sudan required adjustment on a vast scale from nearly all groups of people involved in production for the market – merchants, cultivators, herdsmen, craftsmen, and ruling groups. This is a convenient place to take up the story of one group, and the reactions of other groups will be discussed later.

Although it had been expected for some time, the rapid decline of Sudan trade had immediate and serious repercussions in Tripoli. In 1904 Méhier de Mathuisieulx reported a rash of bankruptcies among Tripoli merchants as a result of the declining trade with the Sudan, price fluctuations on the European market, and competition in the ostrich feather trade from the Cape, where Afrikaner and English farmers raised birds in captivity and were able to produce at a low cost.[43] In an attempt to diversify their activities several Jewish firms had entered the trade in esparto grass, a North African product used in Europe for making paper. By 1906 firms owned by the Nahum and Arbib families were the leading dealers and presumably they had been engaged in this activity for a number of years.[44] But esparto grass trade could accommodate only a limited number of the firms which once handled Sudan trade. By 1911 only eight wholesale firms remained active in Sudan trade, and so the mercantile community had been reduced to a third or a quarter of its former size. And when Sudan trade ended entirely, more drastic forms of adaptation were necessary. A few Jewish merchants left for Khartoum, where they set up import–export businesses of the kind they had run in Tripoli.[45] Others left for Paris, where the Tripoli community had a foothold dating to 1860, when a firm run by César Labi and Ange Arbib set up business selling ostrich feathers forwarded by associates in Tripoli. In 1924 Vadala reported that the community of Tripoli immigrants near Porte St.-Denis included over twenty separate firms and that the recent growth of the community was attributable to the collapse of Tripoli–Kano trade.[46]

Another important reaction, though apparently less common than the move to Paris, was to travel to Kano in an attempt to trace Sudan products to their source.[47] The story of the life of Saul Raccah, who owned the largest groundnut export business in Kano in the 1930s, provides an excellent example of the way that people as well as goods moved along the new maritime route between Tripoli and Kano. Raccah was an Italian Jew from a mercantile family of modest means. When the Sudan trade ended, opportunities in Tripoli disappeared, and so in 1913 he travelled by sea to Lagos and north by rail to Kano, where he found employment with the remnants of a Tripoli firm trading to Manchester. In a short time he was on his own and was able to build up a position of strength for himself in the groundnut trade. Apparently the common pattern among North African merchants in Kano in the 1920s was to travel to North Africa and back by rail and by sea; as before they looked to commercial opportunities in the Central Sudan, but modern means of transport had replaced the old overland routes.[48]

Problems of adjustment were even more complex in the Sahel than in Tripoli. As long as the Tripoli–Kano route survived, Zinder and Djadjidouna had a locational advantage because they were as much as 250 km closer to Tripoli than was Kano, and hence closer to embarkation on cheap seaborne transport. As trans-Saharan trade declined, Kano grew at the expense of the Sahelian towns to its north, not only because it took over functions of bulking and distribution in import–export trade, but also because the arrival of the railway at Kano permitted the large-scale exploitation of agricultural exports for the first time. Even in the case of tanned goat skins, the terms of trade shifted in favour of Kano gatherers, tanners, and exporters because railway shipment made imported cloth cheaper.[49] In addition, Kano continued to benefit from its large and active craft industry, which supplied a large area of the savannah and Sahel with cloth and articles made from leather.

Just how quickly Zinder became a subordinate metropolis is illustrated by two examples of how Kano assumed specialized functions associated with the import–export trade – functions once performed in Zinder. By 1901 Zinder traders only rarely broke bulk from trans-Saharan caravans but watched intead as most imports from Tripoli passed right through Zinder to be unpacked in Kano.[50] The second example concerns the decline of Zinder's tanning industry. Several years after their arrival the French had encouraged over a hundred tanners from Kano to settle in Zinder so that a larger share of the skins headed for Tripoli could be processed locally. In 1915 merchants exporting hides and skins from Zinder found it difficult to have tanning done in Zinder, since many tanners, including those brought north by the French, had moved to Kano or Abeché.[51] This may have been in part a result of the famine of 1914, but it underscores the extent to which Zinder had become dependent on Kano.

Because it was located over 100 km north of Zinder, the Ghadamasi community of Djadjidouna was the first to disperse. As the northernmost of the sub-Saharan enclaves, Djadjidouna had been favoured as a stopping-place for caravans headed north and as the commercial centre of Damergu, a region where wild ostriches abounded. But Djadjidouna's location on the northern fringe also made it extremely vulnerable once the direction of external trade had been reversed. Merchants in Djadjidouna found themselves almost twice as far from Kano, the new point of embarkation, as those in Zinder. In addition, the speciality export of their region, ostrich feathers, was the first product to be exported along the new southern route, beginning in about 1904. To compound their difficulties, ostrich feathers from the Cape began to compete more and more strongly with the Sudan product.[52]

The dispersal from Djadjidouna was rapid, and the movement was probably complete well before the famine of 1914. Most merchants migrated south rather than return to their homes in the oases. Albashir al-Washi, the leader of the Ghadamasi community there and a man of widespread repute, went to Kano, where he was joined by three other former residents of Djadjidouna. Two of the *ikawaren* (black North Africans) – Kaci and Malam Nahamit – came to Zinder. Another merchant, Muhammad Umar, also came to Zinder, though he had been in Djadjidouna for only a few years. The rest, probably not more than half a dozen merchants in all, went to Katsina or Kazaure. The exception was ʿAbd al-Hamid b. Muhammad, known in Tanout as Hamiden, who stayed on alone except for his family.[53]

Meanwhile in Zinder the French attempted to act on their long-standing belief that it would be possible to divert Tripoli–Kano trade westward to Algeria. The French reported that Zinder-based North Africans organized a caravan to Djanet to test the possibility of selling Sudan products there. A little later they also reported that they had 'persuaded', to use the language of the French report, merchants in a caravan travelling north from Agadez to Ghat to go to Djanet. These experiments were said to have failed because the price of skins were not nearly high enough in Algeria to satisfy Zinder merchants and also, as the archival reports imply, because of French interference in the planning of caravans and in contracting for transport animals from the Ahaggar Tuareg. The colonial administration encouraged Zinder merchants to go to Algeria again in 1913, but this time the merchants, who were adamantly opposed, refused.[54]

The Ghadamasi community of Zinder remained intact, but merchants had difficult adjustments to make, especially because the arrival of newcomers from Djadjidouna caused increased competition for the trade that remained. Merchants who had been agents or associates of Ghadamasi firms receiving credit in Tripoli had to do without the usual North African financial backing, and they also had to establish new business contacts in Kano. But the most serious trouble was that they did not enjoy an advantage over the numerous rurally-based, small-scale traders who had been trading between Kano and the Sahel, for decades in some cases. During the dry season any ordinary farmer could join a caravan to go south; and while they did not receive as advantageous a price on imported merchandise as did North Africans, the difference was not great enough to give North Africans a large volume of business. Once the Tripoli–Kano route collapsed all that remained was a tiny southern segment, and North Africans found themselves in an entirely new commercial environment.

The merchants of Zinder tried a variety of solutions to their new problems. Several attempted to stay in the overseas import–export trade, and the reports of colonial officials mention initiatives on the part of North Africans exploring new possibilities. Muhammad Effendi, who arrived in Zinder after 1905 and served as the agent of a prominent Ghadamasi in Tripoli, went to Manchester to approach firms interested in importing feathers and tanned goat skins from the Sudan. During his short stay he acted as an agent for other Zinder-based North Africans who were anxious to develop ties with overseas importers. After returning to Africa he set up a permanent residence in Kano, where he was known as Muhammad Bugreen.[55] Another North African, Salem Salha, took a shipment of skins from Zinder to Kano and on to Lagos on the railway in order to test the profitability of exporting from Zinder through Lagos. As a new entrant in a market already dominated by the Lagos and Kano Trading Company and other Kano-based merchants, Salem Salha was unable to develop this commercial circuit into a profitable business. He went bankrupt several years after his first trip to Lagos, and later he died a poor man.[56]

Most North African merchants were well aware of the opportunities presented to them by the changing conditions of trade – and of the hazards of failing to take advantage of these opportunities. In general they were extremely eager to use new forms of communication and transport. North Africans in Timbuktu requested that the French set up a way to send postal money orders between St.-Louis and Timbuktu so that it would no longer be necessary to wait to buy turn around goods. In Zinder North Africans were among the first to use postal money orders for the same reason. Kano merchants, who pioneered the use of Lugard's postal service, readily adapted to the new conditions, and found a niche for themselves in Kano's commercial structure after the railway arrived.[57]

But for some tradition was slow to die, and they found it difficult to believe that trans-Saharan trade would not revive and thereby give new value to their experience and their contacts in North Africa. In 1915 several Zinder merchants were still waiting to hear about the possibility of delivery of European merchandise they had ordered through Tripoli; about this time bankruptcies became extremely common. Some who failed in commerce stayed in Zinder and lived out their lives as paupers, while others moved to Kano and tried their luck in the North African community there. Muhamman Kane, the eldest of the Zinder merchants at the time field research for this study was done, remembered seeing the son of a wealthy Zinder-based North African in the Kano city market selling indigo-dyed cloth in small quantities, an occupation more typical of people of more humble origin. Muhamman Kane was reminded of a bush Fulani who had come to the city, not the descendant of a merchant who had belonged to a community of rich and powerful expatriates.[58]

Another response to the collapse of desert trade was to concentrate on trade between Kano and Zinder, an approach which worked better than efforts to stay in the overseas import and export trade. The business of Sharif Dodo, a second generation Ghadamasi, is a case in point. In the heyday of trans-Saharan trade, he worked between North Africa and the Sudan in partnership with a full brother and a half brother in Tripoli. By 1904 he had shifted the emphasis of his activities to Kano, and he rarely spent more than several months of each year in Zinder. As time passed he left more and more of his Zinder business in the hands of a representative, communicating with him by mail, and he came to Zinder once a year to close the accounts.[59]

Just five years after the end of trans-Saharan trade, only a handful of the North African merchants of Zinder still had sound businesses. Two successful merchants were Muhammad Salla, a Mujabra Arab who had arrived in Zinder in 1907, and Muhammad Umar, a Ghadamasi who had been in Djadjidouna for a short time. Like Sharif Dodo these as well as other North Africans who stayed active in commerce traded between Zinder and Kano.[60] A very small segment of the old Tripoli–Kano trade route was all that remained, and trade now flowed in the opposite direction.

CONCLUSION

Tripoli–Kano trade ended because transport on the competing route became cheaper after about 1900 and because shipment along the alternative route was safer and more rapid. In addition trade on the southern route was probably taxed at a lower rate. Tripoli–Kano trade failed to be diverted more quickly than it was because Tripoli wholesalers retained their positions as middlemen and continued to perform important functions in the preparation of Sudan products for European and American markets. When desert caravans ceased to ply the old routes, Tripoli wholesalers and Ghadamasi living in the Sudan fit into various levels in a new distribution hierarchy linking Kano and its commercial hinterland to the world market, and some moved into new commercial systems.

CHAPTER V

Adaptation in the Early Colonial Period

THE migration of North African merchants toward Kano and frequent business failures among those who remained behind represent only one aspect of a larger theme in the history of the desert edge during the last hundred years, namely the decline of the desert sector at the expense of the savannah. This shift in resources and opportunities occurred within the context of the introduction of modern transport facilities and the redirection of the import–export trade. The purpose of this chapter is to explore other aspects of colonial rule which contributed to the decline of the desert and Sahel at the expense of the savannah. It will concentrate on southern central Niger, an area where sedentary agriculture was the predominant form of production. The following chapter will focus on the pastoral economy of the desert edge, where colonial policy also determined the direction of long-term economic change.

A recent tendency among historians concentrating on the colonial period has been to play down the extent of social and economic change, especially in the early decades of the colonial era.[1] This generalization has validity for some remote areas of Africa which remained relatively untouched. But in the region being considered, the colonial occupation, aside from permitting the construction of the railway to Kano, affected life in many other ways. The impact of colonial policy was far different from what might be expected, since many aspects of colonial rule reinforced an underlying movement of decline in the northern, desert-edge sector of the Central Sudan.

In Damagaram the new era began on 30 July 1899 when a force of African soldiers recruited in the Western Sudan and led by French officers defeated the cavalry and archers of Damagaram at Tirmini, a village about 10 km west of Zinder.[2] The *Mission Joalland-Meynier* met no further resistance and found Zinder deserted when it entered the city on the next day. When the people of Zinder returned they found that the colonial occupation had little immediate effects on their lives. But French policy set in motion a series of far-reaching changes which eventually affected most areas of political, economic, and social life. The ruling élite were the first to feel the impact. The French levied a head tax almost immediately and relied on the ruling aristocracy to collect it. They replaced Ahmadu Kuren Daga, whom they killed to avenge the deaths of the explorers Cazemajou and Olive in Damagaram in 1898, with Ahmadu 'dan Bassa, another member of the royal family. The new *sarki* was young and ineffectual, which suited the interests of the French, who were inclined toward a policy of direct rule. They suspected Ahmadu of complicity in plots against them in 1903 and again in 1906, when they deposed him, abolished the office of *sarki,* putting in his place as *chef de province* a eunuch who held the title *bellama* and had served the two previous emirs. An account written in 1921 at the occasion of the deposition of the *bellama* stated that bad relations between Ahmadu and the *bellama* began in 1904. Later the *bellama* had a letter made up to look as if it came from the *mahdi* of Satiru in Nigeria and to implicate Ahmadu in plans to overthrow the French. With the help of Lefebvre's interpreter the *bellama* led the French to the letter and convinced them that Ahmadu was plotting to rebel. About the time the city and the barracks were in the greatest state of confusion, Malam Yaro happened to be returning from his country estate on horseback. This was a weekly event, but the sight of Malam Yaro and a large, mounted retinue so alarmed the French that the *bellama* was able to convince them that Malam Yaro had been party to the alleged plans to rebel. These charges against the *bellama* may have been fabricated in 1921 as a pretext to depose him, but they may have been true. Whatever the facts in the suspected rebellion of 1906, the French exiled the *sarki* and jailed five others, including Malam Yaro, and used the occasion to abolish the office of *sarki* for the time being.[3]

THE FAMINE OF 1913/14

Although lower than average rainfall in central Niger affected crop yields several times during the colonial period, only once – in 1913/14 – did severe famine result. The list of famines within living memory begins with several food shortages known as *abaferam* (Kanuri, what can one do), *alagidigo* (Kanuri, a reference to a song), and *Musaram*, a reference to the fact that it occurred shortly after the French killed the Imezureg leader Musa Mai Damergu in July 1901. The famine of 1913/14 was called either *k'ak'ala'ba* (Hausa, literally how [does one] hide [from famine]) or *doguwar yunwa* (Hausa, the long famine). In 1927 a shortage of millet was known either as *mai buhu* (Hausa,'a person with a bag [to buy small quantities of grain]) or *gwajaja,* a word conveying helplessness. Another food shortage occurred in 1929 and is remembered as *mai zarara* (Hausa, raggedly dressed person). *Cin kwaki* or *mai garin kwaki* refers to the time in 1950 when millet was in short supply and people ate *kwaki,* or manioc flour, which was imported from Nigeria. This last crisis was the first and only time that the colonial government involved itself in famine relief in central Niger. Informants are quick to point out that the only real famine was *k'ak'ala'ba* and that others were times of hardship and scarcity: millet was expensive, but death from starvation was uncommon, except in 1913/14.[4]

The chronology of food shortages differs somewhat from what might be expected from an examination of Sahelian rainfall records. Poor rainfall associated with the famine of 1913/14 shows up in the rainfall data as does 1927−9. But another period of lower than average rainfall in the early 1940s seems not to have created problems locally, perhaps because rainfall was better than the Sahelian average or was timed right for good crop yields.[5] (See Table 4.) Conversely 1901 and 1950 were times of local shortages and did not show up in the wider area apparently because of local drought or bad timing of the rains.

The famine of 1913/14 was of course different. A severe drought in the 1913 growing season, which had been preceded by bad years of lesser magnitude, resulted in food deficits across the entire Sudano−Sahelian zone. Judging from the level of Lake Chad and from reports of minor, localized droughts beginning in the 1880s, the climate had been worsening for two or three decades before 1913.[6] With grain reserves already low and livestock weakened, the damage caused by a rainfall deficit was greatly magnified; and of course the fact that the drought affected the entire Western and Central Sudan made matters worse. In Damagaram food shortages became serious in March or April of 1914, just six months after the poor harvest. With the arrival of the growing season many people were too weak to work, and death from starvation became commonplace. People died along the roads as they attempted to flee south, and the living did not have enough strength to bury the dead. Parents who despaired of surviving left their children in the market-place in the hope that benefactors would take them in and feed them. Informants say that as many as two hundred children at a time were seen in the *zongo* market. 'Dan Bade and other wealthy merchants attempted to provide relief; 'Dan Bade alone is said to have paid for the distribution of twenty large bowls of a porridge called *kunu* each day. Some starving children ate and lived but others died.[7]

A mass exodus of people trying to save themselves took place, with emigrants leaving for the south, where rainfall was always greater and the effects of drought less severe. One estimate of the death toll among those who stayed behind was 80,000; three years later many of those who had fled had not yet returned, and it is safe to conclude that many of these died along the roads.[8] Herds were also decimated as pasture became scarce; cattle seem to have succumbed in greater numbers than camels, goats, and sheep.[9]

It is important to emphasize that the famine had a political dimension: the French did nothing to relieve food shortages, and in fact their actions greatly worsened the effects of the drought. They attempted to collect taxes as usual after the deficit harvest of 1913 and were able to bring in a nearly normal amount of revenue.[10] Never having seen the destructive potential of a major Sahelian drought, they probably had very little appreciation of the ultimate effects of their decision. In addition, in early 1913 they had set out on a major campaign to bring Tibesti and the hostile outposts of the Sanūsiyya under their control. Central Niger was one of several sources of supply for the desert campaign, and surviving records indicate that requisitions of grain and transport animals were greater than normal.[11] This arbitrary taxation in kind will be dealt with in greater detail later, but for present purposes it is important to note that the loss of animals was as serious as the loss of grain. Among farmers one effective strategy for survival was to set out for the far southern savannah with animals for sale and to bring back famine food. Some farmers made as many as fifteen trips to southern Zaria; but to do this they needed transport capacity — donkeys or pack oxen.[12] The loss of animals to military requisitions must have ruled out this possibility for some.

French decisions to collect tax as usual and to commandeer resources had important political repercussions for several years after the famine. The responsibility of carrying out French orders fell on the shoulders of the *chefs de canton,* who had no choice but to comply with French orders. But they paid a heavy price for their complicity. The collection of tax before an impending and predictable disaster made them extremely unpopular with their subjects. In fact, they were so completely discredited that they became useless to the French as intermediaries. As a result the French deposed most *chefs de canton* holding office at the time of the famine and replaced them with other appointees. They even gave out gaol sentences to some deposed chiefs.[13]

Although most merchants escaped with their lives, the famine ended several careers and caused considerable hardship for all. The case of Malam Yaro is perhaps atypical because his troubles began earlier, but it none the less illustrates the kind of difficulties which many faced. Because of his alleged complicity in what the French considered to be an attempted rebellion in 1906, he served two years in prison in the Ivory Coast.[14] His imprisonment is somewhat ironic because he had expended considerable energy mollifying French administrators. Whether his close association with the French brought financial gain or loss is unknown, but he must have had considerable difficulty adjusting to the new commercial conditions as trans-Saharan trade declined, especially after his return from the Ivory Coast. But he was still a rich man, and he engaged in various trading activities and invested in a variety of enterprises; among other things he extended mortgages on standing crops and bought crop futures. Many of his debtors went bankrupt or died during the disastrous growing season of 1913, and these losses were the proximate cause of his downfall. Malam Yaro lived into the early 1920s, but when he died little of his wealth remained.[15]

While the prosperity of the merchants allowed them to survive the famine, it also gave them additional responsibilities. Most gave alms to those less fortunate than themselves. Idi Bagindi, the wealthiest of the local merchants based in *birni,* the walled town, spent a good deal of money giving food to the hungry. In an attempt to recover what he lost in this way, he left for Lagos, where he spent several years as a kola landlord. He returned home only after he had accumulated enough capital to start up his trading business once again.[16]

With the famine long-distance trade had come to a standstill, and afterward it recovered to its pre-drought volume very slowly. Under these circumstances merchants who had bad debts or had redistributed their wealth found it difficult to recoup their losses.

Because of depressed conditions merchants found any kind of adaptation immeasurably more difficult than it would have been otherwise. A case in point is the attempt of a Tubu trans-Saharan trader to adjust to new conditions by moving into the kola trade in 1911 or 1912. He suffered a major setback when a shipment of kola spoiled and he had to absorb the loss, but his son insists that he would have been able to recover had it not been for the famine. As it was, he had very little room in which to manoeuvre, and consequently had to give up long-distance trade.[17]

TRADE AND TAXATION

In the early years colonial rule had a varying impact on different segments of the population. Political change was profound, especially from the point of view of those who became intermediaries for the French in the new government – the *sarki*, members of his court, and *chefs de canton*; but many ordinary citizens escaped the direct effects of the new government if they were fortunate. Many remote areas were only slightly affected by the imposition of colonial rule. The incidence of forced labour, requisitions, and the *indigenat*, an infamous criminal code administered by colonial officials, fell more heavily on townspeople rather than those from small villages. And few people even in towns attempted to assimilate French language and culture. As late as the 1920s the only French school offering instruction beyond the first few years was in Zinder. Imposed economic change was as much out of the question as acculturation in other areas, given the small number of French sent out to rule Niger, the meagre resources at their disposal, and the collapse of trans-Saharan trade, which had been the mainstay of the local economy.

French policy on taxation, however, affected everyone who participated in the market economy, and in particular the merchants. Change in the structure of taxation and methods of tax collection was also comparatively rapid. Until 1903 the French relied on the *sarki* and the officials of the court to collect the head tax, caravan tolls, and taxes levied on craftsmen. The colonial government simply superimposed itself at the top of a pre-existing hierarchy, skimming off tax revenue which reached the highest levels. In 1903 the French decided to take a more active role in tax collection in order to be able to increase the revenue at their disposal. They justified this move by saying that the *sarki,* his agents, and his territorial chiefs were keeping too much revenue for themselves and collecting it in an arbitrary and unfair manner.[18]

Although market taxes and caravan tolls under the old regime were abolished in 1903, the French did not fully replace them until 1906. The new market taxes, in particular, had a detrimental effect on trade. Butchers and kola and cloth sellers had to pay a yearly tax, but each animal transaction was theoretically subject to taxation ranging from 3 francs for each cow, horse or camel sold in the market place to 55 centimes for a sheep or goat. The effect of this policy was to drive many of the animal transactions which had once taken place in Niger to markets just south of the Nigerian border. Before the application of the tax, the large market at Myrria, east of Zinder, counted over 2,000 sellers, but by January of 1904 only three or four hundred attended the market.[19] Twenty years later, market taxes remained a serious problem, one which Brévié, the governor-general of Niger, recognized in the economic report for 1923:

In Nigeria, where the markets are free, the English have succeeded in attracting all of the commerce of the colony of Niger. All along the Nigerian border it is possible to notice the absence of markets on the French side, the ruins of abandoned markets, and, on English soil, in immediate proximity to our largest centers of population, very busy markets used especially by our subjects.[20]

The formation of the large markets at Babura, Mai Adua, and Jibiya — all on Nigerian soil and several kilometres from the border — dates back to the twenty-year period when taxes on market transactions were collected in Niger.[21]

The French policy toward caravan tolls was not as self-defeating as levies on markets, but merchants did have a great deal of difficulty with the new system. Under the old regime, the *sarkin shannu* (Hausa, chief of cattle) and other officials of the court collected the *ushiri* or caravan tax. The word *ushiri* means a tenth part, and it referred to the fraction of the salt passing through Zinder collected by the *anastafidet* of the Kel Ewey which he divided between himself and the *sarki*. The *ushiri* on animals and trans-Saharan goods had evolved into fixed payments: 3,000 cowries per load for North African imports and a sliding scale for animals moving south which was the same whether or not they were loaded.[22] In 1903 the French charged the *sarkin shannu*, whose duty was to collect a portion of caravan taxes, with keeping much of the tax he collected for himself. The French had the *sarkin shannu* beheaded and displayed the head of their victim in the Zinder market named *kasuwar kura*. In protest Zinder people refused to use the market, and so a new site had to be found. According to Muhamman Kane, most people at the time were sceptical of the French justification of the execution. In retrospect French motives also appear suspect, since it was in the French interest to get rid of an official who stood in the way of their taking direct control of taxation of trade.[23]

The collection of *ad valorem* tax on trans-Saharan caravans, instituted in 1903, presented few problems. Trans-Saharan commerce had to pass through Djadjidouna, the point where tolls were collected, and even if caravaniers tried to evade the customs post, the presence of a large caravan moving through Damergu could scarcely go undetected. But Zinder-based North Africans complained that the payment of *ad valorem* taxes required that packages be opened.[24] Not only was this inconvenient, but it also strained relations of trust between shippers and the Tuareg who handled consignments of goods.

But the French had more difficulty collecting tax on numerous small caravans of cattle, sheep, and loaded donkeys and pack oxen moving south of Zinder. Unlike the trade to the north, southern traffic was not concentrated in one corridor, but crossed the Nigerian border at hundreds of points. The surveillance of so many export routes forced the French to rely on local personnel to collect tolls. The French sometimes gave out the rights to caravan tolls as political favours; an example is the case of Mamadu Mai Dosso, who received the rights to taxable trade within the canton of Mallaoua.[25] Under this system, some traders paid more than their fair share, and some paid nothing at all. The uncertainty and risk which the arbitrary collection of tolls brought to long-distance trade created an additional burden, and it gave an added boost to the growth of markets across the border in Nigeria. After 1910 the task of collecting caravan tolls fell increasingly to canton chiefs.[26] In this as in other matters, the canton chiefs were frequently caught between the French and their own subjects.

In 1914 the colonial administration established a series of customs posts to tax trade along the border with Nigeria. The personnel of the newly created customs service was recruited largely from the ranks of the *tirailleurs Sénégalais*, and they were unsupervised and poorly trained for the job. The guards of the customs service set up a blockade between Zinder and Tessaoua even though they had no authority to do so; they terrorized a village thought to be harbouring smugglers; and they frequently took bribes. The French administration was well aware that all of this had a detrimental effect on trade. In late 1914 the *commandant* in Zinder wrote that all commercial activity near Tessaoua had ceased, markets were deserted, and people were terrified of the *gardes-frontières*.[27] Matters improved little as time passed, and by 1918 much of the trade of the borderlands had been driven into Nigeria. Recognizing the danger to their own interests, the French abolished export duties in February of 1918, and afterwards all trade flowed across the border untaxed.

MIGRATION

French policy on taxation had a major impact on population movements within the desert-side sector of the Central Sudan. One way to escape the undesirable aspects of French rule was to leave for Nigeria, where the rates of taxation were about the same, but forced labour was less burdensome, and requisitions, market taxes, and military conscription did not exist.[28] The famine added impetus to the southward movement in that many people whose original intention was to return to Niger must have decided to stay in Nigeria once they had seen for themselves the differences in the two regimes. Most local records on forced labour and requisitions in Damagaram and Damergu have been lost or destroyed; but French documents reveal that colonial authorities were concerned about the harshness of their rule in comparison to conditions in Nigeria. When they modified the worst aspects of their administration in the 1920s, they found that many emigrants returned.

This major movement of population toward Nigeria coincided with several other changes in settlement patterns after the colonial occupation. In pre-colonial times the borders of separation between the Sokoto Caliphate and hostile neighbouring states to the north had been largely unoccupied, forming a no-man's-land between Ful'be and Habe. But with the colonial occupation hostilities ceased, and cultivators moved south into sparsely populated land.[29] Farmers also began a process of abandoning fortified, central settlements in favour of small hamlets closer to good agricultural land. In Damagaram and Damergu the movement to dispersed settlement was under way several years after the arrival of the French and received added impetus over a decade later when villagers moved to remote places in efforts to evade conscription into the French colonial army. Movement to remote areas also helped villagers avoid forced labour and requisitions.[30]

Shifts of population to the countryside and toward Nigeria had two principal effects on the activities of merchants. First, the total volume of trade to Niger from Kano was lower than it was before the colonial occupation. Decreased trade was an aspect of depressed conditions in the first several decades of colonial rule, and of course it fitted into the larger pattern of decline in the Sahel at the expense of the savannah. The second effect of these population movements was that they reinforced the decline of market-places north of the colonial boundary and the reciprocal growth of Nigerian border markets.

CURRENCY SPECULATION

Merchants agree that the aspect of French rule which created the greatest difficulties for them was the introduction of French currency. The problem was not that the people of Damagaram refused to accept modern currency, as contemporary observers, and especially colonial administrators, often charged. In fact French currency performed exactly the same functions as the money it replaced, and so in reality it was not an innovation.

The problem resulted instead from a black market, which both local people and French administrators and soldiers used to their advantage. In order to understand how a situation which permitted abuse arose, it is necessary to refer back to early twentieth-century monetary theory. Of particular interest are contradictory notions about the role of currency in the colonies, as well as what appears by modern standards to be a poor understanding of monetary matters. On one hand the French felt that colonial subjects should use French money because it was inherently superior to local currencies, and anything less than a full commitment to encouraging the use of metropolitan currency was thought to betray a lack of seriousness about the self-proclaimed civilizing mission of colonization.[31] But this sense of responsibility was offset by adherence to contemporary monetary theory, which held that metropolitan currency in the colonies represented a potential threat to the mother country in that it might be suddenly repatriated and provoke an inflationary crisis of unknown proportions at home.[32] This theory remained untested since a sudden influx of currency from the colonies did not occur. But the French in particular took great pains to guard against this possibility by controlling transfers of francs to the metropolis and by requiring gold reserves for all money circulating in the colonies. In contrast to the French, the British issued token currency, that is money not backed by reserves. The French refusal to issue token currency until the mid-1920s and then in small quantities relative to the need naturally led to shortages of francs in circulation. These chronic shortages — lasting until the 1940s at least — were at the heart of local problems. In effect Niger was almost totally integrated into the sterling currency zone, and the colony relied heavily on British as well as French specie for private use, and intermittently for payments into the treasury as well.[33]

Money was of course nothing new in the area. Southern Niger was part of a pre-colonial region in which cowries circulated and performed most functions associated with modern money.[34] Pre-colonial money included not only cowries but also Maria Theresa thalers and French five-franc silver pieces. At the turn of the century the rate of exchange was roughly 5,000 cowries for a thaler or a five-franc coin, though exchange rates fluctuated, and speculation was possible. Malam Yaro seems to have been the only Zinder merchant wealthy enough to hoard one or more kinds of coin and take advantage of slight shifts in rates of exchange.[35]

But speculation became a much more serious problem with the introduction of colonial currency. In the early years the French gradually moved to a position where they required French currency to be used in tax payments and other transactions which they controlled, although shortages sometimes forced them to allow the use of British currency. At any rate there was simply not enough French and British currency in circulation to serve these purposes. People continued to rely on cowries and thalers, but shortages of French currency encouraged speculation between cowries and French francs — and even among various forms of French money: coin in small denominations, coin of larger value, and paper.

Profiteering was possible because of severe discrepancies between officially determined exchange rates and the black-market rates which actually prevailed. The first area of disparity was the exchange of cowries and French silver. Until 1910 the colonial administration accepted cowries as payment of taxes, although taxes were assessed in French francs. In 1908 the administration fixed the exchange rate at 6,000 cowries to a five-franc piece, whereas the market rate differed: 7,000 cowries for five francs. This disparity made it advantageous to pay in cowries and gave a windfall profit to those holding cowries when taxes came due. After 1910 the administration accepted only French currency, and so the disparity worked the other way round. When taxes were due, five-franc pieces became as much as 30 per cent more expensive in terms of Maria Theresa thalers and cowries. Now those who were able to hoard French coin to trade for cowries received the windfall profit.[36]

A second kind of imbalance was that French coin in small denominations was worth more than its face value because it was scarce. Few transactions could take place with the exchange of five-franc coins alone, and the demand for one-franc pieces, fifty-centime coins, or those of smaller value far exceeded the supply. The result was that four or four and a half francs in small coin equalled one five-franc piece. Those who held small coins or those who could obtain them at the official exchange rate, namely at the rate of five francs in small coin for a five-franc piece, profited. Some French administrators obtained small coins as they were being introduced into circulation or after they had been paid into the treasury, and sold them back at the black-market rate, reaping a profit of 10 per cent or more on the transaction.[37]

But the introduction of paper currency just before World War I was the occasion for a much more serious misalignment of the official and unofficial rates of exchange between various forms of French currency. Local people had a strong preference for silver currency over paper money, for very good reasons. Silver had an intrinsic value, and should it be demonetized in the future, for whatever reason, it could be melted down and turned into jewellery. More important, its storage properties were far superior to those of paper currency. Those who held savings in paper currency ran the risk of loss in fires or from insect damage, and the latter was a particularly important consideration because termite infestation was common. As a result, on the local market a five-franc bill was worth only two francs silver in the period after the introduction of paper currency until the late 1920s. The value of paper bills fluctuated seasonally, just as the silver franc−cowrie rate had risen and fallen earlier, because the French accepted paper currency when it was time to pay the head tax. At this time the value of a five-franc bill rose to two and a half francs silver, but no higher, because common people did not pay directly to the French, but through intermediaries, namely *chefs de canton* or in the case of people living in

Zinder, through the appointed *chef de province.*[38]

Disparities between official and unofficial rates of exchange gave various groups of the population a chance to profit at the expense of others. This was of course the case with all types of currency imbalance, but the people of Zinder remember conversions between paper and silver coin as the most serious and persistent currency problem. The first group to take advantage of the situation were *chefs de canton*. They collected a large proportion of tax revenue and were able to insist that they receive full value, but they could convert it into paper at the black-market exchange rate, thereby doubling the value of tax revenue at the official rate. Conversions of this kind took place in Zinder, since most paper currency introduced in central Niger went into circulation in the capital. The conversion was technically illegal. But between 1915 and 1925, the period when informants insist that it was common practice, the French prosecuted only one *chef de canton* for changing coin to paper at the black-market rate.[39]

The second group to profit were the French themselves, who condoned illegal currency conversions among local people because they themselves were doing the same thing. Colonial administrators and military personnel received about a third of their pay in coin, and they also did their best to obtain as much additional coinage as they could when it was being introduced into circulation from the treasury. They even went so far as to have relatives and friends in France send them coinage through the mail.[40] By changing coin obtained in these ways to paper at the local black-market rate, they were able to make an automatic profit of 100 per cent or more. Profiteering of this kind began as soon as paper bills were introduced, but it became much easier after the completion of the railway from Kano to Lagos. When French officers returned home through Dakar instead of Lagos, regulations on currency movements had kept profiteering within bounds. But no such check existed at Lagos, and in the absence of border controls between Niger and Nigeria, French personnel could take unlimited amounts of currency with them.[41] The administration tried to control profiteering by prosecuting several blatant offenders, in all cases district officers in charge of *subdivisions*. But profiteering remained a serious problem until the local market exchange rate began to come into line with the official rate in the late 1920s.

The alignment of the two rates of exchange resulted from the introduction of millions of francs' worth of bronze and aluminium alloy coins.[42] These token coins known locally as *ja tamma*, or reddish brown francs, bore the markings of metropolitan *Chambres de commerce*. Since they were not legal tender in France, their export did not offend bullionists. But *ja tamma* were perfectly acceptable to the people of Zinder, who were happy to see the long-awaited alleviation of local monetary problems when they appeared.

The people who lost at the expense of *chefs de canton* and French officials were those who were forced to accept paper currency at its face value but could only convert it at the black-market rate of exchange. The people primarily affected were those who had to deal directly with the French or with the *tirailleurs* on the French payroll. The French also supervised markets and had *tirailleurs* arrest anyone who sold at different prices depending on whether payment was in silver or paper.[43] And the French sent local people acting as their agents, accompanied by *gardes de cercle*, into the countryside to force people to change into paper currency at the official rate.[44] Those who received paper money in an officially supervised transactions took a loss if they had to dispose of it in black-market situations, as most did. For example, if the seller of a garment took a five-franc bill in payment he in fact received only two francs, according to the local rate, unless he could persuade a *chef de canton* to accept the bill at face value, which was unlikely.

Among the merchants, those who suffered most from the introduction of paper currency were the North Africans. Whereas once their sophistication in the manipulation of exchange rates and banking arrangements had been an advantage, after 1910 it quickly became a useless skill. In fact their inability to escape the necessity of using currency was a serious drawback. Since they were based in Zinder and mistrusted by the French, they remained under official scrutiny more than other groups. The French forced them to accept paper currency at the official rate, especially when North Africans sold to French or to *tirailleurs*. Five-franc bills were nearly worthless in Kano, and so North Africans had to change them into silver or obtain trade goods to take to Kano. In either case they took a loss because they held currency worth only 40 per cent or less of its face value. An elderly merchant in Zinder described how North Africans tried to move into the cattle trade in an effort to find a way out of this predicament, but they found that livestock-owners were no more willing than anyone else to accept depreciated currency.[45] In contrast to North Africans, local, rurally-based traders simply exchanged livestock for cloth in Kano, thereby avoiding the pitfalls of the double-tiered ,monetary system.

One interesting if paradoxical effect of the colonial occupation was a levelling of the structure of commerce, as inequalities in the distribution of wealth among merchants were reduced. By 1920 most large-scale merchants of the pre-colonial period were no longer active. Idi Bagindi was an old man when he returned from Lagos. Malam Yaro was impoverished, having lost the remainder of his fortune during the famine. 'Dan Bade died about 1918. As for the North Africans, only a handful were still in business in 1920, and they competed with each other in trade between Kano and Zinder for a market of limited size. North Africans were cut off from their traditional sources of supply and finance, and in addition they had great difficulty adjusting to Niger's multi-tiered monetary system. Other aspects of colonial policy, such as the taxation of trade and the unintentional displacement of population south to Nigeria, affected North Africans and their local counterparts alike. And of course the famine and the severe blow it dealt to the prosperity of the region further limited commercial opportunities.

The decline of large-scale, Zinder-based traders was accompanied by the rising importance of small-scale, rural traders. The people of rural Damaragam needed certain goods, notably cloth or raw cotton, from the south regardless of economic conditions, and in order to buy these necessities they continued to sell animals and grain. With market activity in Niger on the decline, they had to travel to Nigerian border markets or to Kano in order to trade. Whatever collection and distribution continued in Niger increasingly tended to take place outside markets in house trade. Thus an indirect result of the colonial occupation was an increasing involvement in dry-season trade on the part of farmers who sought to supply themselves with items no longer available in cheap and plentiful supply in the markets of Damagaram.[46]

Large-scale commerce survived in Nigeria, where boom conditions in the groundnut trade and a wide variety of other activities offered numerous opportunities for traders to accumulate capital. Commercial possibilities included shuttle trade between the railhead at Kano and large border markets contiguous to Niger, specialization in cattle or kola trade between northern Nigeria and the Yoruba cities, a variety of retail and wholesale activities in Kano or other Nigerian towns, and buying groundnuts for large commercial companies or local exporters.[47] Aside from the North Africans, few Zinder people took advantage of this commercial environment in Nigeria. Apparently, established Kano traders continued to recruit apprentices among the members of their families or among others in their own immediate region. In addition, Zinder people who had some experience in trade were probably handicapped by unfamiliarity with conditions in Kano and by the absence of social contacts and kinship ties.

Thus a combination of unfavourable economic conditions ruined a whole generation of merchants. But the situation began to improve in the 1920s. In the first place the French administration abolished duties on imports and exports on the Niger–Nigerian border, an action which aided recovery from the serious trade depression of 1911–20. Second, the French made a concerted effort to correct the worst abuses of their methods of commandeering produce and animals; this seems to have had the greatest effect on pastoral people, and villagers in Damagaram still had to live with forced labour and requisitions. Third, the monetary situation improved with the introduction of token coinage in the mid 1920s. And finally, the worldwide commercial depression of 1921/2 had only limited effects in Niger. As Nigerian commodity exports slowed, so also did demand for cattle, sheep, and goats from the Sahel. But livestock trade recovered rapidly, responding to the rebound in Nigerian producer incomes as the brief trade depression passed.[48]

The commercial revival of the 1920s set the stage for the emergence of a new generation of Sahelian merchants, but the ruin of their elders left few local sources of capital. Assistance for this new generation of Zinder-based traders came from an unexpected source – from Lieutenant Dufour, a French army officer who took an interest in commerce when still a district officer in Damergu. In 1919 his superiors found out about his commercial activities, reprimanded him, and discharged him from the military.[49] But Dufour remained in Niger and set himself up in business in Zinder. Unlike local traders and those who had been cut off from North African financiers, Dufour had access to capital. In addition to his own funds, he had the backing of a silent partner in France, and, more important, he received supplier credit from European firms in Kano. Dufour used this capital to import cloth from Kano, to export hides and skins (though on a much smaller scale), and to maintain a network of local client traders who travelled to markets and villages in Damagaram and Muniyo, and even as far away as Tahoua, to sell the merchandise Dufour imported.

This network of client traders was the key to Dufour's success. Informants in Zinder called Dufour's agents *'yan balas* (sing. *'dan balas*), using a word borrowed from the French *balance* and referring to the settling of accounts which defined the relations between Dufour and his agents. Dufour gave them merchandise on account, and they were to return to him each day, every week, or once a month depending on how much he trusted them. They presented Dufour with whatever merchandise remained, and they paid for the rest at a predetermined price. The difference between the price of sale and the price paid to Dufour went to the *'dan balas,* and Dufour asked no questions. Many of Dufour's *'yan balas* had sub-clients of their own called *dillalai* (Hausa, sing. *dillali*, meaning a commission seller and not a broker, which is another sense of the word). *Dillalai* received goods to sell, usually on a day-to-day basis, from the *'yan balas.* Dufour extended credit to people he knew and trusted, and they in turn gave out credit on a very short-term basis to people they trusted. Many of the sub-clients got to know Dufour and later became full-fledged *'yan balas* after establishing their reputation with him. Dufour asked only that they have sufficient experience in commerce that they were not likely to be a liability to him.[50]

Dufour used his network of client traders to obtain foreign exchange as well as to dispose of imported merchandise. He obtained bronze-aluminium coins from his friends in the administration and gave them to his agents to exchange them for shillings. The agents fanned out into the countryside in search of shillings which they gave to Dufour when they returned.

But meanwhile Dufour's agents used goods from Dufour or the currency they obtained to finance their own small trading ventures. For example, a client trader might buy sheep and cattle north-east of Zinder with Dufour's money and resell the animals in Zinder.[51] The possibilities for this type of trade were limited only by the need for a sure source of shillings at the ultimate end-point of what might be a complicated set of commercial transactions. It was also helpful to have a source of short-term credit in Zinder in order to be able to give Dufour his money on the appointed day of accounting should private transactions be delayed for some reason. Client traders borrowed money from other merchants, sometimes for periods as short as several hours, but short-term credit was not available to everyone. In the first place capital was scarce and hard to raise. Second, the borrower had to be able to convince the lender of his own credit-worthiness. The borrower had to have a good reputation, and he also had to be able to convince the lender that the venture for which he was using Dufour's capital had a reasonable chance of success.

Dufour's advantage over his competitors in trade between Kano and Zinder was not only his access to capital, but also his ability to obtain currency for buying in Kano at an advantageous rate of exchange. Lacking networks of client traders of the kind Dufour had, the North Africans had the choice between changing francs into shillings in Kano at disadvantageous exchange rates, or finding two-way trade circuits. Two-way barter trade was difficult since the rurally-based *fatake* took a large proportion of the hides and skins destined for the Kano market. Those who had to accept paper currency were at a double disadvantage, since French paper currency brought an even lower rate of exchange than silver francs. With these things in his favour, Dufour easily dominated commerce in Zinder through the 1920s and early 1930s, until his retirement in 1935, when the Société Commerciale de l'Ouest Africain (S.C.O.A.), whose Kano branch had been one of his suppliers, bought out his operation.[52]

Although Dufour came close to monopolizing trade in Zinder until the 1930s, many Zinder merchants were quick to point out the benefits to them of Dufour's presence. Dufour was the source of the wealth of many who later occupied positions of prominence. Among those who first worked for Dufour and later traded on their own were 'Dan Gayi, Ciroma Sulayman, Muhamman Murna, Muhamman Adabar, Mazadu Wudigi, Wurga, and Muhamman Tsofo.[53] Since Dufour asked no questions about how they employed his capital from one accounting to the next, this new generation of town-based merchants worked for him and financed their own trade at the same time, and later had enough trade capital to survive entirely on their own.

But Dufour's business was the precursor of a more pronounced commercial dominance by Europeans which was to develop later. Because of the colonial situation, Dufour threatened local interests much more than North Africans had done in their heyday. Because he was French, he worked the disparity between official and black-market exchange rates to his advantage. In addition, he obtained credit in Kano. Because he traded between Zinder and Kano, his business threatened pre-existing local trade, even that of small-scale rural traders. His advantages included a familiarity with modern business practices, and the backing of large commercial companies such as S.C.O.A. When he turned to lorry transport-ation, he added a technological advantage to an already favourable position. This move in itself foreshadowed troubles to come, since the advent of modern transport forced many small traders out of business.

CONCLUSION

Zinder's merchant community declined in importance as a result of the interplay of a number of factors. With the end of trans-Saharan trade the city lost its collection and distribution network and became a subordinate metropolis, as various commercial functions shifted to Kano. Zinder-based traders no longer played the role they once had because of the diminished importance of commodity exports for the world market, because of the famine, and because certain merchants, the North Africans in particular, suffered under a monetary system which permitted widespread profiteering at their expense. By 1920 the old commercial structure in Zinder had collapsed so completely that the only avenue open to merchants seeking to gain experience and to accumulate trade capital was to try their fortune in Kano or to become the client of a French merchant. Another possibility was to leave the urban setting entirely and enter livestock trade, where growing opportunities partially compensated for Niger's urban trade depression. The structure of commerce in Damagaram had shifted to favour small-scale, rural enterprises and not the relatively large urban firms which had been the rule earlier.

The events of the early colonial period, apart from causing the ruin of a whole generation of merchants, have a wider significance. The end of trans-Saharan trade coincided with climatic downturn to bring about a major reorientation as opportunities shifted to the south. The effect of French colonial rule, which relied on arbitrary taxation in kind, direct taxation, various charges levied on trade and markets, labour service, and military recruitment was to further accentuate differences between the area under French rule and the prosperous area surrounding the railhead at Kano. It is beyond the scope of this study to trace the migration of cultivators who left in response to economic opportunity, or because their only recourse during famine was flight, or because direct and indirect taxation in Niger compared unfavourably with the situation in Nigeria. Nothing less than a full-scale study of immigration in Nigeria and patterns whereby newcomers were either settled in local communities or excluded from opportunities to use land would do justice to this topic.[54] But evidence available from north of the border suggests that the number of immigrants involved was significant, and the movement therefore serves as an indicator of economic decline in the nothern sector of the region.

CHAPTER VI

The Pastoral Economy

THE purpose of this chapter is to examine the evolution of the economy of the desert after the colonial occupation. The principal geographical focus is Tuareg territory in the Aïr massif, the transhumance corridor leading from Aïr to country occupied by Hausa and Kanuri farmers in the south, and the desert oases of Fachi and Bilma, which were visited by Tuareg salt traders. There are two main reasons for including a history of the desert sector of the economy in this study. First, the causes and consequences of the long-term shift of resources and opportunities away from the desert toward the savannah have not been previously researched or analysed. The second reason is that the history of the twentieth century provides an invaluable source of information on economic cycles in the pastoral economy, and it also reveals mechanisms whereby the pastoral sector recovered from the low points in these cycles. Furthermore twentieth-century economic cycles have affected farmers, herders, craftsmen, and traders over a wide area of the steppe and Sahel.

Writing the history of the pastoral economy presents special challenges. Historical sources are sparse, and those which exist give superficial coverage to a variety of unrelated issues. Without doubt the reason for this situation is that nomads moved constantly from place to place with their herds and often used mobility to escape notice by officials and avoid paying taxes. The use of oral sources also involves special difficulties, since interviewing runs the risk of emphasizing the story of a small group and missing the larger picture. Working within the limitations imposed by the sources, this chapter will assemble information on three seemingly diverse topics: (1) the economic impact of colonial policy and antagonism between French and Tuareg; (2) the implications of shifts in relative prices; (3) and movements of population in response to changing economic opportunity. Each topic will be used to develop a periodization and will contribute to an understanding of economic decline and recovery in the pastoral economy.

COLONIAL RULE

Antagonism between the French and their Tuareg subjects played an important role in the decline of the desert sector, though it was of course not the only factor. In order to understand fully why French actions were so damaging, it is necessary to view the wider historical context. In addition, the framework of analysis worked out by Frederik Barth is also helpful.[1] For present purposes Barth's emphasis on the greater potential for growth in the pastoral sector as compared to the agricultural sector should be remembered. According to Barth, 'the picture will rarely be that of an unmodified pastoral buoyancy and agricultural stagnation', though a tendency for real life situations to bear out this theoretical contrast is expected. In fact, in the conditions of the Central Sudan, the risk of drought in the desert must be juxtaposed with the possibility of growth and prosperity. But the key point of analysis is that patterns of growth, decline, and risk differed greatly in the two sectors. The pre-colonial history of Tuareg diversification and involvement in the economy of the savannah demonstrates an adaptation to these conditions.

Differences between the pastoral and agricultural sectors had profound implications for the history of the colonial period as well. In the pastoral sector wealth was concentrated in the hands of the nobles, and as a result it was highly visible to the French. Simply stated, the principal dilemma of the French in the first decade of colonial rule in Niger was to find sufficient revenue to finance their administration, as well as their costly military operations in the desert. The French had hoped to tax trans-Saharan trade, but this was delicate business, since too heavy a burden of taxation would only speed the process of diversion of trade to the new southern route through Nigeria.[2] Hence they levied heavy taxes on trade and markets, but this policy too was self-defeating, since markets relocated just across the border in Nigeria. The only remaining source of income was to be found in the taxation of agricultural production, but this was also an inadequate source of revenue. Indeed, the events of the early colonial period produced a pervasive sense of frustration among colonial rulers at the inability of the *sarki* and his retainers to satisfy the need for an adequate local tax base.

But no such obstacles stood in the way of French actions in the desert, where the concentration of wealth under the control of the nobles encouraged them to take what they needed. And the policy of commandeering camels for French military needs had the supreme virtue of allowing the occupation of the desert to pay for itself. Camel requisitions also served the secondary purpose of undermining the position of the nobles. French reports articulate a preoccupation with the need to intervene on behalf of the lower strata of African societies, both in the desert and among the sedentary population. This justification for colonial rule rested ultimately on egalitarian principles, but military considerations also came into play. The warrior aristocracy was correctly seen as a dangerous segment of the population, the nucleus of any potential resistance.

But the policy of taking camels from nomads created economic dislocation on a vast scale and was a major contributory cause of a crisis which dominated early colonial history. And the policy was short-sighted even from the narrow French point of view, since it ultimately made colonial occupation more troublesome and costly; long run losses from economic decline and the need for increased military expenditures greatly overshadowed short-term gains.

1. Requisitions and Resistance

The most serious challenge to French rule in Niger occurred when a series of loosely connected uprisings broke out first in the Niger bend, then in Dori and the Azawak, and finally in the Aïr massif.[3] The revolt in Aïr represented the greatest threat because it had able central leadership, enjoyed widespread support, used modern weapons captured during the Italian retreat from southern Libya, and was fought on favourable terrain. Kaocen, the leader of the movement, was a member of the Ikazkazen section of the Kel Ewey who had fled to Chad when the French occupied Damergu, had become a member of the Sanūsīyya brotherhood, and had joined Sanūsī resistance to the French in Chad. Kaocen arrived in Agadez in December of 1916 and enlisted the support of the *amenokal* Tegama. An attack on the French garrison at Agadez took its defenders completely by surprise, so that Kaocen and his allies sealed off the French fort and laid seige to it. But they were unable to overcome French defences, and the attackers were finally driven off after a three-month stalemate when a relief column arrived from Zinder. The resistance movement kept going for two years against superior French force but was finally driven into a particularly in-hospitable part of the desert north-east of Aïr in 1918. By this time it had suffered such heavy losses that it ceased to be a serious threat.[4]

Historians have viewed the Aïr revolt in the context of the theme of African resistance to colonial rule, as of course they should. But they have failed to look far enough beyond its military and political significance to appreciate fully its place in the economic history of the desert. The purpose of the present section is to analyse the revolt as an indicator of the detrimental effects of previous bad relations with the French, as an index of stress in the pastoral economy after 1900, and as one of several causes of a major cycle of decline and recovery.

In the first place the arrival of the French imposed a series of far-reaching changes on the Tuareg. Resistance to the initial French penetration from the west in 1899, though not widespread, caused severe disruption in some cases. Sections of the Iullemenden, Kel Gress, and later Imezureg fought the French. Defeated Imezureg and small groups of other confederations fled to Chad, and when they returned, the French forced them to turn over the breech-loading rifles they had acquired and to pay indemnities in kind so as to lessen the likelihood of future resistance.[5]

While handing over rifles and camels represented only a tem-porary burden, regular taxation placed a longer-lasting strain on the political structure. When the French called upon the *amenokal* of Agadez, drum chiefs, and section chiefs to collect head taxes, they were asking them to assume an entirely new role. Before colonial rule the *amenokal* collected tolls from trans-Saharan caravans and from salt traders, and he received tribute from the inhabitants of Agadez, In Gall, and Tegidda-n-tesemt, but only from those of servile status or slave ancestry; nobles were exempt.[6] In order to collect taxes from nobles, Tuareg leaders had to break with tradition, since the role of policeman, judge, and tax collector was an innovation. A principal reason for the establishment of the French garrison in Agadez in 1906 was the impatience of the colonizers with the reluctance of the *amenokal* to accept his new functions.[7] French policy was to move down the hierarchy of seg-mentation, forcing drum chiefs and section leaders to act as intermediaries in fiscal and judicial matters, but they had not yet been able to penetrate to the level of section leaders when the revolt erupted.[8]

But the major source of strain on the nomad economy was the French policy of commandeering transport animals from the Tuareg. The need for camels as remounts for patrols and to run supply caravans greatly exceeded the ability of the French to pay, and in the early years Tuareg never received remuneration. In theory camels were to be returned after being used, but in actual practice the French kept them indefinitely. In addition military commanders had little incentive to take care of the animals, which to the French were nearly costless, and hence many drove camels until they died of exhaustion.[9] Naturally the burden of military requisitions fell in an inequitable way, since commanders took whatever camels happened to be at hand, with little concern for spreading losses evenly. Even when the French used the *manzo* or assistant of the Kel Ewey *anastafidet*, he was forced to resort to the same tactics.[10]

With each successive campaign in the desert, the French needed more transport resources to supply their outposts. Even the small detachment at Bilma, stationed there after 1906, needed supplies from the south; by 1908 requisitions near N'Guigmi, a southern staging area for caravans to the oasis, resulted in the flight of the Tubu population. At about the same time the population of Aïr was being called upon to supply grain and transport animals, though the population base was larger and so the effects of taxation in kind were less pronounced.[11]

But the French decision to occupy the Tibesti *massif* in 1913 had especially grave consequences, in part because it was a large-scale campaign, and in part because it coincided with a period of bad climate. A French force left Bilma headed east to Tibesti in the fall of 1913, just after the arrival of the autumn salt caravan. To mount this expedition the French had requisitioned 400 camels, the services of forty men, and an undisclosed quantity of grain – all from the salt caravan. Most camels succumbed during forced marches in Tibesti; the grain was not reimbursed; and guides and camel drivers, who returned nearly a year later, were not paid for their work.[12] Requisitions became increasingly frequent in 1914 because of the need for re-supply caravans to Tibesti and to other French desert outposts. During the drought, normal channels of supply were inadequate, and not enough food could be obtained on the open market. The anonymous author of the agricultural report for the third quarter of 1914 wrote that at least 60 per cent of the animals used in the convoys between March and July of that year died on the route and the rest were so weak that they could no longer be used.[13] The French took additional camels from the salt caravan which arrived in Bilma in the autumn of 1914. When the news of these requisitions reached Agadez with the return of the salt caravan, the Tuareg were driven to the edge of the revolt.[14]

2. Consequences of the Revolt

Although the revolt in Aïr had political and religious dimensions, without the existence of an economic crisis of major proportions it would never have enjoyed the widespread support it received. Hardship caused by requisitions was great enough in itself, but it was compounded by other factors. The worst incidence of camel loss occurred during the drought of 1911–14, which also cost the Tuareg dearly in herd losses.[15] In a wider perspective the collapse of trans-Saharan trade and disruption caused by the colonial conquest must be taken into account as well.

The revolt and severe measures used by the French to repress it seriously compounded the pre-existing economic crisis and prolonged it for many years. Both the rebels and the French took animals and supplies as they needed them from non-combatants, filled in wells, and laid waste the countryside. The ecological balance of the Aïr, delicate in any case, was tipped toward waste and desolation, and by the end of the fighting most of the country was so impoverished as to be uninhabitable. Many destitute Tuareg fled to the south, and others left for fear they would lose what they had been able to save to that time. Then in 1918 the French began to force the evacuation of the northern Aïr in an effort to prevent future uprisings. Those driven from their homeland, not content to remain in territory ruled by the French, went to Nigeria, where their herds were safe from military requisitions.[16] As many as 30,000 Tuareg left Aïr during and after the revolt, but by 1922 they had begun to return, in part in response to a policy reversal by French authorities, who issued orders to local commanders to take camels only when in the direst need.[17]

But the 'spill over' of Tuareg population in the savannah, especially among low-status Tuareg, was great indeed. In the Zinder *cercle*, for example, a sizeable proportion of the inhabitants of *bugaje* villages south, south-west, and west of Zinder trace the time of their arrival to 1913–18. This was the third of three waves of immigration from the desert after the colonial occupation, each reflecting varying degrees of trouble. The first was a reaction to early French–Tuareg hostilities in 1899–1901, while the second represented a reaction to the occupation of Aïr in 1904. But the wave produced by drought and warfare in 1913–18 overshadowed each of the earlier, lesser movements.[18]

3. The Bilma Salt Trade

The main interest of this study in the Bilma salt trade is that it serves as an index of the level of economic activity in the desert sector. Salt represented a potentially significant share of the earnings of the desert-side sector, and the history of the salt trade provides a hitherto unexplored source of information on the crisis of 1911–18 and the subsequent recovery. In addition, the history of the desert salt trade had an importance of its own, since the recovery after 1918 has often been ignored. Many early twentieth-century observers believed that desert salt trade was or would soon become a casualty of competition from cheap overseas imports, a view often uncritically repeated in recent works.[19] But these observers overlooked the diversity and growing size of the market for desert salt and also misunderstood the constraints on supply.

Before proceeding it is first necessary to consider the organization of the trade as background material, in order to permit an understanding of the responses of traders during the economic crisis. Salt consumed in the Central Sudan in the early twentieth century came from well over 150 separate sources and served a variety of industrial, culinary, medicinal, and other uses, and was fed to animals. By far the most important sources of supply for salts rich in sodium chloride, as opposed to potash (salts with higher concentrations of sulphates and carbonates), were the desert oases of Fachi and Bilma.[20] Bilma is actually the southernmost village in a larger oasis called Kawar, which owes its existence to a rock outcropping extending 80 km in a north–south direction, protecting a narrow strip of land from sand carried by prevailing north-westerly winds. In some places drinking water is available near the surface, and at others the water table carries nearly pure sodium chloride in solution to pits where the water partially evaporates. Because of its north–south orientation and the availability of water, Kawar was a channel for trans-Saharan trade between Borno and the Fazzan.[21] Fachi, a village in an oasis known as Agram, located in the Tenere about 150 km south-west of Bilma, is more isolated than its neighbouring oasis, and the population is smaller.[22] Both Fachi and Bilma belonged to Borno until the eighteenth

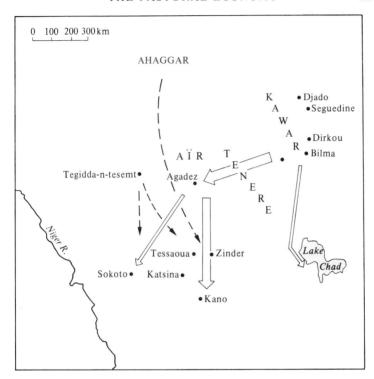

century, and the inhabitants of both villages speak Kanuri. The
Tubu, who carried salt from the oases to Borno, intermarried with
Kanuri, and in the northern villages of Kawar sedentary Tubu
form the dominant group in the population.[23]

The Tuareg of the Aïr gained access to salt from Kawar and
neighbouring oases by degrees. The Tuareg salt trade route moved
successively south over the centuries, with Djado, then Seguidine,
then central Kawar supplying salt to caravans from the Aïr. Tuareg
inroads on desert sources of supply culminated with a successful
attack on Bilma about 1760.[24] The Tuareg then were able to supply
the Hausa states, which displaced Borno as distribution centres for
Saharan salt in the Sudan. In the late eighteenth century, Katsina
was the emporium for salt from Fachi and Bilma, a position taken
over by Kano as the nineteenth century progressed.

Most of the Tuareg of the Aïr participated in the salt trade but
two confederations or drum groups, the Kel Grees and the Kel
Ewey, had an especially intense involvement. The Kel Ewey
attacked the Aïr in the eighteenth century, driving the Kel Grees to

the Adar and Gobir Tudu, areas north of Sokoto and Katsina respectively. The Kel Grees transported salt to the western Sokoto Caliphate, but the Kel Ewey, dominant in the Aïr, were in a position to control the most important branch of the trade route, namely the section between the Aïr and Kano.[25]

The salt trade required a high level of organization because of the absence of wells between the Aïr and the oases, and because of the vulnerability of heavily laden camels to raiding parties. The Tuareg assembled huge caravans at Tabello in the eastern Aïr each year in late October and in March. The Tuareg loaded their camels with millet, cloth, and assorted foodstuffs to trade, their own provisions, and water and fodder for the camels. They had to take enough fodder for the round trip, which averaged thirty days, since no pasture could be found in the Tenere, and the pasture in the oases was sufficient for only a few hundred animals. The largest caravan was the one which set out in October, when the weather was just right for the trip − the worst of the heat was over, but the strong winter winds and sandstorms had not yet begun. The autumn caravan often included something on the order of 20,000 camels, and the main body of the caravan, excluding stragglers, was as much as 25 km long.[26] The order of march reflected the lines of segment-ation within Tuareg society. At the head of the caravan was a representative of the *amenokal* of Aïr; each drum group had a *madugu* who led the sections, each of which had its own *madugu*.[27] Most of the Tuareg who joined the salt caravan were *imrad,* or vassals, trusted with the camels belonging to their master and empowered to act on his behalf.

The Tuareg marched from sunrise until midnight in order to traverse the Tenere as quickly as possible. At midnight they unloaded the camels and camped where they were, so that the caravan was spread out over the space it occupied during the march. The older people slept while the younger men pounded millet and fed the camels from the fodder being carried. When the food had been prepared, the young men woke up their elders, who ate and then took their turn feeding the camels and keeping watch.[28] The caravan reached Fachi after a march of about six days. The Tuareg rested and traded at Fachi for two days, then set out on the four-day march to Bilma.

After the arrival in Bilma, the representative of the *amenokal* met with a representative of the Kanuri people of the oasis to discuss the exchange rates for the various commodities − principally millet traded for salt and millet traded for dates. The exchange rate which prevailed at the end of the previous year's trade usually became the official rate for the next year, but unusual circumstances could cause wider fluctuations. For example, a deficit millet harvest shifted the exchange rate in favour of this commodity, whereas a freak rain squall in the oasis which interfered with salt production had the opposite effect. Buyers and sellers usually followed the officially determined exchange rate, which after all was a reflection of the conditions and supply and demand which applied to the barter. Tuareg salt traders did business with the same Kanuri families from year to year, respecting ties which may have extended back several generations.[29]

The volume of this pre-colonial salt trade is uncertain. In 1870 Nachtigal reported that 70,000 camel loads of salt left the oases.[30] At 95 kg per load of salt, a figure agreed upon in early French sources, this would have amounted to 6,650 metric tons. Nachtigal's estimates of the size of the two main caravans are in accordance with later figures, but he suggests that numerous small caravans accounted for perhaps another 50,000 loads. This is most probably an overestimate, perhaps by a factor of as much as 10, because the desert was dangerous for small caravans, and because the autumn and spring were the best times of the year to travel. French estimates of the annual level of exports just before their arrival range from 10,000 to 25,000 camel loads, but the upper bound seems preferable in light of the first exact figures, which derive from the early customs post at Djadjidouna. In the fiscal year 1903/4 it was reported that 17,930 loads of salt and 184 of dates paid duties, and because of the ease with which caravan movements could be detected in Damergu, it is reasonable to assume that most traffic passing this way was counted.[31] The main branch of the salt route passed through Damergu, with a lesser one going to Kel Gress country in the west. Therefore the Djadjidouna figures represent something like 75 per cent of the yearly total.

After 1908 accurate figures on the autumn caravan are available from Bilma, where loaded camels paid a transit tax. The volume appears not to have changed much, except for a lull in 1906–8 because of increased trouble from raiders. The French began to provide an armed escort in 1907, and the volume responded after 1908. Salt trade peaked in 1913, when tax collectors recorded a total of 26,017 camels returning from the oases, a figure which translates into about 2,470 metric tons of salt and dates. The drought of

1911–14, which was felt most acutely in the growing season of 1913, had a delayed effect on salt trade because millet taken to Bilma in the autumn of 1913 was actually from the 1912 crop. This resulted from the pattern of Tuareg transhumance, since nomads left the fertile savannah in May or June, long before the harvest. The volume of trade declined in 1914 and especially in 1915, when it fell to nearly half the volume of 1913. (See Table 5.) The causes for the decline are threefold: (1) drought and requisitions had reduced the size of the camel herds and cut into Tuareg transport capacity; (2) Tuareg were unwilling to risk the camels they had, given the pattern of requisitions from the salt caravan in 1913 and 1914; (3) and they had difficulty obtaining millet in 1913 and 1914 for use in the caravans of 1914 and 1915.[32] From the point of view of the Tuareg, the decline in the salt trade was serious indeed, especially because French policies and the end of the trans-Saharan trade threatened nearly every other aspect of their economic life. The precipitous decline in 1914 and 1915 was an index of the magnitude of the crisis confronting the pastoral economy.

The revolt completely disrupted the Bilma salt trade. The French were unable to provide escorts for salt caravans until 1919, and in the meantime the desert was so unsafe as to make trade impossible. During the interruption of trade from Bilma, salt from other sources took up the slack. Imports of European salt apparently climbed, although the evidence for this is fragmentary.[33] (See Table 6.) Ahaggar Tuareg, who sided with the French, extended their commitment to salt trade, and brought Amadror salt as far as Kano.[34] The supply of salt from a variety of other sources, ranging from Mangari, Muniyo, the Chad shores, Dallol Fogha, and sites in the Benue basin, must have risen as well, but no detail on volume is available.

However, evidence on trade in Damagaram indicates that increased activity in potash trade probably helped to fill the gap. Many traders who had previously taken potash south towards Nupe shifted to other forms of commerce, especially the cattle trade. But at the same time the crisis in the desert economy brought a vast wave of settlement from the north. The desert was temporarily unable to support its population, and as a result low-status Tuareg who had previously been nomads began to arrive in large numbers and settle to take up farming. Buzu, as the immigrants were called in Hausa, adopted Hausa speech, but they preserved their own customs and brought with them a distinctive form of land use whereby they moved households, animal pens, and cultivated fields along a strip of land each year. Buzu were already well-acquainted with long-distance trade, since many had gone to Bilma with their masters. Lacking camels, Buzu immigrants had to use donkeys. They took millet east to Muniyo and Mangari and returned with potash to sell in Damagaram, Tessaoua, Gobir, or points slightly farther south.[35] Thus during the interruption of the Bilma trade, potash trade had increased and shifted from a primarily north–south orientation to an east–west direction.

In 1918 the volume of the Bilma salt trade began a slow climb back toward the high level recorded for 1913. (See Table 5.) Périé, the author of the most comprehensive of several unpublished monographs on Bilma written by colonial administrators, stated that the principal constraint on the recovery of the salt trade was the size of Tuareg camel herds, and that the volume of salt trade was proportional to the size of the camel population.[36] In the early 1920s herds were only a fraction of their former size, but the population of Aïr began to return in 1922, and herds grew steadily from a low base. Although no data on growth rates in the Nigérien steppe and desert are available, Dahl and Hjort, who have assembled what little information on camel herds in Africa is available, found that reported fertility and mortality rates and age structures imply slow rates of growth, much slower than for cattle.[37] In addition, camels cannot be loaded until they are at least five years of age, and so the breeding of a working population took time.

According to Périé another constraint on salt trade was the threat of camel requisitions. The policy reversal of 1922 encouraged the recovery of trade and remained in effect until 1939, when wartime conditions forced the French to return to their former practice of taking what they could not pay for. Périé noted that the resumption of requisitions had an immediate negative effect on Tuareg participation in salt trade, and the volume dropped. The high level of 1913 was not equalled until unusually large salt caravans were reported in the early 1950s.

The recovery of the desert salt trade took place despite increased competition from overseas imports. The volume of overseas salt imports in the 1920s and 1930s was higher than it had been before the First World War, but the volume of salt from desert sources averaged about twice the level of the overseas imports and increased steadily. (See Table 6.) The series in Tables 5 and 6 are not directly comparable because Table 5 includes dates brought from Fachi and Bilma. Dates and salt from Bilma are lumped together in the official figures, which were given in camel loads. The proportion of dates in the total increased in the long run, but the volume of date exports in the 1930s was typically a quarter or a fifth of the total.

It is important to realize that European imports accounted for only a small proportion of the total salt requirements of the region. Paul Lovejoy has estimated that the pre-colonial Central Sudan produced as much as 10,000 or 16,000 metric tons of salt and potash.[38] Table 6 gives imports into Niger alone, a region much smaller and less populous than the Central Sudan as a whole; nevertheless, imports in the 1920s and 1930s fail even to approach the level of magnitude of Lovejoy's estimates of local production. An economic survey published in 1961 estimated that desert salt still supplied one-third of Niger's total needs, that other local sources accounted for another sixth, and that European salt together with imports from Sine-Saloum in Senegal supplied about half the total.[39] And these estimates for a later period probably understate the volume of local potash production.

Another important reason why European imports failed to undermine desert salt imports is that salt had a variety of uses, and almost pure sodium chloride was used mainly for cooking and seasoning food. Other salts served a variety of medicinal and industrial purposes and were fed to animals.[40] Since animals consumed a large proportion of locally produced salts of all kinds, the growth of herds during the colonial period increased the size of this market substantially. Livestock receive much of their salt requirements through grazing, but cattle sometimes need as much as 20 kg per year. By 1960 the cattle population in Niger had passed 4,000,000, implying an annual consumption of 80,000 tons per year, although actual consumption levels were probably much lower.[41]

RELATIVE PRICES

Data on the volume of the salt trade serve as an index of the seriousness of the damage done by a combination of drought, colonial policy, and warfare. They also show that the period of recovery was drawn out over two or three decades. Further evidence on the magnitude of the crisis and insight into the mechanism of recovery comes from an analysis of shifts in the structure of prices before and after the drought and revolt. Price data, though of necessity inexact, are nevertheless important because quantitative information on the volume of trade in most products or shifts in production is extremely difficult to obtain. Except for figures on the salt trade, no other reliable quantitative data on the desert-edge economy have come to light. Nor is the area to the south better covered with reliable information, despite the fact that it received more attention from the colonial administration.

The absence of data on flows of goods and animals across the Niger–Nigeria border illustrates this problem. Although a customs frontier was in place on the Niger side between 1914 and 1918 and again after 1939, smuggling was so widespread as to render statistics useless. Even in the 1950s and 1960s planners could only guess at the volume of trade crossing the border, and figures from the Nigerian side, derived from veterinary control posts set up after 1934, are equally imprecise.[42]

But if handled carefully price data can serve a useful purpose. Colonial administrators kept a close watch on the prices of exports, and consequently reports of cattle and hides prices are relatively plentiful. But these prices in themselves have little meaning unless compared with the prices of other commodities important in the local economy. The price of millet, a commodity consumed by nearly everyone whether farmer or herder, is reported infrequently. To compound the problem, the price of cloth, another important item in local budgets, is almost never given.[43] Reports of wage rates are also uncommon; nor is it possible to impute returns to labour implicit in the prices of outputs such as grain, animals, or export crops. Hence it is not possible to deal with either the effects of price shifts on patterns of consumption or the impact of changes in real wage rates on choices among various activities. But with an abundance of price data on animals, and some indication of other prices, it is possible to speculate about the effect of changes in prices of outputs on decisions to produce.

Of particular interest here is a dramatic shift in the ratio of pastoral products and millet in favour of pastoral producers after the revolt. (See Table 7.) The prices of salt, dates, slaughter animals, and beasts of burden reached a peak in 1920 or before. Our concern is with relative prices only, so that money prices have been used only to calculate the rate of exchange of pastoral products for millet. The reason for using millet as a common denominator is obvious – all pastoral people in the Central Sudan used and traded for millet, and the exchange rate of products they produced and sold for millet is therefore a relevant one. Simply stated, the jump in the index of export cattle and camels between 1909 and 1920 indicates that cattle traded for ten times more millet in 1920 than in 1909; camels, which were extremely scarce and expensive, bought fifteen times as much millet; and in 1920 salt was worth five times as much as in 1903 when traded for millet.

The only possible explanation for this drastic shift in the terms of trade in favour of pastoral products was that millet production bounced back to or near its long-term average several years after the famine years of 1913 and 1914, but that herd losses caused more lasting damage and were the root causes of scarcities of camels and cattle, and a contributory cause of shortages of salt. While the observed shift in the terms of trade serves as an indicator of trouble in the pastoral sector, it also provides an important insight into a mechanism of recovery. A favourable rate of exchange between pastoral products and millet allowed herders to return to the desert with smaller herds than would have been necessary otherwise, and therefore it encouraged the slow but steady recovery. Few Tuareg had camels to sell, but they were in an advantageous position when they sold cattle, and probably sheep, goats, or donkeys as well. Those who had camels made good profits on salt trade, and hired camel transport brought a good return in Nigeria, where the government paid for these services and traders eagerly sought out Tuareg transporters, especially for the evacuation of the groundnut crop during the dry season. Tuareg had incorporated this kind of dry season work into their transhumance cycle in the nineteenth century and earlier, and they continued to find a ready market for camel transport until lorries became common in Nigeria about 1930.

Scarcities engendered by the revolt in Aïr, the interruption of salt trade, the exile of the Tuareg, and the drought explain high prices of salt and camels, but the causes of high cattle prices relative to millet lie elsewhere. On the supply side, the interruption of trade from Aïr was a minor factor, but more important was the problem of cattle disease. The great rinderpest epizootic of 1887−91 destroyed many animals in what was to become northern Nigeria, but presumably the effect to the north in the Sahel was less pronounced. The bovine population of the Central Sudan was in the process of recovering from this disaster when the drought of 1911−14 struck, and after the drought epizootics of rinderpest and bovine pleuro-pneumonia swept across West Africa with increasing frequency.[44] Disease remained a serious check on the size of the herds until the 1920s and 1930s, when the newly-created veterinary services began to make headway against animal diseases. Important factors on the demand side were rising export earnings in both the forest and savannah in Nigeria, and a ready market for cattle at the port of Lagos during the First World War.[45]

The figures in Table 7 provide some information about long-term change in the economy of the desert edge, especially when they are interpreted in light of other data from colonial archives. For example relative prices of cattle reveal something about change in the cattle industry, a form of production which provided the Sahel with a substantial proportion of its southern exports. From 1920 to 1940 cattle prices fluctuated within wide margins. After peaking in 1920, prices collapsed with the trade recession in 1921.[46] Meat was a highly income-elastic commodity in Africa as elsewhere, and falling real incomes pulled down cattle prices faster than the prices of other agricultural commodities or overseas exports. Cattle prices recovered from their low level with the continuing devaluation of the franc against the pound, since cattle from Niger were being sold in Nigeria. By 1926, when the franc reached its lowest point, cattle prices in Niger had risen fourfold or fivefold from the low level of 1921 and 1922, but they were still below the peak level of 1920.[47] Cattle prices fell again in the early 1930s as a result of the slump in producer incomes with the depression. Cattle prices had fallen to a third or a quarter of their former level in a few short years, according to reports by colonial officials. Administrators also noted that cattle herders, who were being taxed at rates set during more prosperous times, when cattle brought a better price on the market, suffered considerable hardship. In 1934 the French finally adjusted the cattle tax downward to bring it into line with market conditions. Good export earnings and the devaluation of the franc in 1936 brought cattle prices up again in 1936.[48] The French officials who reported these price movements usually felt that cattle prices were changing more rapidly than other prices, though they were unable to assemble the data necessary to confirm their impressions. The relative price movements shown in Table 7, however, do lend support to their observations, especially in the case of the high relative price of cattle in 1926 and 1936 compared to the intervening period.

Because of poor data few definite conclusions about long-term changes in the price structure are warranted. But within the animal series it is clear that camel prices declined against those of slaughter animals.[49] The explanation for this lies either in the declining demand for camels as motor transport became more widespread, or in the rising levels of demand for slaughter animals, or both. Another conclusion, more tentative than the first, is that cattle prices appear to have been rising against those of grain since independence. One study predicted an enormous deficit in the supply of meat available to Nigeria by 1985, a prediction made almost entirely by evaluating the very rapid economic growth of Nigeria and the effect this growth can be expected to have on the levels of demand for beef.[50] This conclusion was reached before the recent drought, which became severe during the growing season of 1972. One of the effects of the drought has been a drastic reduction in the supply of cattle which can only compound the problem and drive the prices of cattle up further.

Another result of long-term change in the price structure along the desert edge was that donkeys became the load-bearing animal most often used, replacing the pack oxen which were so common at the turn of the century.[51] Apparently the very high prices for cattle about 1920 were decisive, since the opportunity cost of taking a steer away from a slaughter herd to be trained as a beast of burden became great enough to be prohibitive. When the market price of slaughter animals reached a certain level, it no longer paid to use animals for transport as long as they brought a good return in herds destined for slaughter or breeding. Instead, it was better to look elsewhere for beasts of burden, and donkeys came into widespread use. If the data in Table 7 are an accurate representation of the actual price trends, it remains a mystery why oxen did not come back into use during the periods of the lowest cattle prices, namely the early 1920s and the 1930s. Perhaps this happened and it escaped notice, or possibly the periods of low prices were too short to have brought back the old way of doing things.

Although the position of cattle nomads appears to have been improving near the end of the colonial period, the situation of the Tuareg, to the extent that they continued to be primarily camel herders, was deteriorating. The declining price of camels against that of other animals reflected the decreasing usefulness of these animals, and the price of Bilma salt began to slump in comparison to other goods in the 1920s and 1930s, just as the volume of trade approached its former peak level. By the late 1930s the ratio of salt to millet prices was well below that of 1900, although it rose again during the war when salt imports from overseas decreased. The terms of trade turned against the Tuareg again in the 1950s, once the volume approached and surpassed the record level of 1913.[52]

Migration in the pastoral sector, though they did not match the size and variety of population movements among sedentary farmers, nevertheless have a historical importance because they indicate shifts in the structure of the economy. One demographic change in the Nigérien desert and steppe after the turn of the century was the arrival of the Fulfulde-speaking cattle nomads. Small groups of Ful'be ventured into southern Damagaram, Maradi, and Adar in pre-colonial times, especially after the rainy season, when it was to their advantage to take cattle far away from cultivated fields to avoid the possibility that cattle might damage standing crops and thereby cause conflicts with farmers. But few went north into the territory occupied by Tuareg. Vast areas of rainy season pasture in the Sahel and southern desert were equally suited to use by cattle nomads or by people who also kept camels, but Tuareg jealously kept this land and its water resources to themselves. After the arrival of the French, however, Tuareg could no longer raid with impunity, and they were therefore powerless to protect the ecological niche which had formerly been theirs alone. Soon after the turn of the century Ful'be began to arrive from Sokoto, Katsina, Gumel, Daura, and Borno, though the largest current was from Sokoto. The principal axis of migration was from south-west to north-east because herdsmen followed the Maradi, Kaba, and Tarka valleys and their tributaries.[53] Once the migration was under way it received additional encouragement in the form of low cattle taxes in the Agadez *cercle,* where the vanguard arrived at its north-easternmost limit in the 1930s. French administrators reported that Ful'be newcomers either paid Tuareg for rights to use wells on an annual basis, bought wells outright, or constructed their own. One Tuareg section leader, who had jurisdiction in conflicts between Ful'be and Tuareg over water and pasture rights, was reported to have been favourably inclined toward Ful'be.[54] The first large capacity wells were dug in the late 1930s, and after the war this programme grew in scope with funds from FERDES — a system of grants and loans from the metropole to aid economic development in the colonies. In the early years of the operation of these large wells, Ful'be used them disproportionately.[55] Ful'be migration to the north has continued in recent times, so that in the thirty years after 1940 the northern limit of transhumance of some Ful'be groups has shifted from 15° latitude to 18° latitude, a distance of over 300 km.[56]

The migration was a gradual process and often represented a shift from semi-sedentary to an almost exclusively nomadic way of life.[57] Among the first arrivals in the north were young herders tending cattle belonging to elders who remained behind in Nigeria to farm. Although many Ful'be divided the labour of their families in this way, they seem to have preferred nomadism when their herds were large enough to support them.

Reversion to nomadism may have been part of a natural cycle, since the Ful'be economy was apparently in the process of recovering from the disastrous effects of the rinderpest epizootic of the early 1890s. The impact of this disease in Damagaram and Damergu is not known; but at the time few Ful'be were to be found anywhere north of the Caliphate, and Tuareg kept fewer cattle than in more recent times. The isolation of Sahelian cattle herds from each other would have helped check the spread of the disease. In parts of the Caliphate and Borno the majority of the bovine population died from rinderpest; the concentration of Ful'be in defensive frontier settlements made their cattle more vulnerable to this highly contagious disease than if they had been more widely dispersed. In Gwandu most pastoral Ful'be lost all their animals or all but one or two and as a result had to take up farming. Apparently the size of Ful'be herds began to recover in the early twentieth century so as to allow an increasing number of Ful'be to take up an exclusively nomadic life. The persistence of outbreaks of rinderpest in the early twentieth century, especially after the drought of 1911–14, probably encouraged migration into the less crowded and therefore less hazardous disease environment of the north. Migration was also encouraged by the availability of pasture in the north at a time when land was becoming increasingly scarce.[58] It also represented a response to a new, egalitarian pattern in the society of the nomads. With the freeing of slaves who farmed and herded, cattle-owners were forced to rely more heavily on their herds, if they lost agricultural labour, and to use the labour of their own families to a greater extent for tending herds.

While the causes of the migration were complex, it must be remembered that favourable price ratios probably played a role. Without doubt Ful'be would have responded to peace, the availability of resources in the desert, and pressure on land in the savannah in any case, but improvement in the ratio of cattle and grain prices aided and speeded the process. Purchases of millet accounted for a large share of the budgets of nomadic Ful'be. Consequently when millet became cheap in terms of animals and animal products, Ful'be were able to buy the millet they needed with a smaller outlay. And hence the shift meant that a given number of people could live by trading from a smaller herd than would otherwise be the case, and so the transition from semi-sedentary to nomadic life could take place sooner.

A favourable shift in terms of trade of animals and animal products for millet indicates a probable improvement in the returns of pastoral production as compared to farming, but unfortunately much less can be said about the costs of production in the two sectors. Since labour constitutes the principal variable cost of production in each of the regimes, opportunity costs associated with using labour should be considered. But so little is known about returns to labour in farming and pastoral production, or in alternative activities such as commerce or craft industries, that this is not possible.

Both the arrival of Ful'be in the desert and Sahel between 1900 and 1960 and the long-term increase in cattle prices relative to camel prices reflected the rise of the cattle industry, a fundamental shift in the desert-edge economy. The commercialization of the Sahelian animal industry will be treated in detail in the following chapter, but for the present purposes it is important to note that the proportion of cattle in Sahelian herds increased over time. Not only were Tuareg joined in their own land by competitors with an almost total specialization in the breeding and raising of cattle; but the Tuareg themselves also began to keep more cattle than they once did, in response to commercial opportunities. Pastures which had been much less intensively grazed came under increasing pressure from cattle, with serious consequences for resources provided by wild rice and other seeds. These plants had formerly provided a sizeable proportion of the diet of pastoralists, but with the increased pressure of cattle on herbaceous plants, they are often destroyed by cattle before they can be gathered for human consumption.[59]

The crisis of 1911−18 did not seriously affect Ful'be migration, except to cause a minor interruption. But the crisis was a key factor in the other major population movement in the desert sector, the migration of Tuareg of low status toward the savannah. Tuareg

resistance to the original occupation of the desert produced minor
waves of immigrants, but the first great exodus occurred during the
crisis of 1911–18 and represented a demographic adjustment to a
reduced scale of economic opportunity. As such this reaction fitted
into a long-term pattern of migration across ecological and ethnic
boundaries in response to changing conditions in the desert. But
another process was also at work, a process whereby Tuareg of low
social status left former relations of social dependence. Several
causes for this second process can be isolated, all confined to the
twentieth century. The first concerns the military power of the
imajeren (nobles), which permitted them to dominate other
segments of society. With the eventual triumph of the French,
imajeren were unable to continue using force to enslave people or as
an implicit threat to keep them in a state of subordination. More-
over, the French had an active interest in levelling Tuareg society.
After 1916 the French policy was to free sedentary Tuareg as
punishment for revolt; and after 1946 the freeing of servile Tuareg
attached to nobles as domestic servants accelerated.[60] And a second
factor was the rise of new economic opportunities for people of
lower status. Recently an observer noted that former *irewelen* and
imrad have used the economic benefits of owning both cattle and
camels to enhance their social status.[61]

While some Tuareg who left former relations of dependence
retained a full or partial commitment to pastoralism, most migrated
to the savannah to take up farming. Those who arrived in the
savannah found rapidly changing conditions. It is beyond the scope
of this study to trace in detail the development of the export
economy of northern Nigeria,[62] but it is none the less important to
consider its main structural features and their impact on the
northern sub-region. The completion of the railway to Kano in 1911
laid the cornerstone for the new colonial economy. This techno-
logically modern commercial infrastructure connected northern
Nigeria to the world economy far more closely than trans-Saharan
caravans once had. The railway permitted large-scale exports of
agricultural products for the first time, and so it determined the
nature of contact between the local agricultural economy and the
industrialized centre in Europe.

This new large-scale import–export trade had an important
impact on the region as a whole. The locational effects of the shift
from desert trade to exports from the Kano railhead have already
been mentioned; peripheral commercial centres such as Djadji-

douna and even Zinder were no longer able to complete with Kano and lost their former positions. Furthermore, the decline of Sahel products in export totals and the growth of agricultural exports from the savannah, groundnuts for the most part, reinforced the effects of this reorientation of trade and had other effects as well. The new export industries used different natural resources than old export activities, and they used labour in a different way. Trans-Saharan trade required transport services in the desert, whereas the new commerce relied upon transportation to and from the railhead.[63] Exports of ostrich feathers once employed villagers in the Sahel, but groundnut exports required land and labour in the savannah. As the research of Jan Hogendorn has demonstrated, the area of land sown in groundnuts near Kano increased immediately after the completion of the railway, as traders and farmers reacted to new opportunities to produce for the market.[64] The land requirements of this commercial agriculture, which spread northward toward and across the Niger border as motor transport developed, combined with population growth in agricultural areas to exert pressure on the supply of available land.[65] In addition opportunities to produce for the export market attracted migrants toward the area served by the Kano railhead, and as the motor transport industry developed, the radius of commercial agriculture spread ouward from Kano. By the early 1930s it was profitable for farmers in southern central Niger to produce groundnuts for export on a large scale. This area also attracted immigrants.[66] Thus migration in response to market forces accentuated movement away from the desert edge because of drought, economic decline, and harsh French rule.

These changes in northern Nigeria and in the border regions to the north produced a new relation between desert and savannah. The desert increasingly took on the role of supplying inputs – principally labour, millet, and animals – for the area of the savannah tied more directly to the world market. The desert assumed the role of the peripheral area, more specialized and more isolated than it had been before these twentieth-century changes. Nevertheless it was linked, though at one remove, to the world economy, since it supplied salt, dates, animals, animal products such as hides and skins, and labour to the area to the south. And these links determined the nature of the impact in the desert and Sahel of closer ties between Europe and northern Nigeria.

It therefore should come as no surprise that the Tuareg network in the savannah – a network based upon a relatively equal and

complementary relation between the two sub-regions in pre-
colonial times – gradually diminished in importance. In the minds
of colonial administrators, economic considerations were not
always in the forefront. Nomads were difficult and troublesome to
administer, and so the French and British had an active interest
in undermining desert–savannah contacts in order to isolate the
nomads and lessen their power. The first development was that the
grain-producing estates of the fertile regions gradually slipped from
Tuareg control. Little detail is available on this process in Nigeria,
but events near Zinder are probably representative. Here the
arrival of a large wave of immigrants from the north between 1911
and 1918, many of whom had severed ties with their former masters,
necessitated an administrative solution to the problem of where
they should fit in the political and fiscal hierarchy. French
authorities systematically transferred the right to tax the inhabitants
of former estates and the new arrivals either to sedentary political
authorities as represented by *chefs de canton,* or to sedentary
Tuareg appointed by the French.[67] By the 1920s most nomadic
Tuareg retained only nominal ties with people who had once been
under their control. Nomads occasionally visited farming villages
but rarely stayed overnight, no longer received grain as tribute, and
were unable to stay for extended periods in case of drought. As time
passed these nominal ties grew weaker still.

   The immediate effect of the dissolution of the Tuareg network
was the loss of revenues from savannah agriculture, but long-term
impact on the land tenure system was without doubt more serious.[68]
As long as nomads had strong ties to settled dependents, the
presence of these servile Tuareg reminded neighbouring farmers,
their local rulers, and the colonial administration of the rights of
nomads to use pasture during the dry season and during drought.
But once these ties were gone the rights of nomads to use savannah
land were unprotected, and colonial administrators and their local
allies could conveniently allow farmers to prevent pastoralists from
using land, thereby giving way to the pressure of population and the
growing need for land for foodstuffs and for commercial agriculture.[69] What was true in Niger was doubly so in Nigeria where the
government felt no responsibility toward inhabitants of another
colony who appeared to have little need of savannah resources.

   Nomads did of course need savannah pasture during drought.
Pastoral nomadism in the pre-colonial Central Sudan should be
understood as a functional adaptation to the marginal and changing

climate. As late as 1911–18, when drought and political disturbances pushed many nomads from the desert, the network in the
savannah was able to absorb many people.[70] The fact that a
southern refuge still existed at this time is certainly an important
factor in explaining why the impact of the drought of 1911–14 on
the Tuareg economy was much less severe than the drought of
1969–73. Desert nomads relied upon region-wide mobility to
spread the risks of their environment over a wider area and over a
number of activities. But the developments of the twentieth century
left intact only a truncated, northern section of the former regional
network.

CONCLUSION

The material in this and the preceding chapter permits an overview
of the process of cyclical economic change in the twentieth century
and the impact of colonial rule on more enduring features of the
Sahelian environment. The great twentieth-century cycle began
with climatic change; after nearly a century of relatively good
climate, dry years became more frequent in the period 1890–1910
and culminated in a general drought in 1911–14. As grave as it was,
this drought in itself was not enough to produce serious social and
economic dislocation. But it coincided with the end of trans-
Saharan trade and with a process of decline in the desert and growth
in the savannah. The effect of French colonial rule, which relied on
arbitrary taxation in kind, direct taxation, various labour services,
and military recruitment during the 1914–18 war, was further to
accentuate differences between desert and savannah and give
added impetus to decline in the desert sector. The magnitude of the
early twentieth-century economic crisis was indicated by the large-
scale migration of herders and farmers to Nigeria, the sedentari-
zation of low-status Tuareg, and the slow rate of recovery as
reflected by the gradual growth of the salt trade. Migration to the
south was an age-old reaction to climatic downturn, but for the first
time an overlay of new economic and political relations weakened
the economy of the desert and provided additional force to the
operation of the north–south gradient.

   The revolt of the Aïr Tuareg fitted into what Ross Dunn has
termed 'a fragmented, contradictory process of attack, compromise, and evasion' in his account of resistance in the pre-
Saharan fringe of Morocco.[71] Dunn's framework of analysis draws

attention to the uncertain environment of the desert, to the shifting and ephemeral nature of alliances in segmentary societies, and to the extreme unpredictability of the French invasion and occupation. As shown by the experience of the Aïr Tuareg, the French army could destroy livestock and other resources and undermine the basis of production. Elsewhere they might establish conditions for permanent peace and expanded trade, but in central Niger the colonial occupation produced economic decline which was further accentuated by the hardships of drought. As in Morocco the arrival of the French created a whole new dimension of uncertainty in what was already a demanding environment:

In short, their coming added to the extreme caprices of nature a whole new set of economic uncertainties. Consequently every tribe and *qsar*, indeed every group, large or small, with shared interests and resources, was obliged to weigh its response to the French army against the effects, for better or worse, on its economic well-being. The crisis produced not an adjournment, but an intensification of the struggle to outwit the environment . . .[72]

Although this conclusion is intended for the Dawi Mani, it might just as well apply to the situation of the Aïr Tuareg throughout the first two decades of the twentieth century.

Perhaps the most striking long-term change in the economy of the desert was a tendency toward specialization. Viewed in time perspective, the crisis of the early colonial period may have been nothing more than the first stage in a series of adaptations to new limits. Drought, the loss of trans-Saharan revenues, and the curtailment of Tuareg political and economic freedom called for adjustment on an unprecedented scale. But as formidable as these pressures were, they constituted only part of a larger pattern in which the economy of the desert became a peripheral adjunct to an expanding, export-oriented economy centring on Kano. By 1950 the half-century cycle of decline and recovery was complete, but the cycle had moved the economy of the Sahel to a far different position. The trend in the desert sector was toward extreme specialization in animal husbandry for markets in Nigeria and toward participation in the growth of the larger region in a limited and peripheral way.

More research needs to be done before comparative conclusions can be certain, but apparently the amplitude of the twentieth-century cycle was greater in the Central Sudan than elsewhere in the West African Sahel. Many local factors were not present elsewhere.

The Central Sudan had a relatively large and dynamic desert sector because of the strong ties within the region, as described in the first chapter, and links to North Africa; because a growing savannah economy made animal husbandry, trade, and transport worth while; and because the products of mining, craft industries, and agriculture reached markets over a wide area. Thus an exceptionally well-developed sector suffered greatly during the first fifteen years of colonial rule, and the revolt in Aïr greatly worsened a pre-existing crisis. Repressive colonial rule produced an especially strong current of emigration because of the presence of an export-oriented economy in northern Nigeria which could absorb labour and other inputs from the Sahel. In short, where the pre-colonial economy was strongest, reorientation to the colonial economy produced the greatest shock.

CHAPTER VII

Livestock Trade

THE preceding chapters show that the period 1900–20 was a time of economic decline both in the desert and in the area of the Sahel and savannah under French rule. But even during this downturn the economy retained a strong involvement in regional trade in the staples of West African markets. In fact, internal trade in salt, livestock, kola, cloth, raw cotton, and local manufactures has always represented a far greater share of local production than had external trade, except for a brief period in the late nineteenth century; and even then the value of trans-Saharan exports and transit trade probably failed to surpass the value of trade in local commodities.[1] Fortunately for the merchants, farmers, herdsmen, and artisans of Damagaram, rapid growth in internal trade partially offset the local economic crisis. Many merchants, especially the North Africans, found it difficult to enter trade networks in which they had no previous experience. But rurally-based *fatake*, who traded on a seasonal basis, and some of their full-time counterparts in Zinder, found new opportunities for profitable trade in livestock, grain, kola, cloth, and potash.

This chapter will focus on livestock trade because this form of commerce became increasingly important in the economy of the desert edge as time passed and because more information is available on it than on other forms of trade. The relative abundance of information on the cattle trade can be misleading; it should be remembered 'that these statistics must be treated with extreme caution. Throughout the period of French rule in Niger administrators realized that export data bore little relation to reality, but they nevertheless felt obliged to report on cattle trade because they considered cattle to be Niger's single most important export. Problems associated with other export series have already been discussed, but it should be remembered that actual cattle exports exceeded officially recorded exports by an unknown margin, perhaps by a factor of three or four. Most other time series on cattle and other livestock are no more reliable. The cattle census, for example, depended on information from tax collectors, and as a result it too was highly suspect. Growth in local slaughter reflected shifts to large markets and improvements in the collection of data as much as increased local consumption. One accurate series is the record of hides and skins exports from southern Nigerian ports, which bears some relation to the production and slaughter of cattle, though it too is subject to fluctuations in a number of extraneous variables. For example, the volume of hides and skins exports rose from a low base by a factor of about 1000 in the period 1900–20; but this increase resulted in part from improved transport and the diversion of former trans-Saharan exports; and these factors over-shadowed change traceable to growth in the size of animal herds or changes in patterns of commercialization. Hides and skins exports rose by a factor of ten between 1920 and the late 1930s, but once again a portion of this increase doubtlessly represents the diversion of hides from local uses rather than rising commercialization.[2] But despite all these difficulties, published and archival material on livestock trade is relatively abundant and provides a point of departure, especially when combined with oral data.

This chapter will discuss livestock trade in networks connecting markets in southwestern Nigeria with areas of savannah and Sahel in the north. These networks incorporated much of northern Nigeria as well as adjacent areas of Niger and Chad and drew from as far north as Mali. In the west they shade off into supply systems channelling cattle toward Accra and Abidjan, and in the east they merge with networks leading towards Igbo country.

COMMERCIALIZATION OF LIVESTOCK

A myth about African pastoralists which has endured outside anthropological circles states that they make decisions about the management of their herds according to a value system calling for large herds for reasons of prestige and social status. According to this myth these conservative social values stand as a formidable barrier to the introduction of modern methods of stock-breeding. As long as keeping large herds has a value in itself, pastoralists seem incapable of taking advantage of opportunities to sell cattle even when it would be in their own interests to do so. As a consequence their herds are larger and contain more adult animals than would be the case if they operated rationally. Pastoralists are therefore seen as peripheral to the exchange economy, unlikely to change on their own, and in need of conversion to habits of calculating profit and loss.[3]

It is unlikely that any human activity can be explained satisfactorily within the framework of economic analysis alone, and without doubt social values influence the behaviour of pastoralists. Nevertheless the economic aspects of herding must also be considered, as anthropologists have long realized. An understanding of pastoral strategies should be framed in the context of the productive goals of herders — to supply themselves with milk and meat and to sell these products and surplus animals to outsiders. In a seminal work on the economic and demographic characteristics of herds, Dahl and Hjort point out that it could be argued that pastoral value systems reflect the economic and ecological conditions in which they earn their livelihood:

> . . . unreliable rainfall leads to great fluctuations in the availability of water and grazing, both seasonally and over longer periods. For a pastoral household it is necessary to keep a margin against the risk of having part of the herds killed from a drought or an epidemic. The number of animals needed to maintain a longtime continuous production is also much larger than the number of animals immediately utilized at a certain period.

> The keeping of large herds is closely linked to the need to protect the household against the effects of drought or epidemics as well as to food requirements during a particular dry period. A sufficient number of animals must survive a disaster in order that the household can exist while the herd is being rebuilt.[4]

Given the risk inherent in a semi-arid, fluctuating environment, it would be foolish to sell too many animals when keeping them represents the only practical way of storing food and of insuring a supply of milk for the pastoral group in the future.

Nevertheless every herd contains animals which can be more readily sold than others. It would be unwise to sell certain animals in the age and sex structure of the herd — milk cows necessary for the food supply of the pastoral group, fertile females critical for the growth potential of the herd, or the few males necessary to breed them. But others, such as mature males and over-age females, can be sold or slaughtered without changing the rate of growth.

It is impossible to over-emphasize the importance of the demographic characteristics of herds, which permit an understanding of many aspects of pastoral strategies, including decisions to keep or sell animals, which type or types of stock to breed, and how to divide the labour of the pastoral family. Dahl and Hjort have assembled and analysed an array of information on demographic variables reported from the field, from East Africa for the most part. They show that small variations in fertility and mortality rates can completely change projected patterns of growth.[5] Fragmentary evidence on herd composition is also available from Niger. A major irony of the history of uninformed discussion about the economic behaviour of pastoralists is that these arguments ignore important empirical evidence from veterinarians, who are especially well placed to know about pastoral strategies. Over the years veterinarians and others have sampled the composition of Sahelian herds by age and sex, and these surveys tend to confirm the notion that herders keep cattle − especially certain categories within the age and sex structure − as a form of capital to ensure the future growth of the herd. The first such report comes from Doutressoule in 1924, who noted that the number of males in Nigérien herds was low and declining over time. In 1928 the *Service de l'Élevage* reported that 60 per cent of the total of Nigérien herds consisted of fertile females and the rest were under-age animals of both sexes, adult males, and a small percentage of over-age and sterile females. In 1939 males which had been weaned constituted only 18 per cent of the total in herds surveyed. In 1945 the ratio of adult males to adult females was reported to have fallen to one to forty on the average. A number of recent surveys have found males of all ages account for as high as 20 or 25 per cent of the total, but among adult animals the percentages are typically between about 3.5 per cent and 8.5 per cent of the herd.[6]

These figures on sex ratios of herds are extremely significant because they indicate that animal husbandry in Niger always had a commercial dimension and that its importance increased considerably over the last fifty years. To be sure the figures represent unscientific sampling and mask variation by region, ethnic group of the herd owner, and other categories; but they are given here to show that male animals were not kept in herds in large numbers and that continual culling of males from herds provided a steady supply of animals for the market. This evidence, especially when juxtaposed with other data on growth of cattle trade over time, shows that it is best to conceive of Sahelian cattle herding as a commercial activity, though of course certain reservations are necessary.

One frequent reaction of agricultural economists who examine data on current patterns of marketing in Niger is the suspicion that herdsmen sell animals too soon, not that they keep them too long. Observers frequently report that most animals reaching the market are males between the ages of two and three and a half years. Ordinarily marketable males should be kept longer, until they are fully grown, which in the conditions of the Sahel would be at least four years from birth. But the practice of selling early can be readily explained by the local disease environment. Where contagious animal disease is common, herders run a risk if they choose to bring an animal to maturity before marketing it.[7] Herders must therefore weigh the risk of losing the animal entirely against the possibility of receiving slightly more money for the animal should it be kept and sold after it has attained its maximum weight.

Another factor which must be considered is the importance of selling cattle in the household budgets of Nigérien herdsmen. In a comprehensive survey of the nomadic population carried out in 1962−4, investigators found that on the average Ful'be households sold two or three head of cattle per year and in some cases additional sheep and goats. The sale of milk, butter, and skins was primarily the concern of women. About one-third of the total income was spent on food, millet for the most part; monetary transaction and barter accounted for about half the estimated expenditure, the rest consisting of subsistence production. Among Tuareg the sale of cattle also represented the main source of monetary income and was used to cover large expenditures − clothing, taxes, and purchases of food, again mainly millet.[8]

The existence of a pool of readily marketable males and the importance of selling animals shows that Sahelian animal husbandry has an important commercial dimension at the level of individual enterprises, and that charges of economically irrational behaviour must take account of local conditions and the basic principles of stock-breeding. The commercial aspect of West African stock-breeding is also obvious at the aggregate level. In a recent study, for example, Polly Hill examined Ghanaian veterinary data to gauge the volume, commercial organization, and seasonal and regional variation in livestock trade to the cattle market at Kumasi, which received a supply of nearly 70,000 head of cattle each year in the period 1962−4. On the basis of evidence from sex ratios, she concluded that the livestock industry of north-western Ghana, where bulls and bullocks averaged only 11 per cent of the number of females, was more highly commercialized than stock-breeding in north-eastern veterinary districts, where the male−female ratio was 54 per cent over-all and cattle herds were smaller than the national average. This regional difference was correlated with a high degree of seasonality of exports to Kumasi from the north-west and a marked regional difference in the scale of operations of cattle traders, with large-scale traders over-represented in the group working between Kumasi and the highly commercialized north-west districts.[9] Ferguson, working with Nigerian livestock data, estimated the take-off ratio of the entire Niger−Nigeria−Chad region to be between 7 to 10 per cent per year.[10] While this seems low in comparison to European or American conditions, where take-off from cattle herds ranges between 20 and 28 per cent per year, it may represent the limit of productivity in West Africa, where mortality from disease is high and seasonal aridity constrains both the rate at which calves are born and the rate of growth and maturation.

NIGER−NIGERIA NETWORKS

Without doubt trade in cattle took place in West Africa for many centuries before the colonial occupation. Animal trade at the desert edge was as old as contact between nomads and their sedentary neighbours, and the scale of the animal trade undoubtedly grew with the gradual arrival of a larger Tamashek-speaking pastoral population in the Sahel and southern desert beginning a thousand years ago. By the end of the nineteenth century the population of the arid lands north of Damagaram including the Aïr had reached perhaps 40,000 or 50,000 souls, and most of these lived almost exclusively from animal husbandry.[11]

The Tuareg of Aïr preferred to eat grain even though they could survive on milk from camels, goats, and cows for extended periods. Milk was extremely scarce during the hot months of March to May, and so most Aïr Tuareg had to trade for grain or obtain it as tribute to last through this period.[12] Farther south, the Tuareg of Damergu, as well as the Tuareg whose transhumance cycle brought them into the savannah each year, obtained some of the grain they needed from their sedentary subjects, and they traded for the rest.

The volume of the cattle trade at the edge of the desert is diffi-cult to determine, but rough estimates are possible. The main item of foreign exchange from the arid regions was of course the desert salt which the Tuareg brought with them on their seasonal

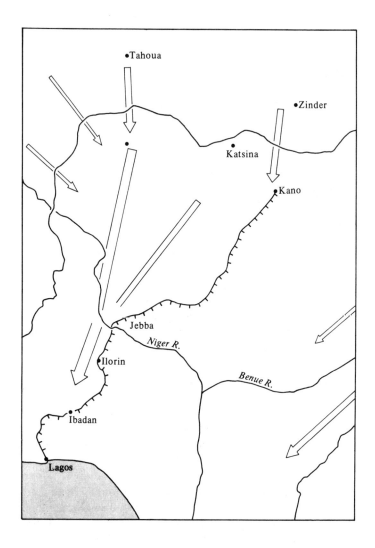

migration to the south. But a subsidiary current of animal trade ran parallel to the salt trade and was almost exclusively an exchange of millet for animals. This trade was carried on by the sedentary Hausa and Dagera of Damergu. In the dry season, they loaded millet from their own fields on pack oxen and took it to Agadez, where they exchanged it for cattle, as well as some sheep, donkeys, and camels. The volume of this trade was probably not much lower than 1,000 metric tons of millet per year, and certainly not over 1,500. At the prices prevailing at the turn of the century, this quantity of millet would have bought between 1,000 and 1,500 head of cattle of average weight.[12] Livestock taken south included sheep, camels, and donkeys, so the estimate of cattle exports has to be lowered to 700 or 1,000 head each year. This figure does not include cattle brought south by Tuareg salt traders, but this was probably not as large as the cattle trade of the Hausa and Dagera. Livestock trade elsewhere in the Nigérien Sahel may have been of the same order of magnitude as trade in the Aïr–Damagaram corridor. The first economic reports filed by the administrators of the western regions of the *Troisième Territoire Militaire* were in agreement that cattle represented the most important item of southbound commerce, but none of the authors were able to give any indication of the volume of trade, or even to hazard a guess.[14]

To the south the volume of trade between savannah and forest is also unknown, but without doubt this segment of the cattle trading network has a long history as well. Trade in forest–savannah networks may have been as great as the movement of livestock south from the desert, since the animal population of the savannah was much larger than in the desert. With the arrival of the Ful'be in Hausaland in the fifteenth century or earlier, the possibility of a marketable surplus in cattle was greatly expanded. Nomadic Ful'be lived primarily on milk from their herds and on grain they obtained in exchange for animals and animal products. As in the case of the Tuareg, the sale of cattle was linked to seasonal transhumance. In recent times sales among northern groups of nomadic Ful'be peaked just before nomads left for rainy season pasture, when they returned, and when they had to pay cattle taxes. Among southern groups of nomads sales were greatest during the rainy season, when cattle traders sought out herdsmen and bought from them to make up for a hiatus in the northern supply.[15] In the savannah sedentary farmers also kept cattle; although per capita ownership of cattle was much lower among sedentary people than among nomads, farmers nevertheless owned a sizeable proportion of the total. In the Adar in the 1960s the sedentary population owned 40 per cent of the total; in northern Nigeria at the same time 20 to 25 per cent belonged to settled farmers, 30 to 35 per cent to semi-sedentary Ful'be, and 40 to 45 per cent to nomads.[16]

Though precise figures cannot be obtained, there is no doubt that pre-colonial cattle trade extended far into the forest. In 1826

Clapperton commented that cattle were sometimes driven across the Niger near Bussa.[17] In 1858, when Samuel Crowther visited Rabba, he reported that Hausa caravans of about 3,000 people and over 1,000 head of cattle were being taken across the river in large craft used for ferries. He also stated that these cattle and other merchandise were headed for the market at Ilorin. At the same time return caravans crossed in the other direction with their beasts of burden — donkeys, pack oxen, and horses. Crowther estimated that on the order of 7,000 animals crossed at Rabba each year during the trade season, and he noted that equal or greater traffic crossed at four other points. Crowther failed to specify what percentage of this total represented animals being taken south for sale as opposed to pack animals to be used for return merchandise. But elsewhere he mentioned that the main items carried by southbound caravans were slaves, silk, natron, and cattle, as well as small numbers of sheep and goats.[18]

Whatever the volume of trade at the turn of the century, it is clear that it grew rapidly between 1900 and 1930. For what they are worth, official statistics on exports from Niger show an increase from 4,779 head of cattle in 1914 to an average of over 40,000 per year in the early 1930s.[19] It is of course not clear whether actual exports increased in proportion to these figures or if better reporting accounted for most of this growth. Apparently something on the order of two-thirds of the cattle being taken from Niger to Nigeria crossed the border without being recorded.[20] In 1934 Nigerian veterinary officials established veterinary control posts along the border to check the spread of contagious disease in trade cattle, and statistics from these control posts show that over 100,000 head of cattle entered Nigeria from Niger and Chad; and of course these figures also understate the actual totals by an unknown margin.[21]

Fortunately the impression of growth in the cattle trade which these imprecise statistics convey can be corroborated by information from other sources. Although the supporting evidence is indirect, it comes from a wide enough variety of sources to be conclusive. First, at the far southern end of the network, demand for slaughter animals increased in the first two decades of the twentieth century as overseas demand for agricultural products from southern Nigeria rose steeply. Exports of cocoa increased rapidly from a low base, and exports of palm products increased sevenfold to a total of over £10,000,000. Export revenue also expanded rapidly in northern Nigeria with the growth of exports of cotton and groundnuts. The growth of real income, especially in the case of cocoa farmers and the gatherers of palm products, probably stimulated demand for beef and the meat of sheep and goats, although no detail on this is available.[22] The growth of towns in Nigeria, especially Lagos and Ibadan, had a similar effect. In general it is clear that cattle-producing areas to the north came to be increasingly closely linked with cities and areas of export production farther south, and that this case fit into the wider pattern in West Africa whereby areas on the periphery supplied inputs of various kinds for export production.

Trade in livestock to Nigerian towns became especially obvious when an unusually large quantity of meat was transported to Lagos during the First World War. This was in part the result of heavy maritime traffic, with some ships putting in at the port just to buy supplies of meat. Nigerian officials estimated that 4,000 head of cattle reached Lagos on the hoof in 1912, before cattle traders began to use the railway. By 1918 the number of cattle transported by rail to Lagos had reached 12,760 head, and cattle exported on the hoof toward the coast probably exceeded this number, if the pattern of later years can be taken as representative of the situation in 1918.[23]

Another indirect indication of the rising volume of the cattle trade was the growth of trade in kola, one of the principal return goods from the south. One variety, *cola accumulata,* was available locally in Yorubaland, but consumers generally preferred *cola nitida,* which had to be imported to Lagos by sea. Imports of *cola nitida* from Sierra Leone began as early as the 1850s, but by 1870 the source of supply had shifted to the east. After the British defeated Asante in 1874, Hausa kola traders began to operate from Accra. With the kola-producing areas of Asante open to the coastal trade, a large volume of commerce became possible, and imports rose sharply to an annual average of over 600 long tons in the late 1890s. At Lagos the Yoruba Saro, or liberated slaves from Sierra Leone, and other traders trans-shipped kola on vessels which steamed up the Niger River to Lokoja, Jebba, and Rabba. Here kola entered the overland caravan trade to the north, and traders from Damagaran were among the buyers in Nupe. The Royal Niger Company excluded the Lagos-based traders from the river in the 1880s, so kola began to follow overland routes north of Lagos, which were generally safe after 1891. Agiri's informants reported seeing Hausa traders on these routes driving donkeys laden with potash and returning from Lagos with loads of kola.[24] Potash remained the principal item of exchange for kola until potash was replaced by cattle after the turn of the century.

The northbound trade in kola was a natural complement to the southbound trade in cattle, except for the transport problem. Cattle are mobile, but kola has to be carried on beasts of burden. No donkeys were available in the forest; traders had to drive donkeys south whether or not they were loaded in order to have transport capacity for the northbound journey. Presumably the demand for potash declined with increased use of imported salt in cooking and to feed to animals, but traders continued to bring potash with them even if they were driving cattle, since transportation of potash was almost without additional cost. Excess southbound transport capacity also helps to explain the growth in the trade of locally-made clothing from Kano to Lagos, a trend noticed by colonial authorities in 1910.[25]

The completion of the railway to Kano in 1911 offered one solution to the different transport requirements of the cattle and kola traders. Cattle and kola could both be carried on the railway as long as traffic moved without excessive delays, and the British colonial authorities set the rates low enough to encourage the rail shipment of both of these commodities. Traders, responding to the high level of demand for cattle in southern Nigeria, and to ready markets for kola in the north, were quick to react, and rail shipment became common.[26]

Another solution to the problem of finding return transport for kola was the use of the river. The wartime demand for cattle in Lagos, and the sustained high level of demand for West African foodstuffs during the post-war commodity boom, drew animals from as far away as the area east and north of the Niger Bend. Cattle export routes from this area followed the Niger River or valleys which fed into it such as the Dallol Bosso and the Dallol Mauri. Traders took cattle south along the river, so that in 1919 in the peak season Niamey control stations recorded an average of 100 head of cattle a day, as well as 150 sheep, from Dori and Hombari in what is now Upper Volta and from the Gao area in Mali.[27] Occasionally traders even took cattle downstream by boat, although apparently this was more common south of Niamey. Having reached their destination, traders sold cattle and bought kola and arranged for a combination of rail and river transport for kola on the return trip. Most river trade took place during the season when the river current

was weakest, when travellers reported seeing many vessels loaded
with merchandise and livestock. Merchants and canoemen camped
on sandbars alongside migratory fishermen at night, so that a string
of camp-fires lit up the entire length of the river in the peak commercial and fishing season.[28] By 1907 river trade in kola, hides and
skins, and potash was flourishing; several years earlier the Niger
Company and Lugard's government river transport service had
begun to compete with each other for traffic, and both carried local
traders and their merchandise, although private companies
apparently did this less frequently than did the government
services.[29] But these transport services probably carried a small
proportion of kola being taken upstream.

The pioneers in the cattle trade from the stretch of the river north
of Say were the *Agalawa* (sing. *Ba'agali*), a Hausa-speaking
professional sub-group of Tuareg origin who practised endogamous
marriage and retained a separate identity.[30] The *Agalawa* specialized in trade, and they had played a key role in the development of
the overland kola trade between Hausaland and the Volta basin in
the nineteenth century. By the end of the century the overland
route was in decline, a casualty of the new and growing trade along
the coast between Accra and Lagos. The *Agalawa* and others
associated with the overland kola trading network had to find new
activities to replace their old commerce; some chose the exchange
of cattle for kola at Lagos, a natural outgrowth of their experience
in the kola trade, while others entered the groundnut buying network centred on Kano.[31]

One of the first merchants to enter the river trade from the area
near Niamey was Alhaji Yahu Isa, a *Ba'agali* whose father and
grandfather had traded potash and kola between Kano and Salaga.[32]
Yahu took up the cattle trade to Lagos at his father's urging some
time before 1910. He bought herds of sheep and cattle and drove
them south-east, parallel to the river, only rarely transporting them
by boat. He sold the animals at Lagos and boarded a ship headed
to Accra with the proceeds of the sale. At Accra he purchased kola
and brought it back to Lagos where he paid import duties and took a
train to Jebba, the rail crossing of the Niger river. Once in Jebba he
found boatmen to take him and his kola up the river toward Say
where he sold the kola and bought cattle to begin the trade cycle
once again.

The overland kola trade survived until about 1930, but in its final
years it was far different from its nineteenth-century form. The

experiences of two twentieth-century kola traders illustrate just how much the old kola trade had changed. One, a *Ba'agali*, traded between Kumasi and the area north of Maradi known as Gobir Tudu; at Kumasi he exchanged animals from the north for kola.[33] The second was Alhaji 'dan Ladi Ahmadu, the son of a kola trader who belonged to one of the Hausa professional groups which had been involved in the kola trade before the advent of the *Agalawa*. 'Dan Ladi and his father joined expeditions of traders travelling between Kano and Asante. They took Kano specialities like sandals and locally-woven cloth to Sokoto, where they sold all of their merchandise for sheep and cattle. They they went south to Kumasi, sold the animals, and bought kola. Some of the members of the expeditions sold kola at Jega, others at Sokoto, and relatively few took kola all the way back home to Kano. The old kola trading network had partially broken up into segments; livestock had assumed a new importance; and potash was no longer the principal return commodity from Kano. Alhaji 'dan Ladi gradually moved away from this trade circuit to the exchange of cattle and sheep from Dori for kola from Kumasi, abandoning all but the far western segment of the old network. Since the locus of his trade had shifted, he moved his home base from Kano to Niamey.[34]

The completion of the railway to Kano changed the geographical pattern of the overland cattle trade, but the shift was delayed until the trade recession of the early 1920s. Judging from the following report by a colonial administrator in Nupe, competition from the railway had little initial effect on the volume of the caravan trade:

From the crowded appearance of the passing trains is deducted the fact that trade must be increasing in leaps and bounds. But with all this the caravan routes at this time of year appear to be crowded as ever with all sorts and conditions of people from the regular Hausa trader to the Asbenawa [Tuareg] and Mangawa [Kanuri-speakers] and people of Damagaram. The articles of export are salt, potash, cattle, sheep, goats and horses transported southward to be exchanged for salt, piece goods and kola nuts.[35]

The slump in the prices of exports of 1921 and 1922 had an adverse effect on all trade, and when conditions returned to normal, the droving routes leading toward the cities of southern Nigeria had shifted to the west, to the area between the railway and the river. Competition from the railway had displaced the overland route westward, and the reason for this is best understood by referring to the strategy of traders taking cattle south on the hoof. They had to be able to sell off animals which became diseased as they passed through tsetse fly country. Near the railway they found relatively few opportunities to sell cattle at a profit because droving routes converged toward the railway from Chad and north-east Nigeria and this ready supply drove down profits. But to the west the over-land route continued to coexist with rail transport farther east because traders used overland and rail shipment for different purposes. Trekking cattle toward the coast required less capital than rail shipment and it also gave traders a chance to take advantage of favourable conditions in local markets along the route. But differing use of transport also depended greatly on geo-graphical factors alone; large-scale traders from Kano relied heavily on the railway, whereas traders from central and eastern Niger and the Sokoto region preferred droving.[36]

Overland cattle routes leading to markets in south-western Nigeria converged on the rail bridge at Jebba because traders could walk cattle across the bridge free of charge, and thereby save the cost of ferrying them from one side of the river to the other.[37] Beginning in the late 1920s, officials recorded the number of animals taken across the bridge. These figures probably greatly understate the actual total volume of cattle trade toward south-western Nigeria, since many cattle must have crossed the river else-where.[38] But they give some indication of volume. The annual average for the 1930s was a little over 89,000 cattle and over 104,000 sheep and goats. (See Table 8.) The number of cattle shipped south on the railway averaged a little less than half of this for the period. Despite incomplete and faulty figures, it seems apparent that the number of trade cattle headed for markets near the coast had increased by a factor of at least four between 1918 and the late 1930s.

Support for the view that cattle trade grew rapidly to the 1930s comes from Ford's work on historical patterns in the occurrence of trypanosomaises in Nigeria.[39] Ford observed a sharp increase in the incidence of sleeping sickness in humans in the 1930s, and sought to explain this rise by referring to disease vectors in the cattle population. He reasoned that rapid growth of the cattle population because of the inauguration of preventive veterinary medicine in Nigeria contributed to the epidemic of sleeping sickness because cattle provided a reservoir for the proliferation of trypanosomiases infections.[40] Both human and animal sleeping sickness increased in the 1930s because growth in human and cattle populations placed both hosts in increasingly close contact along wide fronts with wild-life carriers of the tsetse *glossina mortisans*. The result was epidemic conditions among people and epizootic outbreaks among cattle, neither of which was brought under control until relatively recently with the use of insecticides. But the important point here is that the growth of the cattle population, as indicated by trouble in an eco-system which included humans, cattle, wildlife, and *glossina mortisans*, provided a larger reservoir of animals to be culled from herds, and hence a larger volume of trade than heretofore.

TRADE FROM THE DESERT EDGE

Growth in demand for slaughter animals in the south had reper-cussions after the turn of the century as far away as the desert edge. A case in point is a shift in production and trade in Damergu just before the turn of the century and in the following two decades. The impetus for change may have come from shifts in the costs and returns of pastoral production as compared to farming, but price changes or returns to labour in this early period cannot be docu-mented. However, the increased volume of cattle trade from the Sahel can be traced, and it indicates the remarkable extent to which the market for agricultural staples was integrated over a wide area. And of course the pull of distant markets reached farther in the case of mobile produce such as livestock than in the case of grain, for which transport costs were higher.

Trade in grain and animals played an important role in the economy of pre-colonial Damergu. Sedentary farmers — both Hausa and Dagera – organized trading expeditions to Agadez during the dry season, taking millet north to exchange for cattle, sheep, donkeys, and camels. Returning to Damergu, they sold most of the animals to traders from the south — from Katsina, Tessaoua, Damagaram, and Kano – who took the animals with them when they returned home.[41] The farmers of Damergu kept a small proportion of the animals they obtained through trade in order to provide for the eventuality of crop failure. Rainfall was unreliable at the edge of the desert, and some farmers had poor harvests even in years when the harvests were generally good. Villagers kept their animals in one herd which the young people looked after as it pastured on uncultivated land near the village.

Traders from Damergu rarely went on trading expeditions south of their homeland in pre-colonial times, but the changing conditions of the cattle trade drew them into a network which was new to them. The transition came into two stages, the first beginning in 1896 with the sudden arrival in Damergu of vassal (Kel Ulli) sections of the Tuareg of Ahaggar. Reacting to pressure from the French penetration of the central Sahara from the north, Ahaggar Tuareg initiated trade contacts with the south. They brought high quality salt from the plains of Amadror in the area which is now southern Algeria, along with small amounts of European-made cotton piece goods.[42] They traded for millet, and they also used salt to buy articles manufactured in the Sudan − sandals, swords, mortars for millet, and Kano cloth, to name only a few. The Ahaggar Tuareg had little previous contact with the people of the Sudan, and they lacked a distribution system for salt of the type used by Kel Gress sections in Katsina or the Kel Ewey in Zinder and Kano. The market for Ahaggar salt in Damergu itself was limited. Since it was more suitable than Bilma salt for human consumption, the best markets were in the urban centres of the Sokoto Caliphate. This presented traders in Damergu with an opportunity to become intermediaries in the salt trade. They loaded Ahaggar salt on their pack oxen and headed south for Kano, where they bought locally-made cloth and kola in exchange.[43] The Ahaggar themselves began to come farther into the Sudan after the turn of the century; by the 1920s they came as far as Zinder and possibly even to Kano. The golden age for the Ahaggar salt trade was after the uprising in the Aïr, when the Bilma salt trade was at a standstill.[44]

The second stage of the transition occurred after Hausa and Dagera traders learned of market conditions in Kano. Having taken salt to trade, they soon discovered that they could make better profits on livestock. Just after the turn of the century most of the traders of Damergu had shifted to the cattle trade, leaving the salt trade to the Ahaggar Tuareg.

The new southern trade was especially important for the people of the village of Malam Tilum, the site of one of the most important periodic markets of pre-colonial Damergu. Most of the Ahaggar salt entering the Sudan had passed through this market, and consequently traders from Malam Tilum were the first to take advantage of the new opportunity for trade to the south. By about 1910 villagers had shifted to the cattle trade, and the village counted nearly a dozen successful merchants.[45] Villagers still farmed during the rainy season, but trade gradually replaced farming as the principal activity. Some even traded during the rainy season, and many others traded for a portion of their own grain requirements as they placed less and less emphasis on farming.

Traders from other Damergu villages reacted to the same kinds of opportunities, although they were not as specialized as the people of Malam Tilum. First the relay of Ahaggar salt, then livestock, attracted long-distance traders to segments of the trade network south of their homes. A factor of growing importance after the turn of the century was demand for millet in northern Nigeria, the result of a boom in the export of groundnuts, which competed with millet for land and labour. As early as 1908 the price of millet was high enough to attract supplies from Damagaram and Damergu.[46] Several years later, after a dramatic expansion of the area sown in groundnuts, a French colonial administrator complained that the people of Damergu no longer provided Agadez with an adequate supply of grain, but took millet instead to Kano.[47]

The caravan trade to Agadez, already threatened by new currents of trade south of Damergu, came to a standstill during the revolt of 1916. Just after the rebels attacked the French garrison at Agadez, they surprised two parties of Hausa and Dagera traders at the Aballama well not far to the south, killing a number of traders and taking all animals belonging to the two expeditions.[48]

Normal trade was out of the question until the French put down the last of the resistance in 1918. Nevertheless trade did not resume for at least five years after the end of hostilities, since combatants had filled in the wells along the caravan routes. The journey north from Damergu was still extremely difficult in 1922 on account of the lack of watering-places.[49] Conditions improved after the Tuareg began to return from their exile in Nigeria, but the volume of the trade never regained its former level. The Tuareg themselves traded for most of the grain they consumed; their increased self-reliance in this respect was in part a result of contacts they made in the savannah during the exile of 1916–22.

The animal trade from Damergu was able to continue even after the link from Agadez had been broken because of the arrival of a new group of people in Damergu, the pastoral Ful'be. By 1916 nomadic Ful'be were present in sufficiently large numbers to permit stock-breeding on a much larger scale than before.[50] They came from the south and south-west in a gradual migration of the type which is characteristic of nomads extending the amplitude of their transhumance cycle little by little each year. Nomadic Wo'daa'be groups and Farfaru Ful'be as well, concentrated in Damergu, which became a crossroads for transhumance routes extending north and north-east, and east along the Tarka valley.

The cattle traders of Damergu exchanged cloth, kola, iron tools, and other items for cattle from the nomadic Ful'be. They established long-standing relations with their Ful'be trading partners, and mutual trust was an important element in these relations. Sometimes they advanced goods to the Ful'be in return for a promise of payment in cattle in the future, but credit went both ways. The Ful'be often advanced cattle to traders who promised to bring them cloth when they returned from Kano. Trade sometimes took place in periodic markets, but just as often traders visited Ful'be encampments, where they dealt directly with their trading partners instead of through the brokers who mediated transactions in the market place.[51]

Trade at the edge of the desert followed a seasonal pattern corresponding to the transhumance cycle of the nomadic Ful'be. Most of the trade took place during the dry season, after the Ful'be had returned from the steppe toward the settled area of Damergu. But a small volume of trade also took place during the rainy season, since a few Ful'be groups came up from the south to pasture their cattle on uncultivated land in Damergu. Traders were eager to mount expeditions to Kano during the rainy season, provided they could find cattle for sale and take time off from their farming. Prices were slightly higher in Kano during the rainy season, reflecting the relative scarcity of trade cattle in this season.[52] Apparently a greater proportion of the trade cattle came from the savannah during the rainy season than during the dry season. In northern Nigeria, traders went out from Kano to buy cattle at the encampments of the Ful'be who remained nearby.[53]

CATTLE TRADE IN DAMAGARAM

After 1900 growing southern demand for slaughter animals helped bring about a pronounced shift in patterns of trade in Damergu, as southern markets reached farther north into the desert fringe. The reaction to the south in Damagaram was similar but less dramatic. In Damergu traders formed a new network reaching south toward Kano, but in Damagaram a southern trading network already existed, and so it merely had to be transformed to meet the conditions of the new demand. As in Damergu, full-scale livestock trade from Damagaram came into existence in association with salt trading networks. Traders who joined caravans in the era of Madugu Isa and his companions dealt primarily in potash, but some took livestock south as a secondary commodity. Gradually livestock increased in importance at the expense of potash, and some traders specialized in cattle trade. Informants remember instances of traders dealing exclusively in livestock as early as the 1880s, and specialization became more common as time passed. Many traders from Damagaram took cattle to the large animal market at Ilorin before the turn of the century, and a few even went as far as Lagos.[54] For example, Baba Lushe, then a client of an assimilated North African living in a village south-west of Zinder, went to Lagos three times before the turn of the century. Another trader, probably more representative of average merchants, went to Ilorin several times before 1910, and travelled as far as Lagos shortly afterward.[55] Marion Johnson, writing of the cloth trade in Nupe, notes in passing that Hausa-Nupe trade was in decline in 1890, but that transit trade between Hausaland and Ilorin, which crossed the river at Rabba, was flourishing.[56] Traders from Damagaram may have brought back small quantities of the speciality products of the Nupe textile industry, though these are not mentioned by the French or by informants. The principal return commodities were imported Manchester textiles, kola, and European salt.[57]

At the outset livestock trade from Damagaram had a much wider geographical scope than comparable trade from Damergu, though the two networks overlapped between Damagaram and Kano. But as time passed livestock trade from Damagaram came to more nearly resemble networks originating farther north. By 1920 the railway so completely dominated cattle routes from southern central Niger that Kano became a focal point for most trade from the north and north-east. By 1920 few traders from Damagaram went any farther south than Kano.[58] They either bought animals at periodic markets in Damagaram, Damergu, or Koutous, a region east of Damergu – or they bought directly from herdsmen. Relay trade between the first rank of Sahelian markets – those in Damergu, for example, or the markets at Kazoe and Raffa – and the larger, second order markets located just across the Nigerian border – Mai Adua, Babura, or Mai Gateri, for example – was also a frequent pattern.[59]

Two principal determinants of the size of a cattle market were its location and timing in relation to other, nearby cattle markets. Most rural periodic markets handled some animals, but the important markets are those which permitted traders to drive herds south toward the next important market and arrive the day the market met or the day before. The ideal spacing was 30 or 40 km per day of difference in market scheduling, the distance cattle can be driven in one day without excessive weight loss. Thus a market meeting on a Thursday favoured the development of a market meeting on a Friday 30−40 km to the south on the droving route, or one meeting on Saturday 60−80 km away, and so on.

This process of spatial and temporal selection was illustrated by the rise of a market at Kazoe about 110 km east-north-east of Zinder. Very near Kazoe, at Raffa, was an important cattle market. Since Raffa's market met on Thursday, it was out of phase with Zinder's market, which also met on Thursday. The drive normally took only three days, so a trader would have to wait four days if he wanted to see what prices were like at Zinder. The rise of Zinder's cattle market in the 1940s was accompanied by the rise of the market at Kazoe, very near Raffa, but in phase with Zinder since it met on Mondays. Today traders choose one of two circuits for the first segment of cattle trading expeditions: if they start at Kazoe they come to Zinder, but if they begin at Raffa, they go to Myrria, near Zinder but meeting on Sunday, timed just right for the march of about 75 km.[60]

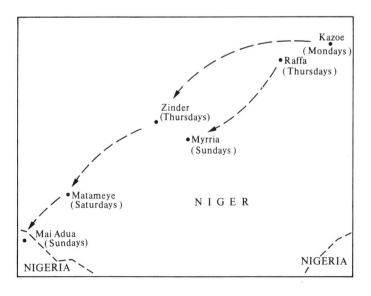

Like their predecessors who traded potash, cattle traders of the early twentieth century operated on a small scale and financed their own activities for the most part. Most lived in small villages, although Zinder people also engaged in small-scale, seasonal trade. When they did, they usually joined forces with people from their village of origin.[61] Traders sometimes worked in partnership with a relative, with full or half siblings for example, but often they traded on their own. They usually had only enough capital to buy a few head of sheep or cattle, but sometimes neighbours gave them an animal to take along in return for a promise to divide the profits from the sale of the animal, with equal shares going to the owner and the trader.[62] Only rarely did traders receive cloth or kola on credit from landlord-brokers living at the southern end of the trade network.[63] This type of credit was much more common after Kano became the southern terminus in the cycles of most traders. In the last few decades of colonial rule, landlord-brokers based in Kano or in market towns like Mai Adua financed a sizeable proportion of the trade from Damagaram, although they probably supplied less than half or a third of the operating capital of each trader they financed, and a smaller fraction of the total trade capacity necessary for livestock imports into Nigeria.

If a trader had a larger herd of trade cattle or more than several donkeys for return goods, he had to employ drovers. These assistants were usually young men from the trader's own village, often relatives, but rarely his own sons. Since young men often looked to their maternal relatives for aid and support, they sometimes became the assistants of their maternal uncles. Several researchers report that elsewhere the employment of a sister's son was the preferred junior–senior relationship for trade, but in Damagaram this kind of arrangement appears to have been only slightly more common than others. Traders sometimes employed the sons of their brothers as clients, but the most common arrangement was simply to employ the son of a friend or distant relative. Another possibility was for an elder brother to take on his younger brother, and this was especially common in the case of full siblings or half brothers who had the same mother.[64] The reluctance of traders to take on their own sons as drovers and apprentices is an extremely important factor in the structure of trading enterprises both in rural Damagaram and in Zinder, and this issue will be treated in detail later.

Cattle traders still travelled in caravans after the turn of the century, but the size of the caravans was smaller than in pre-colonial times. The danger of raiding parties was a thing of the past, but traders still had to guard their merchandise and cattle against thieves and wild animals. Traders travelling alone or in small groups had greater flexibility in the choice of departure times and routes, but they also had to stay awake most of the night standing guard.[65] The members of a caravan took turns keeping watch at night, and travelling in groups had other advantages, such as the company of fellow traders on the long overland marches, and the advice of experienced traders when difficult decisions had to be made.

The institution of *maduganci* also survived, but the role of the caravan leader was far different than in pre-colonial expeditions. One of the principal duties of the *madugu* had been to represent the caravan to the political authorities of the territories through which the caravan passed. The caravan leader collected tolls from each of the traders and presented the transit tax to the local ruler. One of Lugard's first fiscal measures was to take the collection of the caravan tolls away from the Emirs; under the new regime, government agents collected tax from individual traders. In 1914 the British abolished caravan taxes altogether.[66] Occasionally the situation of the caravan did call for leadership, as when the caravan crossed the Niger by ferry. The *madugu* also continued to perform ceremonial duties; in Nupe, for example, the leader of a caravan of cattle traders from Damagaram presented a token gift to the local ruler.[67] But in general *maduganci* were a purely honorary function accorded to a respected elder trader.

Caravan leaders also retained ritual functions, at least in certain special situations. For example, after customs duties were imposed on cattle at the Niger–Nigeria border, traders attempted to smuggle herds across the frontier in order to avoid paying duties. Smuggling was dangerous since traders apprehended by border guards stood to lose all their trading capital. To deal with this risk and uncertainty traders made use of the belief that the *madugu* had the ability to call upon supernatural resources to ensure the safety and success of a trading venture. In the old days traders had followed a particular *madugu* partly because they thought he had *sa'a*, good fortune, or *baraka*, special blessing. During the heyday of pre-colonial caravan trade *madugai* consulted *malamai* to determine the proper time for the caravan to set out in order to avoid misfortune. In the modern form of *maduganci* the caravan leader consulted *malamai* about the proper time to make the risky border crossing. The *madugu* received a fee for these services, part of which was passed along to the *malam*.[68]

After 1940 the cattle trade became less and less the province of the small-scale traders from villages, and professional traders based in Zinder and in towns across the border in Nigeria gained a larger share. Some of the most successful of the rurally-based traders became professionals, and a sub-group of these moved to towns. But those who stayed in the villages with small-scale, seasonal commitments to the cattle trade complained of the disadvantages they suffered in competition with their counterparts who had more capital and more expertise. Villagers resented professional traders most for their ability to make arrangements with the customs officials at the border. Rurally-based traders felt that they had no alternatives other than smuggling or paying export duties, whereas their competitors were able to bribe officials at the border.[69] As the enforcement of the customs frontier became more and more strict in the 1940s and 1950s, the risk associated with smuggling cattle became so great that many rurally-based traders either stopped trading across the border or gave up long-distance trade altogether. Another problem was competition from Nigerian merchants, who occupied a privileged position because their home territory was higher in the collection and distribution hierarchy. By independence Nigerians completely dominated the segment of the cattle routes between Kano and the Niger border, and had made inroads into the segment between Zinder and the border. Many Nigerian traders bought two hundred head of cattle at a time and most transported their herds by lorry. None of the Zinder-based merchants could match this scale of activity or regularly afford to pay for lorry transport.

European merchants tried their hand in the cattle trade from time to time, but they did not offer a serious challenge to the position of the indigenous traders. The case of the Lebanese cattle traders who tried to sell in the Kano market in 1927 is an interesting example of how local merchants might react to competition from outsiders. These Lebanese merchants, who had bought cattle in Zinder, attempted to sell them in Kano but could not find buyers, apparently because everyone in the market had united against them. They were forced to turn back and take losses, selling at the first markets north of Kano where they could find buyers.[70]

Despite this kind of problem, some French merchants operating in Niger entered the cattle trade. Dufour, for example, bought cattle in Zinder, had them slaughtered, and sold the meat to the French in the administration. Occasionally he took cattle to Kano where his African agents sold them for him, but his transactions were never profitable enough to draw him into the cattle trade full time.[71] Bourges, a French merchant who lived in Agadez in the 1920s and 1930s, sometimes bought cattle in Agadez to take to Kano, but he too lost interest after several unprofitable ventures.[72] Bernard Reutsch, a merchant who set up a business in Zinder in 1940 which he still operated in 1972, occasionally bought cattle near Tahoua and sold in Nigerian border markets.[73] Perhaps the best example of the most successful French cattle merchant comes not from Niger but from Mandara country in northern Cameroons, a story told by the merchant himself in a book-length account written under the pseudonym Abu Digu'en (Arabic, the bearded one – the name by which this Frenchman was known locally).[74]

These French merchants knew that they ran the risk of encountering a boycott, or at the very least of not being able to get good prices, if they themselves bought and sold in cattle markets. Accordingly they hired local traders as agents. But this proved to be an unworkable arrangement because it prevented either the French or their agents from making the kind of quick decisions which were necessary in order to make a profit. In other forms of commerce, French merchants worked with African traders who accepted merchandise on account. This arrangement was impossible in the cattle trade because agents had to be able to buy and sell on their own with the financier's money. French merchants were unable to follow the intricate transactions which took place in cattle markets and hence they were unable to tell whether or not subordinates were cheating them.

A major reason why European merchants failed to make inroads in cattle trade was that they were unable to participate as equals in African systems for guaranteeing credit and enforcing contracts. As Abner Cohen has noted, all economic systems which involve credit use various formal and informal mechanisms to organize and maintain credit relations:

These mechanisms are different in form, in the type of pressure they can mobilize on potential defaulters, in the motives they appeal to, and in the interests, sentiments, symbols, myths, norms, values and ideologies which they exploit. There are economic mechanisms, political mechanisms, ritual mechanisms, and moral mechanisms. All these operate in all credit systems. However credit systems vary in the degree to which the different mechanisms are exploited and in the manner in which they are combined.[75]

According to Cohen industrially advanced societies place great emphasis on formal and legal mechanisms to assess solvency of debtors and to uphold contractual agreements. Ritual and primary relations have retained their role in modern western societies despite efforts to reduce all of these mechanisms to contractual relations. But in a pre-industrial society such as colonial Niger or Nigeria, moral and ritual mechanisms had to bear most of the burden for enforcement of contract, assessment of credit worthiness, and control of employees. According to Cohen's analysis, these moral mechanisms expand to fill the gaps in the credit system where economic, political, and legal mechanisms of a formal nature are not effective. To these ends pre-existing primary relations are exploited and new ones are generated.[76]

This was exactly the approach taken by Nigérien cattle traders in cementing relations both within their firms and also in dealings with buyers, sellers, and brokers. Africans had a satisfactory system for controlling clients, which will be examined in the following chapter; but heavy emphasis on the idiom of kinship excluded aliens. Hence Europeans attempting to enter cattle trade in competition with local merchants met a formidable barrier. Relations outside the firm presented similar insurmountable difficulties. European merchants were unable to mobilize primary relations with fellow merchants, brokers, and others to supply themselves with information about the honesty or solvency of potential buyers and sellers.

Thus in the cattle trade Europeans were backward in comparison to Africans. Where so much depended on local, specialized knowledge of markets and upon personal relations between buyers and sellers and within the firm, Europeans lost the competitive advantage which modern business methods and close association with the commercial, colonial economy gave to them in import–export trade. Even if Europeans mastered the techniques necessary for working in African cattle markets, their organizational methods were ill-suited to expanding the cattle trading firm beyond the operations of a single merchant. Furthermore this solitary merchant had to be willing to travel from one market to another or to put complete trust in a subordinate. Even those who enjoyed temporary success, such as the Frenchman who wrote under the pseudonym Abu Digu'en, lacked the patience to continue in a business which required incessant travelling from place to place, especially when greater profits could be made in import–export trade.[77]

The history of the cattle trade provides an example of adaptation in an indigenous distribution system. In early twentieth-century Niger and Nigeria, two contradictory sets of market forces operated: first, demand for livestock increased rapidly in areas of Nigeria where export-led economic growth took place. At the same time the desert–savannah network of the Tuareg, which normally would have transmitted this demand into the pastoral regions of the desert edge, was severely weakened because of conflict with the French. Hence the need for a new commercial system arose, and in response to these early twentieth-century changes, cattle traders from the Sahel and savannah enlarged the geographical scope of a pre-existing long-distance trading system and transformed its organization so that it handled an increased volume of trade. As commercial animal husbandry extended northward into the arid steppe, it drew this area into a progressively closer relation with southern markets for foodstuffs.

CHAPTER VIII

Kinship and the Commercial Enterprise

The preceding chapter provided an over-all view of an African distribution system during a period when an expanded volume of overseas trade from the Central Sudan and from nearer the coast stimulated demand for foodstuffs. This demand, transmitted through pre-existing livestock trading networks, called for adaptation. This chapter and the one following focus on individual firms in a portion of this commercial system as a means of understanding indigenous modes of organization at the level of the enterprise. The main purpose is to explore the capacity for adaptation at the micro-level during a period of rapid economic change. This chapter will survey the organization of commercial firms in Zinder in the late nineteenth and early twentieth century in order to explore the role of kinship in the recruitment and subsequent control of subordinates. The next chapter will set forth the detailed history of a single exceptional enterprise and show how local methods and a propensity for borrowing could combine to permit individual success.

At this point it is necessary to consider the implications for this study of a long-standing debate in the discipline of economic anthropology about the application of liberal economic theory to the study of societies using simple technologies. This debate began with the lines of battle being drawn up between 'substantivists', who argued that Western economic theory was inappropriate in analysis of societies where most people produced most of what they consumed and therefore the market principle could not possibly function to allocate scarce resources; and on the other hand 'formalists', who proclaimed that the scarcity of any resource, even human energy, was enough to make economic theory a useful analytical tool.[1] The opening salvoes produced exaggerated claims on both sides. It is no longer possible to insist, as substantivists once did, that market sectors – that is, areas of economic activity in which supply and demand determine the allocation of resources and the distribution of finished goods – either did not exist or were insignificant throughout pre-colonial Africa. Economic historians have assembled too much data on long-distance trade and production for the market for this claim to be sustained. The pre-colonial Central Sudan is a case in point; among Tuareg pastoralists at least, subsistence production accounted for only roughly half of total output, with the rest being used to purchase items from the south, mainly cloth and millet. And conversely, it is no longer wise to lend too much credence to the inflated claims of the formalists and in doing so deny the importance on one hand of social relations which market transactions sustain and define, and on the other of non-market sources of finished goods and inputs. To take an example once again from the Tuareg economy, nobles demanded payment of tax in millet from sedentary people under their control, and in many cases it would be fruitful to undertake substantivist analysis of redistribution and reciprocity within a larger Tuareg group considered to be an enterprise for the purpose of analysis.

A point of view which seems not to have surfaced in the debate, even among Marxist critics of both camps, is that the two sides are discussing society at different levels.[2] The main problem in assessing the two positions is that empirical studies survey a vast panoply of pre-industrial societies in which either formalist or substantivist analysis, or both, seem appropriate. Firth and others have recognized that substantivists and formalists have sufficiently different interests to observe the same situations, agree on the facts, but still emphasize different aspects of the same phenomena.[3]

But another difference in the two positions, the treatment of activities within firms and households, provides a useful point of departure for clarifying the position taken in this study. Schneider, a self-proclaimed member of the formalist school, sees the main concern of neo-classical micro-economic theory as the interaction of households, defined as consuming units, and firms, or producing units; and within these units decisions about how much to consume or produce or how much land, labour, and capital to use in production.[4] The primary concern of substantivists, on the other hand, appears to be non-market aspects of activity within producing and consuming units. Marxists have also focused attention on households and firms; Terray, for example, argues that an essential characteristic of what he terms the kinship mode of production in pre-capitalist society is that consuming and producing units are homologous — having similar size and organization.[5]

Confusion has arisen because substantivists have failed to recognize that attempts to overrule market forces — to set prices, to limit the circulation of currency or its uses, and to delimit spheres of exchange — can be interpreted as efforts to form very large producing and consuming units. And attempts to form large units within which redistribution and reciprocity govern exchange are not always successful. The king of Dahomey, for example, tried to make the whole kingdom behave as if he were the head of a large household-firm which dealt with outsiders as a block. While Polanyi apparently believed that these efforts were successful, others have expressed scepticism even though they recognize the king's intention.[6]

The approach taken in this study is to espouse elements of the formalist position, but not to accept it in its totality. The main issue is the question of the scale of focus. Thus far the presentation, to be sure, has centred on the market economy. Without doubt an important market sector existed, and it is not necessary to spend time, as Dalton does,[7] arguing about the percentage of aggregate output destined for the market. Whether it was nearer half of total production — as it may have been in the case of some nomads and some slaves — or near a tenth, which seems a more likely global estimate — production for the market is a proper subject of economic history because it represented a force for growth and change, as the case of Damagaram in the nineteenth century shows. But this emphasis on the market sector should not be taken to imply that history may not also be written at a closer focus.

The analysis of patron—client relations within enterprises presented below in the third section owes much to a model worked out by Claude Meillassoux.[8] Reacting against both the substantivist and formalist positions as understood in 1960, Meillassoux developed his model to describe a self-sufficient community entering trade with the outside. This analysis, which I discovered after completing field research, is useful not so much for its treatment of the process of change as for its examination of relations between elder and younger males, flows of resources within productive units, and means by which elder males control younger men by restricting their access to marriage partners. The Meillassoux model permits an understanding of the reason why patron—client relations assumed kinship idioms, and it also focuses attention on important events in the life cycle of commercial firms, or, to use Marxist terminology, in the reproduction of the unit of production.

Informants remember only six traders who operated from Zinder after the turn of the century whose fathers were traders. Three were North Africans: Bedari Zumut's son Abdurahaman; Sharif Bali's son Sharif Dodo; and Muhamad al-Amin's son Mustapha. Another was Malam Yaro, whose career has been described in detail. One was a son of Idi Bagindi, and the last was the son of a Tubu merchant.[9] All but Idi Bagindi's son were directly involved in the trans-Saharan trade or the distribution system connected to it, at least at the beginning of their careers. After the decline of the trans-Saharan trade, very few indeed of the merchants based in Zinder were the sons of traders. Nor were family dynasties any more common in the countryside than in Zinder, for the simple reason that most rural people traded to meet their own consumption needs, and few had any capital to pass on to their sons or to anyone else. Those who did usually moved to the city.[10]

The lack of continuity between fathers and sons is an unexpected finding for a society in which many occupations and trades are inherited, but it is even more extraordinary when compared to the results of research elsewhere in West Africa. Amselle, for example, found that the Kooroko merchants of Mali and northern Ivory Coast recruited their real and classificatory sons and younger brothers into their enterprises. Only when none of these were of the age to trade, or when all had already left, did a trader call on persons outside the family, and then he took maternal relations, affines, or friends into his business. Similarly, Boutillier found that clans consisting of family groups scattered in several trade cities played an important role in the trade systems which he investigated.[11]

Another example of a commercial system in which consanguineal ties were important was the kola trade between Kano and Salaga in the nineteenth century. Sons accompanied their fathers on trading expeditions, learned from them or from other relatives of their fathers' generation, and usually adopted their father's trade specialization. Judging from a recent survey of kola traders based in Kano, this pattern continued to dominate in the twentieth century. In a sample of 150 traders in the local kola market, Lovejoy found that 62 per cent were fourth-generation traders, and that 52 per cent were the descendants of traders who belonged to the commercial reference groups which were prominent in the kola trade during the last century. Descendants of these groups also formed the majority of the richest and most successful traders in the survey. Although the degree of continuity is probably greater in the kola trade than in the merchant community of Kano as a whole, the pioneer kola traders had an important influence on the organization of commerce, and many family firms lasted beyond a single generation.[12]

Historical circumstances offer one explanation for the situation in Zinder. The period of transition during the second decade of the twentieth century was a particularly difficult time for the merchants of Zinder. The end of the trans-Saharan trade, the famine of 1913/14, and the requisitions associated with the Tuareg revolt all took a heavy toll. Many of the merchants of Zinder went bankrupt or stopped trading, and their sons, who might otherwise have been recruited into the profession, had nothing to inherit. Many of the sons also had little inclination to take up commerce, given the difficult conditions of the times.

Another reason for the lack of continuity is the historical importance of the cattle trade, a hazardous form of commerce. Most of the merchants of rural Damagaram participated in the cattle trade at some point in their careers, although it was more important for some than others. In the Zinder cattle market between April and December of 1972, only about 12 per cent of the self-employed traders were the sons of traders, and none were third-generation. Three of the eighty-nine client traders in the sample were the sons of traders, and only one was the grandson of a trader.[13] When asked about the reason for this high rate of turnover from one generation to the next, traders interviewed were unanimous in their opinion that constant exposure to loss over the years was the determining factor.

One major cause of risk in livestock trade was the prevalence of cattle disease, a problem which remained serious until very recently. Epizootics of bovine pleuro-pneumonia, rinderpest, anthrax, and blackwater fever swept through the herds of the Sahel at regular intervals and were especially damaging during the rinderpest epizootic of the 1890s and between 1915 and 1925. Trade cattle often carried these highly contagious diseases from one place to another, and the increasing volume of livestock trade in the early decades of this century seems to have contributed to the severity of outbreaks.[14] At first the quarantine of diseased herds was the only weapon at the disposal of the veterinary services of Niger and Nigeria, which had been created before 1920 to deal with the problem. But veterinarians began to make headway, especially against rinderpest, in the 1930s. Vaccination finally allowed them to gain the upper hand only in the 1960s, when the governments of West Africa, in cooperation with international agencies, organized a massive and coordinated campaign against livestock diseases. By the end of the campaign veterinarians had immunized enough cattle in West Africa to check the spread of disease should it break out. A by-product of this effort was the first estimate of the size of herds which did not depend on data from records of taxation, which consistently underestimate the actual population. Nigérien cattle herds were over 20 per cent larger than anyone had suspected, and Nigerian herds were 50 per cent larger than previously accepted estimates.[15] All along the animal population had included a larger proportion of unvaccinated animals than official figures had indicated, a factor which helps explain why cattle disease had been such a persistent problem.

This high incidence of disease translated into high risk in livestock trade. Merchants could sometimes sell diseased animals along the way, especially when the effects of the disease were gradual, as in the case of trypanosomiasis. But when a contagious disease appeared in a herd of trade cattle, buyers – usually butchers – could not always be found quickly enough for traders to contain losses.[16] Many traders told stories about people in their fathers' or grandfathers' generation who lost all their trade capital when cattle died in the bush before they could be sold.

The creation of the customs frontier between Niger and Nigeria, first in 1914–18 and again in 1937, increased the level of risk and uncertainty. Customs officials confiscated animals belonging to anyone caught trying to smuggle animals across the border. Traders felt that it was impossible to make a profit in the cattle trade if they paid customs duties, since the majority of their competitors failed to pay. They sometimes compromised by paying export duties on some trips but not on others. Naturally only a small fraction of those who smuggled were actually caught, but over the years the number added up.[17] One disaster in the career of a trader was enough to cause bankruptcy, at least until sufficient trade capital could be assembled once again.

Another explanation for the high rate of turnover among merchants was the competitiveness of their undertakings. Since few barriers to entry existed, new entrants continually came into livestock trade, and hence profit margins were narrow. While capital was necessary, lack of familiarity with trade represented a relatively minor problem. Experienced traders tolerated the presence of friends and relatives who went along on expeditions with them and emulated their every move.[18] Landlord-brokers at Kano and other Nigerian markets helped novices sell their cattle and buy return goods, and they even extended credit to those who showed exceptional promise.[19] Since profit margins were close, traders had to rely on their own judgement, and they also needed good fortune. Often a thin line separated success and failure, and here poor communication entered the picture. Often when traders heard rumours of high prices at a distant market they decided to take trade cattle there as quickly as possible. They had no way of knowing whether or not the rumour was true until they arrived, and even if it had been true market conditions might have changed in the meantime. Since traders paid for their own food and that of their drovers, a speculative trip of this kind represented an investment of money as well as time. Should they run out of operating capital they might be force to sell even when prices were unfavourable.[20] A few mistakes caused by bad judgement or unfavourable fluctuations in local markets could be sufficient to put traders out of action.

KINSHIP, INHERITANCE, AND ECONOMIC ACTIVITY

High risk, the absence of barriers to entry, and stiff competition explain the rapid turnover in the cattle trade, but family dynasties were just as rare among local merchants living in Zinder, where the cattle trade was less common than in the countryside. Case histories make it clear that the rarity of second and third-generation traders is not so much the result of historical circumstances or economic factors as an outgrowth of the system of kinship and inheritance within which traders operated. For an explanation of the phenomenon, it is necessary to look beyond the specific context of one branch of commerce to the social structure that determined the form which economic relations could take.

The rules governing the relations among kinfolk in Zinder came from Hausa, Tuareg, and to a lesser extent, Kanuri custom. The people of Zinder belonged to a society which traced descent bilaterally; practised polygynous, virilocal marriage; adhered to a rigid rule of male precedence; and emphasized seniority by birth order. Lineage ties meant little except for those people whose ancestors had held office.[21] The people of Zinder shared these features of their kinship system with the Hausa-speaking people who lived south and west of Damagaram. But they were also strongly influenced by Tuareg custom, with its preference for cousin marriage and tendency to lump all kin of the same generation together. Kanuri kinship was in general compatible with the Hausa system, although its features were not as noticeable in Zinder as those of the Hausa and Tuareg systems, because Kanuri speakers were not as well represented in the population as their northern and western neighbours.[22]

For traders seeking junior partners in their enterprises, an important aspect of the kinship system was the tension characteristic of the father−son relationship. Custom dictated extreme avoidance between a man and his first-born son, and the interaction between the father and his younger sons was only slightly more free. Most young men worked with their fathers in the family farming unit called the *gandu*.[23] They continued to live in their father's compound and to work for him on the family fields even after their marriages, until they had the means to leave and set up a compound of their own. The father redistributed the product of the son's labour as he saw fit, but he was obliged to give his son a share of the land belonging to the *gandu* when the son left to set up his own household. In effect most important goods and resources had already passed to sons before the father's death, so that custom regarding inheritance normally dealt only with personal possessions and trivial amounts of wealth.

But should a person accumulate substantial wealth, inheritance suddenly took on a new meaning in that it had a profound impact on his or her relation with the next generation. Custom and the provisions of Malikite law agreed on the main principles for disposing of estates but they differed in some respects. According to Malikite law, sons were entitled to full shares of the estate, daughters received half shares, and parents and wives of the deceased man received smaller shares. But in Zinder, as in Hausa-land proper, very little wealth actually reached Muslim courts to be divided in this way, since in most cases families saw inheritance as a matter to be worked out among themselves. In addition most local people preferred that daughters receive less than the half shares specified by law. And a final factor was the desire to avoid paying death duties. In the few cases that reached the court for adjudication, some prior division of the estate had usually taken place.[24] These informal arrangements often infringed on the rights of heirs, especially when the sons of the deceased were minors. In one example in Zinder, the nephew of a merchant took most of the estate, promising to keep the wealth in trust for the sons until they came of age; but he squandered the resources of the estate and the sons never received their just shares.[25]

The area of the law in which Maliki jurisprudence and custom converged concerned thé equal division of the estate among male heirs, with preference given to the first descending generation. In local customary law this principle without doubt reflected notions about the balance of work and reward in the *gandu*. Male sons made an important contribution to the support of their father's household, and in return they received money for bridewealth, and eventually land and their freedom. But institutions for a family trading unit similar to the *gandu* did not exist, for reasons which the following case studies will clarify. Trading firms often amassed working capital and wealth for their owners far beyond the trivial sums ordinarily dealt with in customary inheritance. The accumulation of what was often considerable wealth raised the question of whether it properly belonged to the immediate lineage, as did the resources of the *gandu* and personal property as well, according to the rules of customary inheritance and Maliki law; or did it belong to the firm and those who had helped build the firm? The second group was much smaller than the first; and to make matters more complicated, often those with a claim on the resources of the firm did not belong to the immediate lineage of the founder at all.

The first problem was that traders often had to take on employees in order to expand the size of their firms well before their eldest sons were old enough to work. For example traders often married late or needed employees quickly. If they married second and subsequent wives late in life this tended to make for a large average separation in the ages of the father and his sons. The case of Usman 'dan Shaba illustrates this point.[26] Usman was a cattle trader operating from Zinder, active from the 1930s to the 1960s. He began his career as the employee of Muhamman Tsofo, a close friend of his father. Usman accumulated trading capital, partly through gifts from his employer, and partly from dealings of his own on the side. By the time Muhamman Tsofo retired, Usman was trading on his own account. Before he died Muhamman told his own children, who were much younger than his former employee Usman, that he expected them to obey Usman as if he were their own father. Although the children were Muhamman's legal heirs, they actually inherited very little from their father, whereas Usman had received a kind of advance legacy in the form of a start in business and gifts of considerable value. Usman also inherited Muhamman's position in the family and assumed the father's role towards the children, even though he was an outsider. This case demonstrates that a trader had to be able to reward his client, and in order to do so he stepped outside what either custom or Malikite Islamic jurisprudence considered proper. In addition he was probably not able to keep his employee completely honest, and so the employee accumulated wealth regardless of the employer's wishes.

Another example of this kind of role inheritance dates from the turn of the century. 'Dan Maleka, one of the traders from Tessaoua who came to Zinder in response to the trade boom of the 1870s and 1880s, bought a Ful'be war captive named Muhamadu. Muhamadu served faithfully and became a trusted servant. When the French first arrived in Zinder, 'Dan Maleka was away on business. The people of Zinder, expecting the worst from the conquerors, decided to flee, and so Muhamadu had to gather together 'Dan Maleka's family and look after them for the month and a half they spent in exile before deciding to return home. When 'Dan Maleka was reunited with his family, he was so happy with Muhamadu that he decided to free him and arrange a marriage between his former slave and the daughter of his head wife (*uwargida*). 'Dan Maleka's son Muhamman Kane described this practice: 'This is what we do. If you have a slave, and you trust him, and he is a young man, you join him with your daughter and arrange a marriage between them, in order to keep your descendants from leaving your compound. This is what we do, we the people of the west [Tessaoua]. This is what the people of my father's generation did.'[27] Whatever the origin of the custom, the arranged marriage played a very important role in succession and inheritance among Zinder merchants after the turn of the century.

'Dan Maleka also gave Muhamadu authority over his children. 'Dan Maleka's sons, all of whom were younger than Muhamadu, began to behave toward Muhamadu as if he were their elder brother, showing him the respect and deference which both Hausa and Tuareg custom demand from younger brothers (Hausa, *kane*;

Tamashek, *amadrai*) toward their elder male siblings (Hausa, *wa*; Tamashek, *amakar*).[28] It was as if 'Dan Maleka transmitted his role as the head of the family to Muhamadu, the next eldest male member of the family.

Traders' sons had little chance of inheriting enough of their fathers' property to be able to keep the business going even in cases when the father did not designate a successor among his servants or employees. The case of 'Dan Bade, a contemporary of 'Dan Maleka, illustrates this point. 'Dan Bade made his fortune dealing in goat skins specially treated to be used as water bags, and his business continued to do well after the end of the trans-Saharan trade because French military operations in the desert stimulated demand for his product. 'Dan Bade died a few years before 1920 at the age of over 85. His death occasioned a series of bitter disputes within his family over the division of his estate.[29] 'Dan Bade had twenty-four relatives entitled to inherit from him, most of whom were wives and direct descendants. The situation was fraught with difficulties even before 'Dan Bade's death because he was unable to keep a very close account of his wealth. Illiterate and unwilling to trust a scribe, 'Dan Bade kept all of his possessions and money heaped up in a store-room, from which his wives and sons stole large amounts with impunity. When 'Dan Bade died, rivalry among his heirs, who were already very suspicious of each other, prevented them from arriving at an agreement about an equitable division of the estate.

Conflicts between 'Dan Bade and two of his sons further complicated the situation after his death. Sule, the eldest son, had worked for his father and felt that he should have been rewarded more than the younger sons who had nothing to build up their father's estate. Sule also resented the fact that his father had taken a young wife in his old age and spent a good deal of money on her. Relations between 'Dan Bade and the other son, Abdu, were even worse. Abdu got into the habit of drinking millet beer, and this made his father so angry that he tried to banish his son to North Africa. Abdu was in a caravan headed north, in the custody of one of 'Dan Bade's servants, when the *anastafidet* of the Kel Ewey, Jatau, stopped them. In Jatua's opinion, 'Dan Bade had overstepped the rights of a father to discipline his son. Jatau told Abdu to return and gave him a horse, saddle, and clothing. When his son returned. 'Dan Bade confiscated the presents from Jatau, but he dropped the idea of trying to get rid of Abdu. Abdu's first act on hearing of his father's death was to take back the horse, saddle, and clothing – and some other articles as well.

The story of disagreement among heirs and the subsequent division of estates into many small parts was repeated over and over again in Zinder. The courts which enforced Maliki law were not able to win acceptance for the one institution which might have allowed traders to bequeath their businesses intact to their sons, namely the written testament. The people of Zinder considered it possible to draw up a will emunerating persons to whom small articles were to be left, but they considered the will invalid if the division of the estate which it specified was contrary to custom or too far from the dictates of Maliki law.[30] They would therefore not honour a will which gave one son a large share and excluded other heirs. Custom regarding inheritance was much too specific and inflexible for the purposes of the traders, since it dictated that all their possessions should go to the people of their lineage, and none could be reserved for the perpetuation of the business they founded.

Unlike the local people, North Africans relied heavily on the use of written testaments. They commonly made out wills specifying the way they wanted their estates to be divided after their death.[31] Of course if they wanted testaments to be honoured, they had to rely on judges who were sympathetic to their own ideas, and in most cases judges so inclined were North Africans themselves. This is one of the reasons why religious separation in the form of membership in the Sanūsīyya remained so important to a community of strangers who were rapidly assimilating in nearly every other way. Sometimes the North Africans bequeathed most of their property to a son who had been a junior partner in their trading business. This custom, which is related to the willingness of the North Africans to work for their fathers, explains why family firms lasted beyond a single generation much more often among the North Africans and others closely associated with them than among the local people in general.

COMMERCIAL CLIENTAGE

Traders usually recruited their clients, not their sons, into their businesses as junior partners. Clients (Hausa, *barori* or *barwai*, sing. *bara*) were seldom kinfolk of their patrons (*iyayengida*, sing. *ubangida*, literally father of the house).[32] Instead *barori* were often the sons of friends of the *ubangida*, sons of neighbours, people from the same village of origin, or simply young men in search of employment.

Commercial clientage in Zinder had historical roots in patterns of interaction between masters and slaves in the nineteenth century. Like slaves before them, clients in the twentieth century were recruited into the trader's household from outside his immediate kinship group. Like slaves they became quasi-kin whose assimilation into the household of the patron progressed from the moment they entered into a relation with him. As in the case of slaves, the well-being of clients depended more on the status and power of their patron than on their own lowly rank in society. Both clients and slaves could and did rise to positions of prestige in society. In the early 1930s so close were *baranci* (clientage) and *bauta* (slavery) that Zinder people often failed to distinguish between the two terms.[33] The implication is that both English words are misnomers for the institutions and relations to which they refer. Slaves were freer and clients more dependent than these English expressions imply.

Clients began their service doing menial tasks such as fetching wood and water for the trader's household. The next step was for *barori* to accompany their patron on trading expeditions, but once again the work was menial – they tended the pack oxen and donkeys or helped prepare food for the people in the caravan. In the early stages of their service, *barori* went through a process of selection. Those found to be trustworthy received more responsibility, and the *ubangida* allowed them a limited role in trade as part of a test to determine which showed promise. During the trial period, the transactions of the novice took place in the presence of the *ubangida* or one of his close associates. Those who passed the test were allowed to trade on their own with capital borrowed from the *ubangida*. At this stage the *ubangida* and his trusted helpers made frequent checks on the novice to make sure he was not embezzling money or being cheated in transactions. On a regular basis they took back goods which remained unsold and the money owed the *ubangida,* making sure that the balance was in order. The *ubangida* took all of the profit on a sale or exchange, and he redistributed the proceeds among his employees as he saw fit. Clients who were faithful and made good profits for their employer were well rewarded, and they exercised progressively more freedom of action as their loyalty became apparent.[34]

The independence of *barori* represented both an asset, because it added to the supply of labour available to the firm, but also a liability. Employers were not willing to use litigation to regain stolen property. Neither the court of the local judge (*alkali*) nor the *tribunales* of the French colonial judicial system were suited to this purpose. Both judicial systems tended to view disputes between patrons and their clients as intra-family quarrels.[35] In addition those who stole from their employers were likely to leave town, which eliminated the possibility of legal pressure being brought to bear. And if they stayed, they could always claim that they had lost the property innocently, because of their inexperience and lack of familiarity with trade.

The solution adopted by most of the traders of Damagaram was to integrate their *barori* into their own households as fully as possible. The client received food, clothing, and lodging from his employer. Since he was totally dependent, he spent little time away from his patron's compound, even in his free time; control of the client early in his career was possible because he spent so much of his time with the *ubangida*. And as the *bara* gained more independence in business matters, social control over him became more strict. Sanda 'dan Gayi, the younger brother of a successful Zinder trader of the 1930s and 1940s, explained how he and his brother handled subordinates in their enterprise:

A person would have a difficult time finding a chance to steal from us, because in those days it wasn't like now. Everyone was trustworthy. A *bara* whom we took on wasn't really a *bara*, but he was like a relative.
Q. Like a relative −?
A. When we ate meals, we ate with him. When we bought clothing, we bought clothing together. If we went on a trip by truck, we all went together. As for sleeping, if we had a *gida,* we gave it to him. If he was old enough to marry, we would arrange a marriage for him. We were like a single person, we and he. All of our possessions were one. If we went on a trip by horse, he would go along . . .
Q. He was like a relative.
A. With all of this, it was very difficult for a *bara* to steal from us.[36]

In this society, the social control of non-kin necessarily involved creating kinship relationships.

The most important of the bonds which linked *barori* to the *ubangida* were those created by the arranged marriage. Nearly all of the successful traders in Zinder paid bridewealth and made arrangements for the marriages of their clients. This was so much the norm that when one trader failed to provide his client with a wife, the client, seeing that his patron was uncommonly stingy, began stealing from him, left his employ, and had to turn to the patron's wife, with whom he remained on good terms, for someone who would find him a marriage partner.[37] *Barori* were unmarried when they entered the service of their patron. They had no wealth of their own, and received no salary other than food, lodging, and clothing. They were unable to finance their own marriages, since this involved giving gifts of considerable value to the prospective bride and her family. Clients depended on their patrons to pay the bride price, and they also needed their patrons to guarantee the good will of the prospective in-laws. Elder men controlled the access of young men to women of marriageable age, and younger men could seldom make arrangements for a marriage on their own. The prospective bride and her family could back out of the agreement after having accepted some or nearly all of the gifts involved in the bride price, and a young man on his own had no recourse whatsoever.[38] Young men working in the family *gandu* relied on their fathers to make arrangements for the marriage and to pay the bride price. A young man's father could deal with the bride's family as an equal, and a young man who had left home was dependent on his patron for this kind of service.

The *ubangida* were willing to pay the bride price for his clients because a married employee was less of a liability to him than an unmarried man. A married client was a stable member of the community, someone who was much less likely than his unmarried counterparts to pilfer money from his patron to spend on prostitutes. In addition, the family ties which bound a married man usually prevented him from embezzling money and leaving town, an abuse against which the patron had little recourse.

The *ubangida* picked a suitable marriage partner for his client from his relatives and acquaintances. In Zinder the preferred marriage for a loyal and trusted employee was the patron's own daughter. Between 1900 and 1950, fourteen *barori* who later became successful traders in their own right married the daughters of their patrons.[39] The next-best choice was his actual niece, and then came other classificatory 'daughters', defined as kinswomen of the next descending generation. If no relatives were available, the patron turned to the daughters of his close friends, and, failing this source, to the daughters of more distant acquaintances. The patron naturally wanted to find a young bride for his client, and not a divorcee, and this was sometimes a difficult task. Young women of marriageable age remained unmarried only for several years; by the age of fifteen, marriages had been arranged for nearly all of them. Often a patron would have preferred to marry a daughter or a close relative to his client, but none were available.

The purpose of these arranged marriages was to create and maintain ties of real or fictive kinship between patrons and clients, and the reason for the creation of these ties is best understood within the context of the Meillassoux model.[40] Among Hausa farmers, young men in *gandu* gave the product of their labour to their fathers, who in turn provided for the needs of sons. The prestation of goods and services from junior to senior almost always involved a kinship interaction, usually that of father and son. When a young man worked for someone who was not a relative, as in the case of patron and client in trade, the relationship of the two persons necessarily involved elements of the father-son relationship. Clients gave patrons the product of their labour and in return patrons provided food, lodging, and clothing, and paid the bride price and made arrangements for marriages. In this social system younger men were forced to rely upon older men to help them obtain wives, and the power to provide or withhold women was an important element of social control. In some ways patron and client even behaved toward each other like father and son. In the first place *barori* used terms of address appropriate when a son spoke to his father. Second, custom permitted clients to enter the living quarters of their patrons, while patrons were not allowed to enter the rooms of their clients; and this was also analagous to behaviour expected of fathers and sons.[41]

Kinship relationships between *barori* and *ubangida* were of course not always fictive. In some instances clients became the actual son-in-law of the patron. The attitude of a son-in-law (Hausa, *suruki*. The roles like the terminology were reciprocal. Nevertheless, respect, but the *suruki* relationship did not involve the avoidance dictated for father and son, nor the extreme shame and avoidance which a man showed towards his mother-in-law and his wives' elder sisters. The *suruki* relation was classificatory, and all affinal relatives are referred to as *suruki* (plural; feminine singular, *surukuwa*).[42] If a client married one of his patron's consanguineal or maternal relatives, he still considered the patron a classificatory *suruki*. The roles like the terminology were reciprocal. Nevertheless, the rule of deference to elders applied, and in return for his respect the son-in-law received aid and assistance.[43]

The patron played an active part in preserving the marriages of his *barori*. If in the course of an argument the client's wife left her husband and returned to her parents' compound, the patron visited her and tried to persuade her to reconcile the differences with her husband. The patron often went as far as to take sides in marital disputes and exert his authority over the party he considered guilty of wrongdoing.[44] Not only was the patron closely involved in the personal lives of his *barori,* but he also participated in the ceremonial occasions in the lives of the children born to them.

The patron's compound remained the centre of the domestic life of the client even after he moved out and set up a home of his own. The client's wife came to the patron's compound to work with the patron's wife on the evening meal, and all of the women ate this meal together. The men – the patron and all of the *barori*, including those living outside the compound – also ate their evening meal together.[45] To a certain extent, the patron's compound functioned like the home of a rural *mai gida* (household head) with married sons still living at home and working on the *gandu,* since the sons in the *gandu* ate with their father, and their wives helped prepare the food and ate together.

The control of clients through arranged marriages worked two ways. Besides the social ties and kinship roles involved, patrons were able to use the marriage as a reward for services performed. The incentive to be honest and hardworking was strongest in the early stages of the service of unmarried *barori*. Marriages, even those to the patron's real daughter, usually took place within five years of the time a client entered service.[46] Afterwards, the prospect of marriage could no longer serve as an incentive, but the patron held out new rewards. The prospect of receiving gifts of trade capital from their real, fictive, or classificatory father-in-law usually kept *barori* honest.

In most cases where the client married the patron's daughter, informants said that the son-in-law inherited the patron's business. These were not examples of formal inheritance or even pre-heritance, but represent instead the recognition that gifts of trade capital passed from the older man to the younger. In addition the son-in-law received advice and encouragement, and he learned about the technical aspects of trade from his father-in-law. Informal inheritance by sons-in-law constituted the link between generations in the Zinder merchant community which was so noticeably lacking between traders and their own sons.

The relation between the patron and a trusted client usually evolved into something which resembled a partnership. *Barori* received gifts of trade capital from their patrons, and they strove to increase this capital by trading on their own account. Often they handled transactions for themselves and their patrons simultaneously, but patrons and clients never pooled their capital. The traders of Zinder lacked institutions to provide for the division of profits in joint ventures. The only known case of a trading partnership where the members pooled their resources was one in which three independent traders of about the same age agreed to share the profits or losses of their transactions on a rotating basis.[47] Clients who had considerable capital of their own had to accept the assignments which their patrons gave them or break off relations.

The weak point in a system which relied on the bonds created by arranged marriages was the inherent instability of marriage in this social setting. Divorce was so common that many elderly men find it impossible to remember the names of all of their wives, having forgotton all those who did not bear children. Divorce severed the ties which the patron so carefully set up. If they could finance and arrange a marriage by themselves, clients were tempted to set out on their own.

In rural Damagaram, the relationship between father-in-law and son-in-law also had a special meaning, though quite different from its significance to the merchants of Zinder. Madugu Isa married off two of his daughters to caravan leaders of lesser status, but his sons-in-law were not his clients. But they did recognize his authority and seniority, and their marriages expressed their subordination to him. With the decline of *maduganci* in the colonial period, the marriages of a trader's daughters lost their special significance. Few of the rurally-based traders had clients, since the average size of the firm in rural Damagaram was much smaller than in Zinder. Consequently, the marriages of their daughters played no role in the organization of their enterprises.

COMPARATIVE CONTEXTS

Although more research needs to be done, commercial clientage apparently had a wide geographical distribution in West Africa. The research of M. G. Smith in Zaria concentrated on the political rather than the economic functions of clientage, which he found 'coterminus with Hausa political society'.[48] But he also noted that the uses of clientage varied according to the situation, and that sometimes clientage expressed a directly economic relation in which work and reward were balanced. John Works briefly notes that an important Hausa trader in Abeché arranged marriages between trustworthy clients and his daughters. Amselle's study of Kooroko merchants in lower Mali and the upper Ivory Coast describes institutions used by traders to recruit non-relatives into their firms, and these institutions share common features with commercial clientage in Zinder up to a point.[49] The major differences were that Kooroko merchants used explicit contractual agreements about the division of profit between junior and senior partners and used sons and other relatives when they could. More often Zinder merchants had to rely on the creation of social ties, marriage alliances, and kinship analogies to perform the same functions.

Clientage of the economic variety has also been described in the research of Abner Cohen on the Hausa landlords of Ibadan, and once again the institutions are different in important ways from those found in Zinder. Landlords in Ibadan married off their clients for the same reasons as the traders of Zinder, and they also occasionally permitted their daughters to marry their clients, although this appears to have occurred less frequently than in Zinder. The recruitment of clients in Ibadan, however, was completely different from the practice in Zinder. All of the Ibadan landlords had a number of foster sons, and they tended to recruit clients into their businesses among these foster sons.[50] As in Zinder, kinship ties provided the key elements in the control of business clients, but these ties were formed and maintained in entirely different ways. In Ibadan the patron often fostered the first child of his business client. Since fostering one another's children was almost an obligation among close kin, the patron and client entered into a kinship relationship like that between brothers, by virtue of the fostering. In Ibadan a client could be both the foster son of his patron and the 'brother' by analogy because of the fostering of his own first-born son by the patron. But the most important similarity between commercial clientage in Zinder and Ibadan was the reluctance to use sons as junior partners and the need to rely instead on kinship ties which had been created.

At this stage it is impossible to say why certain merchant communities preferred sons as junior partners, as did Hausa kola traders and Kooroko merchants, while others did not. Certain specific explanations for the scarcity of commercial dynasties in

Zinder have been examined, such as hardships during the early years of colonial rule and the risks and uncertainties of the cattle trade. In addition, extreme father–son avoidance in Zinder seems to contrast with Amselle's description of Kooroko families. Prominent Kooroko merchants in Bamako live and work in large groups including their wives, their sons and their families, and in some cases younger brothers of the head merchants and their families. The traditional pattern of inheritance was for wealth to pass from elder to younger brothers until the generation died out, but some merchants successfully used Islamic patterns of inheritance to bequeath wealth to their sons. Sons also received gifts of money which had been collected at their baptism, saved and invested for them by a woman from their mother's patrilineage, and given to them when they become adults to enable them to begin trading.[51] The testimony of Zinder merchants calls special attention to patterns of inheritance as an explanation for the failure to incorporate sons into trading businesses, and this explanation makes sense in light of a comparison with the North African mercantile community of Zinder, where the larger number of father–son businesses follows from the willingness of merchants to bequeath a disproportionately large share of wealth to a son who had been active in the business. But if inheritance explains the pattern in Zinder, why should Hausa kola merchants, who presumably have similar customs regarding inheritance, act differently? In fact, inheritance among Hausa kola traders may differ significantly from patterns in Zinder and Ibadan and thus account for a different attitude toward sons as junior partners. But this question cannot be answered with certainty until further research is done on inheritance in other communities of Hausa merchants.

Unfortunately a number of unanswered questions remain in other areas as well. Presumably Zinder's system of commercial clientage evolved in response to the particular needs of a city where trade had a special importance. A preliminary investigation at Tessaoûa, just 100 km to the west, revealed that arranged marriages and marriages between traders' daughters and clients, key institutions in Zinder, were unknown. The assumption that commercial clientage of the type found in Zinder had a limited distribution is therefore probably valid, but much less is known about the historical evolution of the institution. A logical hypothesis is that the growth of trade of all kinds in the middle and late nineteenth century forced adaptation and the response was to form larger firms by using slave employees and marrying them to daughters, as the earliest known examples of 'Dan Bade and the father of Muhamman Kane illustrate. The institution was then modified to suit the changing conditions of the early twentieth century, and it has continued to evolve. For example, Al-Hajj Mukhtar, whose case will be discussed in detail in the following chapter, built a commercial enterprise which retained something of the old system of clientage, but he also paid salaries to employees and also willed his business to a son who had taken an active interest in it from his youth.

WOMEN

One lapse of the Meillassoux model of family enterprise is that it treats women as the objects of transactions which define the nature of relations between younger and older men. The model does apply to Damagaram and Damergu in the sense that women had little scope for independent social and economic life outside the household, but exceptional cases where women did enter into production for the market economy can be instructive. In addition the model also provides the correct framework for viewing most production by women within the household, namely that they gave their labour to elder men who then redistributed the product. But once again exceptions can be instructive, and more detail is desirable. Perhaps this is an appropriate place to consider the role of women in commercial enterprises and in the economy in general.

First it must be emphasized that this was a society in which most women were subordinate to men and had little freedom of action. Most spent their lives in the households of first their fathers and then their husbands. Rural women farmed on *gandu* land and on their own plots called *gayauna* or *gamana,* marketing produce from these private plots to buy clothing or condiments for food. Both rural and urban women also gathered wood and carried water to their compounds. In some cases husbands secluded their wives according to Muslim custom, but this was rare in the period covered by this study because most husbands could not afford it; husbands with secluded wives had to pay servants to carry water and gather wood. Women were free from the day-to-day supervision of men when they entered the status of *karuanci,* which can be translated roughly as prostitution, a translation which obscures the fact that this status was both less shameful and less permanent than a corresponding situation in western societies.[52] Many women became *karuwai* between marriages rather than return to the compound of their father, which was usually the only alternative for a divorced woman.

Household duties included preparing food, cleaning, craft occupations, and the arduous task of pounding millet to remove the outer shell of the grain. Among Tuareg and Ful'be, women milked the animals, set up camp, prepared food, gathered wild grain and berries, sold milk and butter, wove mats, and made household implements. Hausa women sometimes bought, stocked, and resold grain, operating from their compounds, and a small percentage of the production of the household was marketed – for example, prepared food or the products of craft industries. Most marketed craft items were made by men, but women made pottery, wove mats, made cooking utensils, and spun thread for their own use and for sale. Before the era of machine-made cloth a large female labour force was needed to spin, since twice as much labour was necessary for spinning as for weaving. Traders returning from Zaria with cotton often loaned it to women who worked in groups and repaid traders in thread, keeping some for their own use.[53]

Some women also participated in long-distance trade, and most relied on commercial clientage as men did. Early examples of trade by women are provided by the servile Tuareg landlady-brokers who operated in Zinder before and after the turn of the century and later in Agadez. They traded grain as did their guests, and they fitted into a larger pattern throughout the Central Sudan of house trade in grain by women. Women in general suffered from several handicaps in long-distance trade, among them difficulties and dangers involved in travel and the inability to enter easily into business relations with men. But women could use clients, and the pattern was that elder women worked the system of arranged marriages to ensure the honesty and loyalty of younger clients just as their male counterparts did. An example of this is provided by a rural woman who sponsored a client trader named Gwanda.[54] Gwanda had worked for a small-scale rural merchant named Bra Lagos who was active in the southern cattle trade in the 1930s and 1940s. When Bra Lagos refused to arrange a marriage for Gwanda, he left and began working for his patron's former wife, who was willing to find Gwanda a wife. Earlier examples of the use of clients and former slaves to trade include several Dagera women. Azumi, who came to Damagaram and moved on to Damergu in the time of

Sarki Tanimu, and later became the head of a large household, had clients who traded millet for potash and returned from Zaria with cotton, which her slaves spun and wove. She marketed some cotton and finished cloth not needed in her household. Two other Dagera women of Damergu, Kelzu Ganduram and Magaram Karama, whose wealth dated from the early twentieth century and was traced to large millet harvests, had clients who traded grain to Agadez and returned with animals. Perhaps the largest operation was run by a woman trader named Mairam Hadisa who ran a large network of clients from Yanduna in Nigeria in the Daura Emirate. Working in the 1930s and 1940s, she was a groundnut weigher for several Lebanese buyers and had two overlapping networks of clients who bought cattle or skins in Niger and sold them in Kano or Zaria, in the case of cattle usually at rural markets. Her clients worked either in the northern branch of her network or in the southern branch. Unfortunately people in Damagaram were too remote from her operations to be able to provide detail on her firm.[55]

CONCLUSION

Despite the lack of detailed historical information and incomplete data on comparative cases, the Zinder commercial community provides an important example to illustrate that fluidity and adaptation were as much a part of the network of relationships which made up the kinship system as were rigidity and conservatism. In certain respects the kinship system stood in the way of solutions to problems associated with enlarging the scale of economic enterprises and assuring their continuity, and yet adaptation in other areas permitted solutions to be worked out. Furthermore, where economic change resulted in new forms of accumulation of wealth, the rules of inheritance took on new meaning and set up a potential conflict between those whose intent was to preserve the assets of the firm and those who stood to benefit from a wider, customary distribution of the estate.

Another conclusion that can be drawn from the Zinder case studies is that the substantivist and formalist positions greatly understate the complexity of relations between market and non-market sectors in at least one West African economy. In the Zinder merchant community most enterprises relied almost totally on the sale of commercial services to allow them to purchase food, clothing, shelter, and other necessities. In other words their subsistence production was negligible. Yet these enterprises, which can be described as participating fully in the market sector, also relied heavily on non-market sources of labour and used non-market channels, namely kinship ties, for the accumulation of capital.[56] The reason for this reliance on kinship and fictive kinship was not the absence of capital or labour markets, since both existed in the early twentieth century, as the complex transactions of merchants working with Dufour and other examples from the tape collection demonstrate. The reason centred instead on organizational problems within the firm such as the control of subordinates and also on the need for continuity from one generation to the next.

CHAPTER IX

A Commercial Biography

Economic hardship in the early colonial period, and in particular during the years 1911–20, had repercussions for people in all walks of life, especially the merchants. The new generation which rebuilt afterwards began their careers almost to a person as clients of Dufour. They rebuilt on local models, using kinship and commercial clientage if they enlarged the scale of their operations beyond the activities of a single person. This reliance on local experience set a limit on the degree of expansion possible as compared to European commercial companies. Similarly the structure of colonial commerce created barriers, since European companies had the advantages of ready access to credit, ability to influence prices of imports and exports, and experience in large-scale business organization. Even local European enterprises, such as the one owned by Dufour, benefited from an association with giant European commercial companies.

But limitations on the scale of activity were not absolute, as demonstrated by the case of Al-Hajj Mukhtar b. Sharif Bashir, who began trading about 1910 and emerged at the end of the colonial period at the head of a modern, large-scale enterprise. The life of this local merchant reads as a remarkable story of innovation in adverse conditions, and as such has a value in its own right. Nevertheless it would be unwise to weave the entire narrative of the period around the accomplishments of one person, an approach which implies, as a critic of the entrepreneurial school of history has charged, that an individual made a unique contribution.[1] It also neglects external economic circumstances. There are, however, several good reasons for including a detailed account of the commercial activities of Mukhtar in this study. First, the growth of the firm he headed represents the next step in the process of growth in the scale of economic units described in the preceding chapter, since he relied to an extent on local relations and institutions to recruit and control employees, although he modified these and other aspects of local economic organization. Second, even though he was the most successful merchant of the time and hence represents an exceptional case, his life shows that considerable scope for innovative behaviour remained even where colonial relations placed formidable restrictions on local participation in economic life. And finally a purely practical reason for including an account of Mukhtar's business must be considered. At the time I conducted research a sizeable portion of Mukhtar's business records survived, and I was able to gain access to them. These documents constitute the largest single collection of material on economic activity of any kind in the 1930s and 1940s. Given the fact that other archival material has been lost and what remains is dispersed and incomplete, it would be senseless not to exploit fully the information contained in Mukhtar's papers. In addition, it was possible to complete the story by interviewing his family, employees, associates, and rivals.

Little is known about Al-Hajj Mukhtar's early life, except that he was born in Zinder about 1892, the son of Sharif Bashir, a Ghadamasi who made a living not from trade, but by taking alms from his countrymen. Sharif Bashir had spent a short time in the Ghadamasi community at Djajdidouna, but he moved to Zinder before 1890. Mukhtar's mother was a Kanuri woman from a village near Lake Chad who met and married Sharif Bashir in Zinder. As a child Mukhtar completed Koranic school and several years of French primary school.[2]

Mukhtar began trading in 1910 when his father died. Although he was only eighteen years old at the time, as a single able-bodied male the responsibility of supporting the family fell on his shoulders. Muhammad Salla, the most successful of the Ghadamasi in Zinder at the time, helped Mukhtar get started.[3] Muhammad Salla married one of Mukhtar's younger sisters, the opposite of the usual pattern in Zinder wherein the subordinate married into the family of the patron. It is difficult to determine the exact relation between Mukhtar and his patron in the early years, since informants closest to Mukhtar tended to minimize the extent of his dependence. But the most anyone outside Mukhtar's family or business claimed was that he received a loan which enabled him to buy camels and go to Kano to trade for kola, sugar, and cloth to take to N'Guigmi, where he then set up regular trading activities. Mukhtar repaid this loan quickly, and it is fairly certain that he was never one of Muhammad

Salla's regular clients.

By moving to N'Guigmi Mukhtar was able to escape the unfavourable situation of the other North African merchants working in the overseas import–export trade. Kano–Zinder trade circuits were overcrowded, and retail trade in Kano itself offered few opportunities to newcomers. Those who stayed in Zinder were conspicuous enough to French authorities that they often became victims of currency profiteering.[4] Once North Africans had been forced to accept paper currency, they could only dispose of it locally

at a loss, and French currency was also worthless in Kano. The irony of the situation was that interregional trade, especially livestock trade, was on the upswing. Though local trade was inaccessible to most North Africans, Mukhtar was just beginning his career and had therefore invested little time in establishing business contacts in Zinder. He was free of the kind of ties which bound many older men, and besides his maternal relatives lived near N'Guigmi. By leaving the capital of the territory he was able to overcome difficulties encountered by many other North Africans in their efforts to break into internal trade, and he moved to an area where possibilities for commerce were much more open.

At N'Guigmi Mukhtar sold primarily to the French military personnel and to African troops whom they commanded. Because he found few competitors for the trade of this small military outpost, he was able to make a good profit on the goods he imported from Kano. One of Mukhtar's clients, a trader named Abdullahi, took camel caravans of kola, cloth, and imported foodstuffs to Bilma, where another garrison was stationed. Another employee, Alhaji Jibaje, who was to remain with Mukhtar until Mukhtar's death in 1971, tended the small retail store which Mukhtar maintained at N'Guigmi.[5] Mukhtar himself made regular trips to Kano to buy supplies.

The return trade from N'Guigmi to Kano was also profitable. At first he took hides to Kano, but later he moved into the livestock trade. Jibaje, who accompanied him on a trading expedition which turned out to be especially profitable, gave the following account of what happened. They were taking a herd of cattle to Kano on the droving route and had gone about half the distance when news reached them that a severe epizootic of cattle disease had broken out in the area they had to cross. They were faced with a choice between turning back and accepting a loss on the expedition, since the cattle would have to be sold near the point where they had been bought, or going ahead and risking loss of the herd to disease. Mukhtar decided to push ahead toward Kano but to travel at a very slow pace so that his herd would have the maximum possible resistance to disease. They arrived to find the Kano cattle market nearly deserted and the price being paid for cattle from the north about twice its normal level.[6]

Soon afterwards Mukhtar diversified his enterprise by moving in other new directions. Although he still lived in N'Guigmi he returned to Zinder from time to time, and there he bought wheat futures. Since wheat could be sold at a profit in Kano, he had it shipped there after taking delivery. Mukhtar engaged an assistant in Kano, a Hausa trader named Gajere, who sold wheat and kept the proceeds until Mukhtar arrived on one of his regular visits.[7] Gajere had been an employee of the landlord who had lodged and provided brokerage services for Mukhtar in the early days of the Kano–N'Guigmi trade. This landlord had died suddenly, and creditors descended on his house to take what they could. Once Mukhtar had arrived in Kano to find Gajere destitute and alone in the empty compound. Mukhtar decided to take on Gajere as a client, and deeply indebted to his patron, Gajere remained a faithful and trusted assistant for many years and continued to act as Mukhtar's agent in Kano.[8]

The first major expansion of Mukhtar's business occurred in 1932 when he moved back to Zinder. He knew from experience that supplying military posts could be an extremely profitable business, and he realized that he could easily enlarge his scale of operations by dealing with a larger post. Zinder was also a logical choice for the headquarters of the new business because of its strategic location on the newly completed road from Kano. Mukhtar left Jibaje in N'Guigmi to supervise the activities of the firm in eastern Niger and to maintain contacts built up over the years. Mukhtar concentrated on establishing new ties. From Zinder he entered into relations with independent traders in Agadez and in towns west of Zinder. These traders placed orders by letter or by telegraph; those who were not literate in French or Arabic had letters written for them, and postal employees translated messages into French for transmission by telegraph. Traders often paid for merchandise they received by postal money order.[9] Mukhtar shipped goods to his correspondents by camel caravan. Since he had married several Tuareg women, he could call upon Tuareg in-laws or groups associated with them to run these caravans.[10]

This distribution system took very little of his time and attention. The accounting system was simple, since Mukhtar kept only a file of correspondence and a record of transactions and debts.[11] Because he asked for payment on delivery or soon thereafter, he did not have to follow the movements of his correspondents nearly as closely as he would have to have done if he had advanced goods to them on credit. Close supervision would also have been necessary had Mukhtar's correspondents actually been his clients or employees. As it was, his time was free for other activities.

Mukhtar divided his efforts in Zinder between a retail outlet for imported merchandise and competitive bidding for the supply of gasoline, oil, cloth, and foodstuffs to the military garrison and colonial administration of Zinder. Mukhtar bought supplies for the French in Kano from European-owned commercial companies – the United Africa Company and its subsidiaries, principally the Compagnie du Niger Français (C.N.F.); Patterson, Zochonis and Co., Ltd.; and the Société Commerciale de l'Ouest Africain (S.C.O.A.); and several Kano-based firms, such as Ambrosini and Co., and A. J. Tangalakis and Co.[12] These firms supplied him with gasoline and oil for the French in Zinder and for shipment to French posts in Agadez and Bilma which sometimes placed orders through Mukhtar. They also furnished him with all of the goods he sold at the retail level in Zinder or shipped to the independent traders who constituted his distributive system. Mukhtar maintained contact with Kano wholesalers by making frequent trips there himself, by using Gajere as a contact, or by mail and telegram. He bargained with Kano companies to obtain the best price and informed competitors when the prices seemed too high. Once he complained when he lost a bid for the supply of gasoline to the French based on a Kano price which he considered too high. He ordered goods well in advance of the expected date of delivery in Kano, since consignments destined for merchants in Niger had to be cleared through customs at Lagos as merchandise in transit, or else they were subject to Nigerian import duties.[13]

Mukhtar's main competitors in the early 1930s were two merchants based in Zinder, the Frenchman Dufour and a Greek merchant named Petrokocino. Mukhtar and his competitors all bought from the same wholesalers in Kano. Dufour maintained a large network of client traders in and around Zinder, and he probably did a larger volume of business than Mukhtar in the Zinder area itself. Petrokocino's business appears to have been the smallest of the three. Mukhtar probably did more business than Dufour because he maintained a widespread distribution network and was able to tap markets for imports throughout eastern and central Niger.

Mukhtar's records are of course an invaluable source for the study of his remarkable career, but they raise almost as many questions as they answer. For example, surviving records for 1936, a year in which the bills from suppliers seem to have been filed systematically, show an annual turnover on the import side of over

£6,000 at Kano prices, which were the starting point for Mukhtar.[14] Bills from S.C.O.A. and some United Africa Company affiliates are missing, and it is impossible to come up with anything but a very rough estimate of Mukhtar's annual turnover in 1936, but it seems to have been substantial. The records for other years are even more sparse, and as a result nothing is known about the evolution of the size of Mukhtar's business over time. Judging from the situation in 1936, cotton piece goods appear to have made up 80 to 90 per cent of the value of his imports, but once again it is impossible to resolve this question with any degree of accuracy. Lacking data on the retail prices of his imports, calculation of the rates of return or profit margins is of course out of the question. Nevertheless, the main lines along which his business evolved are clear, in spite of the lack of detail.

The need to adapt to an increasingly competitive situation arose in 1935, when the three largest commercial companies operating in West Africa — S.C.O.A., C.F.A.O., and the United Africa Company, acting through its subsidiary C.N.F. — established branches in Niger.[15] These companies brought merchandise within the reach of merchants whom Mukhtar had been serving, even those as far away as Bilma and Agadez. S.C.O.A. and C.N.F., which set up branches in Zinder, were able to import merchandise at lower prices than Mukhtar because they dealt directly without intermediaries. In addition, the Kano branches of S.C.O.A. and C.N.F. refused to sell to Mukhtar at prices which would undercut their own operations in Zinder, and all outlets related to C.N.F. through its parent company, U.A.C., co-operated in this effort. Nevertheless they continued to sell to Mukhtar, though at disadvantageous prices. The following excerpt from an interview with Mukhtar's son suggests why he was able to hold his own:

Q. Did competition from S.C.O.A. and C.N.F. present real difficulties?
A. No . . . because he was here before them, and people knew him, and after all he was a local man and people had to help him. By the time S.C.O.A. and C.N.F. arrived he already had enough money to be able to trade all over Niger.[16]

He had already built up a strong competitive position which he used as a base.

Another factor which permitted Mukhtar's survival was that the arrival of European commercial companies coincided with a period of prosperity. Most important was a rapid increase in the volume of groundnut exports from central Niger, which generated income for imports and created commercial opportunities in the groundnut export trade. Farmers had grown groundnuts for local consumption before the colonial occupation, but cultivation of the crop for export was associated with the arrival of modern transport facilities, when in the late 1920s improvements in the road network north of Kano permitted purchases to be taken by lorry to the railhead at Kano. The real growth of the groundnut export trade occurred in the early 1930s as a result of higher producer prices made possible by a combination of competition among buying companies operating from Kano, better roads, price supports from France, and the establishment of regulated groundnut markets in the Magaria subdivision.[17]

Although data for terms of trade indices of exports and imports in central Niger cannot be assembled, apparently favourable barter terms of trade also contributed to prosperity in the mid-1930s. By 1935 the market for African agricultural commodities had rebounded from the lows of the depression. Prices of products exported from Niger through Nigeria were given a further boost by the devaluation of the franc in 1936.[18] With the general commodity recovery the price of hides rose, and rising incomes among producers of export crops near the coast influenced cattle prices, which rose sharply in the late 1930s. With the spread of groundnut cultivation in Niger, the rising price of groundnuts on the international commodity market was also an important factor. In 1936 the terms of trade of groundnuts for cotton piece goods, the imported merchandise most commonly bought by Nigérien producers, was unusually favourable.[19]

Mukhtar responded to the challenge to his established position in wholesale and retail import trade by moving into the groundnut trade, a step facilitated by boom conditions in this branch of commerce. In the early days of the trade buying was often a simple exchange of cloth for the export crop. Groundnut-buying therefore enabled Mukhtar to stay in the import business and to utilize contacts and expertise he had built up since moving to the Zinder area, but he had to accept agricultural produce as payment. In short, the locus of demand for imports had suddenly shifted to groundnut markets, and Mukhtar was quick to respond. He began buying at Matameye, on the road between Zinder and Kano, and later bought also at Baban Tapki, a small market near Zinder. During the war he moved into the rest of the important groundnut markets in central Niger – Sassoumbroum, Dungass, Magaria, and the market in Zinder itself. Mukhtar had no lack of competition in groundnut trade; besides S.C.O.A., C.F.A.O., and C.N.F., Lebanese and Ghadamasi from Kano also bought in Niger. At Matameye, in 1937, seven of twelve buyers were based in Nigeria, and in the same year five of eleven buyers in the Zinder market were also Nigerians.[20]

Mukhtar turned to modern methods of transportation in order to be able to compete with S.C.O.A., C.N.F., and Nigerian buyers. Until the middle and late 1930s, camel caravans had carried most of

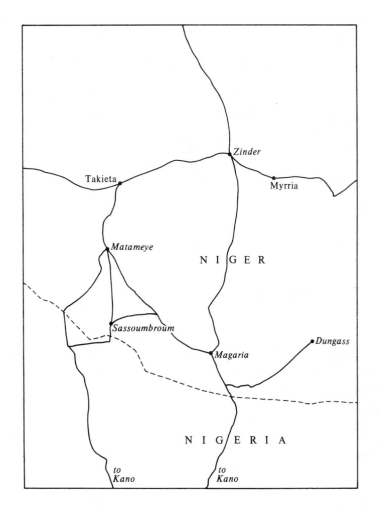

the commercial traffic between Zinder and Kano. Because of the
poor condition of the roads in Niger, lorries often bogged down in
the sand during the dry season or in the mud during the rains. The
roads in Nigeria were generally better, but Zinder was more than
100 kilometres from the Nigerian border. As late as 1936 the bulk of
the groundnut crop − much of which was bought in markets
relatively inaccessible to lorries − was carried into Nigeria, usually
as far as Kano, by camel caravans.[21] By the late 1930s some of the
Lebanese and North Africans from Kano who bought in Niger
owned their own lorries, and others paid Kano-based entrepreneurs
specializing in road haulage. When Mukhtar began buying groundnuts for export, he contracted with Tuareg for the transport of his
stocks to Kano. He also gave consignments of goods to Muhammad
Bugreen, a North African merchant based in Kano with whom he
had a long-standing business relation.[22] By 1938 Mukhtar had two
Dodge lorries of his own, each with carrying capacity of 3½ tons.
After the war he bought a 3½-ton Chevrolet, a 4½-ton Citroen,
and two 3½-ton Renaults. One of the Dodges which he had
purchased in 1937 or 1938 was still in good working condition in
1949.[23] These lorries carried the groundnuts Mukhtar bought and
returned imports which were allotted to him under the aegis of
S.C.O.A.'s import quotas, and he also accepted consignments of
goods for other Zinder merchants and commercial companies.

World War II brought about several changes in Mukhtar's
business, the first of which was an expansion of his marketing
operations to include Libya and Algeria. Fighting in the Mediterranean theatre cut off most of North Africa from European sources
of supply, and shortages of cloth in particular became acute. As the
war progressed, merchants based in Libya and southern and central
Algeria turned to sub-Saharan Africa for supplies of imported
cloth. Mukhtar already had correspondents in Agadez and Bilma,
some of whom were North Africans. Mukhtar used these contacts,
and developed new ones, to exploit the new demand from the
north.[24] From Zinder he relayed cloth and other merchandise north
toward the desert. The chief constraint on the growth of the
Saharan business was the difficulty of obtaining supplies in Kano.
In 1941 the British in Nigeria sealed the border with Niger as a
sanction against the colonial government of *Afrique Occidentale
Française,* which sided with the Vichy regime. Like all other
attempts to control trade across the border, this one was ineffective,
but it did produce temporary scarcities and delays in filling orders

at a time which called for quick action.[25]

A much more serious check on the expansion of Mukhtar's business during the war was the quota system which tied him to S.C.O.A. and limited him to a fixed quantity of imported merchandise. He was unable to take full advantage of the sudden growth of the Saharan market, although he may have been able to smuggle cloth across the border and ship it north. Demand in North Africa collapsed in 1943 when the area fell to the allies and began to receive supplies from Europe. Quotas ceased to be a serious problem for Mukhtar once Saharan demand was gone, though they remained in place until 1950.[26] The quota system left Mukhtar with a fair share of the retail market in Zinder; in fact, he was often unable to take deliveries on all of the merchandise allotted to him.

Another result of wartime conditions was an intensification of Mukhtar's tendency to invest in real estate. Investment in houses for rental income was a good way to employ capital which would have been idle otherwise. Furthermore, managing income property took very little time, since most of Mukhtar's holdings were concentrated in a small area of Zinder.[27] When opportunities for commerce opened up after the war, Mukhtar was free to devote nearly all of his attention to trade since his real property holdings, though extensive, were easily manageable.

With the end of the war Mukhtar turned once again to exporting groundnuts. He had capital well beyond what was required to finance exports to France, as opposed to dealing through an intermediary exporter as he had before.[28] Since exporting involved complex accounting operations, he needed help in this area, but he could avail himself of the services of the newly opened Zinder branch of the Banque de l'Afrique Occidentale. He was already familiar with bank transactions, since he had used the Bank of British West Africa in Kano. But the presence of a bank branch in Zinder enabled him to use its services more fully, and the B.A.O. offered him technical help with exporting. The bank did some of the accounting necessary, and bank personnel helped with the rest in their spare time. Bank employees also advised Mukhtar on how to invest his money, and it was at their urging, for example, that he bought shares of stock in Renault.[29]

Once wartime quotas were finally lifted in 1950, Mukhtar began importing certain items directly from France. Before the war he had imported small quantities of merchandise on his own − tobacco,

perfume, and automobile replacement parts. After the war one
company which took delivery of Mukhtar's stocks of groundnuts
offered to ship cloth in return.[30] He accepted and apparently continued to import from these sources through the 1950s, though his
business records are not clear on how long this practice lasted.

Mukhtar's share of the export market probably declined to
between 5 and 10 per cent of the groundnut crop of central Niger,
although this is a very rough estimate. C.F.A.O. joined S.C.O.A.
and C.N.F. in Zinder to tap the export trade; the French merchants
Reutsch and Chaverini bought in competition with Mukhtar; and
several Lebanese buyers, some based in Zinder, others in Kano,
were also active. During the 1950s Mukhtar probably derived a
larger share of his income from rental properties than before. But
he emerged at the time of independence in a relatively strong
position. In 1960/1 he bought and exported a larger tonnage of
groundnuts than any of the Lebanese buyers except Nabib Chamchoum. In central Niger his exports were the seventh greatest,
after Chamchoum, the three large companies, and the two local
French merchants. Seven years later Mukhtar still ranked sixth
among the buyers of central Niger, and seventh in the whole
country.[31] Mukhtar's son Bashir, who inherited the business, still
exported when research was conducted in 1972.

THE ORGANIZATION OF THE FIRM

Mukhtar never employed more than about ten at any given time,
most of whom were drivers and helpers. Only three employees were
in positions of trust: Jibaje, who left N'Guigmi to manage
Mukhtar's retail outlet in Zinder; Amadou Chaibou, a man who
was literate in both French and Arabic and helped with bookkeeping, and was also in charge of buying groundnuts for export;
and Amadou Yaro Malam, Mukhtar's head driver, who was
entrusted with some important business transactions. To control his
employees Mukhtar used methods commonly employed by other
African traders in Zinder, as the following portion of an interview
with Mukhtar's son shows:

The employees are more or less — those who have been with him from the
beginning have always been faithful to him. Because they find — for
example, Jibaje, he had been with us 56 years. And there has been no
problem with them.
Q. And the drivers?

A. Yes, all those who began with him finished with him. They were always faithful, the drivers and the drivers' helpers. He was a good boss to them, he gave them everything he possibly could have. Besides, he considered them 'his children − Jibaje, Adamou, and the others − he paid for their marriages, he took them on the pilgrimage to Mecca, he gave them houses, he did everything for them. He thought of them as his own children. I think that from this they saw they weren't dealing with a boss, but with a father, and they had every reason to really care for his property and watch over it.

Q. And the employees such as the drivers − did he arrange marriages for them?

A. Yes, even for the drivers. For example, his driver, the one who drove him around, who was related to him, a maternal cousin.

Q. Is it Yaro −?

A. Yaro Malam, his cousin.[32]

Mukhtar included Amadou Yaro Malam, Jibaje, and Amadou Chaibou in his will, leaving them substantial sums of money and giving them rights of ownership in the houses in which they lived, which had belonged to him. This was a departure from the usual pattern of inheritance in Zinder, but the use of written testaments was accepted practice among the North Africans.

The status of drivers and drivers' helpers fell somewhere between employees and clients. Mukhtar paid them a monthly salary, but he also paid their taxes, gave them gifts of cloth on special occasions, and paid bridewealth for their marriages, at least for those who had worked for him for some time. Nevertheless a relatively fast turnover characterized this category of employee; some stayed for only a year or so; but at any given time perhaps half the drivers and assistants employed had been with him for five or ten years.[33]

At first Mukhtar used a rudimentary accounting system, but this seems not to have impaired the growth of his enterprise. Up to 1942 his records consisted of copies of waybills which accompanied merchandise delivered to independent traders or to the French, as well as bills or receipts from Kano. In the case of suppliers, records of transactions with each company were kept in separate folders; but the records of sales and deliveries to Mukhtar's customers were seldom filed according to customer. This system was essentially the same as the one used by North African merchants in trans-Saharan trade, as well as a few Sudanese traders associated with the trans-Saharan network − Malam Yaro, for example. As in the case of trans-Saharan trade, the waybills and receipts served well as records of debts, but they were inadequate for the purposes of determining prices, drawing up balance sheets, or controlling the activities of employees. To keep control of employees he relied on bonds of trust and loyalty and local institutions of commercial clientage, rather than on his accounting system.

But accounting took on greater importance as time passed. In 1942 Mukhtar began keeping an integrated record of business activities in the form of a register of receipts.[34] He did this not to be better able to manage his business, but for tax purposes, since the colonial administration had introduced a transactions tax. He drew up the register of receipts each year with the help of postal and bank employees.[35] Once begun, the exercise proved useful, and modern bookkeeping played a progressively greater role. Accounting permitted overseas import and export activities, for example, and during the period when he did business directly with overseas firms, he hired not only bank employees but also professional accountants for specific tasks.

CONCLUSION

Essential ingredients in Mukhtar's success were his outstanding intelligence and his ability to conceive of possibilities to move in new directions, as well as a willingness to act on these perceptions. If an explanation for his remarkable career were to be sought in one aspect of his life, it would be his cosmopolitan background and the ability to learn from all cultures with which he came into contact. Mukhtar spoke all the languages of business in Niger. He attended French primary school, and he married the daughter of a French soldier and a local woman. His association with French culture enabled him to form lasting friendships with many French administrators, and these personal relations with colonial administrators were often useful to him in that officials aided his efforts to collect bad debts or enforce contractual agreements.[36] He spoke Hausa and was literate in Arabic and French, and he hired secretaries who handled correspondence in French, Arabic, and English. He was equally at home in the world of European commercial companies or the realm of Africans who traded cattle, kola, and other staples of West African internal trade. He adapted quickly to new conditions created by the commercial crisis of 1911–20 and to the rapidly changing situation in the 1930s when Nigérien groundnut exports took off. He survived in the face of competition because he could combine resources in ways that others could not. He made deliveries by using his own lorries or hired motor transport, but he could also arrange with affinal relatives to hire camel caravans when necessary. The same flexibility was also apparent in the way he combined labour and specialized services. He used the local institutions of commercial clientage, but he also hired accountants and relied on a modern banking system. While no single aspect of his business was in a strict sense an innovation, the creativity of his approach lay in the combination of many relations, ideas, and modes of organization from different sources.

While it is necessary to remember the role of these personal qualities, external economic circumstances also entered the picture. Elsewhere in Africa many entrepreneurs succumbed to competition from Europeans operating on a small scale, Lebanese, or giant commercial companies, with the commercial depressions of the 1880s, World War I, 1921/2, and the thirties taking a heavy toll. But the particular situation of the Sahel, where a large volume of trade in the staple commodities of internal long-distance trade existed alongside external import-export trade, created a greater degree of freedom. Because he was willing to take considerable risks in livestock trade, Mukhtar was able to accumulate capital which was the basis for his activities in external trade. Managerial and entrepreneurial talent enabled him to exploit this special relationship between internal and external trade in the Sahelian economy and create a niche for himself among expatriates and international companies.

CHAPTER X

The Open Economy 1930–1960

It is important to emphasize that very few people indeed fared as well under colonial rule as Al-Hajj Mukhtar. All historical studies must face and acknowledge the problem that success is more easily documented than failure. The fact that Mukhtar had many employees and several who remained with him for decades, that he was literate, and that he and his heirs saved his business records means that his accomplishments will not easily be forgotten. This is, of course, not the case when we turn our attention to countless other persons of lesser status – peasant farmers, small-scale merchants and retailers, craftsmen, and labourers. The purpose of this chapter is to describe the structure of the economy in the late colonial period, to review, briefly, opportunities in farming and craft production, to survey the range of positions open to local people in the urban, commercial sector, and finally to discuss relations between commerce and the rest of the economy.

A useful framework for discussing the economy of central Niger between 1930 and 1960 is the concept of the open economy, a model of relations between the centre and the periphery first formulated by Seers and amended and developed by Hopkins in his application of the concept to the colonial economy of West Africa.[1] The principal features of the ideal type open economy are the following. First, open economies export a limited range of primary products in exchange for a broad variety of manufactured goods. Second, one or more sectors of the economy, such as commerce or mining, are dominated by expatriate interests. Third, economic policy is dictated by the desire of the metropolitan power to maintain a smooth flow in the exchange of primary products for manufactured goods. Fourth, the metropolitan power minimizes its fiscal obligations by insisting on balanced budgets, with revenues deriving primarily from the taxation of trade. Fifth, banking arrangements are concerned mainly with financing the activities of expatriate interests. According to the model the long-term growth of the open economy is largely determined by the size of export earnings and the degree of responsiveness of demand for imports to changes in income. Although growth can occur, little structural transformation takes place because of built-in restrictions on the volume of investment, a consequence of the limited focus of expatriate activity in both public and private sectors.

Applied to central Niger, this model accurately describes the dependence of the area on the metropolitan French economy. Beginning in the 1930s, groundnut exports dominated the totals, and a chain of collection and distribution linked peasant farmers with European manufacturers and consumers. Expatriate interests had controlled commerce since the days of Dufour, but this domination took on new meaning with the arrival of C.F.A.O., S.C.O.A., and C.N.F. Both public economic policy as determined by the French administration, and private activities such as banking, aimed at assuring a steady flow of primary products in exchange for imported merchandise. Finally, the structure of the economy changed little in the period under consideration. At the end as in the beginning, groundnuts were the main export crop; expatriate commercial interests dominated exchange; and the main sources of revenue for the government were taxation of import trade and head taxes which drew in large part on earnings from the sale of groundnuts. As indicated by the model, an important reason for the lack of structural transformation was the reluctance of either government or private interests to invest in activities outside the import–export circuit. In the early decades of the century the region failed to generate much revenue, and the colonial policy of maintaining balanced budgets dictated that little could be invested. With the boom in exports came a semi-public lending agency, the Banque de l'Afrique Occidentale, but it was concerned only with financing a limited range of activities in the export sector. The area received little aid from the outside even in the 1950s when France made large sums of money available to the colonies under the F.I.D.E.S. and F.E.R.D.E.S. programmes.[2] By 1960 public investment from France began to reach central Niger, for the most part in the form of spending on health and education. Large-scale spending on processing plants for manufacturing groundnut oil and for the construction and improvement of roads began only after independence.

But the implantation of the peasant export economy in the first place represented a break with the past. Groundnut cultivation, which began in earnest in the 1930s, transformed the structure of opportunity in agriculture and changed the lives of Nigérien farmers. In the area which receives enough moisture for ground-nuts, which is limited to territory south of Zinder for the most part, farmers had cultivated the crop for local consumption before the colonial occupation, and without doubt small quantities entered long-distance trading networks. But exports of the crop on a larger scale had to await the arrival of the railway at Kano in 1911. The early boom in groundnut exports affected mainly the area near the railhead, but it also had a farther reach.[3] In 1915 colonial authorities reported that farmers along the southern border of Niger took groundnuts to Kano by head-loading or on donkey or camel caravans. Villagers interviewed by Collins also confirmed the early date of exports from Niger, though undoubtedly only a small volume was traded.[4] In 1927 a Hausa agent of C.N.F. in Kano arrived in Magaria, a town near the Nigerian border in the heart of the Niger groundnut region, to purchase. By 1928 roads connected Magaria to the Nigerian road network, and about the same time a Lebanese merchant arrived in Magaria to buy groundnuts for U.A.C. and other large exporters in Kano.[5]

Another factor which affected Nigérien farmers was a major change in the structure of groundnut-buying in Nigeria. Whereas buyers had been content to stay in central locations and let peasant producers come to them, better roads permitted increased com-petition, and in the late 1920s both the large commercial companies and their Lebanese competitors moved eagerly into outlying areas. The giant European companies in particular began to acquire leases on commercial property in towns on the periphery of the main groundnut-buying area. This extra measure of competition, a result of declining profit margins during the depression and improvements in the road network surrounding Kano, encouraged both European companies and their Lebanese competitors to move north toward the Niger border. By the end of 1930 both groups had installed warehouses and shops on 129 of these outlying sites in Nigeria, one-third of which had been acquired in 1930 alone. The U.A.C., the largest of the exporters, held rights to over half the trading plots.[6]

The arrival of new buyers set the scene, but the real growth of groundnut production occurred in the mid-1930s as a result of French policy. In the first place, the French established permanent groundnut markets in Magaria, Dungass, and Sassoumbroum in

1932, and another began at Matameye in 1935. Records from these markets serve as an indicator of local production, though it must be realized that after their establishment, as before, production from either Niger or Nigeria could be marketed across the border. In the mid 1930s markets in Niger attracted Nigerian produce because of the French decision to support the price of groundnuts between 1933 and 1937. In 1934 buyers in Magaria offered significantly higher prices than competitors in Nigeria. Accordingly the volume of purchases in Niger, which had previously remained below 7,000 tons, quadrupled. The volume nearly doubled again during the buying season of 1935/6. These spectacular increases, coupled with new restrictions on buying in Nigeria, attracted S.C.O.A., C.N.F., and C.F.A.O. to Magaria to compete with the Lebanese already there.[7]

It is not clear what proportion of the rising totals of the 1930s resulted from increased production in Niger as opposed to purchases of groundnuts grown in Nigeria or portions of the local crop which had previously been marketed in Nigeria. But higher prices can be expected to have had an effect on decisions to produce, and in fact the findings of Collins, who interviewed in villages in the Magaria region, confirm this expectation. According to his informants, local production rose sharply in the 1930s because of price incentives, and most farmers who grew groundnuts for sale lived near one of the four markets.[8] This indicates that the cost of transportation entered into decisions about whether or not to produce. When the period of favourable incentives ended in 1937 some farmers stopped growing groundnuts, but between 1943 and 1945 many were forced to plant groundnuts on what the French called *champs groupées*. In many instances groundnut cultivation in areas remote from the commercial sites began during this period of obligatory production. In the late 1940s the positive incentive of favourable prices returned. A commercial infrastructure was already in place, and in addition the road network had been improved in the meantime.[9]

In the late 1940s and early 1950s the colonial administration, often at the request of the *commandant* at Magaria, made gradual improvements in conditions in the groundnut markets. In 1948 the administration decreed that the four markets in the Magaria subdivision had to stay open permanently during the buying season. Previously buying companies had taken weighers and scales from place to place, so that each market was open only one day each week. It was reported that farmers were often cheated or had money stolen from them in the confusion and crowds. In 1955 the administration issued comprehensive regulations applying to buyers and sub-buyers. In the following year six new markets were created in the Magaria region despite the opposition of the expatriate commercial interests. The large European companies were content to remain in the central market sites and let producers come to them, in effect passing along transport costs to these farmers. But the administration, and in particular R. de Sablet, the *commandant* at Magaria, saw the establishment of new markets, and the resultant increase in the price paid to producers, as an integral part of efforts to promote economic development.[10]

The issue of economic development in a peasant export economy is obviously a complex one, and one aspect of the situation in Niger which needs to be considered is the position of the peasant farmer in the commercial hierarchy. In particular, what fraction of the revenue generated by groundnut exports reached the hands of peasant farmers? Although good data are not available, it seems that most profit remained with the commercial interests. It is possible to see small changes for the better as commerce came under inreasingly strict control and new markets were created, forcing buying companies to assume costs of transport from the newer, more remote markets. It should be added that these gains have not led very far. In a later period the independent Nigérien government created the Société Nigérien de Commercialisation de l'Arachide (SONARA) which functioned like a marketing board, dividing the considerable profits of exporting groundnuts between the twenty-two companies which held half the shares in this semi-public agency, and government agencies, which held the other half interest.[11] Although the creation of SONARA reduced commercial profits, it also created an export tax by diverting revenue to the government.[12] These levies and profits were far more important in determining the structure of opportunities for income from groundnut cultivation than the rather slight changes in producer prices in the 1950s and after independence as a result of fluctuations in the world market, French and Common Market price supports, or the continuation of the process of market reform begun after World War II.

Equally important to producers was the structure of commerce below the buying companies. Sub-buyers occupied the first level, and these were often Lebanese or others from Nigeria who bought from producers and sold their purchases to buying companies at the end of the season. Nigerian entrepreneurs occupied positions from the 1930s but were forced out by the reforms of 1955. Below the sub-buyers were weighers, though often weighers worked for expatriate companies rather than for sub-buyers. Expatriate companies or sub-buyers gave weighers advances of money or cotton piece goods with which to buy and then took charge of produce after weighers had placed it in sacks of a specified weight. They then credited the account of the weigher with the produce received. Buying was highly competitive, and weighers often distributed gifts or loans to farmers to induce them to market with them. Weighers also dealt with intermediaries called *madugai,* a term originally applied to caravan leaders, but in this instance referring to people who either resembled client traders working for weighers or were independent transporters. Some *madugai* bought on their own account in areas away from groundnut markets at a price lower than the market price, then resold at the market, taking as profit the difference in prices. Others acted as clients of weighers in that they distributed gifts and loans with the understanding that recipients would market with the weigher who financed the loans or gifts. Farmers who had donkeys of their own or could borrow them transported groundnuts to market themselves, often making a number of trips in one market season because they did not have enough animals to carry their entire crop in one trip. Weighers sometimes distributed jute bags to farmers through their networks of *madugai,* thereby sparing farmers the expense of leather bags (*taiki*) often used to transport groundnuts and other agricultural produce. If the jute bags were lost, the weigher had to pay for them since they belonged to the buying company for which the weigher worked.[13]

The most important unanswered question concerning the position of farmers in the export economy concerns rural indebtedness. Nicolas, who conducted a full-scale investigation of credit in the Maradi region, found that lending was extremely widespread – in fact nearly everyone borrows or lends. In Nicolas's sample alone, an unknown proportion of the total of loans made at the time he conducted the study amounted to one-fortieth of the value of the groundnuts marketed in the Maradi region in 1967/8. Most loans were granted just before or during the growing season, and most repaid during the groundnut marketing season. Rates of interest were astronomical, with most ranging from 20 to

70 per cent, but some lenders received as much as 370 to 380 per cent.[14] The wide extent of rural indebtedness, its obvious relation to inequality, the seasonal pattern of borrowing, and the position of weighers as lenders raises important historical questions about relations between groundnut marketing and indebtedness. Unfortunately this study cannot answer these questions, nor does Collins's work. Neither does the literature generated by post-independence efforts to replace many of the functions of weighers with officials elected by rural co-operatives.[15] This lack of information is a pity because the issue of indebtedness goes to the heart of the structure of the open economy and the degree to which risk in this economy is passed to peasant producers, while commercial interests and the government take the profits.

Another aspect of the open economy in central Niger was its impact on domestic craft industries and small-scale local manufacturing. It was noted in an earlier chapter that central Niger lost its tanning industry as trans-Saharan trade declined, and the industry survived on a limited basis in the later period to satisfy local rather than export needs for leather. An expatriate established a modern tannery in Zinder after independence to serve the export market. The import–export trade also had a large impact on the local cloth industry. A major downturn in this industry, too, occurred with the arrival of the railway at Kano; but it made a short-term comeback during World War I. It also benefited from fluctuations in the exchange rate, as in 1923, when imported cloth became temporarily more expensive than usual. Local cloth production received its final boost during World War II, when imports were scarce and expensive.[16] All local crafts, and in particular the cloth industry, seem to have suffered from competition during a period of increasing volume in import–export trade between 1921 and 1940. The *commandant* at Zinder reported that the number of weavers declined from 1548 to about 200 in this period, and he also noted decreases, though less sharp, in the numbers of tanners, leather-workers, and blacksmiths.[17] A further decline may have taken place with the post-war growth of the groundnut export trade and rising imports. However a number of speciality products continue to be made. Local pottery, for example, is superior to imported enamel ware for some purposes, such as the storage of drinking-water; local weavers still produce decorative cloth blankets in strips which are sewn together; and leather-workers still produce sandals and a variety of other products.[18]

COMMERCE

The presentation thus far has shown that opportunities in farming and craft industries were limited. What chances for local people to participate in higher levels of the economy remained? Specifically, what were the possibilities in commerce, the sector of the economy which determined what other activities took place and drew the lion's share of the profit from them?

In order to describe the evolution of commerce as it was related to the peasant export economy, it is necessary to go back to the period before the arrival of S.C.O.A. and C.N.F. in Zinder. The main locus of commercial opportunity for local merchants was the circuit between Kano and points in Niger, especially Zinder. In this respect the activities of Al-Hajj Mukhtar were entirely typical of a wider pattern, although he was exceptionally fortunate; most others operated on a much smaller scale. Far more representative was an enterprise run by Alhaji Usman 'dan Haladu, who began trading skins between central Niger and Kano in 1930. In Kano he sold to C.F.A.O. and continued to do so after S.C.O.A. and C.N.F. set up branches in Zinder in 1935. But in 1940 C.F.A.O. joined its rivals in Zinder. Alhaji Usman described the situation he faced:

I had been doing business with C.F.A.O. in Kano. C.F.A.O. opened a branch in Zinder, and they told me I no longer had the right to trade in Kano. They told me I would have to take payment for hides and skins which I turned in at Kano in Zinder, and that I would have to accept an unfavourable exchange rate. I did this once, then transferred all of my business to the Zinder branch.[19]

Later the manager of C.F.A.O. in Zinder offered Usman a job as a weigher in a groundnut market, which he accepted. As this example illustrates, the arrival of the expatriate companies severely limited the opportunities for local and long-distance trade destined for overseas markets, and for some forms of internal trade as well. Profitable trade in cloth between Zinder and Kano was no longer possible, except for Mukhtar, who had a well-established position in the market.

Like Alhaji Usman, most prominent traders of the 1930s became groundnut weighers and were therefore little more than employees of the large European companies.[20] Although success was possible in this niche, weighers operated with several important restrictions on their freedom. They bought on commission, but until the mid-1950s the rate of commission was set after the buying season. They had to strike the right balance between conservative and aggressive buying, and chance often determined which policy was the right one. If a buying company thought that a weigher was in debt and could not possibly repay, it could dismiss him in the middle of the buying season. Often weighers ended up the season in debt, but in some instances buying companies might agree to carry the debt over until the next season in the hope that next year's purchases would allow the weigher to work his way out of debt. This was virtually the only way to recover money from a weigher.[21]

The large-scale participation of Lebanese, Tripolitanian, and Hausa merchants from Nigeria as sub-buyers in the groundnut export trade also limited opportunities for the advancement of locals. Lebanese had moved eagerly into Nigérien groundnut-buying along with large European companies in the late 1920s and early 1930s. Lebanese who did not already have a firm foothold in the groundnut trade in Nigeria, especially new arrivals from the home country, found it best to set up on the periphery, and some came to Niger. Few established permanent residences, and all who did so lived in Magaria. The first Lebanese to set up shops in Zinder arrived later, in the 1940s.[22] The presence of Lebanese merchants, and to a lesser extent the participation of a few Tripolitanian and Hausa sub-buyers from Kano, blocked several natural avenues of expansion for local merchants, since the former occupied intermediate positions in the collection and distribution hierarchy. The situation changed somewhat in 1955 when the colonial administration issued a regulation stating that all groundnut-buyers had to have a permanent commercial establishment in Niger, thereby restricting merchants based in Nigeria

The response of the weighers to their unfavourable situation was to form the Syndicat des Acheteurs d'Arachides, an organization based in Zinder. The members of the association formulated their position and sent letters listing grievances to the governor of Niger in the hope that the French would be favourably inclined to their cause. The *syndicat* asked (1) that entry into the groundnut-buying trade be limited by law, (2) that groundnut weighers be paid in money and not in merchandise, (3) that a uniform price be enforced in the groundnut markets, (4) that the days groundnut markets were to be open be regulated by law, and (5) that exporting companies be prevented from sacking weighers without compensation in the middle of the buying season.[23] A major breakthrough occurred when Djibo Bakary, the secretary of the newly-formed Union

Démocratique Nigérienne and Niger's foremost trade unionist, espoused the cause of the groundnut-buyers.[24] Djibo had already masterminded a series of successful strikes in the early 1950s and was backed by the French Confédération Générale du Travail. The French could not easily ignore Djibo, and, besides, they recognized that the groundnut-weighers had real grievances against the exporting companies. The new governor who arrived in 1955, Jean Ramadier, was sympathetic to the cause of the Zinder weighers, and he initiated a series of reforms which incorporated a large part of the programme of the groundnut-buyers' *syndicat*, with the exception of the provision that entry into the trade be limited.[25]

More important than favourable treatment from the French, however, was the growing political influence of the groundnut-buyers as a group. Their enthusiastic support for Djibo Bakary carried weight with the peasants and helped Djibo's *Sawaba* party win majorities in the Tessaoua and Zinder *cercles* during the referendum of 1958, at a time when support for Djibo in the rest of Niger had completely eroded.[26] The significance of this was not lost on the French, and especially not on the leaders of the Niger branch of the Rassemblement Démocratique Africain who were to inherit the government of the territory. It is clear that traders received favourable treatment from the government after independence, although from the records now available it is impossible to determine what form these favours took.

A final reorganization of commerce falls outside the period covered by this study, but it will be discussed because it shows a continuation of the process whereby Nigériens gained higher positions. SONARA, the semi-public exporting agency created in 1962, treated all buyers alike, and as a result Africans made impressive gains. By 1968 many merchants who had once been sub-buyers or weighers for S.C.O.A., C.N.F., or C.F.A.O. were buying on a scale which approached the level of purchases of their former employers. Alhaji Ali Ilia, for example, who began his career as a buyer for C.N.F., bought nearly as much as Mukhtar in the 1967/8 season. African buyers had also made gains relative to the Lebanese. Both the number of Lebanese buyers and their share of the market declined between 1961 and 1968.[27] Along with the state monopoly on groundnut exporting, the political influence of African merchants must have been a factor, although it is not yet clear just how African merchants were able to bring their newly found power to bear in their own interests.

Another adjunct to the peasant export economy where Africans made post-war gains was the motor-transport industry. In Nigeria European firms had found that they could not make a profit running their own transport, and consequently they deliberately relegated motor transport to African and Lebanese entrepreneurs, and were content to take profits on importing and selling lorries. Local merchants were able to operate at a profit by making frequent stops in order to include short-distance freight along with longer hauls.[28] Lorries had become common in Northern Nigeria during the late 1920s, but their use spread slowly into Niger because transport by camel caravan remained cheaper given the poor condition of most roads. Of the Zinder-based merchants, only Mukhtar and 'Dan Gayi owned lorries before World War II. Motor transport grew in importance with the post-war export boom and improvements in roads. Another major stimulus came in the mid 1950s with *Opération Hirondelle,* a government sponsored programme designed to channel Nigérien groundnut exports from the area west of Maradi, and part of the eastern purchases as well, through Dahomey instead of through Nigeria. Maradi was about equidistant from both Lagos and Cotonou, but the route to the Nigerian port was much cheaper, with about four-fifths of the distance covered by railway, compared with only one-third of the distance in Dahomey (from Parakou to Cotonou). By subsidizing groundnut haulage and return loads, the French hoped to increase tonnage on under-utilized railway and port facilities in Dahomey and to divert exports from the Nigerian railway, which was overburdened and unable to guarantee space for Nigérien exports.[29] *Opération Hirondelle* resulted in a sudden increase in the volume of road haulage available to shippers, and a slightly higher than normal rate structure on freight shipped through Dahomey.

At first growth in the motor-transport industry benefited only local Europeans and the Lebanese, but Africans gradually worked their way into competitive positions. Africans who already owned vehicles could apply for licences to carry a share of traffic subsidized by *Opération Hirondelle.* Since quotas were based on existing capacity,[30] Africans, with more restricted access to capital than their competitors, were initially at a disadvantage because they were less able to expand their lorry fleets in anticipation of contracts. African transporters chose to deal with this handicap, and a quota system in general, through Djibo Bakary.[31] In the short run they had little success, but their position improved after independence. Like groundnut-weighers, transporters benefited from the creation of SONARA, since this state-controlled corporation handled most of its own haulage and subcontracted to transporters. Africans had already learned to make a profit on mixed loads and short hauls, and they readily adjusted to the new situation. In addition they found themselves on an equal footing, and sometimes in a favoured position, when bidding for SONARA contracts.

Among those in the expanded transport industry were two of Mukhtar's elder sister's sons, Abdurahaman Diallo and his full brother Bohari. Both had worked for Mukhtar early in their careers, but he set them up in business for themselves. The sale of a lorry at a nominal price, for example, enabled Abdurahaman to go out on his own.[32] Mukhtar's nephews staked out positions in the transport business, but his son Bashir, who was much younger than Abdurahaman or Bohari, stayed with groundnut exports, which had been his father's primary interest.

The corollary of the domination of export trade by foreign firms was their control of imports, and this changed little as independence approached. In the 1950s all imported hardware, European processed foodstuffs, machinery, and automobiles were sold by foreign owned firms. A large proportion of imported cotton piece goods, merchandise destined for mass consumption, was also handled by foreign importers. At the same time some Lebanese merchants were losing their position in the export trade, others moved into retail cloth-selling. Cotton piece goods passed down a distribution hierarchy familiar in descriptions of African colonial economies; with French firms at the top and Lebanese in intermediate positions, Africans were relegated to the lowest level. To be sure the situation of Africans had improved somewhat in comparison to what it had been in the days when Dufour dominated import–export trade, since in the late 1950s more merchants financed their own operations. But on the average this was no more than a modest change, considering the low turnover and meagre levels of income which characterized the businesses of most Africans. Capital accumulation was all but impossible among retail market sellers, haberdashers (*masu koli*), sellers of soap, cigarettes, candy, and sundry small items (*masu tebur*), and retail *dillali* (commission sellers, not brokers, which is a separate meaning of the word). African-owned shops were rare, and where they existed they seldom had a wider variety of goods than those sold by *koli* and *tebur* retailers. Only recent North African immigrants had shops rivalling the Lebanese in terms of size and variety of wares.

Kola and livestock trade remained in the hands of Africans, but both evolved into one-way, single commodity lines of commerce. Kola merchants bought large bundles (*huhu*) of kola in Kano, paid for motor transport, and returned to Zinder to subdivide the bundles and sell to other wholesalers and retailers. Cattle merchants also preferred to return with money rather than with merchandise. Merchants often sent their drovers ahead with the herds on the hoof, then found lorry transport for themselves so that they would arrive at one of the large collection markets in Nigeria at the same time the herd arrived.[33] By returning with the money from the sales immediately after the sale of their herds, they were able to keep their capital turning over more rapidly than if they went on to Kano to buy kola wholesale.

The opportunities open to rurally-based cattle traders were also more limited in the closing years of the colonial period than they had been before. Traders from villages no longer crossed the Nigerian border regularly, but traded instead between the northernmost markets, usually near the northern limit of non-irrigated agriculture, and collection markets, either at Zinder or in southern Damagaram.[34] Of course nothing prevented them from trading alongside the large-scale traders from Zinder or from towns in Nigeria, and often they did. But the skill of the professional traders, combined with their access to capital, ability to manipulate the customs authorities, and knowledge of market conditions made them formidable competitors. Few rurally-based traders were able to accumulate enough capital to make the transition to professional traders. But the few that did usually took up residence in Zinder, where the proximity of the region's largest markets gave them access to the information about market conditions in Nigeria which was so vital to the success of their operations.

By the end of the colonial period, all but the last vestige of the long-distance trade of the past had disappeared. Cattle traders rarely went as far as Kano; most of the valuable commodities, including staples of the past like millet, cloth, and kola were trans-ported by truck; and large-scale wholesalers had taken over the kola trade, once the province of *fatake* who traded seasonally. Many potash traders gave up their traditional occupation when Nigerian customs officials began charging export duties on potash shortly after the war. The people of one village south of Zinder began to trade in the fronds of the dum-palm (*goruba*), called *kaba*. Palm fronds were the raw material for many articles of local manufacture in wide use, such as mats, baskets, hats, and various kinds of rope. *Kaba* was in short supply in northern Damagaram and Damergu, and in Kano as well, and so *fatake* alternated trips in the dry season between northern and southern markets. On trips to Kano, the average trader, who had four or five donkey loads of *kaba*, could make enough on the sale to buy six or eight yards of cheap cotton cloth.[35] This was, of course, a very meagre return on the labour of gathering the palm fronds and making the ten-day round trip on foot to Kano.

Therefore, by independence one historically important link between agriculture and commerce, namely small-scale dry-season trade, had almost completely disappeared. What other flows of resources, talent, and products between the sectors remained? The population living in rural areas and supported by agriculture continued to supply labour to commercial activities. For example, merchants hired drovers from rural areas; weighers hired labourers for moving and sacking groundnuts; and as shown in Chapter VIII, merchants recruited clients from rural as well as urban areas. Wealthy merchants and other city-dwellers built expensive houses, and builders used labour supplied mostly by rural people seeking dry-season employment. In the later period as before, the urban, commercial sector created demand for foodstuffs and animals from rural areas. But the flow of capital from agriculture was relatively limited. First, dry-season trade by small-scale farmers diminished in importance. And second, from interviews it is clear that only rarely could people have been said to be wealthy before they entered commerce, and these exceptional cases all date from before 1910.[36]

Despite inadequate data it can be said with some certainty that flows of resources in the other direction, that is from commerce to agriculture, were not important in the twentieth century. In this analysis it is important to distinguish between the two levels of commerce: first rural, seasonal, small-scale traders, and second the urban, professional merchants whose enterprises were the subject of Chapter VIII. Urban merchants were notable in that they evolved a means of distinguishing between the wealth of the firm, which in some cases was considerable, and the property of the patrilineage. These urban commercial firms contrasted with economic activity in other sectors, which remained on a small scale and did not necessitate the incorporation of people outside the immediate kinship group. Capital accumulated in these urban, large-scale firms tended to stay in commerce and be built up over the years and the generations, although of course some wealth was dissipated among heirs, as case studies have shown. But despite this 'leakage', capital accumulated in large-scale commerce has tended to stay in this sector. Merchants had great difficulty reinvesting wealth in productive activities in other sectors of the economy. The rapid growth of exports of groundnuts from central Niger during the 1930s would seem to have created opportunities to reinvest commercial profits in agriculture. In fact few of the large-scale merchants invested in land, and those who did produced little more than the needs of their family and clients. A few of the richest merchants had sizeable networks of clients, but they used these extended networks to collect groundnuts for sale rather than to mobilize labour on the land. Land could be bought and sold, but evidently hiring labour was not a workable solution, either because the costs of supervision were too great or because potential profits were not large enough to attract investment; but this is a subject for future research.

In a similar manner other obstacles prevented investment in stock-breeding. Because of seasonal variation in the availability of water and pasture, the only way to raise large herds was to move from place to place to take advantage of good pasture where it could be found. Nomadism was the most efficient way to raise large herds, but sedentary farmers often owned a few animals and sometimes entrusted their cattle to nomadic Ful'be herders for several months or longer. This arrangement was less than ideal because farmers often suspected herders of dishonesty: that is, reporting that animals had succumbed to disease when in reality herders had sold them; substituting sickly calves for strong ones; or engaging in other underhand practices. These suspicions reflect the inability of outsiders to oversee the activities of nomads, and although they may sometimes be unfounded, they represent a major barrier to investment in stock-breeding. Of the merchants in the sample none after Malam Yaro invested in breeding herds.

CONCLUSION

A peasant export economy developed more slowly in south central Niger than in other regions of Africa, and the first significant increases in groundnut production occurred during the depression.

By the mid-1930s competition among buyers, improved transport facilities in Nigeria, and price supports for purchases in Niger combined to provide price incentives for Nigérien farmers. At present there is no evidence to suggest that declining opportunities in non-agricultural pursuits had much to do with increased production of groundnuts, nor that the production and trade of cattle slumped so as to force labour back into agriculture.[36] As time passed farmers from more remote areas produced for export markets, but even with the growth of the export economy in the 1950s rural economic opportunity failed to diversify. Peasant farmers, who were taxed heavily in comparison to merchants, also had to bear considerable risks inherent in farming in a region where climate was unreliable, although the magnitude of the risk involved was not apparent during the relatively good climate of the 1930s to the 1960s and became evident only later. Under the pressure of competition from imports, local industries, and in particular spinning and weaving, dwindled to insignificance. The only exceptions were certain local specialities such as pottery and leather crafts. Commerce was the only sector of the economy where profits were large enough to permit the evolution of large-scale indigenous enterprise. Nigériens occupied positions once held by expatriate merchants, but the modest progress of local people should not gloss over the lack of structural change in the peasant export economy and the similarity of the role of commerce in 1935 and 1960.

When applied to central Niger, the model of the open economy adequately describes the peasant export sector, but it fails to take account of pastoral activities and livestock trade, both of which were important in the area long before groundnut exports and in all likelihood will overshadow groundnut cultivation in the future. Livestock trade falls outside the provisions of the model because it is not destined for overseas markets, because the colonial government found it difficult to tax both stock-breeders and livestock traders, and because livestock trade did not come under expatriate control. What is needed is a more complex description of centre-periphery relations. Chapter VI, which dealt with the pastoral economy, indicated some implications of increasing specialization within the pastoral sector, competition of pastoral and sedentary land use, and the long-term modification of modes of interdependence between pastoral and sedentary production. The extensive treatment of livestock trade in Chapter VII pointed out that economic growth in areas closely linked to the international economy had spin-off effects farther away, and that production of animal protein in the Sahel depended on the growth of markets nearer the coast.

Conclusion

This book tells the story of people whose lives were transformed at a time of changing relations between an isolated region of the West African Sahel, a wider West African region, and the world economy. In the nineteenth century Damagaram and Damergu participated in desert-edge regional trade which arose from the differing production of various ecological zones and the specialization of their inhabitants. Zinder and the surrounding countryside became a crossroads for both regional trade in staple items such as animals, kola, salt, dates, cloth, and the products of other local craft industries, and for the import – export trade of desert caravans. The prosperity of a major trans-Saharan route encouraged the growth of local production for the market and trade in these staple items, and in the 1870s a shift in external trade allowed scope for peasant exports and foreshadowed greater peasant participation in export activities in the twentieth century. Toward the end of the century traders from Damagaram, who had hitherto limited themselves to networks along the desert edge and in the northern Sokoto Caliphate, began to enter southern trading networks in greater numbers. And so for the first time traders from the northern edge of Hausa settlement began to participate fully in a general process of Hausa commercial expansion which had begun earlier and reflected vigorous indigenous economic growth.

Within each of the two major productive regimes – pastoral nomadism and sedentary agriculture – social stratification was a major determinant of the organization of production. For example the Tuareg, the masters of the desert sector, combined market and non-market sources to obtain grain; they traded desert products in savannah markets, but they also used force to enslave agricultural labourers and demand tribute from other sedentary farmers under their control. Hausa and Kanuri who ruled sedentary states also dominated servile agricultural labourers living on plantations, and taxed the remaining population of sedentary farmers. But the prevalence of relations of inequality should not obscure the countervailing principle of social mobility, since slaves in both systems could and did improve their lot. In the Tuareg system, people of servile strata had to be free to move in order to save themselves in case of drought and to take advantage of seasonal pasture and seasonal opportunities to trade. Constant supervision of slaves was therefore impossible, and they could use private earnings to better their condition. The status of slave, as was the case with other low-status positions in the Tuareg social hierarchy, referred not to a permanent position, but rather to recent entry into desert society, incomplete acculturation, and limited claims on scarce productive resources. During drought, low-status Tuareg, who had only tenuous access to resources, had to leave the desert and take up farming temporarily. In the case of trade specialists living in urban communities, upward mobility was common. And the same was true among people recruited into the households of traders of backgrounds other than Tuareg, as case studies among the merchants of Zinder have demonstrated. Among sedentary farmers a major instrument of upward mobility was conversion to Islam; sedentary states raided and enslaved outlying non-Muslim people, but the descendants of these slaves who had been forcibly integrated into the economy of the central area of the Caliphate and its northern neighbours usually converted to Islam.

Available evidence does not indicate major change in the institutions of slavery in the desert sector in the last half of the nineteenth century. But it is clear that the rise of exports of ostrich feathers and tanned goat skins did enhance the power of the Imezureg, a Tuareg group well placed to benefit from the taxation of the dry-season export earnings of peasants they controlled. Although available evidence on the sedentary sector is far from clear, the blockage of overseas exports of slaves may have promoted increase use of slaves on plantations in Damagaram, in all probability through the mechanism of declining relative prices for slaves, especially during the period of general economic prosperity and military success after 1870.

The twentieth century ushered in a series of far-reaching changes which combined to bring about severe decline in the desert-edge sector. The colonial occupation coincided with a climatic downturn which culminated in a devastating drought in 1911–14. Conflict between the French and Tuareg, while reflecting an existing economic crisis brought on by requisitions of camels, also greatly worsened its effects. The Tuareg economy was so seriously affected that some forms of economic activity such as the salt trade were still in the process of recovering to their former level in 1950. The period 1900–20 was also a time of trouble for sedentary farmers because bad climate coincided with taxation of trade and with black market currency profiteering. In addition the reorientation of trade which occurred when the railroad reached Kano affected both sectors. The collapse of trans-Saharan trade deprived desert people of revenue they once earned from escorting and providing transport for passing caravans. In the savannah and Sahel exports of ostrich feathers ceased, a casualty of changing European fashion, and Sahelian exporters of tanned skins lost their locational advantage. Producers nearer the railway received better prices for hides and skins, and in addition the advent of modern transport made over-seas exports of groundnuts possible and profitable. Economic decline in Niger contrasted sharply with growth in Nigeria, where the drought of 1911–14 was less severe and therefore constituted a much less serious shock to the economy than in Niger.

The economic crisis of the early colonial period interrupted a pattern of pre-colonial economic growth in which desert and savannah shared a relatively equal footing. Whereas both Hausa and Tuareg trading networks participated in a general expansion of internal commerce in the nineteenth century, after the revolt of 1916 the Tuareg network lay in ruins. Previously the Tuareg system had formed an important link between desert and savannah. But when southern demand for livestock increased in the twentieth century, Hausa merchants transmitted the pull of these southern markets into the Sahel by extending the capacity and geographical scope of their networks. The release of servile labour from the desert during and after the revolt of 1916 added a new element to savannah trade, but by and large these newly arrived *bugaje* entered the lowest level of savannah commerce, namely the exchange of grain for potash. Few *bugaje* had the capital to trade animals, and none had camels to make the trek to Bilma for salt. Hence the main regional impact of the decline of the Tuareg network was to provide further stimulus to Hausa commercial expansion which had been under way for over a century and a half.

Although economic decline during the period 1900–20 affected all branches of commerce, livestock trade escaped the worst effects of the depressed conditions for a number of reasons. First, cattle are mobile merchandise, so that the remoteness of the Sahel from modern transportation and its disadvantages compared to northern Nigeria were of little consequence. In Nigeria the mobility of livestock enabled old methods of taking animals to market to compete with modern transport, and so droving routes co-existed with rail and lorry transport. Second, livestock trade remained relatively free from government taxation or control, and this was especially significant during the period between about 1910 and 1920 when the French taxed trade heavily. Third, cattle and other stock from the Sahel continued to be marketed despite the drought and the crisis in the Tuareg economy because Ful'be moved north to take advantage of pasture in the Sahel and steppe. Hence a small flow of migrants against the main southward current of migration allowed livestock production and trade to continue near its former level. Finally, livestock trade survived because merchants could barter cloth, iron tools, pottery, and articles manufactured from leather and wood for stock, thereby avoiding problems inherent in monetary transactions at a time of massive redistribution of wealth that took place because of currency profiteering.

Perhaps the most important conclusion about the early colonial period, aside from findings about the severity, causes, and consequences of the economic crisis in central Niger, concerns the impact of monetary policy. This study has been able to document the effects of profiteering made possible by scarcities of money and disparities between official and unofficial exchange rates at all levels in the currency – between francs and sterling, between francs and cowries, between paper and silver francs, and between French coins of large and small denominations. Hints of profiteering of a similar nature appear in the historical literature of the early colonial period elsewhere in Africa, but this is a subject for future research. Another unanswered question of a larger scope concerns the economic effects of forty years of extreme monetary tightness, as indicated by the willingness of the French authorities to accept sterling in tax payments into the treasury. This, too, is a topic for future research.

Economic growth began again in central Niger in the 1920s and 1930s but within a far different structural framework. The brief revival of trans-Saharan trade between 1870 and 1900 had been financed by capital from Europe and North Africa, but Ghadamasi and their associates in the Sudan operated without the networks of dependent local traders which came to be the hallmark of the new export trade. The new era began with an expatriate French merchant dominating commerce in Zinder, and he was followed in 1935 by international trading companies such as S.C.O.A., which had been attracted to Niger by the development of groundnut exports. A peasant export economy took root late in Niger because of the remoteness of the area, and it arrived during the height of the depression. Although the depression would seem to be the least favourable time for growth of exports, French price supports for groundnuts encouraged large-scale production in Niger for the first time in 1933–7 and contrasted sharply with depressed conditions elsewhere in Africa in other commodity markets.

The transition to a peasant export economy, as most previous interaction between the Central Sudan and the world economy, lagged behind similar developments in coastal regions. In the Central Sudan the shift from slave exports to legitimate trade, which began earlier on the coast, took place gradually between 1850 and 1880. In some areas increasingly close contact with the world economy produced a rapid rise in the volume of import–export trade between 1870 and 1914; this also occurred in the Central Sudan, but the growth of trade from the northern, desert-side sector was cut short by decline on trans-Saharan routes after 1900.

Although sources for economic history between 1935 and 1960 are more sparse than for the earlier period, certain conclusions about the economy of central Niger are warranted. First, the structure of the economy changed little in this quarter-century, with exports of groundnuts continuing to dominate opportunities for export income in sedentary agriculture and exports of livestock predominant in the pastoral sector. Second, commerce was the only noticeably profitable activity and the only sector of the economy in which profits allowed the accumulation of wealth to be inherited or passed on within indigenous firms. Only in commerce was it possible to create units of production larger than those usually found in agriculture and craft industries, where the largest unit might include a man, his married sons, their womenfolk, and their dependants. Third, merchants of local origin used their familiarity with local markets and applied political pressure to move up in the commercial hierarchy and occupy positions once taken exclusively by expatriates and Nigerians.

The concluding sections in the chapters of this book provide summaries of findings, and so it would perhaps be more useful to the reader to use the remaining space to assess the limits of available historical source material. A question of general importance concerns historical change in the welfare of ordinary farmers and herders: was their life richer, less hazardous, and easier in 1960 than in 1850? Economic historians have had little success answering this question for other regions of Africa, and this study runs up against similar obstacles. To be sure once the colonizers had imposed peace on their own terms the danger of warfare and slave raiding sub- sided; but acceptance of the terms of the colonizers was not without cost, as this study has demonstrated. And various segments of the population, including those at the lowest level, suffered. A crude accounting of costs and benefits is of course fruitless, and other approaches to the issue of welfare are no more useful. It is impossible to generate an appropriate physiological measure of welfare, such as the incidence of malnutrition or other kinds of material deprivation for any period covered by this study. Nor can economic indices of welfare be assessed, such as levels of income, or changes in income, changes in distribution of income, or the net effects of increasing overseas trade in the period after World War II. For example, a case for improved welfare at the lowest levels of society cannot be argued on the basis of gains from trade. Such an argument would contend that farmers and herders received greater revenues from trade as they participated more fully in regional and international networks: but this study has also raised issues which suggest that a large part of this added income may have been used to purchase items once produced locally. For example local craft industries declined and the scope open to rurally-based small-scale traders, who once travelled to supply themselves with cloth and raw cotton, decreased as time passed.

Perhaps the most that can be said about historical change in welfare is a rough periodization which attempts to follow the experience of various groups. The first two decades of the century represented a time of troubles for most who came into contact with the colonial administration or felt the impact of its policies. Especially hard hit were Tuareg nomads, while Ful'be fared better and migrated northward against the main flow as most other branches of pastoral activity declined. Among sedentary farmers those who fared best were people who turned to cattle trade and managed to stay in business despite the hazards of their occupation. From 1920 to 1940 the situation improved for most except those engaged in local cloth production, who had to look for other dry season occupations. In this period newly sedentarized Tuareg of low status adjusted to their new environment; urban merchants, including the remnants of the North African trading community, following adjustments before 1920 which had proved catastrophic to some, by and large found places in import–export trade. An élite of local merchants, with Al-Hajj Mukhtar in the vanguard, worked their way into groundnut trade. Following World War II renewed growth in the export sector permitted further gains by this élite of merchants and road transporters. Exceptionally good climate in the late 1950s and 1960s, as shown by rainfall records throughout the Sudano-Sahelian zone and by levels of Lake Chad, benefited farmers, who pushed the margin of cultivated land northward, and herders, whose nomadic life enabled them to exploit the seasonal pasture and water resources of the steppe and southern desert.

In the period covered by this study aridity replaced remoteness as the principal constraint on economic growth. An unanswered question, though it is perhaps about the future more than the past, concerns the effects on the ecosystem of extreme specialization in the production of livestock and groundnuts for regional or overseas exports. Given current techniques of production and patterns of access to resources, is the human and animal population of central Niger large enough to cause irreversible deterioration of vegetation and serious wind and water erosion of the soil? Some pessimistic views of the future of the Sahel also point to various means by which human activity can affect the atmosphere and even lead to changes in the climate.

In order to answer these questions more and better research is needed. Because almost no reliable information is available on historical changes in the level of population, economic history and historical demography have little to contribute to the narrow issue of population loads. But the crude hypothesis of inexorably advancing desert should be rejected out of hand because it ignores historical patterns of decline and recovery. In addition, support for this hypothesis usually refers to a base period in the 1950s and 1960s when the climate was exceptionally favourable, or in the more enlightened versions of the argument, to the nineteenth century, which was also a time of good climate.[1]

Arguments which refer only to population growth and the effects of overgrazing and overcropping represent a regrettably unilinear view of historical economic change. This study suggests an alternative framework for evaluating the present problems of the Sahel. In order to develop this framework, it is necessary to refer to the functions of the pre-colonial Tuareg economic network and to changes which interfered with these functions. The Tuareg network had a special importance far out of proportion to the number of people it encompassed or the size of its output because it permitted economic integration on a regional scale. In particular, the Tuareg system permitted reactions to drought at all levels of society; it allowed warrior aristocrats to shift labour between stock-breeding, agriculture, and commerce; and it permitted them to reinvest the profits of animal husbandry in less risky enterprises in the savannah. The system had considerable drawbacks when viewed from the bottom instead of from the top, since it perpetuated an unequal distribution of wealth and power and caused suffering among those brought into the system as slaves. But whatever the drawbacks, it guaranteed its members, including those at the lowest levels of society, access to savannah resources – pasture and water for herders and land to farm for those who lost their herds during drought. The Tuareg system disintegrated because it became increasingly anachronistic as time passed, both because it relied on servile labour and because nomads represented a locus of military power which was a real danger to the French administration. Although social stratification was repugnant to Europeans, they were willing to overlook the forms of servility they found in Tuareg society or to undermine them gradually. But the lesson of the revolt in 1916 was that the military power of the Tuareg, which was based both on geographical mobility and on the control of people and resources, could not be tolerated.

It is of course neither possible nor desirable to encourage stratification and the use of dependent labour to reappear. But other and more fundamental principles of desert–savannah interdependence must be recognized. In the past not only finished products but also factors of production such as labour and capital moved between sectors of the economy. This study has demonstrated how this pattern of interdependence was upset over the last eighty years by a chronic crisis in the pastoral economy, the weakening of Tuareg commercial networks in the savannah, changes in the patterns of access to land, new forms of taxation, and the rise of commercial agriculture in the savannah. In the twentieth century capital accumulated in the commercial sector has tended to stay in this sector rather than flowing to agriculture or being invested in live-stock. The main reason for the isolation of commerce in recent times is that entrepreneurs who might otherwise look for agricultural or pastoral investments have no effective way of controlling labour except within commercial enterprises. For agricultural investments, hired labour was a solution, but little capital accumulated in the commercial sector has been reinvested in this way. The explanation may be found in the costs of supervision involved in using hired labour, or in other factors which cause decreasing returns to scale. Or perhaps potential profits in agriculture are low compared to commerce; in any case, this is a topic for future research. In the case of limited reinvestment in livestock, the explanation is almost certainly to be found in the absence of suitable means for controlling labour. In the environment of central Niger large-scale stock breeding requires transhumance, and sedentary farmers or merchants have been unwilling to trust nomads with more than a few head of cattle, given the risk involved and the difficulty of ascertaining the truth should herders claim that animals entrusted to them have died or been lost or stolen.

The economic history of central Niger has several clear implications for development policy. First, it is essential to find new means of assuring pastoralists of access to savannah resources during drought. Second, planners should make efforts to encourage reinvestment of commercial capital in agriculture and stock-breeding. Third, indigenous models for controlling labour such as those found in commercial enterprises merit further investigation for possible modification and application in non-commercial settings.

TABLE 1: Sudan Exports in Transit through Tripoli (£000)

	Ivory	Ostrich feathers	Tanned goat skins	Total
	£	£	£	£
1862	10	3	—	—
1863	13	6	—	—
1864	17	10	1.5	28.5
1865	15	12	1.5	28.5
1866	12	7	1	20
1867	—	—	—	—
1868	—	—	—	—
1869	25	12	2.1	39
1870	25	16	1.5	42.5
1871	40	30	8	78
1872	35	45	8	88
1873	30	40	—	—
1874	50	115	—	—
1875	60	125	—	—
1876	60	132	—	—
1877	—	—	—	—
1878	31	187	3.5	222
1879	21	235	11	267
1880	24	167.5	7.5	194
1881	16	152.5	12	181
1882	14	179	8	201
1883	15	236	11	262
1884	8	184	3	195
1885	12	85	4	101
1886	28	30	4	62
1887	20	15	5.5	40.5
1888	24.5	40	9	73.5
1889	18	55	15	88
1890	22	95	18	135
1891	30	80	17	127
1892	—	—	—	—
1893	28	56	38	122
1894	22	48	44	114
1895	8	45	51	104
1896	7	55	49	110.5
1897	7	66	48	121
1898	1.5	70	65	136.5
1899	4.5	58	59	121.5
1900	6	54	58.5	118.5
1901	2	28	49	79
1902	—	—	—	—
1903	3	21	43	64
1904	2	23	37	60

Sources: British consular estimates found in the Parliamentary Papers; for 1901,

TABLE 2: Indices of Ostrich Feather Imports to Tripoli, 1870–1900
(base = 1871)

	Index of Volume	Index of Price
1870	68.8	77.5
1871	100.0	100.0
1872	129.7	129.7
1873	115.8	115.8
1874	381.8	100.4
1875	379.3	109.8
1876	402.2	109.3
1877	—˙	—
1878	360.1	173.1
1879	399.6	196.0
1880	281.4	192.4
1881	289.0	175.8
1882	380.3	156.9
1883	554.0	141.9
1884	556.7	110.2
1885	312.6	90.6
1886	117.4	85.1
1887	70.5	70.8
1888	234.6	56.8
1889	389.2	47.1
1890	552.9	57.3
1891	424.7	62.7
1892	—	—
1893	395.1	47.2
1894	327.6	48.8
1895	316.6	47.3
1896	411.9	44.5
1897	487.3	45.1
1898	522.1	44.7
1899	374.1	60.9
1900	352.4	55.2
1901	181.6	52.8
1902	133.8	56.1
1903	100.2	55.8

Sources: Value of Tripoli imports from Table 1; prices of ostrich feathers at London from 'Statistical Abstract for the United Kingdom, 1870–1884', Parliamentary Papers, 1884–5, vol. 82; 'Statistical Abstract, 1884–1898', Parliamentary Papers, 1899, vol. 104; 'Statistical Abstract, 1891–1905', Parliamentary Papers, 1905, vol. 130.

TABLE 3: Exports of Tanned Goat Skins from Zinder 1905 to 1912, including Transit

	Trans-Saharan Exports	Coastal Exports
	kg	
1905	30,400	—
1906	65,500	—
1907	74,480	—
1908	124,640	—
1909	87,870	—
1910	—	—
1911	17,190	—
1912	—	11,400

Source: ADZ, Rapport commercial, 2ᵉ trimestre 1912.

TABLE 4: Twentieth-Century Droughts in the Central Sudan

Dates	Location	Severity
1900–3	Asawak	moderate
1901	Central Niger	slight
1911–14	Entire Sudano-Sahelian Zone	extremely serious
1927	Hausaland	moderate
1929	Central Niger	slight
1930–1	Western Niger	moderate drought but famine from locusts
1941–4	Hausaland	slight
1950–1	Central Niger, Hausaland	slight
1969–73	Entire Sudano-Sahelian Zone	extremely serious

Sources: E. Bernus, 'Drought in the Niger Republic', *Savanna*, 2 (1973), 129–31; Michael Mortimore, 'Famine in Hausaland, 1973', *Savanna*, 2 (1973), 103–7; A. T. Grove, 'A Note on the Remarkably Low Rainfall of the Sudan Zone in 1913', *Savanna*, 2 (1973), 133–8; A. T. Grove, 'Desertification in the African Environment', *African Affairs*, 73 (1974), 137–51; W. Gerald Matlock and E. Lendell Cockrum, *A Framework for Evaluating Strategies for the Development of the Sahel-Sudan Region: Vol. II, A Framework for Agricultural Development Planning*, Center for Policy Alternatives, Report No. CPA-74-9 (Cambridge, Mass.), 78–9; see also Sharon E. Nicholson, 'A Climatic Chronology for Africa: Synthesis of Geological, Historical, and Meteorological Information and Data', Ph.D. dissertation, University of Wisconsin–Madison, 1976.

TABLE 5: Volume of Trade in Salt and Dates from Fachi and Bilma,
1908–1953[1]

	Annual Total	Autumn Caravan
		metric tons
1908	n.a.	1,425
1911	n.a.	2,232
1912	2,472	2,232
1913	n.a.	2,375
1914	n.a.	1,900
1915	n.a.	1,235
1916	n.a.	n.a.
1917	n.a.	0
1918	n.a.	19
1919	n.a.	66
1920	456	323
1921	613	433
1922	755	644
1923	767	592
1924	814	719
1925	815	737
1926	n.a.	715
1927	n.a.	920
1928	n.a.	963
1929	n.a.	968
1930	n.a.	n.a.
1931	n.a.	1,010
1932	1,086	787
1933	1,189	821
1934	1,470	1,064
1935	1,432	821
1936	1,786	1,254
1937	1,672	1,048
1938	2,086	1,611
1939	1.331	788
1940	1,448	1,030
1941	n.a.	n.a.
1942	n.a.	1,833
1951	n.a.	2,470
1952	n.a.	1,805
1953	n.a.	2,185

[1]The tonnage was computed from the count of the number of camels returning from the oases loaded on the average with 95 kg each, a figure generally agreed upon in early French archival and printed sources. The count of the number of camels can be considered to be accurate since loaded camels were subject to a tax levied and collected by the French.

Sources:
1908: Archives Nationales du Sénégal, ID 203, 'Rapport du Lieut. Ronjat au sujet de l'escorte de la caravane de Fachi, 1908'.
1911: Archives Nationales du Sénégal, 2G 12-18, Niger, Rapport politique, 1911.
1912: Archives Nationales du Niger, Monographies – Bilma, Monographie de Bilma, 1912, unsigned, Bilma, 31 Dec., 1912; Archives Nationales de France – Section Outre-Mer, Niger, Rapport politique, 4e trimestre, 1912.
1913–14: Archives Nationales du Sénégal, 11G 16, Mourin, 'Rapport sur l'exploitation des salines et mares de natron au Territoire Militaire du Niger en 1915'.
1915: Archives Nationales du Sénégal, 2G 15-11, Niger, Rapport d'ensemble, 1915.
1917–19: Archives Nationales du Sénégal, 2G 19-9, Niger, Rapport économique d'ensemble 1919.
1920–40: Archives Nationales du Niger, Monographies – Bilma, J. Périé, 'Carnet monographique du canton de Bilma, 1941'.
1941–2: Archives Nationales du Niger, Monographies – Bilma, P. Gentil, 'Aux confins du Niger et du Tchad', 1943.
1951: Archives Nationales du Niger, Monographies – Bilma, Lejeune, 'Carnet monographique du canton de Kawar', 20 Aug. 1952.
1952–3: Jean Questiaux, 'Quelques aspects de l'économie salinière dans les territoires d'Afrique nord-occidentale et centrale', unpublished doctoral thesis, University of Algiers, 1957.

TABLE 6: Overseas Imports of Salt into Niger, 1913–1937

Salt Imports
metric tons

1913	12
1914	37
1916	61
1917	137
1918	45
1924	153
1925	128
1926	206
1928	630
1929	365
1930	470
1931	135
1932	285
1933	351
1934	372
1935	477
1936	683
1937	312

Sources: ANS, 2G 14-11, Niger, Rapport d'ensemble, 1914; ANS, 2G 16-12, Niger Rapport d'ensemble, 1916; ANS, 2G 18-6, Niger, Rapport d'ensemble, 1918; A.O.F., *Statistiques commerciales de l'A.O.F. en 1928* (Paris, 1929); A.O.F., Agence Économique, *Annuaire statistique* (Paris, 1934), I. 66; 1935, II. 68; 1936, II. 69; 1938, III. 70.

TABLE 7: Index of Terms of Trade of Pastoral Products for Millet

	Three-year-old export steer (1903=100)	Pack camel, average size (1908=100)	Salt, by weight (1903=100)
1903	100		100
1908	26	100	
1909	48	154	
1920	425	2,350	511
1926	91	302	
1934[1]	29	161	16
1935[1]	27	120	14
1936[1]	59	255	22
1937	79	460	
1938[2]	104		111
1940[2]			122
1941[2]	128	510	166
1949	28	37	
1952	85		
1957	68		22
1960	57		22
1966	108		

[1]Average prices of produce exported from Zinder to Nigeria.

[2]Range of prices in a series of transactions which took place in Tanout, adjusted for geographical differential from Zinder by raising cattle, camel, and salt prices by 10 per cent.

Sources: See Appendix.

TABLE 8: Volume of Trade in Cattle, Sheep, and Goats Crossing the
Rail Bridge at Jebba, on the Hoof and by Rail, 1928–1950

	Cattle			Sheep and Goats		
	Hoof	Rail	Total	Hoof	Rail	Total
1928	67,968					
1929	70,922					
1930	73,520					
1932	90,291	39,895	130,186			
1933	103,967	46,921	150,888			
1934	91,225	23,730·	114,955			
1936	100,847	23,590	124,437	79,198	10,946	90,144
1937	94,396	32,104	126,400	85,000	27,455	112,455
1938	69,812	31,582	101,399	86,000	18,663	104,663
1939	88,233	37,523	125,756	93,387	17,200	110,587
1940–1	96,538	62,798	159,336	100,116		
1941–2		54,026				
1944		75,317				
1946–7		62,269				
1948		87,634				
1949		107,635				
1950		109,341				

Sources: PRO, CO/651/36, Northern Nigeria, 'Annual Report of the Veterinary
Department, 1933'; CO/657/38, Veterinary Report, 1934; CO/657/50, Trade
Report, 1938; CO/657/47, Veterinary Report, 1939; CO/657/54, Annual Report for
the Government Railway, 1940–1; CO/657/58, Annual Railway Report, 1946;
CO/657/56, Annual Report, 1944; CO/657/63, Agriculture Report, 1948;
CO/657/65, Veterinary Report, 1950. PRO, CO/657/31, Nigeria, Annual Report of
the Northern Provinces; CO/657/27, Annual Report of the Northern Provinces,
1930; CO/657/36, Veterinary Report, 1933; R. Scott, 'Production for Trade', in *The
Native Economies of Northern Nigeria*, ed. M. Perham (London, 1945), 277.

APPENDIX I

Prices of Millet, Cattle, Camels, and Salt in Zinder

Money circulated freely in the economy of pre-colonial Damagaram, with cowries and Maria Theresa thalers serving as the medium of exchange. For several decades in the early twentieth century, these currencies were used simultaneously with French money, and Maria Theresa thalers still circulate today, at least in limited quantities. Despite the fact that money played an important role in the economy, the relative prices of goods are preferable for the purposes of economic history. The first problem with price series is that the price of one commodity cannot be taken in isolation. When a large volume of trade takes place across an ecological frontier, the determinant of product mix and the allocation of resources is best represented by the terms of trade of one good for another. The second problem with prices expressed in money is the persistent inflation of the French franc, especially after 1940. A suitable price deflator would be derived from a cost of living index based on the budget of the average family. Throughout most of the period in question, the average Nigérien consumer bought almost no manufactured goods from overseas save cloth. Nomadic Ful'be bought cloth manufactured in Kano, not in Europe, for the most part. For this reason, the use of French price deflators is unwarranted, since they are weighted according to the budgets of French consumers. No long-term African cost of living index is available, and none can be constructed for Niger because of the paucity of price data on cloth. Money prices of key commodities are listed here for reference in the event of more data becoming available.

TABLE 9: Post-harvest Millet Prices in Zinder, 1903–1962

current price in French francs
(CFA 1949 and after)

	kg
1902	0.10
1903	0.075
1908	0.12–0.15
1909	0.05–0.12
1915	0.04
1917	0.04
1918	0.04
1920	0.05
1926	0.35
1934[1]	0.35
1935[1]	0.40
1936[1]	0.25
1938	0.24
1940	0.30
1941	0.37
1949	15.0
1952	10.0–10.5
1957	15.0
1960	20.0
1966	15.0

Sources:
1902: Guy Nicolas, 'Circulation des richesses et participation sociale dans une société Hausa du Niger' (Bordeaux, 1967, mimeographed), 222.
1908, 1909, 1915: Nicolas, 'Circulation', 222.
1917: ADZ, Commandant Zinder to Commandant Magaria, 14 Mar. 1918.
1920: ADZ, Administrateur, *Cercle* Zinder to Governor, Territory of Niger, 1 Aug. 1922.
1926: ADZ, Économie Générale, Procès-verbal de réunion du conseil des notables, 27 Apr. 1926.
1934, 1935, 1936: ANS, 2G 36–7, Niger, 'Rapport économique, 1936'.
1938–1941: ASTa, Register for local expenditures, 1938–42.
1949: ADZ, file marked 'Situation alimentaire', Chef de la subdivision centrale to Commandant Zinder, 21 Dec. 1949.
1952: ADZ, Ville de Zinder, Commandant de Police, Rapport Mensuel, janvier 1952.
1957, 1960: République du Niger, Ministère des Affaires Économiques, *Bulletin trimestriel de statistique*, no. 6, 11.
1966: personal experience.

[1]Average prices of produce exported from Zinder to Nigeria.

TABLE 10: Post-harvest Cattle Prices in Zinder, 1903–1966

current price in French francs
(CFA 1949 and after)

	head
1903	66
1908	30
1909	30
1911	40
1916	30–55
1920	150–225
1921	110–150
1926	175–400
1927	200–250
1934[1]	90
1935[1]	92
1936[1]	130
1938	150–275
1941	200–400
1949	3,500–4,000
1952	7,500
1957	9,000
1960	12,000
1966	18,444–10,400

Sources:
1903: ADZ, 'Rapport Agricole, juin 1903'.
1908: ADZ, 'Rapport Commercial, 4e trimestre 1908'.
1909: ADZ, 'Rapport Commercial, 3e trimestre 1909'.
1911: ADZ, 'Rapport Commercial, 4e trimestre 1911'.
1916: ADZ, Commandant Zinder to Commissaire du Gouvernement Général AOF au Niger, 21 June 1916.
1920: ANS, 2G 20-12, Niger, 'Rapport d'ensemble, 1920'.
1921: ANS, 2G 21-5, Niger, 'Situation Économique, 1921'.
1926: ADZ, file marked 'Économie Générale,' Procès-verbal de réunion du Conseil des Notables, 27 Apr. 1926.
1927: ANS, 2G 27-9(1), Niger, 'Notice Économique, 3e trimestre 1927'.
1934–6: ANS, 2G 36-7, Niger, 'Rapport Économique, 1936'.
1938–41: ASTa, Register for local expenditures, 1938–42.
1949: ADZ, file marked 'Situation alimentaire', Chef de la subdivision centrale to Commandant de Cercle, Zinder, 21 Dec. 1949.
1952: R. Larrat, *Problèmes de la viande en AOF: les principaux marchés: zones de production Haute Volta, Niger* (Paris, 1954–5), II. 38.
1957–60: République Française, Secrétariat d'État aux Affaires Étrangères, *Approvisionnement en viandes de l'Afrique Centre Ouest* (Paris, 1968), I. 336–7.
1966: République Française, *Approvisionnement en viandes*, I. 291.

[1]Average prices of produce exported from Zinder to Nigeria.

Table 11: Post-harvest Camel Prices in Zinder, 1908–1949

current price in French francs
(CFA for 1949)

	head
1908	100
1909	80
1920	750–1,000
1921	500–750
1926	400–1,500
1934[1]	410
1935[1]	350
1936[1]	475
1936	750–1,000
1941	1,000–1,500
1949	3,500–5,000

Sources:

1908: ADZ, 'Rapport Commercial, 4e trimestre 1908'.
1909: ADZ, 'Rapport Commercial, 3e trimestre 1909'.
1920: ANS, 2G 20-12, Niger, 'Rapport d'ensemble, 1920'.
1921: ANS, 2G 21-5, Niger, 'Situation Économique, 1921'.
1926: ADZ, file marked 'Économie Générale', Procès-verbal de la réunion du conseil des notables, 27 Apr. 1926; Dugald Campbell, *On the Trail of the Veiled Tuareg* (London, 1928), 67.
1934–6: ANS, 2G 36-7, Niger, 'Rapport Économique, 1936'.
1936: ANS, 2G 37-47, Niger, Service Zootechnique, 'Rapport Annuel, 1937'.
1941: AAN, Monographs of Zinder, Puliani, 'Rapport sur le recensement du canton de Guidimouni', 17 Oct. 1941.
1949: ADZ, file marked 'Situation Alimentaire', Chef de la subdivision centrale to Commandant de Cercle, 21 Dec. 1949.

[1]Average prices of produce exported from Zinder to Nigeria.

TABLE 12: Post-harvest Salt Prices in Zinder, 1903–60

current price in French francs
(CFA 1949 and after)

	kg
	kg
1903	0.70
1920	2.0–2.6
1934[1]	0.53
1935[1]	0.55
1936[1]	0.50
1938	2.0
1940	3.0
1941	5.0
1957	30.0
1960	30.0

Sources:
1903: ADZ, 'Rapport Agricole, juin 1903'.
1920: ANS, 2G 21-5, Niger, 'Situation Économique, 1921'.
1934–6: ANS, 2G 36-7, Niger, 'Rapport Économique, 1936'.
1938–41: ASTa, Register for local expenditures, 1938–42.
1957: J. Questiaux, 'Quelques aspects de l'économie salinière dans les territoires d'Afrique nord-occidentale et centrale', doctoral thesis, University of Algiers, 1957, 156.
1960: Companie Générale des Recherches pour l'Afrique, 'Analyse des Courants d'Échange' (Paris, 1961, mimeographed), vol. 1, 25.

[1]Average prices of produce exported from Zinder to Nigeria.

APPENDIX II

Results of a Survey of the Zinder Cattle Market, April–December 1972

1. *Translation of the Questionnaire (originally in Hausa)*

Name	Father's name
Age	
Ethnic origin	
Residence:	village
	canton
Occupation:	rainy season
	dry season
Father's occupation:	rainy season
	dry season

Where did father live and work?

Is father still alive?

Father's present residence

If father was a trader, what form of commerce did he engage in?

Grandfather's occupation (paternal):	rainy season
	dry season

Where did grandfather live and work?

Is grandfather still alive?

Grandfather's present residence

Do you trade on your own account?

If you have a patron, is he a relative?

What relation is he to you?

Patron's name?   Patron's father's name

Patron's present residence

Is your patron the son of a cattle trader or a *dillali*?

If you are a *dillali*, where do you work? Which markets?

If you are a cattle trader, where do you work? Which markets do you visit?

Do you learn to trade from a relative
or from someone who is not from
your kinship group? If from a relative,
which one?

2. *Ethnic groups of Client Traders Surveyed by Region*

	Hausa	Ful'be	Buzu	Kanuri	No response
Tanout	1	0	2	7	6
Zinder (city)	0	0	3	0	0
Matameye-Magaria	14	0	9	2	9
Zinder (area)	11	0	4	4	14
Nigeria	5	0	0	0	0
Total	31	0	18	13	29

3. *Partnerships and Kinship*

Partnership with:

Father	2	Father-in-law	0
Uncle	7	Cousin	3
Elder brother, same father	3	Brother (not specified)	11
Elder brother, different father	1	Brother (not specified) same father	4
Younger brother, same father	4	Wife	1
		Relative, not specified	5
Younger brother, different father	1	No response	24
Partner not related	49		

Notes

INTRODUCTION

1. Sahel means shore in Arabic, and if the desert is thought of as an ocean, the word is an apt metaphor for the land at the southern desert edge. In this study the term refers to an east–west strip of land extending 100 or 200 kilometres either side of an ecological frontier which divides a northern, arid region suitable only for pastoral nomadism from the southern, fertile lands where rainfall is sufficient for cultivation. The usage is therefore more restricted than that of journalists and planners, who often use Sahel to refer to the desert-edge countries of West Africa.
2. E. W. Bovill, *Caravans of the Old Sahara: An Introduction to the History of the Western Sudan* (London, 1933); revised as *The Golden Trade of the Moors* (London, 1958); and revised and with additional material by Robin Hallett (London, 1968).
3. A. Adu Boahen, *Britain, the Sahara and the Western Sudan 1788–1861* (Oxford, 1964).
4. J.-L. Miège, *Le Maroc et l'Europe*, 4 vols. (Paris, 1961–3).
5. C. W. Newbury, 'North African and Western Sudan Trade in the Nineteenth Century: A Re-evaluation', *Journal of African History*, 7 (1966), 233–46; Marion Johnson, 'Calico Caravans', *Journal of African History*, 17 (1976), 95–117.
6. Louis Brenner, 'The North African Trading Community in the Nineteenth-Century Central Sudan', in *Aspects of West African Islam*, ed. D. F. McCall and N. R. Bennett (Boston, 1971), 137–71.
7. Johnson, 'Calico Caravans', 95–117.
8. Philip D. Curtin, *Economic Change in Precolonial Africa: Senegambia in the Era of the Slave Trade* (Madison, 1975).
9. A. G. Hopkins, *An Economic History of West Africa* (New York, 1973), 243–53; Paul E. Lovejoy, 'The Hausa Kola Trade (1700–1900): A Commercial System in the Continental Exchange of West Africa', Ph.D. dissertation, University of Wisconsin–Madison, 1973; J. S. Hogendorn, 'The Origins of the Groundnut Trade in Northern Nigeria', Ph.D. dissertation, London School of Economics, 1966; and Jan S. Hogendorn, *Nigerian Groundnut Exports: Origins and Early Development* (London and Zaria, 1978).

CHAPTER I

1. Frederik Barth, 'A General Perspective on Nomad-Sedentary Relations in the Middle East', in *The Desert and the Sown: Nomads in the Wider Society*, ed. Cynthia Nelson (Berkeley, 1973), 11–22; see also Frederik Barth, *Ethnic Groups and Boundaries* (Bergen, 1969), introduction and *passim*.
2. A good though non-historical introduction to climate and physical environment

in West Africa is found in W. B. Morgan and J. C. Pugh, *West Africa* (London, 1969), 176–206.

3. H. T. Norris, *The Tuaregs: Their Islamic Legacy and Its Diffusion in the Sahel* (Warminster, 1975), 13–14, 75–6; Johannes Nicolaisen, *Structures politiques et sociales des Touaregs de l'Air et de l'Ahaggar*, trans. S. Bernus (Paris, 1962), 21–36; Pierre Bonte, 'Esclavage et relations de dépendence chez les Touaregs Kel Gress', in *L'Esclavage en Afrique précoloniale*, ed. Claude Meillassaux (Paris, 1975), 51–2; for a history of climate in the Central Sudan, see Paul E. Lovejoy and Stephen Baier, 'The Desert-Side Economy of the Central Sudan', *International Journal of African Historical Studies*, 8 (1975), 551–81; and Sharon E. Nicholson, 'A Climatic Chronology for Africa: Synthesis of Geological, Historical, and Meteorological Information and Data', Ph.D. dissertation, University of Wisconsin–Madison, 1976, 123–5, 127–30, 134–45, and *passim*.

4. Camille–Charles Jean, *Les Touaregs du sud-est, leur rôle dans la politique saharienne* (Paris, 1909), 175–6; Lloyd C. Briggs, *Tribes of the Sahara* (Cambridge, Mass., 1960), 146.

5. Jean, *Touaregs du sud-est*, 102–11; Nicolaisen, *Structures politiques*, 28; Henri Lhote, *Les Touaregs du Hoggar* (Paris, 1955), 157.

6. Nicolaisen, *Structures politiques*, 27; Norris, *Tuaregs*, 74–5.

7. C. C. Stewart, 'Southern Saharan Scholarship and the *Bilad al-Sudan*', *Journal of African History*, 17 (1976), 73–94.

8. The discussion of stratification which follows is based on Nicolaisen, *Ecology and Culture of the Pastoral Tuareg* (Copenhagen, 1963), 439–46; Nicolaisen, *Structures politiques*, 100–7; Francis Rennell of Rodd, *People of the Veil* (London, 1926), 135–40; E. Bernus, 'Les Touaregs du sahel nigérien', *Cahiers d'Outre-Mer*, 19 (1966), 13–15; J. Clauzel, 'Les Hiérarchies sociales en pays touareg', *Travaux de l'Institut des Recherches Sahariennes*, 21 (1962), 120–75; A Richer, *Les Touaregs du Niger (région Tombouctou-Gao), les Ouilliminden* (Paris, 1924), 3–5; André Bourgeot, 'Idéologie et appelations ethniques: l'exemple Twareg', *Cahiers d'Études Africaines*, 48 (1972), 533–53. An extended discussion of the position of nobles at the head of enterprises with diverse economic activities is found in Lovejoy and Baier, 'Desert-Side Economy', 551–81. For a fuller treatment of Tuareg stratification, see Stephen Baier and Paul E. Lovejoy, 'The Tuareg of the Central Sudan: Gradations in Servility at the Desert Edge', in *Slavery in Africa: Historical and Anthropological Perspectives*, ed. Suzanne Miers and Igor Kopytoff (Madison, 1977), 391–411.

9. Bernus, 'Touaregs du sahel', 14–16; Lhote, *Touaregs du Hoggar*, 207; Guy Mainet, 'L'Élevage dans la région de Maradi', *Cahiers d'Outre-Mer*, 69 (1965), 32–72; Nicolaisen, *Structures politiques*, 100–7.

10. Henri Gaden, 'Notice sur la résidence de Zinder', *Revue des Troupes Coloniales*, 2, No. 17 (1903), 632; Rennell of Rodd, *People of the Veil*, 135–6; Clauzel, 'Hiérarchies sociales', 143–5; interview with Wuru 'dan Tambari Mayaki, 12 Oct. 1972 (tape 39).

11. Henri Duveyrier, *Les Touaregs du nord* (Paris, 1864), 334–5; Briggs, *Tribes*, 136–7; Rennell of Rodd, *People of the Veil*, 136–8; F. Nicolas, 'Notes sur la société et l'état chez les Twareg du Dinnink', *Bull. IFAN*, 1, No. 2–3 (1939), 580.

12. Nicolaisen, *Structures politiques*, 105; Clauzel, 'Hiérarchies sociales', 149–50; Lhote, *Touaregs du Hoggar*, 203–4, 208.

13. Jean Chapelle, *Nomades noirs du Sahara* (Paris, 1957), 344–74 and *passim*; Lieutenant Grall, 'Le Secteur nord du cercle de Gouré', *Bull. IFAN*, 7 (1945), 16–20; Joseph H. Greenberg, *The Languages of Africa* (Bloomington, Indiana, 1966), 163–77.

14. Chapelle, *Nomades noirs*, 113–14; Paul E. Lovejoy, 'The Hausa Kola Trade: A

Commercial System in the Continental Exchange of West Africa', Ph.D. dissertation, University of Wisconsin–Madison, 1973, 120; Y. Urvoy, *Histoire des populations du Soudan central* (Paris, 1936), 187–8; Louis Brenner, *The Shehus of Kukawa: A History of the Al-Kanemi Dynasty of Bornu* (London, 1973), 24; Capitaine Grandin, 'Notes sur l'industrie et le commerce du sel au Kawar et en Agram', *Bull. IFAN*, 13 (1951), 490–1.

15. Greenberg, *Languages of Africa*, 163–77; D. J. Stenning, *Savannah Nomads: A Study of the Wodaabe Pastoral Fulani of Western Bornu Province* (London, 1959), 7–21; Marguerite Dupire, *Peuls nomades, étude descriptive des Wodaabe du sahel nigérien* (Paris, 1962), 28; S. Hogben and A. M. H. Kirk-Greene, *The Emirates of Northern Nigeria* (London, 1966), 429.

16. Dupire, *Peuls nomades*, 23, 39, 130–2; C. E. Hopen, *The Pastoral Ful'be Family in Gwandu* (London, 1958), 17–40, 147–57; Marguerite Dupire, *Facteurs humaines de l'économie pastorale*, Études Nigériennes No. 6 (Paris, 1962).

17. Dupire, *Peuls nomades*, 155; 207, 215, 305; Hopen, *Pastoral Ful'be Family*, 139; Marguerite Dupire, 'Exploitation du sol, communautés résidentielles et organisation lignagère des pasteurs woDaaBe (Niger)', in *Pastoralism in Tropical Africa*, ed. T. Monod (London, 1975), 322–7. See also Marguerite Dupire, *Organisation sociale des Peuls, étude d'ethnographie comparée* (Paris, 1970).

18. August Tilho, *Documents scientifiques de la mission Tilho* (Paris, 1910–14), II, 403–55; on the eastern Sokoto Caliphate, see Victor N. Low, *Three Nigerian Emirates: A Study in Oral History* (Evanston, Illinois, 1972); for Borno, see Brenner, *Shehus of Kukawa*; for Damergu, see Stephen Baier, 'Trans-Saharan Trade and the Sahel: Damergu, 1870–1930', *Journal of African History*, 18 (1977), 37–60; for the far north-western fringe of Hausa settlement, see Marc-Henri Piault, *Histoire mawri, introduction à l'étude des processus constitutifs d'un état* (Paris, 1970); see also Guy Nicolas, 'Les Catégories d'ethnie et de fraction ethnique au sein du système social hausa', *Cahiers d'Études Africaines*, 15 (1975), 415–17.

19. Guy Nicolas and Guy Mainet, *La Vallée du Gulbi de Maradi, enquête socio-économique*, Documents des Études Nigériennes No. 16 (Bordeaux, 1964), 113–229.

20. Polly Hill, *Rural Hausa: A Village and a Setting* (Cambridge, 1972), 38.

21. Hill, *Rural Hausa*, 38–56; Nicolas and Mainet, *Gulbi de Maradi*, 164–5, 167 [as cited in Hill]; and Guy Nicolas, *Circulation des richesses et participation sociale dans une société hausa du Niger* (Bordeaux, 1967), 24–5, 57 [as cited in Hill].

22. Henri Raulin, 'Travail et régimes fonciers au Niger', *Cahiers de l'Institut de Science Économique Appliquée*, 166 (1965), 19–39; Hill, *Rural Hausa*, 40, 240–1, and *passim*; Roberta Ann Dunbar, 'Slavery and the Evolution of Nineteenth-Century Damagaram (Zinder, Niger)', in *Slavery in Africa: Historical and Anthropological Perspectives*, ed. Suzanne Miers and Igor Kopytoff (Madison, Wisconsin, 1977), 167–8; Mary Smith, *Baba of Karo: A Woman of the Muslim Hausa* (New York, 1954); 40–4.

23. T. Monod, 'Introduction', *Pastoralism in Tropical Africa* (London, 1975), 102. The best classification, which uses both occupation (herding, herding with agriculture, agriculture with herding, and agriculture) as well as residence pattern (nomadic, semi-nomadic, semi-sedentary, and sedentary) appears in Victor Piché and Joel Gregory, 'Pour une mise en contexte de la famine: le cas du Liptako-Gourma', in *Drought in Africa 2*, ed. David Dalby, R. J. Harrison Church, and Fatima Bezzaz (London, 1977), 174–5. Piché and Gregory note concentration at either end of the spectrum except for Ful'be, who may be found in all categories.

24. Michael Horowitz, 'Herdsman and Husbandman in Niger: Values and

Strategies', in *Pastoralism in Tropical Africa*, 397–401.
25. Baier, 'Trans-Saharan Trade and the Sahel', 46–54.
26. Dupire, *Peuls nomades*, 39.
27. Morgan and Pugh, *West Africa*, 356–72.
28. Joseph P. Smaldone, *Warfare in the Sokoto Caliphate: Historical and Sociological Perspectives* (Cambridge, 1977), 149.
29. Smaldone, *Warfare*, 39–53 and *passim*.
30. Cf. Jack Goody, *Technology, Tradition, and the State in Africa* (London, 1971), 21–56.
31. Smaldone, *Warfare*, 54–68.
32. The literature on the *jihad* of Usuman 'dan Fodio is vast, but several works are especially important. See Mervyn Hiskett, *The Sword of Truth: The Life and Times of Shehu Usuman Dan Fodio* (New York, 1973), 15–115; Murray Last, *The Sokoto Caliphate* (Longmans, 1967), 3–141; Marilyn R. Waldman, 'The Fulani *Jihad*: A Reassessment', *Journal of African History*, 6, No. 3 (1965), 333–55.
33. Paul E. Lovejoy, 'The Role of the Wangara in the Economic Transformation of the Central Sudan in the Fifteenth and Sixteenth Centuries', *Journal of African History*, 19 (1978), 183; Finn Fuglestad, 'A Reconstruction of Hausa History Before the Jihad', *Journal of African History*, 19 (1978), 319–40. Information on North African contacts is from Mark Dyer, personal communication about a forthcoming study using both written Arabic documentation and archeological sources.
34. Waldman, 'Fulani *Jihad*', 355; Smaldone, *Warfare*, 29–37.
35. M. G. Smith, 'A Hausa Kingdom: Maradi under Dan Baskore, 1854–1875', in *West African Kingdoms in the Nineteenth Century*, ed. D. Forde and P. Kaberry (London, 1967), 93–122; Philippe David, *Maradi, l'ancien état et l'ancienne ville*, Études Nigeriennes No. 18 (Paris-Niamey, 1965), 6–103.
36. Paul E. Lovejoy, 'Plantations in the Economy of the Sokoto Caliphate', *Journal of African History*, 19 (1978), 341–68; and Jan Hogendorn, 'The Economics of Slave Use on Two "Plantations" in the Zaria Emirate of the Sokoto Caliphate', *International Journal of African Historical Studies*, 10 (1977), 369–83; J. S. Hogendorn, 'Slave Acquisition and Delivery in Precolonial Hausaland', in *West African Culture Dynamics: Archeological and Historical Perspectives* (The Hague and Chicago, 1979). For a description of the economic history project conducted in 1975–6, see Paul Lovejoy and Jan Hogendorn, 'Oral Data Collection and the Economic History of the Central Savanna', *Savanna*, 7 (1978), 71–4.
37. Lovejoy, 'Plantations', 349 ff.
38. Nicolas, 'Catégories d'ethnie', 403–4; Guy Nicolas, *Dynamique sociale et appréhension du monde au sein d'une société hausa* (Paris, 1975), 11–217; see also Fuglestad, 'Hausa History Before the Jihad', 338–9.
39. Roberta Ann Dunbar, 'Damagaram (Zinder, Niger), 1812–1906: The History of a Central Sudanic Kingdom', Ph.D. dissertation, University of California at Los Angeles, 1970, 43–56.
40. Nicolas, *Dynamique sociale*, 38–40, 523–77; Nicolas, 'Catégories d'ethnie', 404. For Gobir, see especially Guy Nicolas, 'Fondements magico-religieux du pouvoir politique dans la principauté hausa du Gobir', *Journal de la Société des Africanistes*, 34 (1969), 199–232.
41. For an extended discussion of desert-savannah trade, see Lovejoy and Baier, 'Desert-Side Economy', 554–71.
42. Heinrich Barth, *Travels and Discoveries in North and Central Africa* (1857–59: reprinted ed., London: F. Cass, 1965), I. 389–94; Gaden, 'Notice', 626–8; Nicolaisen, *Pastoral Tuareg*, 209–17; and Dunbar, 'Damagaram', 203 ff.

43. Djibo Hamane, *Contribution à l'étude de l'histoire des états hausa: l'Adar précolonial (République du Niger)*, Études Nigériennes No. 38 (Niamey, 1975); Pierre Bonte, *L'Élevage et le commerce du bétail dans l'Ader-Doutchi-Majya*, Étude Nigériennes No. 23 (Niamey, 1967), 46 ff.; Capitaine Grandin, 'Notes sur l'industrie et le commerce du sel au Kawar et en Agram', *Bull. IFAN*, 13 (1951), 524; Commandant Gadel, 'Notes sur Bilma et les oasis environnantes', *Revue coloniale*, 7, No. 51 (1907), 374; Nicolaisen, *Pastoral Tuareg*, 209–16, 481–2.

44. For a detailed description of the Tuareg network, see Lovejoy and Baier, 'Desert-Side Economy', 564 ff.

45. Interview with Kelilan Gaja, 19 Apr. 1972 (tape 11); Bernus, 'Tuareg du sahel nigérien', 15.

46. Lovejoy and Baier, 'Desert-Side Economy', 562–3, 569–71; while this description applies to the Kel Ewey network, on the Kel Gress see Bonte, 'Esclavage et relations de dépendence'; see also Lina Brock, 'Innovation of Winter Season Vegetable Gardening among the Tamejirt, an Iklan Group of Northern Adar and Southern Azawagh Regions, Department of Tahoua, Republic of Niger', in *Colloquium on the Effects of Drought on the Productive Strategies of Sudan-Sahelian Herdsmen and Farmers*, Report of the Institute for Development Anthropology, Inc. (Binghamton, N.Y., 1976), 26–31.

47. Lovejoy, 'Hausa Kola Trade', *passim*; Paul E. Lovejoy, 'The Wholesale Kola Trade of Kano', *African Urban Notes*, 5 (1970), 129–42.

48. Marion Johnson, 'Cloth on the Banks of the Niger', *Journal of the Historical Society of Nigeria*, 6 (1973), 353–64; Paul E. Lovejoy, 'Interregional Monetary Flows in the Precolonial Trade of Nigeria', *Journal of African History*, 15 (1974), 565–74.

49. E. and S. Bernus, *Du sel et des dattes, introduction à l'étude de la communauté d'In Gall et de Tegidda-n-Tesemt*, Études Nigériennes No. 31 (Niamey, 1972), 1–46.

50. For salt production in the region, see Paul E. Lovejoy, 'The Salt Industry of the Central Sudan: A Preliminary Survey', paper presented at the Seminar on the Economic History of the Central Savannah of West Africa, Kano, 5–10, Jan. 1976; and Paul E. Lovejoy, 'The Borno Salt Industry', paper presented at the annual conference of the Canadian Association of African Studies, Ottowa, 2–5 May 1978. Research on mining was conducted in 1974–5 by David Tambo, a doctoral candidate at the University of Wisconsin–Madison.

51. Philip Shea, 'The Development of an Export-Oriented Dyed Cloth Industry in the Kano Emirate in the Nineteenth Century', Ph.D. dissertation, University of Wisconsin–Madison, 1975, 53–94.

52. Lovejoy, 'Plantations', 341–68.

53. Paul E. Lovejoy, 'The Kambarin Beriberi: The formation of a Specialized Group of Hausa Kola Traders in the Nineteenth Century', *Journal of African History*, 14 (1973), 633–52.

54. Lovejoy and Baier, 'Desert-Side Economy', 570–5.

55. A. T. Grove, 'A Note on the Remarkably Low Rainfall of the Sudan Zone in 1913'; *Savanna*, 2, No. 2 (1973), 133–8; E. Bernus, 'Drought in the Niger Republic', *Savanna*, 2, No. 2 (1973), 129–32; A. T. Grove, 'Desertification in the African Environment', *African Affairs*, 73 (1974), 143–4.

56. Jean Maley, 'Mécanisme des changements climatiques aux basses latitudes', *Palaeogeography, Palaeoclimatology, and Palaeoecology* 14 (1973), 218.

57. Nicholson, 'Climatic Chronology', 159–76; Grove, 'Remarkably Low Rainfall', 133–8.

58. Baier, 'Trans-Saharan Trade and the Sahel', 47–51.

59. Rennell of Rodd, *People of the Veil*, 136; Jean Bétrix, *La Pénétration touareg* (Paris, 1911), 8; F. Nicolas, 'La Transhumance chez les Iullemmeden de l'Est',

Travaux de l'Institut des Recherches Sahariennes, 4 (1947), 113.

60. E. de Bary, *Le Dernier Rapport d'un Européen sur Ghât et les Touareg de l'Aïr (Journal de voyage d'Erwin de Bary, 1876–1877)*, trans. H. Schirmer (Paris, 1898), 101, 106; Dunbar, 'Damagaram', 205–6.

61. For more detail on the drought-recovery cycle, see Stephen Baier, 'Droughts and Economic Cycles among the Tuareg of the Sahel', paper presented at the annual meeting of the Social Science History Association, Philadelphia, 30 Oct. 1976.

62. For similar strategies of returning to pastoral life, though without the mechanism of social stratification, see Diouldé Laya, 'Interviews with Herders and Livestock-Owners in the Sahel', *African Environment*, 1, No. 2 (1975), 49–93.

63. For recent static analyses of stratification, see Bourgeot, 'Idéologie et appelations ethniques', 533–53; and Robert F. Murphy, 'Tuareg Kinship', *American Anthropologist*, 69 (1967), 164.

64. Gudrun Dahl and Anders Hjort, *Having Herds: Pastoral Herd Growth and Household Economy* (Stockholm, 1976), 113–30.

CHAPTER II

1. For more detail on migration to Damergu, see Stephen Baier, 'Trans-Saharan Trade and the Sahel: Damergu, 1870–1930', *Journal of African History*, 18 (1977), 47–54. See also Yehoshua Rash, 'Des colonisateurs sans enthousiasme: les premières années françaises au Damerghou', *Revue Française d'Histoire d'Outre-Mer*, 59 (1972), 5–69; and 59 (1972), 240–308; André Salifou, 'Rivalités tribales et intervention française au Damerghou', unpublished paper, August 1971; and ANN, Tanout, Y. Riou, 'Les Touaregs du cercle de Tanout'. A chronology of droughts in the Central Sudan and a discussion of cycles of drought and recovery appears in Paul E. Lovejoy and Stephen Baier, 'The Desert-Side Economy of the Central Sudan', *International Journal of African Historical Studies*, 8 (1975), 551–81. The local climate improved somewhat more rapidly in the early nineteenth century than elsewhere in Africa; Sharon E. Nicolson, 'A Climatic Chronology for Africa: Synthesis of Geological, Historical, and Meteorological Information and Data', Ph.D. dissertation, University of Wisconsin–Madison, 1976; Sharon E. Nicholson, 'Saharan Climates in Historic Times,' in *The Sahara and the Nile*, ed. M. A. J. Williams and H. Faure (Rotterdam, 1979).

2. Interview with Wuru Tambari Mayaki, 14 Oct. 1972 (tape 41 and 42); Fokondo Mala, 13 Oct. 1972 (tape 40); and Atari Madiguburi, 14 Oct. 1972 (tape 40 and 41); see also Salifou, 'Rivalités tribales', 4–5.

3. Roberta Ann Dunbar, 'Damagaram (Zinder, Niger), 1812–1906: The History of a Central Sudanic Kingdom', Ph.D. dissertation, U.C.L.A., 1970, 17–20. For the early history of Damagaram, see also André Salifou, *Le Damagaram ou sultanat de Zinder au xixe siècle*, Études Nigériennes No. 27 (Niamey, 1971), 37–49; and August Tilho, *Documents scientifiques de la mission Tilho* (Paris, 1908), II. 436 ff.; and E. Séré des Rivières, *Histoire du Niger* (Paris, 1965), 134.

4. Heinrich Barth, *Travels and Discoveries in North and Central Africa* (1857–59: reprinted., London: F. Cass, 1965), I. 478–9; Hugh Clapperton, *Narrative of Travels and Discoveries in Northern and Central Africa* (London, 1826), II. 121–2; Usufu Bala Usman, 'The Transformation of Katsina, *c.*1796–1903: The Overthrow of the Sarauta system and the Establishment and Evolution of the Emirate', Ph.D. dissertation, Ahmadu Bello University, 1974, 466–9. Usufu Usman argues that the assertions of Barth and Clapperton that trade declined in Katsina after the *jihad* must be treated with caution, but he presents evidence

which indicates that North African and Tuareg merchants moved from Katsina to Kano. Important forms of interregional trade, such as trade in tobacco grown in Katsina, may not have declined. See also Philip Shea, 'The Development of Export-Oriented Dyed Cloth Industry in Kano Emirate in the Nineteenth Century', Ph.D. dissertation, University of Wisconsin–Madison, 1975, 34–6.

5. Marion Johnson, 'Calico Caravans: The Tripoli-Kano Trade after 1880', *Journal of African History*, 17 (1976), 95–118.

6. Baier, 'Trans-Saharan Trade and the Sahel', 39–41.

7. Johnson, 'Calico Caravans', 100; see also Thomas Jago, Report on the Trade and Commerce of Tripoli for 1896, House of Commons, Session of 1897, vol. 94; R. Dickson, Report on the Trade and Commerce of Tripoli for 1898, House of Commons, Session of 1899, vol. 103.

8. USNA, RG59, T40, W. Gaines to the Department of State, 31 Mar. 1852: Gaines reported that Tripoli slave exports declined from over 2,000 slaves per year in 1847 and 1848 to 450 slaves in 1851 but gives no reason for the decline. According to a personal communication from Mark Dyer, French archives and related published material yield figures of the same order of magnitude for the early 1850s. How many of these slaves arrived from the direction of Kano is unknown, but Richardson reported a caravan of 1,000 slaves from Kano in 1846; see James Richardson, *Travels in the Great Desert of Sahara in the Years of 1845 and 1846* (London, 1848), II. 115, 310 (as cited in Ralph Austen, 'The Transsaharan Slave Trade: A Tentative Census', in *The Uncommon Market: Essays in the Economic History of the Atlantic Slave Trade*, ed. J. S. Hogendorn and H. Gemery (New York, 1979). Austen's paper, which assembles data from a wide variety of sources to give an overview of trans-Saharan slave trade, provides estimates showing a greater volume of trade in the nineteenth century than in any previous century. Exports to Libya, Egypt, and Morocco were high in the nineteenth century, but by the 1870s, Austen concludes, most Libyan traffic followed the Benghazi–Wadai route to the east, which was less easily monitored by European abolitionists than the Tripoli–Kano route. In the early 1850s Richardson estimated that not more than 150 or 200 slaves left Damagaram or passed through in transit for North Africa; see James Richardson, *Narrative of a Mission to Central Africa* (London, 1853), II. 273. During his residence in Ghadames Dickson estimated the volume of slave trade passing through the oasis at 500 per year; see C. H. Dickson, 'Account of Ghadames', *Journal of the Royal Geographical Society*, 30 (1860), 260.

9. USNA, RG59, T 40 Michel Vidal to the Department of State, 27 July 1876; see also Vidal's dispatches of 1 Mar. 1875, 26 Aug. 1875, and of 15 July, 1876.

10. A. G. Hopkins, 'Economic Imperialism in West Africa: Lagos, 1880–1892', *Economic History Review*, 12 (1968), 587–90; A. G. Hopkins, *An Economic History of West Africa* (New York, 1973), 125–46; David Northrup, 'The Compatibility of the Slave and Palm Oil Trades in the Bight of Biafra', *Journal of African History*, 17 (1976), 353–64; K. O. Dike, *Trade and Politics in the Niger Delta 1830–1885* (Oxford, 1956); and A. J. H. Latham, *Old Calabar 1600–1891* (Oxford, 1973).

11. For more detail, see Baier, 'Trans-Saharan Trade and the Sahel', 37–60.

12. Interview with ᶜAbd al-Hamid b. Muhammad, 24 May 1972 (tape 13); Gaden, 'Notice', 654.

13. Baier, 'Trans-Saharan Trade and the Sahel', 51–8.

14. F.O. 101/88, Thomas S. Jago, 'Supplementary Report for the Year 1897 on the Vilayet of Tripoli'; Thomas S. Jago, Report on the Trade and Economic State of the Vilayet of Tripoli for the Past Forty Years, House of Commons, Session of 1902, vol. 103; Johnson, 'Calico Caravans', 100.

15. Barth, *Travels*, I. 517–23; Capitaine Moll, 'Situation économique de la région de

Zinder', *Renseignements coloniaux* (9 Dec. 1901), 197–8, as cited in Johnson, 'Calico Caravans', 102.

16. USNA, RG59, T 40, Cuthbert Jones to the Department of State, 19 June 1880 and 5 Aug. 1879.
17. Interview with Malam Ali Yaro, 13 May 1972 (tape 18 and 19).
18. USNA, RG59, T 40, Cuthbert Jones to the Department of State, 9 July 1880.
19. Richardson, *Travels*, II. 117.
20. This and what follows is based on Dunbar, 'Damagaram', 43–4, and to a lesser extent on Salifou, *Damagaram*, 59–83, 147.
21. Joseph P. Smaldone, *Warfare in the Sokoto Caliphate: Historical and Sociological Perspectives* (Cambridge, 1977), 110–24, 159–60.
22. Smaldone, *Warfare*, 95–101; USNA, RG59, T 40, Cuthbert Jones to the Department of State, 26 Oct. 1880; Parmenio Bettoli, 'Tripoli Commerciale', *L'Esploratore*, 6, No. 7 (1882), 267.
23. Smaldone, *Warfare*, 100–1; Humphrey J. Fisher and Virginia Rowland, 'Firearms in the Central Sudan', *Journal of African History*, 12 (1971), 215–39. For the Sanūsīyya and the Benghazi–Wadai route, see Dennis D. Cordell, 'Eastern Libya, Wadai and the Sanūsīyya: A Ṭarīqa and a Trade Route', *Journal of African History* 18 (1977), 21–36.
24. Smaldone, *Warfare*, 99; Tilho, *Documents scientifiques*, 444–5.
25. Dunbar, 'Damagaram', 43–4.
26. Dunbar, 'Damagaram', 44.
27. Roberta Ann Dunbar, 'Slavery and the Evolution of Nineteenth-Century Damagaram (Zinder, Niger)', in *Slavery in Africa: Historical and Anthropological Perspectives*, ed. Suzanne Miers and Igor Kopytoff (Madison, Wisconsin, 1977), 160–8.
28. Interview with Malam Ali Yaro, 13 May 1972 (tape 18 and 19) and 3 Nov. 1972 (tape 44).
29. Dunbar, 'Damagaram', 28, 46, 192.
30. Interview with Kelilan Gaja, 18 Apr. 1972 (tape 10); Kasko Ahamat, 25 May 1972 (tape 14 and 16); Dodo Mai Zaga, 7 Apr. 1972 (tape 3); see also Henri Gadan, 'Notice sur la résidence de Zinder', *Revue des Troupes Coloniales*, 2 (1903), 626–8.
31. Dunbar, 'Damagaram', 204–5.
32. Interview with Muhamman Kane, 30 May 1972 (tape 37 and 38) and 3 Dec. 1972 (tape 49); Illali Ali, 17 May 1972 (tape 20); and Cillo Alassan, 6 Oct. 1972 (tape 36).
33. Estimates of the level of salt trade just before the colonial occupation range from 10,000 loads per year to 25,000; see chapter 5, n. 31 for a list of sources. The first accurate figure comes from tax collection in Damergu during the 1903/4 fiscal year, when 17,930 loads of salt were recorded: ANS, 2G 4-3, Cercle de Zinder, Rapport commercial, 2e trimestre 1904. The value of salt in Damagaram was about 1 franc or 1,000 cowries per kg Gaden, 'Notice', 779; and ADZ, Rapport commercial, 2e trimestre 1903.
34. ADZ, Rapport commercial, 4e trimestre 1903.
35. Interview with Dodo Mai Zaga, 7 Apr. 1972 (tape 3); Alhaji Katche Ango, 6 May 1972 (tape 5); Alhaji Ali Yaro, 13 May 1972 (tape 18), and 3 Nov. 1972 (tape 44); and Muhamman Kane, 30 May 1972 (tape 37 and 38), and 3 Dec. 1972 (tape 49).
36. P. Gamory-Dubourdeau, 'Étude sur la création des cantons de sédentarisation dans le cercle de Zinder, et particulièrement dans la subdivision centrale (arrondissement de Mirria)', *BCEHSAOF*, 8, (1924), 239–58; Barth, *Travels*, III. 77.
37. Interview with Kelilan Gaja, 18 Apr. 1972 (tape 10), and 19 Apr. 1972 (tape 11);

Kasko Ahamat, 25 May 1972 (tape 14 and 16); Wuru Tambari Mayaki, 12 Oct. 1972 (tape 39), and 14 Oct. 1972 (tape 41 and 42).
38. Interview with Abdu 'dan Dabba, 9 Nov. 1972 (tape 45); Malam Ali Yaro, 3 Nov. 1972 (tape 44); and Dunbar, 'Damagaram', 28, 160–1.
39. Interview with Muhamman Kane, 3 Dec. 1972 (tape 49).
40. Dunbar, 'Damagaram', 160–1.
41. Richardson, *Narrative*, II. 182–5, 192–3; Dunbar, 'Damagaram', 124–7.
42. Dunbar, 'Damagaram', 44–56. On Tuareg alliances, see also interview with Kasko Ahamat, 25 May 1972 (tape 14 and 16).
43. P. L. Monteil, *De Saint-Louis à Tripoli par le Tchad* (Paris, 1894), 342 [as cited in Dunbar].
44. Dunbar, 'Damagaram', 70–81; Tilho, *Documents scientifiques*, II. 447–52; Louis Brenner, *The Shehus of Kukawa: A History of the Al-Kanemi Dynasty of Bornu* (London, 1973), 122–3.
45. Interviews with Muhamman Kane, 21 May 1972 (tape 34), 8 Oct. 1972 (tape 39), 3 Dec. 1972 (tape 49), and 4 Dec. 1972 (tape 49). Muhamman Kane, born before 1890, is the son of 'dan Maleka.
46. Interview with Musa Sidi, 21 Sept. 1972 (tape 34); Cillo Alassan, 20 Oct. 1972 (tape 42); and Lawan Sidi, 14 Nov. 1972 (tape 46).
47. Paul E. Lovejoy, 'Interregional Monetary Flows in the Precolonial Trade of Nigeria', *Journal of African History*, 15 (1974), 569, 579.
48. Interview of Ma'azu Isa, 28 Aug. 1972 (tape 29), and 11 Sept. 1972 (tape 32).
49. Interview with Sami Sharubutu, 11 May 1972 (tape 4); Ilia Ilias, 18 Sept. 1972 (tape 8 and 34). These men are the sons of the persons allied by marriage to Madugu Isa. Although other traders in precolonial Damagaram used the title *madugu*, informants agreed that only Isa, Sharubutu, and Ilias were caravan leaders of sufficient stature to lead caravans on their own.
50. Interview with Ilali Ali, 17 May 1972 (tape 20), and 15 Sept. 1972 (tape 9).
51. For a more detailed description of the role of caravan leaders in pre-colonial trade, see Paul E. Lovejoy, 'The Hausa Kola Trade (1700–1900): A Commercial System in the Continental Exchange of West Africa', Ph.D. dissertation, University of Wisconsin–Madison, 1973, chapter 5.
52. See Lovejoy, 'Hausa Kola Trade', chapter 5.
53. Interview with Isa Kadir, 11 Sept. 1972 (tape 33).
54. Interview with Ma'azu Isa, 28 Aug. 1972 (tape 29). Caravans led by Madugu Isa introduced salt of European origin into Damagaram. For trade in Ilorin at the turn of the century, see C. W. Newbury, *British Policy towards West Africa: Select Documents, 1875–1914* (London, 1971), 460–1, 471–3; and Marion Johnson, 'Cloth on the Banks of the Niger', *Journal of the Historical Society of Nigeria*, 6 (1973), 362–3; for the shipment of kola by sea beginning in 1890, see Lovejoy, 'Hausa Kola Trade', 195–7.
55. Interview with Suley Sami, 30 Sept. 1972 (tape 4); and Ma'azu Isa, 28 Aug. 1972 (tape 29).
56. ADZ, Rapport sur le marché de Myrria, Aug. 1900; interview with Garba Surkule, 29 Nov. 1972 (tape 33). For a description of the Zinder market, see Fernand Foureau, *D'Alger au Congo par le Tchad* (Paris, 1902), 528.
57. Interview with Ahmadu Galdi, 25 Apr. 1972 (tape 12); and Foureau, *D'Alger au Congo*, 528.
58. Interview with Garba Surkule, 29 Nov. 1972 (tape 33).

CHAPTER III

1. Henri Duveyrier, *Les Touregs du nord* (Paris, 1864), 256. Hausa-speaking people rarely distinguished between North Africans, calling them all *larabawa* (sg., *balarabe*). Only occasionally did Hausa refer to North Africans with names reflecting true North African reference groups, but *Adamusawa* (Hausa, meaning people from Ghadames) was a term known to most Hausa who had dealings with North Africans in the Sudan.
2. F.O. 101/88, Thomas S. Jago, 'Supplementary Report for the Year 1897 for the Vilayet of Tripoli'.
3. Leo Africanus, *The History and Description of Africa*, trans. John Pary, ed. Robert Brown (London, 1896), III. 797. Other early references to Ghadamasi pre-eminence include Royal ·Geographic Society, *Records of the African Association 1788–1831* ed. Robin Hallett (London, 1964), 82; Dixon Denham and Hugh Clapperton, *Narrative of Travels and Discoveries in Northern and Central Africa in the Years 1822, 1823, and 1824* (London, 1826), 45; and M. Mauroy, *Du commerce des peuples de l'Afrique septentrionale* (Paris, 1845), 199.
4. Heinrich Barth, *Travels and Discoveries in North and Central Africa* (1857–9: reprint ed., F. Cass, 1965), I. 507; Duveyrier, *Touaregs du nord*, 256–7. See also Denham and Clapperton, *Narrative*, 45; Louis Brenner, 'The North African Trading Community in the Nineteenth-Century Central Sudan', in *Aspects of West African Islam*, ed. D. F. McCall and N. R. Bennett (Boston University Papers on Africa, Volume 5. Boston: 1971), 147–8; James Richardson, *Travels in the Great Desert of Sahara in the Years of 1845 and 1846* (London, 1848), I. 350–1, II. 3; Henri Duveyrier, *Sahara algérien et tunisien: journal de route publié et annoté par C. Maunoir et H. Schirmer* (Paris, 1905), 165 ff.
5. Mohammed El-Hachaichi, *Voyage au pays Senoussiya* (Paris, 1912), 220–2.
6. Lloyd Fallers, ed., *Immigrants and Associations* (The Hague, 1967). The best theoretical work on the concept of the trade diaspora is Abner Cohen, 'Cultural Strategies in the Organization of Trading Diasporas', in *The Development of Indigenous Trade and Markets in West Africa*, ed. Claude Meillassoux (London, 1971), 266–81. See also Abner Cohen, *Custom and Politics in Urban Africa: A Study of Hausa Migrants in Yoruba Towns* (London, 1969). For an application of the concept and an extended analysis, see Philip Curtin, *Economic Change in Precolonial Africa: Senegambia in the Era of the Slave Trade* (Madison, Wisconsin, 1975), especially 59 ff.
7. Information on brokers, who were known by the Kanuri word *fatomai* (sg., *fatoma*) is scattered throughout the interviews I taped in Damagaram, but for representative examples see interviews with Muhamman 'dan Jawo, 14 Sept. 1972 (tape 9) and Usman 'dan Shaba, 6 Sept. 1972 (tape 24). For information on the role of Tuareg landlady-brokers, see Paul E. Lovejoy and Stephen Baier, 'The Desert-Side Economy of the Central Sudan', *International Journal of African Historical Studies*, 8 (1975), 551–81.
8. For the production and trade of Ghadames today, see Lars Eldblom, *Structure foncière, organisation et structure sociale: une étude comparative sur la vie socio-économique dans les trois oasis lybiennes de Ghat, Mourzouk, et particulièrement Ghadamès*, translated by Yvonne Richter and Marianne Melrad (Lund, 1968), 47–57.
9. On Mujabra and Zuwaya, see Dennis D. Cordell, 'Eastern Lybia, Wadai, and the Sanūsīyya: A Tarīqa and a Trade Route', *Journal of African History*, 18 (1977), 21–36; and F.O. 101/99, Justin Alvarez to the Foreign Office, 11 Nov. 1901; F.O. 101/99 Justin Alvarez to the Foreign Office, 7 June 1901. For Sawkna, see Richardson, *Travels*, II. 412–3. On the Bani-Mzab, see Marcel Mercier, 'Mzab', in *The Encyclopedia of Islam* (Leyden,1913), supplement, 164.

10. Interview with Muhamman Kane, 17 Nov. 1972 (tape 46) and Alhaji Ali Yaro, 3 Nov. 1972 (tape 44). The inventory lists were known as *taskara* in Zinder and as *teskra* in Ghat. This is probably the Arabic word *tadhkira*, meaning paper, message, or permit. See M. Brûlard, 'Aperçu sur le commerce caravanier Tripolitaine-Ghat-Niger vers la fin du XIXe siècle', *Bulletin de Liaison Saharienne*, 9 (1958), 208, 214n; Roberta Ann Dunbar, 'Damagaram (Zinder, Niger), 1812–1906: The History of a Central Sudanic Kingdom', Ph.D. dissertation, University of California at Los Angeles, 1970, p. 204.
11. J. Étiévant, 'Le commerce tripolitain dans le centre africain', *Afrique Française*, 9 (Sept. 1910), 280.
12. A. Adu Boahen, *Britain, the Sahara and the Western Sudan* (London, 1964), 112 ff.
13. According to Muhamman Kane (interview of 17 Nov. 1972, tape 46), Tuareg led camels carrying trans-Saharan consignments through the streets of the North African quarter in Zinder past merchants who carefully read the addresses on the bundles of merchandise and claimed any that had been sent to them; see also Brûlard, 'Aperçu', 209.
14. El-Hachaichi, *Voyage*, 27, 113–14, 225; Richardson, *Travels*, I. 32, 232–3, 260 (both as cited in Brenner, 'North African Trading Community', 147n). See also H. Méhier de Malthuisieulx, 'Une mission en Tripolitaine', *Renseignements Coloniaux*, Jan. 1904, p. 31. In 1911 the El-Tseni family was still the most important mercantile group in Ghadames; see Léon Pervinquière, *La tripolitaine interdite* (Paris, 1912), 184.
15. G. Méry, 'Renseignements commerciaux sur le mouvement des échanges entre la Tripolitaine et le Soudan central', *Bulletin du Comité de l'Afrique Française*, Sept. 1893, 3. See also Duveyrier, *Sahara*, 190.
16. ADZ, Dossier marked 'Renseignements 1906–1909', entries under 'Cherif Dodo' for 1906, 1908, and 1918; ADZ, Correspondence, Commandant Zinder to Resident at Kano, 6 Apr. 1924; M. Laizé, 'L'Islam dans le territoire militaire du Niger', *BCEHSAOF*, 1919, 181–3; Dunbar, 'Damagaram', 201; interview with Gani Maburu and Habu Abdallah, 2 September 1972 (tape 30); Alhaji Ali Yaro, May 13, 1972 (tape 18 and 19). A name included in the list of Tripoli merchants given by Méhier de Mathuisieulx as Guéraba is probably to be identified with the Guenaba family, See also Dunbar, 'Damagaram', 199.
17. El-Hachaichi, *Voyage*, 240–2.
18. Interview with Abdurahaman Bedari, 7 Aug. 1972 (tape 32), who is the son of Bedari Zumut; with Muhamman Kane (interview of 11 Nov. 1972, tape 46 and 47), who identified Zammit as the Ghadamasi employer of Bedari Zumut. Mustapha Zammit is mentioned by Parmenio Bettoli, 'Tripoli Commerciale', *L'Esploratore*, 6 (1882), 266; and by the American consul at Tripoli: see United States National Archives (hereafter USNA), RG59, T 40, Michel Vidal to the Department of State, 25 July 1876, and 27 July 1876.
19. Méry, 'Renseignements commerciaux', 3.
20. Dunbar, 'Damagaran', 193–8; James Richardson, *Narrative of a Mission to Central Africa* (London, 1853), 179–82. Richardson, who was in Zinder in 1851, reported conversations with Sharif Kabir, the wealthiest of the Zinder merchants, and with merchants from Murzuk. Heinrich Barth spent over a month in Zinder in December 1852 and January 1853, but wrote very little about the city because he used the time to organize his notes; see Barth, *Travels*, III. 72–6.
21. James Richardson, *Travels*, II. 411. For a history of the conflict between the Awlad Sulayman and the Turks, see Dennis D. Cordell, 'The Awlad Sulayman of Chad and Libya: A Study of Raiding and Power in the Chad Basin in the Nineteenth Century', M.A. thesis, University of Wisconsin–Madison, 1972.

22. Interview with Gani Maburu, 10 May 1972 (tape 23); and interview with Gani Maburu and Habu Adballah, 2 Sept. 1972 (tape 30).
23. Duveyrier, *Sahara*, 165.
24. Fernand Foureau, *D'Alger au Congo par le Tchad: Mission saharienne Foureau-Lamy* (Paris, 1902), 525–6; Émile Reibell, *Carnet de route de la mission saharienne Foureau-Lamy* (Paris, 1931), 219. The estimate of the number of Ghadamasi living in Tuareg settlements is based principally on interviews with Muhamman Kane, 20 May 1972 (tape 15), 17 Nov. 1972 (tape 46), and 18 Nov. 1972 (tape 46 and 47).
25. El-Hachaichi, *Voyage*, 221; Henri Gaden, 'Notice sur la résidence de Zinder', *Revue des Troupes Coloniales*, 2, No. 17 (1903), 654; Capitaine Moll, 'Situation économique de la région de Zinder', *Renseignements Coloniaux* (9 Dec. 1901), 199; interview with ᶜAbd al-Hamid b. Muhammad, 24 May 1972 (tape 13); Umbatu Gangan, 18 Aug. 1972 (tape 27); and Fokondo Mala, 13 Oct. 1972 (tape 40).
26. E. E. Evans-Pritchard, *The Sanusi of Cyrenaica* (London, 1949), *passim*.
27. Cordell, 'Eastern Libya, Wadai and the Sanūsīyya', 31.
28. Duveyrier, *Les Toureg du nord*, 303; M. Laizé, 'L'Islam dans le Territoire Militaire du Niger', *BCEHSAOF* (1919), 180–3; interview with Gani Maburu, 10 May 1972 (tape 23), and 2 Sept. 1972 (tape 30); Almahadi Atalib, 1 June 1972 (tape 16), who is the son of Shaikh Talib b. Mubarak, the *muqaddam* of the mosque at Djadjidouna appointed by al-Sunni. This Shaikh Talib is not to be confused with another man of the same name said to have founded the Sanūsī mosque in Kano; see Muhammad Uba Adamu and John Lavers, 'Notes on the Influence of North Africa Traders in Kano', *Kano Studies*, 1, No. 4 (1968), 47n. The account of Gani Maburu (10 May 1972, tape 23) attributes the founding of the Kano mosque to al-Sunni himself. See also Dunbar, 'Damagaram', 199.
29. Laizé, 'Islam', 182; on the activities of al-Sunni before he arrived in Zinder, see PRO, F.O. 101/88, Thomas Jago to F.O., 1 Dec. 1898. For background on the Awlad Sulayman, see Dennis D. Cordell, 'The Awlad Sulayman of Libya and Chad'. For peace-keeping activities on the Benghazi–Wadai route, see Cordell, 'Eastern Libya, Wadai, and the Sanūsīyya', 28 ff.
30. Laizé, 'Islam', 183.
31. Interview with Abdurahaman Bedari, 7 Aug. 1972 (tape 32).
32. Interview with Malam Almahadi Atalib, 6 June 1972 (tape 16).
33. Malam Yaro is mentioned in passing in Dunbar, 'Damagaram', 208. For a detailed study, see André Salifou, 'Malan Yaroh, un grand négociant du Soudan central à la fin du XIXe siècle', *Journal de la Société des Africanistes*, 42 (1972), 7–27. Information on the marriage of Malam Yaro's father is from an interview with Muhamman Kane, 4 Dec. 1972 (tape 50). André Salifou ('Malan Yaroh', 8–9) argues that Malam Yaro's father was of free origin, taking the testimony of Alhaji Ali Yaro, Malam Yaro's son, at face value, despite the general reluctance of people to admit servile origins. Malam Yaro is mentioned frequently in early French sources; see for example Gaden, 'Notice', 781; Foureau, *D'Alger au Congo*, 522 ff.; Reibell, *Carnet de route*, 229–33; ANS, 2G 2–13, Troisième Territoire Militaire, Rapports Politiques Mensuels, Zinder 1902, Mois de Juillet; and ADZ, Sultanat, 'Rapport sur la sauvegarde des biens du Sultan et de ses complices', n.d.
34. The story of Malam Yaro's early life is from an interview with Kelilan Gaja, 18 Apr. 1972 (tape 10).
35. Interview with Fokondo Mala, 13 Oct. 1972 (tape 40).
36. Interview with Alhaji Ali Yaro, 13 May 1972 (tape 18); and Alhaji Katche Ango, 6 May 1972 (tape 5).

37. Salifou, 'Malan Yaroh', 13n.; interview with Alhaji Ali Yaro, 13 May 1972 (tape 18).
38. Interview with Alhaji Ali Yaro, 3 Nov. 1972 (tape 44).
39. For the use of orders of payment in Islamic societies, see Eliahu Ashtor, 'Banking Instruments between the Muslim East and the Christian West', *Journal of European Economic History*, 1 (1972), 553–73. On the use of delegation of credit by European travellers in the Sahara, see Lucie G. Colvin, 'The Commerce of Hausaland, 1780–1833', in *Aspects of West African Islam*, ed. D. F. McCall and N. R. Bennett (Boston, 1971), 119.
40. Interview with Abba Musa, 16 May 1972 (tape 6 and 7).
41. August Tilho, *Documents scientifiques de la mission Tilho* (Paris, 1908), II. 445–7; Joseph Smaldone, 'The Firearms Trade in the Central Sudan in the Nineteenth Century', in *Aspects of West African Islam*, ed. D. F. McCall and N. R. Bennett (Boston, 1971), 162.
42. Information on the Tubu trade diaspora is principally from Abba Musa, interviewed 16 May 1972 (tape 6 and 7); Abba Musa's father made the trip to the Fazzan and beyond several times. Trade carried by the Tubu attracted the interest of the French. See ANF-OM, Afrique Occidentale, NS 61, Telegram from Merlin at Gorée to Ministre des Colonies, 17 Oct. 1906; ADZ, Rapport du Chef de Battion Mouret sur la situation politique générale pendant le mois de mai 1908.
43. A European traveller of the late nineteenth century considered this route too dangerous to take. See Charles Robinson, *Hausa-land or Fifteen Hundred Miles Through the Central Soudan* (London, 1896), 122.
44. Johannes Nicolaisen, *Ecology and Culture of the Pastoral Tuareg* (Copenhagen, 1963), 210–12; M. Gast, 'Évolution de la vie économique et structures sociales en Ahaggar', *Travaux de l'Institut des Recherches Sahariennes*, 24 (1965), 130; Foureau, *D'Alger au Congo*, 564; Jeremy Keenan, *The Tuareg: People of Ahaggar* (London, 1977), 139–40.
45. Raphael Patai, *The Tents of Jacob: The Diaspora of Yesterday and Today* (Englewood Cliffs, New Jersey, 1971), 201; Nahoum Slousch, 'Les Juifs en Tripolitaine', *Revue du Monde Musulman*, 2 (1907), 28; R. Vadala, 'L'Émigration maltaise en pays musulmans', *Revue du Monde Musulman*, 14 (1911), 41–3. On the Jewish community of Tunis see Allesandro Triulzi, 'Italian-Speaking Communities in Early Nineteenth Century Tunis', *Revue de l'Orient Musulman et de la Méditerranée*, 9 (1971), 156–8.
46. An extensive list of Tripoli merchants and their affiliations to various European consulates is found in USNA, RG59, T 40, Michel Vidal to the Department of State, 1 July 1876, and 7 July 1876.
47. Méhier de Mathuisieulx, 'Mission', 31; ANF-AE, Rais to Ministère des Affaires Étrangères, 5 July 1905. The same families were apparently prominent in 1880; see USNA, RG59, T 40, Cuthbert Jones to the Department of State, 12 July 1880, which transmits a letter of protest from Jewish merchants dated 17 June 1880; this letter replied to an article by Jones appearing in the *American Exporter* in February 1880 which impugned the honesty of the Tripoli Jewish community.
48. USNA, RG59, T 40, Cuthbert Jones to the Department of State, 1 Oct. 1878.
49. USNA, RG59, T 40, Cuthbert Jones to the Department of State, 6 Oct. 1879; Cuthbert Jones, 'Warning to American Exporters', *American Exporter*, Feb. 1880; USNA, RG59, T 40, Cuthbert Jones to the Department of State, 12 July 1880 (this transmits the translation of a letter of protest which first appeared in the Maltese newspaper *Risorgimento*).
50. William Coffin, 'The Cotton Goods Trade, Tripoli-in-Barbary', *Monthly Consular and Trade Reports* (U.S.), No. 347 (Aug. 1909), 69–70.

51. Charles Wellington Furlong, *The Gateway to the Sahara: Observations and Experiences in Tripoli* (New York, 1909), 175–6; Thomas S. Jago, 'Report on the Trade and Economy of the Vilayet of Tripoli in Northern Africa, in the Past Forty Years', House of Commons, Sessional Papers, 1902, vol. 103, p. 7; for earlier examples of Tripoli finance, see L. Charles Féraud, *Annales tripolitaines* (Tunis, 1927), 409–11; and Richardson, *Travels*, I. 350, II. 18.

52. Anon., 'Le Commerce tripolitaine dans la région du Lac Tchad et le Sokoto', *Renseignements Coloniaux*, Aug. 1898; FO 101/88, Thomas S. Jago, 'Supplementary Report for the Year 1897 on the Vilayet of Tripoli'; A. de Calassanti-Motylinski, *Le Dialecte berbère de R'edames* (Paris, 1904), 287–8.

53. According to Bettoli ('Tripoli Commerciale', 614), some merchants never went beyond Ghat. See also Richardson, *Travels*, I. 352, II. 18, 420; USNA, RG59, T 40, Cuthbert Jones to the Department of State, 6 Oct. 1879.

54. For a list of political authorities to whom tolls had to be paid at mid-century, see Richardson, *Travels*, I. 175.

55. Thomas Jago, 'Report on the Trade and Economic State of the Vilayet of Tripoli during the Past Forty Years', House of Commons, Sessional Papers, 1902, vol. 102, p. 7; Furlong, *Gateway to the Sahara*, 175–6.

56. Noel Temple Moore, 'Report on the Trade and Commerce of Tripoli for 1891', House of Commons, Sessional Papers, 1892, vol. 84, p. 7; on the previous page Moore explained that by Arabs he meant 'Ghadamsenes, an intelligent and business-like tribe . . .'

57. J. B. d'Attonoux, 'Tripoli et les voies commerciales du Soudan', *Annales de Géographie*, 5 (1895–6), 196; 'Le Commerce tripolitaine dans la région du Lac Tchad', 209.

58. Bettoli, 'Tripoli Commerciale', 266–8. The equal division of profit between financiers and caravaniers is confirmed by Henri Méhier de Mathuisieulx, *A travers la Tripolitaine* (Paris, 1912), 98.

59. Étiévant, 'Le commerce tripolitain', 281.

60. C. W. Newbury, 'North African and Western Sudan Trade in the Nineteenth Century: A Reevaluation', *Journal of African History*, 7 (1966), 238; H. Mircher, *Mission de Ghadamès (septembre, octobre, novembre, et décembre, 1862). Rapports officiels et documents à l'appui* (Alger, 1863), 52–3.

61. Méhier de Mathuisieulx, *A travers la Tripolitaine*, 99.

62. F. R. Drummond-Hay, 'Report on the Trade and Commerce of Tripoli for the Year 1888', House of Commons, Sessional Papers, 1899, vol. 81, p. 2; Noel Temple Moore, 'Report on the Trade and Commerce of Tripoli for 1891', House of Commons, Sessional Papers, 1892, vol. 84, p. 5.

63. Dunbar, 'Damagaram', 204.

64. For Wadai, see Cordell, 'Eastern Libya, Wadai, and the Sanūsīyya', 23–4; on Damagaram, see Dunbar, 'Damagaram', 219; Joseph P. Smaldone, 'The Firearms Trade in the Central Sudan in the Nineteenth Century', in *Aspects of West African Islam*, ed. D. F. McCall and N. R. Bennett (Boston, 1971), 147; Tilho, *Documents scientifiques*, II. 446 (as cited in Smaldone).

65. Dunbar ('Damagaram', 203) reports that Malam Yaro had a monopoly on gun imports before the turn of the century.

66. Méry, 'Renseignements commerciaux', 3; Johnson, 'Calico Caravans', 110.

67. Méhier de Mathuisieulx, 'Mission', 31; ANF-AE, Rais to Affaires Étrangères, 5 July 1905; Slousch, 'Juifs', 28–34; Nahum Slousch, 'Tripoli', *Revue du Monde Musulman*, 6 (1908), 272–9. Moll ('Situation économique', 198) reported that English firms with branches in Tripoli financed a portion of the trade; he may be referring to Wardel Riley and possibly other firms, or he may simply be mistaken, the result of receiving information at a great distance. Similarly Étiévant ('Commerce tripolitain', 280) mentions the presence of Turkish,

Jewish, or European firms in Tripoli with agents in the Sudan.
68. For more information on trade in hides and skins, most of which went to the U.S., see Thomas S. Jago, 'Report on the Trade and Commerce of Tripoli for the Year 1894', House of Commons, Sessional Papers, 1895, vol. 101, p. 5; John Q. Wood, 'Commerce and Industries of Tripoli-in-Barbary', *Daily Consular and Trade Reports* (U.S.), 164 (13 July 1912), 226–35; Johnson, 'Calico Caravans', 108; William Coffin, 'Tripoli-in-Barbary: Review of Trade Conditions', in *Commercial Relations of the United States with Foreign Countries* (Washington, D.C., 1911); and William Coffin, 'Sudan Tanned Skins', *Monthly Consular and Trade Reports* (U.S.), 349 (Oct. 1909), 122–3.
69. Newbury, 'North African and Western Sudan Trade', 239–40.

CHAPTER IV

1. C. W. Newbury, 'North African and Western Sudan Trade in the Nineteenth Century: A Reinterpretation', *Journal of African History*, 7 (1966), 233–46.
2. Marion Johnson, 'Calico Caravans: Tripoli-Kano Trade after 1880', *Journal of African History*, 17 (1976), 95–117; see also Stephen Baier, 'Trans-Saharan Trade and the Sahel: Damergu, 1870–1930', *Journal of African History*, 18 (1977), 37–60.
3. Dennis D. Cordell, 'Eastern Libya, Wadai and the Sanūsīyya: A Ṭarīqa and a Trade Route', *Journal of African History*, 18 (1977), 21–36; Jean Ferrandi, *Le Centre-Africain français* (Paris, 1930), 67–94.
4. Roberta Ann Dunbar, 'Damagaram (Zinder, Niger), 1812–1906: The History of a Central Sudanic Kingdom', Ph.D. dissertation, University of California at Los Angeles, 1970, 206.
5. Thomas S. Jago, 'Report on the Trade and Economic State of the Vilayet of Tripoli in Northern Africa, during the Past Forty Years', House of Commons, Sessional Papers, 1902, Vol. 103, 7.
6. PRO, FO 101/88, Thomas Jago to F.O., 1 Dec. 1898.
7. PRO, FO 101/91, Thomas S. Jago to F.O., 24 Feb. 1900, as cited in Dunbar, 'Damagaram', 100.
8. NNAK, SNP 7, 1538/1908, Kano Province Annual Report, 1907. Most ivory from central Africa may have gone north by way of Wadai, since very little of this product shows up in the early Zinder trade figures, as for example in ADZ, Rapport commercial, 3e trimestre 1903.
9. ANF-AE, AOF, Ns60, Lacau to Delcassé, 22 Apr. 1904.
10. H. Méhier de Mathuisieulx; *La Tripolitaine d'hier et de demain* (Paris, 1912), 187–8; H. Méhier de Mathuisieulx, *À travers la Tripolitaine* (Paris, 1912), 99.
11. On rivalry between Kel Ewey and Imezureg, see Stephen Baier, 'Trans-Saharan Trade and the Sahel: Damergu, 1870–1930', *Journal of African History*, 18 (1977), 37–60. Yehoshua Rash, 'Des colonisateurs sans enthousiasme: les premières années françaises au Damerghou', *Revue Française d'Histoire d'Outre-Mer*, 59 (1972).
12. Rash, 'Damerghou', 271–5; Francis Rennell of Rodd, *People of the Veil* (London, 1926), 50–1; and Charles Furlong, *The Gateway to the Sahara: Observations and Experiences in Tripoli* (New York, 1909), 81–2, 205–7. While travelling in Tripolitania, Furlong spoke with one of the few North Africans to survive the Farak raid, and Furlong's account relays information from this source.
13. Johnson, 'Calico Caravans', 112.
14. PRO, FO 101/91, Thomas Jago to F.O. 20 Apr. 1901 and 27 Apr. 1901.
15. ANF-AE, AOF, NS59, Rais to Delcassé, 30 Nov. 1903.

16. Johnson, 'Calico Caravans', 113–15.
17. Jeremy Keenan, *The Tuareg: People of Ahaggar* (London, 1977), 63–85; Pierre Boyer, 'L'odyssée d'une tribu saharienne: les Djeramna (1881–1929)', *Revue de l'Occident Musulman et de la Méditerranée*, 10 (1971), 27–54.
18. Joseph P. Smaldone, *Warfare in the Sokoto Caliphate: Historical and Sociological Perspectives* (Cambridge, 1977), 100–1.
19. Parmenio Bettoli, 'Tripoli Commerciale', *L'Esploratore*, 6 (1882), 267; imports of Winchester rifles are also mentiqned in USNA, RG59, T 40, Cuthbert Jones to the Department of State, 26 Oct. 1880. In an earlier dispatch Jones reported that 60 or 70 gunsmiths in Tripoli were employed full time mounting smuggled gun barrels which were often mistaken for barrels of local manufacture; these would have been muskets, and therefore had a much less significant effect on power relations in the desert than did modern weapons; USNA, RG59, T40, Cuthbert Jones to the Department of State, 6 Oct. 1879. For a later report indicating the importance of repeating rifles in the successful defence of a caravan against attack, see Méhier de Mathuisieulx, *La Tripolitaine d'hier et de demain*, 187–8.
20. Smaldone, *Warfare*, 101; Joseph P. Smaldone, 'The Firearms Trade in the Central Sudan in the Nineteenth Century', in *Aspects of West Africa Islam*, ed. D. F. McCall and N. R. Bennett (Boston, 1971), 161–2; see also Humphrey J. Fisher and Virginia Rowland, 'Firearms in the Central Sudan', *Journal of African History*, 12 (1971), 233–4, 230.
21. Dennis D. Cordell, 'The Awlad Sulayman of Chad and Lybia: A Study of Raiding and Power in the Chad Basin in the Nineteenth Century', M.A. thesis, University of Wisconsin–Madison, 1972.
22. Philip Curtin, *Economic Change in Precolonial Africa: Senegambia in the Era of the Slave Trade* (Madison, 1975), 278.
23. J. Étiévant, 'Le Commerce tripolitain dans le Centre africain', *Afrique Française*, 9 (Sept. 1910), 280–1; see also Stephen Baier, 'Local Transportation in the Economy of the Central Sudan, 1900–1930', paper presented at the Conference on the Economic History of the Central Savannah of West Africa, Kano, 10 Jan. 1976.
24. Henri Gaden, 'Notice sur la résidence de Zinder', *Revue des Troupes Coloniales*, 2 (1903), 790; ANS, 6F4, 'Comparaison des prix de revient à Zinder des marchandises achetées par les commerçants arabes', n.d.
25. Curtin, *Economic Change*, 280; Jacques Meniaud, *Haut-Sénégal-Niger (Soudan Français)* (Paris, 1912), I. 118–19, as cited in Curtin.
26. ANS, 6F4, 'Comparaison des prix de revient à Zinder des marchandises achetées par les commerçantes arabes', n.d.
27. A. G. Hopkins, *An Economic History of West Africa* (New York, 1973), 74–5; J. C. Anene, 'Liaison and Competition between Sea and Land Routes in International Trade from the Fifteenth Century', in *Les Grandes Voies maritimes dans le monde, xve-xixe siècles* (Paris, 1965), 204–5.
28. PRO, Northern Nigeria Correspondence, Niger Co. to the Undersecretary of State, 27 Aug. 1907; Memo by Lugard on river transport, 9 July 1906; Niger Company Papers, Vol. 7, Earl of Scarborough to Miller, 27 Feb. 1905.
29. Niger Company Papers, Vol. 12, Watts to Directors, 28 Mar. 1908.
30. ADZ, Capt. Paupelain, 'Rapport au sujet de l'ousourou [caravan tax]', 30 June 1912.
31. Étiévant, 'Commerce tripolitain', 279. The value of skins per load comes from ADZ, Rapport commercial, 3e trimestre 1909.
32. Méry, 'Renseignements commerciaux', 2.
33. NNAK, SNP 7 1538/1908, Kano Province Annual Report for 1907.
34. John Q. Wood, 'Commerce and Industries of Tripoli-in-Barbary', *Daily*

Consular and Trade Reports (U.S.), No. 164 (13 July 1912), 227–8; Johnson, 'Calico Caravans', 106.
35. ADZ, Rapport commercial, 2e trimestre 1904.
36. ADZ, Rapport commercial, 4e trimestre 1908, 1er trimestre 1909; 2e trimestre 1909; 3e trimestre 1909.
37. ADZ, Rapport commercial, 3e trimestre 1912.
38. NNAK, SNP 7, 1538/1908, Kano Province Annual Report for 1907; see also Johnson, 'Calico Caravans', 114–15.
39. ADZ, Rapport commercial, 3e trimestre 1908.
40. ADZ, 'Résident Zinder à pétitionnaires de la lettre écrite de Kano le 20 moharam 1322', 17 Apr. 1904; ADZ, Rapport commercial, 3e trimestre 1908; Johnson, 'Calico Caravans', 115; ADZ, Rapport commercial, 2e trimestre 1912.
41. ADZ, Rapport commercial, 1er trimestre 1909; Rapport commercial, 2e trimestre 1911; Rapport commercial, 1 Feb. 1912; Rapport commercial, 2e trimestre 1912; and interview.with Katché Ango, 6 May 1972 (tape 5).
42. PRO, Northern Nigeria Correspondence, Memo by Lugard on caravans tolls, 9 July 1906; Lugard to C.O., 2 Oct. 1905.
43. H. Méhier de Mathuisieulx, 'Une mission en Tripolitaine', *Renseignements Coloniaux*, Jan. 1904, 31–2.
44. PRO, FO 101/92, Perry, Bury and Co. to Marquis of Landsdowne, 16 Apr. 1902; Furlong, *Gateway to the Sudan*, 182; and John Q. Wood, 'Commerce and Industries of Tripoli-in-Barbary', *Daily Consular and Trade Reports* (U.S.), 164 (13 July 1912), 228.
45. Nahum Slousch, *The Jews of North Africa* (Philadelphia, 1944), 108.
46. R. Vadala, 'Une colonie tripolitaine à Paris dans le commerce des plumes d'autriche', *Renseignements Coloniaux*, Feb. 1924, 89.
47. D. A Schultze, *The Sultanate of Bornu*, trans. by P. A. Benton (London, 1913), 218n.
48. W. K. Hancock, *Survey of British Commonwealth Affairs* (London, 1942), II. 215, 215n., 216, 216n.
49. The price at Kano of one kind of imported cloth dropped 25 per cent the year the railway was completed; ADZ, Capt. Paupelain, 'Rapport au sujet de l'ousourou [caravan tax]', 30 June 1912.
50. Capt. Moll, 'Situation économique de la région de Zinder', *Renseignements Coloniaux*, Dec. 1901, 198; ADZ, Rapport commercial, 3e trimestre 1908.
51. ADZ, Rapport commercial, 4e trimestre 1915; Rapport commercial, 2e trimestre 1912; Rapport commercial, 1 Feb. 1912; John A. Works, *Pilgrims in a Strange Land: Hausa Communities in Chad* (New York, 1976), 87.
52. Anene, 'Liaison and Competition', 204–5; NNAK, SNP 7, 1538/1908, Kano Province Annual Report for 1907; Johnson, 'Calico Caravans', 114–15.
53. Interview with Malam Almahdi Atalib, 1 June 1972 (tape 16); 17 Aug. 1972 (tape 27); and 19 Aug. 1972 (tape 28 and 29); interview with cAbd al-Hamid b. Muhammad, 24 May 1972 (tape 13); and summary of a conversation with Abdurahman Bedari, 24 Oct. 1972 (tape 43). Mohammed el-Hachaichi (*Voyage au pays Senoussia* [Paris, 1912], 221) lists Albashir al-Washi among the inhabitants of Djadjidouna in the 1890s and adds that he was a 'personnage considérable, jouissant d'une grande influence parmi les Ghadamsia'.
54. For early French interest in the revival of Algerian trade, see Newbury, 'North African and Western Sudan Trade', 233 ff.; for a later effort, see ANF-AE, Rais to Affaires Étrangères, 5 July 1905; for Zinder, see ADZ, Commandant of Niger to Commandant of Agadez Cercle, 12 June 1909 and 9 July 1909; Rapport du chef de bataillon Mouret sur la politique générale pendant le mois de Février 1909; and Rapport commercial, 3e trimestre 1913. See also ANS, 2G 8 18, Haut-Sénégal-Niger, Rapport politique, 2e trimestre 1908.

55. ANS, 6F4, Rapport sur le mouvement caravanier entre le terroitoire du Niger, les oasis, et la Tripolitaine, signed de Maugras (?), n.d.; interview with Muhamman Kane, 20 May 1972 (tape 15) and 17 Nov. 1972 (tape 46); ADZ, Rapport commercial, 2e trimestre 1911; Rapport commercial, 2e trimestre 1912.
56. ADZ, Rapport commercial, 2e trimestre 1912; interview with Muhamman Kane, 17 Nov. 1972 (tape 46) and 18 Nov. 1972 (tape 46 and 47).
57. Baillaud, *Sur les routes du Soudan*, 111; Étiévant, 'Commerce tripolitain', 282; Anene, 'Liaison and Competition', 204–5; and Johnson, 'Calico Caravans', 114–16.
58. ADZ, Rapport commercial, 2e trimestre 1915; Rapport commercial, 4e trimestre 1915; Rapport politique, 4e trimestre 1915; interview with Muhamman Kane, 17 Nov. 1972 (tape 46) and 18 Nov. 1972 (tape 46 and 47).
59. Interview with Gani Maburu, 19 May 1972 (tape 23) and 2 Sept. 1972 (tape 30); ADZ, ledger marked simply 'Renseignements', entries under 'Cherif Dodo' dated 1906, 1908, and 1918; ADZ, Commandant of Zinder *cercle* to Resident of Kano, 6 Apr. 1924; ADZ, Commandant of Zinder *cercle* to Dufour (a local merchant), 24 June 1924; M. Laizé, 'L'Islam dans le Territoire Militaire du Niger', *BCESHAOF* (1919), 180–2.
60. Interview with cAbd al-Hamid b. Muhammad, 24 May, 1972 (tape 13); Muhamman Kane, 20 May 1972 (tape 15) and 8 Oct. 1972 (tape 39); Malam Almahdi Atalib, 1 June 1972 (tape 16); ADZ, ledger marked 'Renseignements', entries under 'Mohammed Lamine Ettourki', 'Boubakar', 'Cherif Ganaba', 'Mohammed Ben Salla'; see also Étiévant, 'Commerce tripolitain', 277–82; most of Étiévant's information came from Muhammad Salla.

CHAPTER V

1. See for example Michael Crowder, *West Africa under Colonial Rule* (London, 1968), 7–10.
2. Jules Joalland, *Le Drame de Dankori: mission Voulet-Chanoine; mission Joalland-Meynier* (Paris, 1930), 106–43; and Octave Meynier, *La mission Joalland-Meynier* (Paris, 1947), 75–7. For a good general political and administrative history of Niger, see E. Séré des Rivières, *Histoire du Niger* (Paris, 1965).
3. ADZ, file marked 'Bellama, 1921' in the dossier 'Sultanat'; also 'Rapport du Capitaine Lagaillarde, Commandant du Cercle de Zinder, sur les faits reprochés au Chef de Province Bellama', 23 Mar. 1921; Lefebvre to Commandant of Territory, 18 May 1904; Mukhtar b. Sharif to Commandant of Zinder *cercle*, 12 Sept. 1937. See also ADZ, dossier 'Sultanat', 'Fiches de renseignements, Sultan Ahmadu dan Bassa'; 'Fiches de renseignements, Bellama'; 'Fiches de renseignements, Sarkin Makada Ali', Interview with Muhamman Kane, 4 Dec. 1972 (tape 49 and 50); Haruna Muhamman, 31 Oct. 1972 (tape 44); Malam Ali Yaro, 13 May 1972 (tape 18 and 19) and 3 Nov. 1972 (tape 44). See also Roberta Ann Dunbar, 'Damagaram (Zinder, Niger), 1812–1906; The History of a Central Sundanic Kingdom', Ph.D. dissertation, University of California at Los Angeles, 1970, pp. 111–17.
4. Interview with Atari Madiguburi, 14 Oct. 1972 (tape 40 and 41); Amadu 'dan Mai, 14 Oct. 1972 (tape 41); Malam Musa Sidi, 21 Sept. 1972 (tape 34); Lawan Sidi, 13 Nov. 1972 (tape 45); Usman 'dan Shaba, 23 Nov. 1972 (tape 47). For a famine in western Niger caused by insects, not drought, see Finn Fuglestad, 'La Grande Famine de 1931 dans l'ouest nigérien', *Revue Française d'Histoire d'Outre-Mer*, 61 (1974), 18–33. The list of famines in twentieth-century Damagram coincides with the list given by Polly Hill only in 1913/14 and 1927;

see Polly Hill, *Rural Hausa: A Village and a Setting* (Cambridge, 1972), 231, 284.

5. For an introduction to the Sahelian rainfall regime and a note on the sensitivity of sorghum to deficit rainfall, see Derek Winstanley, 'Climatic Changes and the Future of the Sahel', in *The Politics of a Natural Disaster: The Case of the Sahel Drought*, ed. Michael Glantz (Praeger, 1976), 189–213, and especially 191.

6. Jean Maley, 'Mécanisme de changements climatiques aux basses latitudes', *Palaeogeography, Palaeoclimatology, Palaeoecology*, 14 (1973), 193–227; Paul E. Lovejoy and Stephen Baier, 'The Desert-Side Economy of the Central Sudan', *International Journal of African Historical Studies*, 8 (1975), 553–83; reprinted in *The Politics of a Natural Disaster*, ed. Glantz, 145–75; A. T. Grove, 'A Note on the Remarkably Low Rainfall of the Sudan Zone in 1913', *Savanna*, 2 (1973), 133–8; E. Bernus, 'Drought in the Niger Republic', *Savanna*, 2 (1973), 129–33; A. T. Grove, 'Desertification in the African Environment', *African Affairs*, 73 (1974), 143; Stephen Baier, 'Economic History and Development: Drought and the Sahelian Economies of Niger', *African Economic History*, 1 (1976), 1–19.

7. Interview with Muhamman Kane, 17 Nov. 1972 (tape 46); Usman 'dan Shaba, 9 June 1972 (tape 24); and Gilbert Vieillard, 'Coutumiers du cercle de Zinder, 1932', in *Coutumier juridique de l'Afrique Occidentale Française* (Paris, 1939), III. 139.

8. ANS, 2G 14–11, Niger, Rapport d'ensemble, 1914. According to Marty (ANS, 11G 16, Paul Marty, 'Note sur la question musulmane jointe au rapport politique [Niger?] du 3e trimestre 1916'), the population of the Zinder *cercle* at the time was about 350,000. It should be emphasized that estimates of both population and famine deaths represent only rough guesses.

9. ANS, 2G 14-4, Niger, Rapport agricole, 2e trimestre 1914.

10. ADZ, Rapport du Capitaine Milot, commandant du cercle de Zinder, sur une tournée, Septembre–Octobre 1913.

11. ANN, TC 21, Telegram from Intendance Zinder to Intendance Dakar, 12 Dec. 1913; ADZ, Rapport commercial, 4e trimestre 1912; ANN, TC 21, Loffler, Rapport sur les opérations de Tibesti; ANF-OM, Affaires politiques, C518 Dr20, Simon to Governor General of AOF, 28 Feb. 1919.

12. Interview with Malam Musa Sidi, 21 Sept. 1972 (tape 34); and Habu Taliya, 13 Oct. 1972 (tape 40).

13. ADZ, 'Rapport du Capt. Ferrière, Commandant du cercle, au sujet des faits ayant motivé l'envoi du nommé Serkin N'Go chef du canton de Myrriah avant le tribunal de cercle', 1914; and ten other similar reports dated 1914 and 1915 entered in the registers of correspondence kept in the Zinder archives. See also ADZ, Rapport politique, 3e trimestre 1914; Rapport politique, 2e trimestre 1915; and dossier marked 'Renseignements' containing information on *chefs de canton*.

14. ADZ, dossier marked 'Renseignements', entry on Malam Yaro, 1906–9.

15. Interview with Sarkin Dawaki Ibrahim Muhamman, 31 Mar. 1972 (tape 1 and 2).

16. Interview with Abdurahman Idi Bagindi, 27 Oct. 1972 (tape 43).

17. Interview with Aba Musa, 8 May 1972 (tape 6).

18. ADZ, Rapport politique, July 1903. This is the basis for accounts of pre-colonial taxation appearing in Gilbert Vieillard, 'Coutumiers du cercle de Zinder', 119; and Dunbar, 'Damagaram', 157; and in Henri Gaden, 'Notice sur la résidence de Zinder', *Revue des Troupes Coloniales*, 2 (1903), 765–7.

19. ADZ, Rapport commercial, 2e trimestre 1904; Rapport commercial 1er trimestre 1904; Commandant Zinder to Sgt. Nignon at Gangara, 6 May 1907; 'Rapport sur les marchés du cercle', 1 Jul 1911; and Rapport commercial, 1 Feb. 1912.

20. ANS, 2G 23-22, Niger, Rapport économique annuel, 1923; additional information on the movement of market transactions to Nigeria is found in ADZ, 'Rapport sur les marchés du cercle', 1 July 1911.
21. Derrick Thom, 'The Niger-Nigeria Borderlands: A Politico-Geographical Analysis of Boundary Influence upon the Hausa', Ph.D. dissertation, Michigan State University, 1970, pp. 193–6.
22. ADZ, Rapport politique, July 1903; Gaden, 'Notice', 767; Dunbar, 'Damagaram', 162.
23. Interview with Muhamman Kane, 4 Dec. 1972 (tape 49 and 50). Guy Nicolas ('Circulation des richesses et participation sociale dans une société Hausa du Niger' [Bordeaux, cyclostyled, 1967], 229) argues that the execution of sarkin shannu was one of several French measures beneficial to trade. This follows the claim of the official reports, but these same reports begin to complain about the exodus of trade and markets to Nigeria at about the same time; see for example ADZ, Rapport commercial, 2e trimestre 1904.
24. ADZ, 'Résident Zinder à pétitionnaires de la lettre écrite de Kano le 20 moharam 1322', 4 Apr. 1904.
25. ADZ, Commandant Zinder to Lafarge, Subdivision Magaria, 3 Apr. 1908; Mamadu Mai Dosso was beaten publicly and jailed for alleged tax abuse. See account of Muhamman Kane, 24 Nov. 1972 (tape 47 and 48). For collection of tax on the border, see ADZ, Compte rendu, relations Nigéria, Apr. 1912.
26. ADZ, Rapport commercial, 1er trimestre 1912.
27. ADZ, Rapport commercial, 4e trimestre 1914; at the same time the French were setting up a customs frontier on their side of the border, the British eliminated taxes on potash, salt, and livestock, the principal southbound exports; see C. W. Newbury, British Policy towards West Africa: Select Documents 1875–1914 (London, 1971), 474–5.
28. For a detailed discussion of Niger-Nigeria migration, see Thom, 'Niger–Nigeria Borderlands', 133 ff.; Derrick J. Thom, The Niger–Nigeria Boundary 1890–1906: A Study of Ethnic Frontiers and a Colonial Boundary (Athens, Ohio, Papers in International Studies, Africa series, No. 23, 1975). On military recruitment, see ADZ dossier marked 'Sultanat', Mukhtar b. Sharif to Commandant du cercle, 5 Sept. 1937; ANS, 11G 16, No. 27, Renseignements recueillis au sujet de la guerre actuelle au territoire militaire du Niger, Zinder, 22 Sept. 1916; ADZ, Rapport politique, 2e trimestre 1918; NNAK, SNP 8/5 28/1918, Gowers to SNP, 15 Mar. 1918. For migration into British territory elsewhere, see A. I. Asiwaju, 'Migrations as Revolt: The Example of the Ivory Coast and Upper Volta before 1945', Journal of African History, 17 (1976), 577–94.
29. Thom, 'Niger–Nigeria Borderlands', 140.
30. ADZ, 'Rapport du Chef de Bataillon Mouret sur la politique générale pendant le mois d'avril 1908', 20 June 1908. Fortified central settlements were known as agama in Hausa; see interview with Lawan Sidi, 14 Nov. 1972 (tape 46).
31. ADZ, 'Rapport sur la circulation des monnaies françaises et anglaises dans le cercle de Zinder', Oct. 1910.
32. For an excellent survey of monetary policy in the early colonial period, see A. G. Hopkins, 'The Creation of a Colonial Monetary System: The Origins of the West African Currency Board', International Journal of African Historical Studies, 3 (1970), 101–33; for a statement of French monetary thought in the early twentieth century, see Emile Baillaud, 'La Question monétaire en Afrique occidentale', Annales des Sciences Politiques, 20 (Sept. 1905), 561–77.
33. For currency shortages in Niger in the 1920s and 1930s, see ANS, 2G 27-7, Rapport économique d'ensemble 1927; ANS, 2G 24–36, Rapport économique annuel 1934; ANS, 2G 29–39, Rapport économique annuel 1939; ANN,

Rapports de tournées, Maradi, Paumelle, 1 June 1945. John Works reports that after over twenty years of colonial rule in Abeché, the currency in use in the 1930s was still Egyptian pounds; see John Works, *Pilgrims in a Strange Land: Hausa Communities in Chad* (New York, 1976), 176.

34. Paul E. Lovejoy, 'Interregional Monetary Flows in the Precolonial Trade of Nigeria', *Journal of African History*, 15 (1974), 563–86.

35. Dunbar, 'Damagaram', 203, 213–14.

36. A good summary of early Niger currency shortages and speculation is found in Maurice Abadie, *La Colonie du Niger* (Paris, 1927), 303–5. On the cowrie–franc exchange rate, see ADZ, 'Rapport sur la circulation des monnaies françaises et anglaises dans le cercle de Zinder', Oct. 1910; Rapport commercial, 4e trimestre 1909; Rapport commercial, 1er trimestre 1910; Rapport commercial, 4e trimestre, 1910; Rapport commercial, 1er trimestre 1911.

37. ADZ, Rapport commercial, 4e trimestre 1910; interview with Muhamman Kane, 17 Nov. 1972 (tape 46); see also Abadie, *Colonie du Niger*, 304–5.

38. ANS, 2G 21-5, Niger, Situation économique 1921; Abadie (*Colonie du Niger*, 303–5) felt that at the time he wrote scarcities of coin in small denominations had become much less of a problem than it once was; but spot reports from Zinder and Tanout indicate that a five-franc bill exchanged for as little as 3.25 francs in coin: ADZ, dossier marked 'Economie générale', Procès-verbal de réunion du conseil des notables, 27 Apr. 1926; and Subdivision de Tanout, Rapport économique, 2e trimestre 1927. Paper currency was also depreciated in Nigeria: see NNAK, SNP 10/9, 120p/1921, Kano Province Report for 1920–1.

39. Interview with Muhamman Kane, 17 Nov. 1972 (tape 46).

40. Abadie, *Colonie du Niger*, 304.

41. Interview with Muhamman Kane, 17 Nov. 1972 (tape 46).

42. Abadie, *Colonie du Niger*, 304; ANS, 2G 24-12, Niger, Rapport économique d'ensemble, 1924.

43. Interview with Muhamman Kane, 17 Nov. 1972 (tape 46); Rapport commercial, 3e trimestre 1911. Muhamman Kane told of being arrested for suspicion of selling cloth at different prices depending on whether the mode of payment was paper or silver.

44. Interview with Mato Sarki, 7 Dec. 1972 (tape 52).

45. ADZ, Compte rendu, relations avec la Nigéria, Apr. 1912; interview with Muhamman Kane, 17 Nov. 1972 (tape 46) and 18 Nov. 1972 (tape 46 and 47).

46. Interview with Kanta Kolo, 13 Oct. 1972 (tape 40); and Suley Sami, 30 Sept. 1972 (tape 35).

47. Jan. S. Hogendorn, 'The Origins of the Groundnut Trade in Northern Nigeria', Ph.D. dissertation, London School of Economics, 1966. pp. 14 ff.; NNAK, Kano Province annual Reports; interview with Muhamman 'dan Jawo, 14 Sept. 1972 (tape 9).

48. ANS, 2G 22-88, Niger, Bulletin économique mensuel, juillet 1922; ANS, 2G 22-28, Niger, Rapport économique d'ensemble, 1922.

49. ASTA, Commissaire du Gouvernement Général de l'AOF to Commandant Zinder, 12 Nov. 1919.

50. Interview with Alhaji Katche Ango, 6 May 1972 (tape 5); Abba Musa, 8 May 1972 (tape 6); Abba Musa, one of Zinder's few locally born Christians, worked for Dufour for a number of years in the 1920s. See also interview with Muhamman Kane, 22 May 1972 (tape 37); Muhamman Kane began as a *dillali* for one of Dufour's agents and then worked his way up to the status of an agent. See also interview with Usman 'dan Shaba, 9 June 1972 (tape 24); and Abdu 'dan Kalla, 15 Aug. 1972 (tape 27); Abdu is the brother of Ciroma Sulayman, one of the most successful of the group who worked for Dufour. See also interview with

Bernard Ruetsch, 11 Aug. 1972 (tape 25); and Sarkin Kasuwa Garba Adabar, 4
Sept. 1972 (tape 30 and 31).

51. Interview with Usman 'dan Shaba, 9 June 1972 (tape 24); and 22 Nov. 1972 (tape
47). Usman's patron, Muhamman Tsofo, used Dufour's capital to trade sheep
and cattle between Raffa or Kazoe and Zinder or Myrria.

52. Interview with Bernard Ruetsch, 11 Aug. 1972 (tape 25); and private business
papers of Al-Hajj Mukhtar b. Sharif Bashir (see chapter 9), to Christian and
Co., 12 Apr. 1972.

53. Interview with Abba Musa, 8 May 1972 (tape 6); Kasum Wurga, 1 Nov. 1972
(tape 44); and Sanda 'dan Gayi, 31 Oct. 1972 (tape 43 and 44).

54. See M. J. Mortimore, 'Population Distribution, Settlement, and Soils in Kano
Province, Northern Nigeria 1931–62', in *The Population of Tropical Africa*, ed.
John C. Caldwell and Chukuba Okonjo (London, 1968), 305; and Polly Hill,
Population, Prosperity, and Poverty: Rural Kano 1900 and 1970 (Cambridge,
1977), 55–66.

CHAPTER VI

1. Frederik Barth, 'A General Perspective on Nomad-Sedentary Relations in
the Middle East', in *The Desert and the Sown: Nomads in the Wider Society*, ed.
Cynthia Nelson (Berkeley, 1973), 11–21.

2. Guy Nicolas, 'Circulation des richesses et participation sociale dans une société
Hausa du Niger' (Bordeaux, cyclostyled, 1967), 226.

3. A. Richer, *Les Touaregs du Niger (Région de Timbouctou-Gao): Les
Oulliminden* (Paris, 1924), 267–305; F. Nicolas, *Tamesna: Les Ioullimmenden
de l'est* (Paris, 1950), 90–101; Guy Pineau, 'La guerre de Kaossen, 1916–1919',
Afrique Littéraire et Artistique, 10 (1970), 50–5; Finn Fuglestad, 'Les Révoltes
des Touaregs du Niger (1916–1917)', *Cahiers d'Études Africaines*, 49 (1973),
82–120. See also Jide Osuntokun, 'Nigeria's Colonial Government and the
Islamic Insurgency in French West Africa, 1914–1918', *Cahiers d'Études
Africaines*, 15 (1975), 85–94.

4. H. T. Norris, *The Tuaregs: Their Islamic Legacy and its Diffusion in the Sahel*
(Warminster, 1975), 162–73; André Salifou, *Kaoussan ou la révolte senoussiste*,
Études Nigériennes No. 33 (Niamey 1973), 55–157; see also Fuglestad,
'Révoltes', 113–14.

5. ADZ, Commandant Zinder to Commandant Damerghou, 11 Mar. 1903;
Rapport politique, Apr. 1903.

6. Norris, *Tuaregs*, 74–5; J. Étiévant, 'Le Commerce tripolitain dans le centre
africain', *Afrique française*, 9 (Sept. 1910), 279.

7. Camille-Charles Jean, *Les Touaregs du sud-est: l'Air* (Paris, 1909), 14–31; E.
Séré des Rivières, *Histoire du Niger* (Paris, 1965), 213–14; Johannes Nicolaisen,
Structures politiques et sociales des Touaregs de l'Air et de l'Ahaggar, Études
Nigériennes No. 7 (Paris, 1962), 27.

8. F. Nicolas, 'Contribution à l'étude des Twareg de l'Aïr;, in *Contribution à l'étude
de l'Aïr* (Paris, 1952),˙ 462; ADZ, Commandant Zinder to Commandant
Damerghou, 2 Mar. 1903; Jean, *Touaregs du sud-est*, 49–52, 148–70. For a study
of the rising power of religious leaders as a class, see Norris, *Tuaregs*, 145–63;
Norris views the rise of these leaders in the context of processes beginning well
before the arrival of the French. Fuglestad ('Les Révoltes', 93–4) emphasizes
the actions of the French, who favoured religious over military classes. see also
E. Bernus, 'Les Touaregs du sahel nigérien', *Cahiers d'Outre-Mer*, 19 (1966),
12; J. Clauzel, 'Les Hiérarchies sociales en pays Touareg', *Travaux de l'Institut
des Recherches Sahariennes*, 21 (1962), 136; Francis Rennell of Rodd, *People of*

the Veil (London, 1926), 142; and E. Bernus, 'Les Composantes géographiques et sociales des types d'élevage en milieu touareg', in *Pastoralism in Tropical Africa*, ed. T. Monod (London, 1975), 236–8.

9. ANN, TC 4, Peroz, Circulaire No. 1, 16 June 1901; ADZ, Haut-Sénégal-Niger, Région de Zinder, Rapport du chef de bataillon Mouret sur la politique générale pendant le mois de Mars 1908; Méchet to Commandant Damerghou, 28 Feb. 1918.

10. For the activities of Manzo Kandarka, see interview with Alhaji Ali Yaro 13 May 1972 (tape 18 and 19); and Abdu 'dan Dabba, 23 Oct. 1972 (tape 42) and 9 Nov. 1972 (tape 45).

11. ADZ, Haut-Sénégal-Niger, Région Zinder, Rapport du chef de bataillon Mouret sur la politique générale, Feb. 1908; ANN, TC 30, Agades, Rapport politique, Aug. 1908.

12. ANN, TC 21, Loffler, Rapport sur les opérations de Tibesti; ANS, 2G 15-11, Niger, Rapport d'ensemble, 1915.

13. ANS, 2G 14-4 Niger, Rapport agricole, 3ᵉ trimestre 1914. The author of this report wrote: 'L'élevage des chameaux traverse une crise très sérieuse. Beaucoup de ces animaux ont succombé pendant la période de ravitaillement particulièrement dans les transports absolument nécessaires, destinés aux troupes du Tibesti en Mars, Avril, Mai, Juin et Juillet, dont les résultats arrivent seulement à notre connaissance. On peut dire que sur un millier d'animaux de transport, les trois cinquièmes sont morts et les deux cinquièmes restant sont rentrés dans leurs pâturages inutilisables pour au moins une année.'

14. ANS, 2G 15-2, Niger, Venel, Rapport politique, 1ᵉʳ trimestre 1915; AAN, TC 21, Loffler, Rapport sur les opérations de Tibesti.

15. ADZ, Rapport agricole, 4ᵉ trimestre 1915; the anonymous author of this report gives equal weight to the Tibesti requisitions and the drought as causes of severe losses to camel herds in Damergu. Rennell of Rodd (*People of the Veil*, 205) estimated the losses from requisitions for the Tibesti campaign at 23,000 camels among the herds of the Aïr Tuareg alone.

16. NNAK, SNP 8/5, 65/1918, Mourin to Lugard, 28 Dec. 1917; SNP 10/5 88p/1917, Laforgue to Goldsmith, 15 May 1917; SNP 10/5 88p/1917, Brice-Smith to D. O. Hadeija, 26 Jan. 1917; Rennell of Rodd, *People of the Veil*, 360–1.

17. Rennell of Rodd, *People of the Veil*, 361; ANN, Fonferrier, Étude historique, Agadez, 1920; ANS, 2G 22-28, Niger Rapport commercial 4ᵉ trimestre 1922; ANS, 2G 24-12, Niger Rapport économique d'ensemble, 1924; ADZ, Commandant Zinder to Commandant subdivision Tanout, 26 Feb. 1924; the import of this last report bears extensive quotation: 'Je ne saurais trop vous recommander d'agir avec la plus grande circonspection en matière de réquisition d'animaux de transport. C'est là une des questions qui intéressent le plus les indigènes et qui provoquent le plus de critiques à l'égard de notre administration. S'il convient en effet que nos transports s'effectuent normalement, il ne faut néanmoins pas perdre de vue que la réquisition indispose les populations pour lesquelles elle est une gêne et une charge indéniables. C'est cette raison qui a motivé en 1918 et 1919 le départ en Nigéria de 25 à 30.000 Touaregs parmi ceux qui possèdent le plus de chameaux et qu'il est difficile aujourd'hui de faire rentrer sur notre territoire tant qu'ils craignent d'être soumis de nouveau à des réquisitions dont ils ont conservé un souvenir déplorable. Nos anciens administrés, qui suivent très attentivement nos méthodes établissent tout naturellement une comparaison entre notre système de réquisition et le régime libre dont ils jouissent actuellement en Nigéria.'

18. P. Gamory-Dubourdeau, 'Étude sur la création des cantons de sédentarisation dans le cercle de Zinder, et particulièrement dans la subdivision centrale (arrondissement de Mirria)', *BCEHSAOF*, 8 (1924), 239–58.

19. For mistaken early forecasts, see E. D. Morel, *The Affairs of West Africa* (London, 1902), 62; ANS, 2G 24-12, Niger, Rapport économique d'ensemble, 1924; ANS, 2G 35-36, Niger, Rapport économique annuel, 1935; for mistaken later accounts, see E. W. Bovill, *The Golden Trade of the Moors* (2nd edn., New York, 1968), 242; Jean Suret-Canale, *French Colonialism in Tropical Africa*, trans. Till Gottheiner (London, 1971), 190; Nicolas, 'Circulation des richesses', 211n; Johannes Nicolaisen, *Ecology and Culture of the Pastoral Tuareg* (Copenhagen, 1963), 215; and A. Adu Boahen, *Britain, The Sahara and the Western Sudan* (London, 1964), 23–4.

20. For a general survey of the salt industry, see Paul E. Lovejoy, 'The Salt Industry of the Central Sudan: A Preliminary Survey', paper presented at the Seminar on the Economic History of the Central Savannah of West Africa, Kano, 5–10 Jan. 1976. In addition to Bilma and Fachi, another source of sodium chloride was Tegidda-n-tesemt; see Edmund Bernus and Suzanne Bernus, *Du sel et des dattes: introduction à l'étude de la communauté d'InGall et de Tegidda-n-tesemt*, Études Nigériennes No. 31 (Niamey, 1972), 1–46. Other Nigérien sources include Manga country west of Damagaram: see Fernand Foureau, *Documents scientifiques de la mission saharienne* (Paris, 1905), 580–2; the Dallol Fogha: ANN, Michel Perron, La Rivière de sel du Fogha; the Aïr massif, which produced a salt called *agha*: see Rennell of Rodd, *People of the Veil*, 125, 441; and interview with Mato Sarki, 7 Dec. 1972 (tape 52); and the Ahaggar massif to the north: see interview with Ma'azu 'dan Madugu Isa, 28 Aug. 1972 (tape 29). On the taxation of Niger salt production from various sources, see ANS, 11G 16, Mourin, Rapport sur l'exploitation des salines et des mares de natron du Territoire Militaire du Niger en 1915; ANN, Boubou Hama, Enquête sur le sel – situation du sel au Niger (Niamey, mimeographed, 1954).

21. P.-L. Monteil, *De Saint-Louis à Tripoli par le Lac Tchad* (Paris, 1894), 393–8; ANN, Pierre Gentil, Aux confins du Niger et du Tchad: Bilma-Kaouar-Agram-Djado, 1943; Périé, Carnet monographique du cercle de Bilma, 1941; ANN, Monographie de Bilma, 1912; Lieut. Le Sourd, 'Tarikh el Kawar', *Bull. IFAN*, 8 (1946), 1–54.

22. ANN, Notice succincte sur l'oasis d'Agram, 1907.

23. Capitaine Grandin, 'Notes sur l'industrie et le commerce du sel au Kawar et en Agram', *Bull. IFAN*, 13 (1951), 488–533; Henri Gadel, 'Notes sur Bilma et les oasis environnantes', *Revue Coloniale*, 7 (June 1907), 361–86; Yves Urvoy, *Histoire des populations du Soudan central* (Paris, 1936), 187–8; and ANN, Monographie de Bilma, 1912. At the turn of the century a small Tubu salt caravan plied the direct route between Bilma and Zinder; see Fernand Foureau, *D'Alger au Congo par le Tchad: mission saharienne Foureau-Lamy* (Paris, 1902), 531; for early Tubu salt trade, see Louis Brenner, *The Shehus of Kukawa: A History of the Al-Kanemi Dynasty of Bornu* (London, 1973), 24; and Paul E. Lovejoy, 'The Hausa Kola Trade (1700–1900): a Commercial System in the Continental Exchange of West Africa', Ph.D. dissertation, University of Wisconsin–Madison, 1973, p. 120n.

24. Rennell of Rodd, *People of the Veil*, 415; Grandin, 'Notes', 490–1; Urvoy, *Histoire*, 187–8; Lovejoy, 'Hausa Kola Trade', 120n.

25. A good general summary of early Tuareg history is found in Johannes Nicolaisen, *Structures politiques et sociales des Touareg de l'Air et de l'Ahaggar*, Études Nigériennes No. 7 (Niamey, 1960), 21–8; on the migration of the Kel Gress, see E. Bernus, 'Les Touareg du sahel nigérien', 11–2. On late eighteenth-century salt trade to Katsina, see Lovejoy, 'Hausa Kola Trade', 93–5; and Royal Geographical Society, *Records of the African Association 1788–1831*, ed. R. Hallett (London, 1964), 95. Kawar villages paid nominal tribute to either Kel Gress or Kel Ewey sections. See Gadel, 'Notes sur Bilma', 374–5.

26. ANS, 1D 203, Rapport du Lieut. Ronjat au sujet de l'escorte de la caravane de Fachi, 9 Nov. 1908; ANS, 1D 203, Rapport du chef de bataillon Bétrix sur la tournée d'exploration Agadez-Fachi, 29 Sept.–3 Nov. 1907; ANN, Dario, Monographie du cercle d'Agades reproduite par le capitaine Bonaccorsi, 18 Apr. 1913; ANN, Notice succincte sur l'oasis d'Agram, 1907; ANN, Pierre Gentil, Aux confins du Niger et du Tchad: Bilma-Kawar-Agram-Djado, 1943. General descriptions of salt caravans are also found in Le Sourd, 'Tarikh', 32–6; Grandin, 'Notes', 517–27; and Capitaine Fonferrier, 'Étude historique sur le movement caravanier dans le cercle d'Agades', BCEHSAOF, 7 (1923), 303–4. See also Heinrich Barth, Travels and Discoveries in North and Central Africa (New York, 1857; rpt. London 1965), I. 374, 517, 573 ff.; Gustav Nachtigal, Sahara und Sudan (Berlin, 1879), I. 535; and Paul Staudinger, Im Herzen des Hausaländer (Berlin 1889), 610 ff.
27. Interview with Kelilan Gaja, 18 Apr. 1972 (tape 10) and 19 Apr. 1972 (tape 11). Further information on madugai in the salt trade is found in the interview with Kasko Ahamat, 25 May 1972 (tape 14 and 15); ANS, 1D 203, Rapport du chef de bataillon Bétrix sur la tournée d'exploration Agades-Fachi, 29 Sept—3 Nov. 1907.
28. Interview with Abdu Agali, 7 Oct. 1972 (tape 34).
29. Interview with Kelilan Gaja, 19 Apr. 1972 (tape 11); Abdu Agali, 7 Oct. 1972 (tape 34); and Grandin, 'Notes', 510–27.
30. Gustav Nachtigal, Sahara und Sudan (Berlin, 1879), I. 535 (as cited in Lovejoy, 'Salt Industry', 23).
31. ANS, 2G 4-3, Cercle de Zinder, Rapport commercial, 2ᵉ trimestre 1904.
32. ANS, 11G 16, Mourin, Rapport sur l'exploitation des salines et mares de natron au Territoire Militaire du Niger en 1915.
33. ANS, 2G 17-11, Niger, Rapport d'ensemble, 1917.
34. F. Nicolas, 'Le voilement des Twareg (anagad)', in Contribution à l'étude de l'Aïr (Paris, 1950), 498.
35. Gamory-Dubourdeau, 'Cantons de sédentarisation', 249–57; Guy Nicolas, 'Un village bouzou au Niger: étude d'un terroir', Cahiers d'Outre-Mer 58 (1962), 138–65; and interview with Alhassan Muhamman, 28 Aug. 1972 (tape 29); and Ibrahim Muhamman, 28 Aug. 1972 (tape 29).
36. ANN, J. Périé, Carnet monographique du cercle de Bilma: ressources économiques, 1941.
37. Gudrun Dahl and Anders Hjort, Having Herds (Stockholm, 1976), 77–86.
38. Lovejoy, 'Salt Industry', 28.
39. Compagnie Générale des Recherches pour l'Afrique, 'Analyse des courants d'échange' (Paris, mimeographed, 1961), I. 105–6; Boubou Hama, 'Enquête', 31.
40. Lovejoy, 'Salt Industry', 2–6.
41. Estimation of average salt requirements is from Jean Questiaux, 'Quelques aspects de l'économie salinière dans les territoires d'Afrique nord-occidentale et centrale', doctoral thesis, Université d'Alger, 1957, p. 35. Estimates of the cattle population of Niger are from H. E. Lepissier, I. M. MacFarlane, and S. J. Henstra, 'Rapport technique sur le déroulement de la compagne conjointe contre la peste bovine en Afrique centrale et de l'ouest' (Dakar, mimeographed, 1969).
42. PRO CO 657/38, Nigeria, Annual Report of the Veterinary Department 1934.
43. For price data on cotton imports see G. K. Helleiner, Peasant Agriculture, Government and Economic Growth in Nigeria (Homewood, Ill., 1966), 516, 523. For price indices compiled by Helleiner and weighted heavily for cotton piece goods, see Helleiner, 494.
44. Afrique Occidentale Française, Agence Economique, Bulletin de

Renseignements, Aug. 1922, 183–6. See also John Ford, *The Role of Trypanosomiases in African Ecology: A Study of the Tsetse Fly Problem* (Oxford, 1971), 394, 404, 430, 441. Ford gives exaggerated emphasis to the rinderpest epizootic of the late 1880s as a determinant of the size of the cattle population in the early colonial period. Few sources on the severity of the rinderpest epizootic are available, and no solidly based estimates of the effects of the disease can be made. See F. W. de St. Croix, *The Fulani of Northern Nigeria* (1945; reprinted Farnborough, 1972), 12–13; and D. J. Stenning, *Savannah Nomads* (London, 1959), 3–5. It is possible that rinderpest in the 1880s was considerably more severe in the Sokoto Caliphate than it was in Damagaram, but evidence from oral sources in Damagaram suggests that the epizootic was not severe enough to have the kind of effect on the cattle population for which Ford argues. Relative price data suggests that cattle were not particularly scarce by 1900, and that epizootics after 1913, combined with high demand for slaughter animals, were a more serious check on the growth of the herds than the rinderpest epizootic of the 1880s.

45. Helleiner, *Peasant Agriculture*, 76–107, 501; Northern Nigeria Gazette, 29 June 1912; NNAK, SNP 10/7 93p/1919, Kano Province Annual Report, 1918.

46. ANS, 2G 21-15, Niger, Rapport annuel d'ensemble, 1921.

47. ANS, 2G 26-26, Niger, Service zootechnique, rapport annuel, 1926.

48. ANS, 2G 36-7, Niger, Rapport économique annuel, 1936. Cattle prices rose in 1936 in Kano, reaching a point about 15 per cent above the level of the previous year: NNAK, SNP 17/3 27810, Kano Province Annual Report, 1936. On cattle taxes, see ANS, 2G 34-36, Niger, Rapport économique annuel, 1934.

49. R. Larrat, *Problèmes de la viande en Afrique Occidentale Française; les principaux marchés; zones de production: Haute Volta, Niger* (Paris, 1954–5), II. 38. Average prices of cattle and sheep increased by factors of 23 and 25, respectively, between 1938 and 1953; camel prices rose by a factor of 17 in the same period.

50. République Française, Secrétaire d'État aux Affaires Étrangères, 'Approvisionnement en viandes de l'Afrique Centre Ouest: analyse de la situation actuelle et projections' (Paris, Mimeographed, 1969), 245.

51. See for example H. Gaden, 'Notice sur la résidence de Zinder', *Revue des Troupes Coloniales*, 2 (1903), 650–1.

52. In 1942 11 kg of millet were needed to buy 1 kg of salt; see ASTa, Livre Journal Budget Local 1938–1945, entries for 1942. By 1960 3 kg of millet would buy 1 kg of Bilma salt: Companie Générale des Recherches pour l'Afrique, 'Analyse', vol. 1, 25; Archives of the Ministry of Rural Economy, Niamey, Service de l'Agriculture, 'Rapport Annuel, 1962', part 1, p. 19.

53. ADZ, Commandant Zinder to Commandant Région, 1 July 1908; ANN, Subdivision Tanout, Rapport politique, 2e trimestre 1934; ADZ, dossier marked 'Sultanat', Brouin to Governor General, 8 Apr. 1953 and Azemia to Commandant Maradi, 30 Mar. 1953; and Marguerite Dupire, *Organisation sociale des Peul: étude d'ethnographie comparée* (Paris, 1970), 222–8.

54. ANN, Saint-Léon, Rapport du recensement des Peuls et des Igdalen du cercle d'Agadez, Jan.–Mar. 1948; ANN, Geyer, Rapport annuel: contrôle des Peuls nomadisants, Agadez, 21 May 1953.

55. ANN, Lafitte, Carnet monographique, cercle d'Agadez, 1940–1; ADZ, Brouin to Governor General, 8 Apr. 1953.

56. E. Bernus, 'Human Geography in the Sahelian Zone', in *The Sahel: Ecological Approaches to Land Use* (Paris, 1975), 70.

57. D. J. Stenning, *Savannah Nomads* (London, 1959), 4–7; C. E. Hopen, *The Pastoral Ful'be Family in Gwandu* (London, 1958), *passim*; Marguerite Dupire, *Peul nomades: étude descriptive des Wod'aabe du sahel nigérien* (Paris, 1962),

21 ff., 39, 130–2, and *passim*. And Florence Adebisi Okediji, 'An Economic History of the Hausa-Fulani Emirates of Northern Nigeria, 1900–1939', Ph.D. dissertation, Indiana University, 1970, pp. 22–56.

58. ADZ, Commandant Maradi to Governor of Niger, 27 Mar. 1953.
59. On the increasing importance of cattle ownership, see Bernus 'Les Composantes géographiques et sociales', in *Pastoralism in Tropical Africa*, ed. T. Monod, 229–44. For change in plant cover as a result of the growing cattle population, see Bernus, 'Human Geography in the Sahelian Zone', 70.
60. R. Capot-Rey, *Le Sahara français* (Paris, 1953), 289; Nicolaisen, *Structures politiques*, 100; Bernus, 'Tuaregs du sahel nigérien', 16.
61. Bernus, 'Composantes géographiques et sociales', 236–7. For a survey of Tuareg household budgets in the early 1960s, see M. F. Ganon, 'The Nomads of Niger', in *Population Growth and Socioeconomic Change in West Africa*, ed. John C. Caldwell (New York, 1975), 700.
62. See Helleiner, *Peasant Agriculture*, 1–23, 107–18, 126–32.

63. See Stephen Baier, 'Local Transportation in the Economy of the Central Sudan, 1900–1930', paper presented at the Conference on the Economic History of the Central Savannah of West Africa, Kano, 5–10 Jan. 1976.

64. Jan S. Hogendorn, 'New Views on the Origins of Northern Nigerian Groundnut (Peanut) Exporting', paper presented at the Seminar on the Economic History of the Central Savannah of West Africa, Kano, 5–10 Jan. 1976.

65. Pierre Bonte, *L'Élevage et le commerce du bétail dans l'Ader-Doutchi-Majya*, Études Nigériennes No. 23 (Niamey, 1967), 102. ADZ, Commandant Maradi to Governor Niger, 27 Mar. 1953; ANN, Subdivision Tanout, Rapport politique, 2e trimestre 1934; S. Diarra, 'Les Problèmes de contact entre les pasteurs peul et les agriculteurs dans le Niger central', in *Pastoralism in Tropical Africa*, ed. Monod, 284–97. See also Claude Raynaut, 'Le Cas de la région de Maradi', in *Sécheresses et famines du Sahel* (Paris, 1975), 6–11.

66. ADZ, Rapport commercial, 4e trimestre 1915; ADZ, subdivision Magaria, Rapport économique, 3e trimestre 1928; interview with Manzo Muhamman Abubakar, 5 June 1972 (tape 16) and 6 Dec. 1972 (tape 51); Yves Péhaut, 'L'Arachide au Niger', in *Étude d'économie africaine*, ed. D.-G. Lavroff (Paris, 1970), 41–70.

67. Gamory-Dubourdeau, 'Cantons de sédentarisation', 239–58; see also Guy Nicolas, 'Les Catégories d'ethnie et de fraction ethnique au sein du système social hausa, *Cahiers d'Études Africaines*, 15 (1975), 399–442.

68. A full study of the evolution of land tenure systems in Central Niger has not been done, but see Nicolas ('Un village bouzou', 138–65) for a description of a novel system evolved by low-status nomads who settled in Kantché, south-west of Zinder. The best survey of Nigérien land tenure appears in H. Raulin, 'Travail et régimes fonciers au Niger', *Cahiers de l'Institut de Science Économique Appliquée*, 166 (1965), 19–39. For land tenure systems as related to master–servant relations among Malian Tuareg, see P. Idiart, 'Métayage et régimes fonciers dans la région de Faguibine (Cercle de Goundam – Soudan)', *Études Rurales*, 2 (1961), 37–59, and 3 (1961), 21–44.

69. For population pressure on land, see ADZ, Dossier 'Sultanat', Commandant subdivision Dakoro to Commandant Maradi, 30 Mar. 1953; AAN, Subdivision Tanout, Rapport politique, 2e trimestre 1934.

70. NAAK, SNP 10/5 88p/1917, Laforgue, Chargé d'affaires du gouvernement générale du territoire militaire du Niger à M. Goldsmith, Lieutenant Governor Northern Nigeria, 15 May 1917; Jide Osuntokun, 'Nigeria's Colonial Government and the Islamic Insurgency in French West Africa, 1914–1918', *Cahiers d'Études Africaines*, 15 (1975), 85–94.

71. Ross E. Dunn, *Resistance in the Desert: Moroccan Responses to French Imperialism 1881–1912* (London and Madison, Wisconsin, 1977), 225.
72. Dunn, *Resistance in the Desert*, 225.

CHAPTER VII

1. In Kano in 1910, when imports had already begun to arrive from the coast in quantity, Kano cloth still accounted for 90 per cent of local consumption; and the most valuable export was cattle, while kola was the most significant import; see NNAK, SNP 7/11 3835/1910, Kano Province Half-Year Report, 30 June 1910; and E. D. Morel, *The Affairs of West Africa* (London, 1902), 65–7.
2. PRO, CO/657/1, F. D. Lugard, Report on the Blue Book, 1914, p. 8.
3. Examples of statements of this position can be found in International Monetary Fund, *Surveys of African Economies; Vol. 3: Benin, Ivory Coast, Mauritania, Niger, Senegal, Togo, Upper Volta* (Washington, 1970), 421; Victor D. Dubois, 'The Drought in West Africa: Evolution, Causes, and Physical Consequences', American Universities Field Staff, West Africa Series, 15, No. 1, 7.
4. Gudrun Dahl and Anders Hjort, *Having Herds: Pastoral Herd Growth and Household Economy* (Stockholm, 1976), 17; another discussion of the herd as insurance is found in Randall Baker, 'Development and the Pastoral Peoples of Karamoja, North-Eastern Uganda', in *Pastoralism in Tropical Africa*, ed. T. Monod (London, 1975), 191. For an analysis of the herd as capital, see Harold K. Schneider, 'Economics in East African Aboriginal Societies', in *Economic Transition in Africa*, ed. M. Herskovits and M. Harwitz (Evanston, Ill, 1964), 53–76.
5. Dahl and Hjort, *Having Herds*, chapters 2–5.
6. Georges Doutressoule, *L'Élevage au Niger* (Mortain, 1924), 45; Gouvernement Général de l'Afrique Occidentale Française, *Problèmes de la viande en AOF: II, Niger*, p. 7; Denis Danset, 'La Commercialisation du bétail et de la viande au Niger' (Niamey, mimeographed, 1964); Pierre Bonte, *L'Élevage et le commerce du bétail dans l'Ader-Doutchi-Majya*, Études Nigériennes No. 23 (Niamey, 1967), 26–7.
7. République Française, Secrétaire d'État aux Affaires Étrangères, 'Approvisionnement en viandes de l'Afrique Centre Ouest' (Paris, mimeographed, 1969), 59.
8. M. R. Ganon, 'The Nomads of Niger', in *Population Growth and Socioeconomic Change in West Africa*, ed. John C. Caldwell (New York, 1975), 699–700. An earlier and more limited study yielded a similar budget for selected Tuareg and Ful'be households: see ANN, Saint-Léon, Rapport du recensement des Peuls et des Igdalen du cercle d'Agadez, Janvier–Mars 1948.
9. Polly Hill, 'The Northern Ghanaian Cattle Trade', in *Studies in Rural Capitalism in West Africa* (Cambridge, 1970), 92–131.
10. W. Ferguson, 'Nigerian Livestock Problems', in *Markets and Marketing in West Africa* (Edinburgh, 1966), 82–3; H. J. Mittendorf and S. G. Wilson, *Livestock and Meat Marketing in Africa*, F.A.O. publ. no. 14235-R-1 (Rome, 1961), 10; Dahl and Hjort, *Having Herds*, 66–9, 82–4, 102–6.
11. Estimates of the population of Aïr and surrounding areas are found in Johannes Nicolaisen, *Ecology and Culture of the Pastoral Tuareg* (Copenhagen, 1963), 8; Francis Rennell of Rodd, *People of the Veil* (London, 1926), 402; and Camille-Charles Jean, *Les Touaregs du sud-est: l'Aïr* (Paris, 1909), 100–17. The best account of the early history of the Tuareg is found in H. T. Norris, *The Tuaregs: Their Islamic Legacy and its Diffusion in the Sahel* (Warminster, 1975), 1–161.
12. Nicolaisen (*Pastoral Tuareg*, 213) estimated that the millet consumed may have averaged as high as 100 kg per person per year.

13. H. Gaden, 'Notice sur la résidence de Zinder', *Revue des Troupes Coloniales*, 2 (1903), 650–4. Gaden reported that caravans of 2,000 to 3,000 pack oxen left four or five times a year from Damergu. Assuming each animal carried 100 kg, the volume of millet traded ranged from 800 to 1,500 metric tons. See also Capitaine Fonferrier, 'Études historiques sur le mouvement caravanier dans le cercle d'Agadez', *Bulletin CEHSAOF*, 7 (1923), 302–3; and Stephen Baier, 'Trans-Saharan Trade and the Sahel: Damergu, 1870–1930', *Journal of African History*, 18 (1977), 51 ff.

14. ANS, 2G 4-3, Cercle du Djerma, Rapport agricole, 2e trimestre 1904; Cercle du Djerma, Rapport commercial 3e trimestre 1904; Cercle de Tahoua, Rapport agricole, 1er trimestre 1904; Cercle de Gouré, Rapport agricole, 1 Mar. 1904; ADZ, Rapport commercial, 3e trimestre 1903; ANN, Joly, Monographie du cercle de Tahoua, 22 Aug. 1901.

15. Bonte, *L'Élevage et le commerce du bétail*, 136–43; Florence Adebisi Okediji, 'An Economic History of the Hausa-Fulani Emirates of Northern Nigeria, 1900–1939', Ph.D. dissertation, Indiana University, 1970, pp. 235–6.

16. Bonte, *L'Élevage et le commerce du bétail*, 16–9; Okediji, 'Economic History', 252n.

17. Hugh Clapperton, *Journal of a Second Expedition into the Interior of Africa, from the Bight of Benin to Soccatoo* (London, 1829), 115.

18. Samuel Crowther and John Taylor, *The Gospel on the Banks of the Niger* (London, 1859), 148–9, 201–2, 208–9, 213.

19. France, Office Colonial, Ministère des Colonies, *Statistiques du Commerce des Colonies Françaises pour l'année 1914* (Paris, 1915); ANS, 2G33–36, Niger, Rapport zootechnique, 1933.

20. A.O.F., *Problèmes de la viande*, 60–2; ANS, 2G 34-42, Niger, Rapport annuel, élevage et état sanitaire, 11.

21. PRO, CO/657/38, Annual Report of the Veterinary Department, 1934; CO/657/38, Annual Report on the Social and Economic Progress of the People of Nigeria, p. 46.

22. G. K. Helleiner, *Peasant Agriculture, Government, and Economic Growth in Nigeria* (New York, 1966), 76–134, 501; P. T. Bauer, *West African Trade*, 2nd edn. (New York, 1963), 195–201. It is generally agreed that demand for meat is income elastic; see Companie Générale des Recherches pour l'Afrique, 'Analyse des courants d'échanges' (Paris, mimeographed, 1961), 38.

23. PRO, CO/586/4, Northern Nigeria Gazette, 29 June 1912; NNAK, SNP 10/7 93p/1919, Kano Province Annual Report, 1918.

24. Information on the coastal kola trade is from Babatunde Aremu Agiri, 'Kola in Western Nigeria, 1850–1950: A History of the Cultivation of Cola Nitida in Egba–Owode, Ijebu–Remo, Iwo, and Ota Areas', Ph.D. dissertation, University of Wisconsin–Madison, 1972, pp. 64–70. See also Paul E. Lovejoy, 'The Wholesale Kola Trade of Kano', *African Urban Notes*, 5 (1970), 129–31.

25. NNAK, SNP 7/12 951/1911, Kano Province Annual Report, 1910.

26. NNAK, SNP 10/7 93p/1919, Kano Province Annual Report, 1918; NNAK, Kanoprof. 5/1 628, Kano Province Annual Report, 1930.

27. ANS, 2G 19-19, Niger Service Zootechnique, Rapport, 4e trimestre 1919. A recent investigator implies that Malian cattle trade came into existence with the growth of cities in a later period: see J. Dirck Stryker, 'The Malian Cattle Industry', *Journal of Modern African Studies*, 12 (1974), 448–9. This seems highly unlikely in view of material in French colonial archives.

28. F. W. H. Migeod, *Through Nigeria to Lake Chad* (London, 1924), 38.

29. PRO, Northern Nigeria Correspondence, Niger Co. to Undersecretary of State, 25 July 1907, and 26 Aug. 1907. European imports accounted for only 4 per cent of imports cleared for passage at Jegga; see CO, Confidential Prints, African 845/31, Governor of Southern Nigeria to Secretary of State, 10 May 1907.

30. Paul E. Lovejoy, 'The Hausa Kola Trade (1700–1900); A Commercial System in the Continental Exchange of West Africa', Ph.D. dissertation, University of Wisconsin–Madison, 1973, pp. 131–67.

31. For the decline of the overland kola trade, see Lovejoy, 'Wholesale Kola Trade', 130.

32. Interview with Alhaji Yahu Isa, 10 Feb. 1972 (tape 1).

33. Interview with Ma'azu Isa, 28 Aug. 1972 (tape 39 and 40).

34. Interview with Alhaji Amadu 'dan Ladi, 8 Feb. 1972 (tape 1).

35. NNAK, Minprof 7/7 39/1912, Niger Province Annual Report, 1912.

36. Interview with Suley Ekade, 1 Oct. 1972 (tape 36); Sani Fari, 30 Sept. 1972 (tape 36); and Suley Sami, 30 Sept. 1972 (tape 35). All were cattle traders who travelled between Tessaoua (north of Katsina) to Lagos.

37. Interview with Suley Sami, 30 Sept. 1972 (tape 35).

38. One source estimates that 200,000 head of cattle were imported into the southern provinces of Nigeria in 1934; see PRO, CO/657/38, Annual Report on the Social and Economic Progress of the People of Nigeria, 1934.

39. John Ford, *The Role of Trypanosomiases in African Ecology: A Study of the Tsetse Fly Problem* (London, 1971), 367–441.

40. The annual reports of the Veterinary Department of Northern Nigeria document progress against animal disease. By 1927 rinderpest serum was being administered to cattle in six locations, and 95,000 head of cattle were being treated each year; see PRO, CO/657/23, Annual Report of the Veterinary Department, 1927. Similar progress was being made in Niger, though at a slower pace; see ANS, 2G 34–42, Rapport annuel sur l'élevage et l'état sanitaire du bétail, 1934. Ford (*Role of Trypanosomiases*, 367–441) relies on highly suspect Nigerian census data to document growth of the human population. For a critical analysis of census data, see Helleiner, *Peasant Agriculture*, 395–7.

41. Gaden, 'Notice', 650-4; Fonferrier, 'Études historiques', 302–3; interview with Guntu Nomo, 13 Oct. 1972 (tape 40); Usman Saidu, 13 Oct. 1972 (tape 40).

42. Interview with Haruna Biriam, 14 Oct. 1972 (tape 41); Jeremy Keenan, *The Tuareg: People of Ahaggar* (London, 1977), 139–40. For an account of economic forces in Ahaggar which led to increased emphasis on trade towards the Sudan, see M. Gast, 'Évolution de la vie économique et structures sociales en Ahaggar', *Travaux de l'Institut des Recherches Sahariennes*, 24 (1965), 134.

43. Interview with Haruna Biriam, 14 Oct. 1972 (tape 41).

44. Dugald Campbell (*On the Trail of the Veiled Tuareg* [London, 1928], 74) reported seeing Ahaggar Tuareg in Zinder in 1926. On the increase in Ahaggar economic power and social prestige during the revolt, see F. Nicolas, 'Le Voilement des Twareg (*amgad*)', in *Contribution à l'étude de l'Aïr* (Paris, 1950), 497–503. Other sources on salt trade from Ahaggar include Fernand Foureau, *D'Alger au Congo par le Tchad: mission saharienne Foureau-Lamy* (Paris, 1902), 554; Nicolaisen, *Pastoral Tuareg*, 210–12; ADZ, Rapport commercial 4e trimestre 1903; ADZ, Subdivision Tanout, Rapport économique, 4e trimestre 1922; and numerous taped oral sources.

45. Interview with Atari Madiguburi, 14 Oct. 1972 (tape 40 and 41); Fokondo Mala, 13 Oct. 1972 (tape 40); Kanta Kolo, 13 Oct. 1972 (tape 40); each of these were cattle traders themselves, as were their fathers. See also accounts of Umbutu Gangan, 18 Aug. 1972 (tape 27); and Isan Talha, 19 Aug. 1972 (tape 28). The village of Malam Tilum lost its market when the water supply became inadequate during and after the drought of 1911–14; the site of the market moved to Gangara; see ANN, Réponse à télégramme-lettre officiel no. 2225 a.p. du 5 août 1934, Tanout, 27 Aug. 1934.

46. ADZ Rapport sur les marchés du cercle, 1 July 1911.

47. ADZ, Rapport commercial, 1 Feb. 1911; ADZ, Rapport commercial, 4e

trimestre 1911; interview with Atari Madiguburi, 14 Oct. 1972 (tape 41).

48. Interview with Atari Madiguburi, 14 Oct. 1972 (tape 41).

49. See Rennell of Rodd, *People of the Veil*, 60, who travelled north from Damergu in 1922.

50. ADZ, dossier marked 'Sultanat', Brouin to Governor of Niger, 8 Apr. 1953; Eldridge Mohammadou, 'Les Peuls du Niger oriental: groupes ethniques et dialectes', *Camelang*, 2 (1969), 57–93; ANN, Tanout, Rapport politique, 2e trimestre 1934.

51. Interview with Fokondo Mala, 13 Oct. 1972 (tape 40); Kanto Kolo, 13 Oct. 1972 (tape 40).

52. Interview with Abdu 'dan Dabba, 9 Nov. 1972 (tape 45).

53. Okediji, 'Economic History', 235–6.

54. ADZ, Commandant Zinder to Commandant Niamey, 28 Sept. 1903; ADZ, Rapport commercial, July 1903; ADZ, Rapport commercial, 3e trimestre 1903. Okediji's informants stressed the importance of Ilorin as the major southern cattle market in the years before the turn of the century; see Okediji, 'Economic History', 224.

55. Interview with Muhammad 'dan Jawo, 9 Sept. 1972 (tape 9); Alhaji Adamu Abdumumuni, 8 May 1972 (tape 7); Malam Cillo Alassan, 9 May 1972 (tape and 8); Malam Lawan Sidi, 12 May 1972 (tape 21 and 22); and Malam Musa Gambo, 31 Oct. 1972 (tape 43).

56. Marion Johnson, 'Cloth on the Banks of the Niger', *Journal of the Historical Society of Nigeria*, 6 (1973), 353–64.

57. ADZ, Rapport commercial, 3e trimestre 1903; ADZ, Commandant Zinder to Commandant Niamey, 28 Sept. 1903; interview with Malam Musa 'dan Gambo, 31 Oct. 1972 (tape 43).

58. Interview with Alhaji Adamu Abdumumuni, 8 May 1972 (tape 7). Traders from the area west of Damagaram more frequently continued to travel south of Kano; see the account of Suley Ekade, 1 Oct. 1972 (tape 36), who took cattle overland to Lagos and Ibadan, shipped animals (including sheep and goats) by rail, and also took them south by truck.

59. Interview with Usman 'dan Shaba, 9 June 1972 (tape 24); and Musa 'dan Maduga, 14 June 1972 (tape 24).

60. Interview with Usman 'dan Shaba, 9 June 1972 (tape 24); and Musa 'dan Maduga, 14 June 1972 (tape 24).

61. Interview with Musa 'dan Gambo, 31 Oct. 1972 (tape 43).

62. Interview with Alhaji Adamu Abdumumuni, 8 May 1972 (tape 7). See also Guy Nicolas, 'La pratique traditionnelle du crédit au sein d'une société sub-saharienne, vallée de Maradi, Niger', *Cultures et Développement*, 6 (1974), 737–73.

63. For an exceptional case, see the account of Mani 'dan Tambai, interviewed 6 Sept. 1972 (tape 31); interview with Lushe Bukari, 11 Sept. 1972 (tape 33).

64. For examples of traders who learned their occupations from elder brothers, see interview with Cillo Alassan, 9 May 1972 (tape 7 and 8); Isan Talha, 19 Aug. 1972 (tape 28); Isa Kadir, 11 Sept. 1972 (tape 33); and Isufu Abande, 14 Aug. 1972 (tape 25 and 26). For cases of apprenticeship to paternal uncles, see interview with Sharubutu Isa, 6 Sept. 1972 (tape 32); to maternal uncles, see interview with Garba Surkule, 29 Nov. 1972 (tape 33). When asked about apprenticeship many traders insisted that the village was the trading unit and that they learned from many villagers who had experience; kinship played a role only to the extent that people consider all fellow villagers distant kinfolk. See interview with Haruna Muhamman, 31 Oct. 1972 (tape 44); Sami Sharubutu, 11 May 1972 (tape 4); 'dan Rugu Awakas, 6 Sept. 1972 (tape 31).

65. Interview with Alhaji Sali Amadu, 30 Sept. 1972 (tape 35 and 36); Sami

Sharubutu, 11 May 1972 (tape 4); Malam Kulu Malia, 30 Sept. 1972 (tape 35). On the decreasing size of caravans, see also A. G. Hopkins, *An Economic History of West Africa* (New York, 1973), 63.

66. C. W. Newbury, *British Policy Towards West Africa: Select Documents, 1875–1914* (Oxford, 1971), 474–5; interview with Cillo Alassan, 20 Oct. 1972 (tape 36).

67. On the river crossing, see interview with Mutari Nuhu, 30 Sept. 1972 (tape 35); and Suli Sami, 30 Sept. 1972 (tape 35); on the caravan leader as intermediary in the payment of tolls, see interview with Cillo Alassan, 20 Oct. 1972 (tape 36).

68. Interview with Isufu Abande, 14 Aug. 1972 (tape 25 and 26); for a detailed account of the functioning of pre-colonial caravans and the role of the *madugu*, see Lovejoy, 'Hausa Kola Trade', 178–86.

69. Interview with Isufu Abande, 14 Aug. 1972 (tape 25 and 26); Alhaji Nahum Muhamman, 15 June 1972 (tape 24); and Sharubutu Isa, 6 Sept. 1972 (tape 13).

70. ANS, 2G 27-29, Niger, Service Zootechnique, Rapport annuel 1927, p. 27; and interview with Lawan Sidi, 12 May 1972 (tape 21 and 22).

71. Interview with Usman 'dan Shaba, 9 June 1972 (tape 24).

72. Interview with Bernard Ruetsch, 11 Aug. 1972 (tape 25); Dugald Campbell, *On the Trail of the Veiled Tuareg* (London, 1926), 110. Campbell visited Bourges in Agadez. Like Dufour, Bourges was a retired military man; he had been a hero in the fight against Kaocen during the revolt of 1916–18.

73. Interview with Bernard Ruetsch, 11 Aug. 1972 (tape 25).

74. Abou Digu'en [pseud.], *Mon voyage au Soudan tchadien* (Paris, [1929]), 64–70, 90, 129, 131, 142; and on cattle trade from Mao in Chad, see ibid., 192, 226–30.

75. Abner Cohen, *Custom and Politics in Urban Africa: Hausa Migrants in Yoruba Towns* (London, 1868), 84.

76. Cohen, *Custom and Politics*, 84–5.

77. Abou Digu'en, *Voyage au Soudan, passim.*

CHAPTER VIII

1. For a review of the two positions, see E. E. LeClair and H. K. Schneider, eds., *Economic Anthropology: Readings in Theory and Analysis* (New York, 1968), especially reprints of articles by K. Polanyi, George Dalton, Robins Burling, Edward E. LeClair, Scott Cook, and Frank Cancain. Recent statements of each position can be found in Harold K. Schneider, *Economic Man: The Anthropology of Economics* (New York, 1974), 1–42; and George Dalton, review of A. G. Hopkins, *An Economic History of West Africa* in *African Economic History*, 1 (1976), 51–101.

2. Claude Meillassoux, 'Essai d'interprétation du phénomène économique dans les sociétés traditionelles d'auto-subsistence', *Cahiers d'Études Africaines*, 4 (1960), 38–67; Georges Dupré and Pierre-Philippe Rey, 'Reflections on the Pertinence of a Theory of the History of Exchange', *Economy and Society*, 2 (1973), 131–63, trans. Elizabeth Hindress.

3. Raymond Firth, 'Introduction', to *Themes in Economic Anthropology*, ed. Raymond Firth (London, 1967), 3 ff.

4. Schneider, *Economic Man*, 43–7.

5. Emmanuel Terray, *Maxism and 'Primitive' Societies* (London, 1972), trans. Mary Klopper, 151–2.

6. Robin Law, 'Royal Monopoly and Private Enterprise in the Atlantic Trade: The Case of Dahomey', *Journal of African History*, 18 (1977), 555–77. Polanyi's argument is presented in Karl Polanyi, *Dahomey and the Slave Trade: An Analysis of an Archaic Economy* (Seattle, 1966), 3–139, esp. 94.

7. George Dalton, review of A. G. Hopkins, *An Economic History of West Africa* in *African Economic History*, 1 (1976), 51–101.

8. Meillassoux, 'Essai d'interprétation du phénomène économique', 37–67.
9. Interview with Abdurahaman Bedari, 7 Aug. 1972 (tape 32); Hajiya 'yar Idi Bagindi and Abdurahaman Idi Bagindi, 27 Oct. 1972 (tape 43); Alhaji Ali Yaro, 13 May 1972 (tape 18 and 19), and 3 Nov. 1972 (tape 44); Gani Maburu, 10 May 1972 (tape 30); and Muhamman Kane, 17 Nov. 1972 (tape 46).
10. Interview with Malam Lawan Sidi, 12 May 1972 (tape 21 and 22).
11. Jean-Loup Amselle, 'Parenté et commerce chez les Kooroko', in *The Development of Indigenous Trade and Markets in West Africa*, ed. Claude Meillassoux (London, 1971), 256–8; see also Amselle, 'Les Réseaux marchands Kooroko', *African Urban Notes*, 5 (1970), 143–58; and Jean-Loup Amselle, *Les Négociants de la savanne: histoire et organisation sociale des Kooroko (Mali)* (Paris, 1977), 151–206. Jean-Louis Boutillier, 'La Cité marchande de Bouna dans l'ensemble économique Ouest-Africain', in *The Development of Indigenous Trade and Markets*, 244–5.
12. Paul E. Lovejoy, 'The Hausa Kola Trade (1700–1900): A Commercial System in the Continental Exchange of West Africa', Ph.D. dissertation, University of Wisconsin–Madison, 1973, 131–65; and Lovejoy 'The Wholesale Kola Trade of Kano', *African Urban Notes*, 5 (1970), 138–42.
13. For other results of the survey, see appendix II.
14. The major epizootics took place in the 1880s 1914/15, 1916/17, 1919–20, 1921, and 1925. See Georges Doutressoule, *L'Élevage au Niger* (Mortain, 1924), 44, 57–61; ANF-OM, Agence des Colonies, C141 Dr99, Niger, Service Zootechnique, Rapport annuel, 1933; PRO, CO/567/18, Northern Nigeria, Veterinary Report for 1926.
15. H. E. Lepissier, I. M. MacFarlane, and S. J. Henstra, 'Rapport technique sur le déroulement de la compagne conjointe contre la peste bovine en Afrique Centrale et de l'Ouest (1961–69)' (Dakar: cyclostyled, 1969 [?]. For a description of the progress of the veterinary departments in the 1930s, see John Ford, *The Role of Tryanosomiases in African Ecology* (London, 1971), 406–8.
16. For a strategy of buying and selling to make up for losses from disease, see interview with Malam Cillo Alassan, 6 Nov. 1972 (tape 36); and Suley Ekade, 1 Oct. 1972 (tape 36).
17. Interview with Alhaji Nahum Muhamman, 15 June 1972 (tape 24); Isufu Abande, 14 Aug. 1972 (tape 25 and 26); Abdu 'dan Dabba, 23 Nov. 1972 (tape 42); and Ma'azu Isa, 28 Aug. 1972 (tape 29).
18. Interview with Isufu Abande, 14 Aug. 1972 (tape 25 and 26); Isufu had an informal apprenticeship of this kind with Madugu Isa of Tunduku near Tirmini, Abdu Genu of Garurua near Tirmini, and Sami Sharubutu (interview with the latter is found on tape 4).
19. For a detailed account of the services provided by the *fatoma* Muhamman Labe, a Kano landlord-broker visited by many Damagaram and Damergu traders, see interview with Isufu Abande, 14 Aug. 1972 (tape 25 and 26). For a Zinder landlord, see interview with Isan Talha, 19 Aug. 1972 (tape 28); nearly all traders visiting Kano used landlords, in contrast to those who came to the Zinder market, who usually did not use landlords. Only Abdu 'dan Dabba (interview of 23 Nov. 1972, tape 42) was able to get along in Kano without a landlord.
20. Interview with Malam Lawan Sidi, 5 May 1972 (tape 21 and 22), 13 Nov. 1972 (tape 45), and 14 Nov. 1972 (tape 46).
21. M. G. Smith, 'The Hausa System of Social Status', *Africa* 29 (1959), 239–51; M. G. Smith, *The Economy of the Hausa Communities of Zaria* (London, 1955), 41–7; M. G. Smith, *Government in Zazau 1800–1950* (London, 1960), *passim*; for an ethnography of Zinder written in the 1930s, see Gilbert Vieillard, 'Coutumiers du cercle de Zinder', in *Coutumiers juridiques de l'Afrique Occidentale Française*, 5 vols. (Paris, 1939), III. 97–179.

22. Ronald Cohen, *Dominance and Defiance: A Study of Marital Instability in an Islamic African Society* (Washington, 1971), 23–64; Robert Murphy, 'Tuareg Kinship', *American Anthropologist* 69 (1967), 163–70; and Johannes Nicolaisen, *Ecology and Culture of the Pastoral Tuareg of Air and Ahaggar* (Copenhagen, 1962), 447–77 and *passim*.

23. Polly Hill, *Rural Hausa: A Village and a Setting* (Cambridge, 1972), 36–56; and Smith, *Economy of the Hausa Communities*, 31 ff. For the *gandu* in Damagaram, see Guy Nicolas, 'Circulation des richesses et participation sociale dans une société Hausa du Niger' (Bordeaux: cyclostyled, 1967), 24–5, 57.

24. M. G. Smith, 'Hausa Inheritance and Succession', in *Studies in the Laws of Succession in Nigeria*, ed. J. Derrett (London, 1965), 281 ff; Vieillard, 'Coutumier', 154–9; an excellent summary of literature on Hausa inheritance appears in Hill, *Rural Hausa*, 270–2.

25. Interview with Muhamman Kane, 8 Oct. 1972 (tape 39).

26. Interview with Usman 'dan Shaba, 9 June 1972 (tape 33), and 23 Nov. 1972 (tape 47). For an analysis of family firms in a different context, see Burton Benedict, 'Family Firms and Economic Development', *Southwestern Journal of Anthropology*, 24 (1968), 1–19; Benedict sees two crises in the development of family firms, the first occurring when sons reach maturity and wish a greater role in decision making, and the second when the firm has grown to the point that outsiders must be incorporated.

27. Interview with Muhamman Kane, 20 May 1972 (tape 15), 24 November 1972 (tape 47 & 48), 3 Dec. 1972 (tape 49). Muhamman Kane is the son of 'dan Maleka, and at 88 years of age was the eldest living member of the Zinder merchant community at the time field research was done. The quotation is from the interview of 24 Nov.

28. Interview with Muhamman Kane, 8 Oct. 1972 (tape 39), and 24 Nov. 1972 (tape 47 and 48). A special relationship between a man and his father's slave or client also recurs among the Tuareg; see interviews with Isan Talha, 19 Aug. 1972 (tape 28), and 27 Oct. 1972 (tape 43); and Sarkin Kasuwa Garba Adabar, 4 Sept. 1972 (tape 30 and 31).

29. Interview with Muhamman Kane, 24 Nov. 1972 (tape 47 and 48), 3 Dec. 1972 (tape 49), and 4 Dec. 1972 (tape 49 and 50). For a similar case in which wealth was dissipated at the death of a Hausa merchant of Abeché, see John Works, *Pilgrims in a Strange Land: Hausa Communities in Chad* (New York, 1976), 70–1.

30. Vieillard, 'Coutumier', 159.

31. Interview with Bashir Mukhtar, 1 Dec. 1972 (tape 51). The use of written wills was also common among North Africans living in Kano; see C. W. Rowling, *Report on Land Tenure, Kano Province* (Kaduna, 1949).

32. *Bara* may be translated 'servant' or 'retainer' as well as client. Much useful information on clientage is found in Smith, *Government in Zazau*, 8–9, 83, 245–60. See also Smith, *Economy of the Hausa Communities*, 95; and Hill, *Rural Hausa*, 72–4, 207–8.

33. Vieillard, 'Coutumier', 166. For slavery in nineteenth-century Damagaram, see Roberta Ann Dunbar, 'Slavery and the Evolution of Nineteenth-Century Damagaram', in *Slavery in Africa: Historical and Anthropological Perspectives*, ed. Suzanne Miers and Igor Kopytoff (Madison, 1977), 155–80; see also Stephen Baier and Paul E. Lovejoy, 'The Tuareg of the Central Sudan: Gradations in Servility at the Desert Edge', in *Slavery in Africa*, ed. Miers and Kopytoff, 391–414.

34. Interview with Kasum Wurga, 1 Nov. 1972 (tape 44); Sanda 'dan Gayi, 31 Oct. 1972 (tape 43 and 44); and Usman 'dan Shaba, 9 June 1972 (tape 24).

35. ADZ, Commandant at Zinder to Jegou, 10 Sept. 1908.

36. Interview with Sanda 'dan Gayi, 31 Oct. 1972 (tape 43 and 44).

37. Interview with Malam Lawan Sidi, 13 Nov. 1972 (tape 45).
38. Smith, *Government in Zazau*, 255–7.
39. Interview with Mato Sarki, 7 Dec. 1972 (tape 52). Manzo Kandarka married the daughter of his patron; see interview with Abdu 'dan Dabba, 9 Nov. 1972 (tape 45). Manzo Kandarka's client married his patron's daughter, as explained in the same interview. Idi Bagindi married off one of his daughters to a client; see account of Hajiya 'yar Idi Bagindi, and Abdurahaman Idi Bagindi, 27 Oct. 1972 (tape 43). 'Dan Gayi married the daughter of his patron, Shariff Dodo; see interview with Sanda 'dan Gayi, 31 Oct. 1972 (tape 43 and 44). Ali Ilia married the daughter of his patron, 'dan Gayi (from the same interview). Madugu Isa of Ruwan Gao married one of Babna Lushe's classificatory daughters, as in the account of Muhaman 'dan Jawo, 14 Sept. 1972 (tape 9). 'Dan Zara married the daughter of his patron, Ciroma Sulayman; see interview with Barma Usman Muhamman, 6 Dec. 1972 (tape 52). Two of 'dan Maleka's clients married his daughters; see interview with Muhamman Kane, 24 Nov. 1972 (tape 47 and 48). Madugu Kato married the daughter of his patron; see account of Alhaji Adamu Abdumumuni, 8 May 1972 (tape 7). Muhamman Murna married the daughter of Ciroma Sulayman, his patron; see interview with Ilali Ali, 17 May 1972 (tape 20), and 15 Sept. 1972 (tape 9). Ma'azu Isa married his daughter off to a foster son who was his junior trading partner; see account of Ma'azu Isa, 11 Sept. 1972 (tape 32). Muhamman Adabar married his patron's daughter; see account of Sarkin Kasuwa Garba Adabar, 4 Sept. 1972 (tape 31 and 32). Bazindire married the daughter of his patron Nomo; see interview with Muhamman Kane, 24 Nov. 1972 (tape 47 and 48).
40. Meillassoux, 'Phénomène économique,' 57.
41. Interview with Mato Sarki, 7 Dec. 1972 (tape 52).
42. Smith, *Economy of the Hausa Communities*, 49–50.
43. Nicolas, 'Circulation des richesses', 29.
44. Interview with Usman 'dan Shaba, 23 Nov. 1972 (tape 47); and Mato Sarki, 7 Dec. 1972 (tape 52).
45. Interview with Sarkin Dogari Haruna Salau, 29 Nov. 1972 (tape 51) and Sanda 'dan Gayi, 31 Oct. 1972 (tape 43 and 44).
46. Interview with Abdu 'dan Kalla, 15 Aug. 1972 (tape 27).
47. Interview with Usman 'dan Shaba, 23 Nov. 1972 (tape 47) and 9 June 1972 (tape 24). The partnership involved Barmo, Bukari Dukusuru, and Muhaman Tsofo; the last was Usman 'dan Shaba's patron.
48. Smith, *Government in Zazau*, 260.
49. Works, *Pilgrims*, 70–1; Amselle, 'Parenté et commerce', 143–58.
50. Abner Cohen, *Custom and Politics in Urban Africa: A Study of Hausa Migrants in Yoruba Towns* (London, 1969), 83–7. Fostering occurred in Zinder, but it seldom played a role in the recruitment of traders into the enterprise. In an exceptional case Muhamman Murna fostered Garba, the son of Muhamman Adabar; see interview with Garba Adabar, 4 Sept. 1972 (tape 30 and 31). For examples of fostering among rural traders see accounts of Ilia Ilias, 18 Sept. 1972 (tape 8 and 34); Ilali Ali, 15 Sept. 1972 (tape 9); and Ma'azu Isa, 28 Aug. 1972 (tape 29).
51. Amselle, *Les Négociants de la savanne*, 163–4, 177–80.
52. On the division of labour in agriculture, see Jacqueline Nicolas, *Les Juments de dieux, rites de possession et condition féminine en pays hausa: vallée de Maradi, Niger*, Études Nigériennes No. 21 (Niamey, 1966), 17 ff.; Hill, *Rural Hausa*, 249–52. For prostitution, see Colette Piault, *Contribution à l'étude de la vie quotidienne de la femme mauri*, Études Nigériennes No. 10 (Niamey, 1965), 100–2, 125–33; Cohen, *Custom and Politics*, 55 ff.; and Suzanne Bernus, *Particularismes ethniques en milieu urbain, l'exemple de Niamey* (Paris, 1969), 143–64.

53. Interview with Ma'azu Isa, 28 Aug. 1972 (tape 29). According to Muhamman Kane (interview of 20 May 1972, tape 15) the women of urban households spun thread to sell to weavers and gave their husbands one-tenth of their profit. For the impact of competition from machine made cloth on the local West African cloth industry, see Marion Johnson, 'Technology, Competition, and African Crafts', in *The Imperial Impact: Studies in the Economic History of Africa and India*, ed. Clive Dewey and A. G. Hopkins (London, 1978), 243–58.
54. Interview with Lawan Sidi, 12 May 1972 (tape 21 and 22).
55. Interview with Musa Sidi, 21 Sept. 1972 (tape 34); Umbutu Gangan, 18 Aug. 1972 (tape 27); and Lawan Sidi, 12 May 1972 (tape 21 and 22) and 13 Nov. 1972 (tape 45).
56. The work of Sara Berry has called attention to the importance of non-market sources of capital and labour in the expansion of cocoa farming in western Nigeria; see Sara Berry, *Cocoa, Custom, and Socio-Economic Change in Rural Western Nigeria* (London, 1975), 7–8.

CHAPTER IX

1. Robert Paul Thomas, 'The Automobile Industry and Its Tycoon', *Explorations in Economic History*, 6 (1969), 139–40. For recent studies of African entrepreneurs, see John R. Harris, 'Some Problems in Identifying the Role of Entrepreneurship in Economic Development', *Explorations in Economic History*, 7 (1970), 347–69; and Peter Marris and Anthony Somerset, *African Businessmen: A Study of Entrepreneurship and Development in Kenya* (London, 1971), 2–3.
2. Interview with Bashir Mukhtar, 1 Dec. 1972 (tape 51), who is Mukhtar's son and the heir of his business. See also interview with Alhaji Jibaje Ali, 7 June 1972 (tape 17 and 19).
3. Muhammad Salla is mentioned in the account of J. Étiévant, 'Le Commerce tripolitain dans le centre africain', *Afrique Française* 9, Sept. 1910, 281–2. For Mukhtar's relation with Muhammad Salla, see interviews with Alhaji Jibaje Ali, 7 June 1972 (tape 17 and 19); and Muhamman Kane, 17 Nov. 1972 (tape 46).
4. Interview with Muhamman Kane, 17 Nov. 1972 (tape 46). For a detailed description of black market currency transactions, see chapter IV.
5. Interview with Alhaji Jibaje Ali, 7 June 1972 (tape 17 and 19), and 7 Oct. 1972 (tape 34). The business records of Al-hajj Mukhtar have been preserved and are kept in his office, which is now occupied by his son Bashir. These papers consist for the most part of business correspondence, records of debts, and accounts of transactions, but a small number of personal letters have also been kept. Among telegrams in Mukhtar's files were those he received from Jibaje in N'Guigmi and Abdullahi in Bilma; for example, telegrams dated 9 May 1934 and 13 Feb. 1934.
6. Interview with Alhaji Jibaje, 7 June 1972 (tape 17 and 19); and Mani Abdou, 5 June 1972 (tape 16).
7. Interview with Muhamman Kane, 17 Nov. 1972 (tape 46); and Bashir Mukhtar, 1 Dec. 1972 (tape 51).
8. Mukhtar papers, telegram to Gajere Mouapak, Kano, no date; interview with Alhaji Jibaje Ali, 7 June 1972 (tape 17 and 19).
9. Mukhtar papers, file of telegrams received between 17 Jan. 1933 and 4 July 1935. Copies of communications by telegram for earlier and later periods could not be located.
10. Mukhtar papers, record debts from Feb. 1939 to May 1945; Mukhtar to manager of the co-operative at Bilma, 21 Aug. 1934; Lieut. Périquet, représentant de

l'artillerie to Mukhtar, 24 Jan. 1934; interview with Abdu Agali, 7 Oct. 1972 (tape 34), who is one of Mukhtar's wives' half-brothers.

11. Mukhtar kept his records in chronological order rather than filing them separately for each debtor and creditor. This system probably changed after 1945, when Mukhtar modernized his accounting system, but it is not possible to be certain because records for the later period could not be found.

12. Mukhtar to the director of the Niger Co. (C.N.F.), 16 Sept. 1934; Mukhtar to Patterson, Zochonis and Co., 6 Sept. 1935; S.C.O.A. Kano branch to Mukhtar, 21 Nov. 1934; Mandrides and Logios to Mukhtar, 12 Sept. 1934. For background on these firms see A. G. Hopkins, *An Economic History of West Africa* (New York, 1973), 199–200; J. Mars, 'Extra-territorial Enterprises', in *Mining, Commerce, and Finance in Nigeria*, ed. Margery Perham (London, 1947), 43–58; and P. T. Bauer, *West African Trade: A Study of Competition, Oligopoly and Monopoly in a Changing Economy* (New York, 1967), 65–86, 195–227. For general background on S.C.O.A. and C.F.A.O., see Catherine Coquery-Vidrovitch, 'L'Impact des intérêts coloniaux: S.C.O.A. et C.F.A.O. dans l'Ouest Africain', *Journal of African History*, 16 (1975), 595–621.

13. Mukhtar papers, P. Pon, director of S.C.O.A. Kano branch to Mukhtar, 3 Sept. 1934; statement from the Bank of British West Africa, 31 Dec. 1947.

14. Mukhtar papers, receipts from 1936 from files for A. J. Tangalakis and Co., Patterson, Zochonis and Co., and J. Christian and Co.

15. Mukhtar papers, Mukhtar to the director of the Niger Co. (C.N.F.), 16 Sept. 1934.

16. Interview with Bashir Mukhtar, 1 Dec. 1972 (tape 51).

17. John D. Collins, 'Government and Groundnut Marketing in Rural Hausa Niger: The 1930s to the 1970s in Magaria', Ph.D. dissertation, The Johns Hopkins University, 1974, 18–48; ADZ, Économie générale, Subdivision Magaria, Rapport économique 3ᵉ trimestre 1928; NNAK, SNP 17/2 14686, Kano Province Annual Report, 1930.

18. ANS. 2G 36-7, Niger, Rapport économique 1936.

19. Bauer, *West African Trade*, 412; G. K. Helleiner, *Peasant Agriculture, Government and Economic Growth in Nigeria* (Homewood, Ill., 1966), 500.

20. Mukhtar papers, Mukhtar to the Commandant at Zinder, 28 Sept. 1936; Mukhtar to the Commandant at Zinder, 28 June 1938; map referred to in the letter of 28 Sept. 1936; maps of plots in groundnut markets in Zinder and Matameye, 1937; interview with Alhaji Jibaje, 7 June 1972 (tape 17 and 19).

21. ANS, 2G 36 7, Niger, Rapport économique, 1936; NNAK, SNP 17/2 14686, Kano Province Annual Report, 1930; for motor transport in Nigeria, see J. Mars, 'Extra-territorial Enterprises', 121.

22. Muhammad Bugreen had passed through Zinder about the time trans-Saharan trade ended as an agent of a Tripoli merchant remembered in Zinder only as 'Effendi', Muhammad Bugreen was known as Muhammad Effendi. He is said to have travelled to Manchester as an agent of Zinder-based North Africans. See ANS, 6F4, Rapport sur le mouvement caravanier entre le territoire du Niger, les oasis, et la Tripolitaine', signed DeMaugras (?), undated; the nature of the business relation between Mukhtar and Muhammad Bugreen is unclear; some claim that Mukhtar received loans: interview with Muhamman Kane, 17 Nov. 1972 (tape 46). See also interview with Alhaji Jibaje, 7 June 1972 (tape 17 and 19); Mukhtar papers, notebook containing duplicates of waybills, Mar. 1940; ADZ, Situation alimentaire, Mukhtar to Commandant at Zinder, 22 June 1950.

23. Mukhtar papers, Mukhtar to Governor of Niger in care of chef de subdivision, Travaux Publiques du Niger-Est, 14 Jan. 1949; S.C.O.A. Kano branch to Mukhtar, 21 Oct. 1937.

24. Mukhtar papers, record of debts from Feb. 1939 to May 1945. For trade in cloth

from Nigeria toward North Africa, see interview with Alhaji Saley Ahmadu, 30 Sept. 1972 (tape 35 and 36).

25. Interview with Bernard Ruetsch, 11 Aug. 1972 (tape 25); NNAK, SNP 17/4 34242, Kano Province Annual Report, 1941.

26. Mukhtar papers, Mukhtar to Michel Gastine, 1 Jan. 1949; Mukhtar to the Commandant at Zinder, 19 Nov. 1948; S.C.O.A. Zinder branch to Mukhtar, 30 July 1949.

27. Mukhtar papers, receipts for rent payments, 19 May 1939 to 1 Jan. 1956.

28. Bashir Mukhtar remembers seeing a bank statement in 1945 reporting a balance of 336,000,000 metropolitan francs; interview of 1 Dec. 1972 (tape 51).

29. Interview with Bashir Mukhtar, 1 Dec. 1972 (tape 51); Mukhtar papers, Mukhtar to Pierre Souchette, 5 Feb. 1949.

30. Mukhtar papers, Mukhtar to J. Brassos, Oran, 30 Sept. 1935; Mukhtar to Société Job, 72 Boulevard Strasbourg, Toulouse, 6 Sept. 1935; Mukhtar to Louis Dreyfus, Hertschtel and Co., Paris, 25 May 1950; Mukhtar to Central Pièces Accessoires, La Garenne, 15 Mar. 1950.

31. Yves Péhaut, 'L'Arachide au Niger', in *Étude d'économie africaine*, ed. D.-G. Lavroff (Paris, 1970), 66, 89.

32. Interview with Bashir Mukhtar, 1 Dec. 1972 (tape 51).

33. Mukhtar papers, Mukhtar to Commandant at Zinder, 15 Jan. 1949, 9 Feb. 1947, 27 June 1938, 4 Jan. 1939, and 9 Apr. 1941; in these letters Mukhtar listed the names of his employees, their occupational classification, and in some cases their place of birth.

34. Mukhtar papers, Mukhtar to Pierre Souchette, 5 Feb. 1949; Mukhtar to the Commandant at Zinder, 29 Jan. 1940.

35. Interview with Bashir Mukhtar, 1 Dec. 1972 (tape 51).

36. Mukhtar papers, Mukhtar to Bruin, 29 May 1955; Mukhtar received a personal letter from General de Gaulle thanking him for a gift which Mukhtar gave him when de Gaulle came through Zinder on a tour in the early 1950s. Numerous letters on personal matters show that Mukhtar corresponded with friends in the administration and military after they were transferred from Niger. On his use of the administration to collect bad debts, see Mukhtar to Colonel commandant la bataillon des tirailleurs sénégalais, 10 Aug. 1934; and ADZ, Sultanat, Mukhtar to Commandant at Zinder, 10 Feb. 1939.

CHAPTER X

1. A. G. Hopkins, *An Economic History of West Africa* (New York, 1973), 167–71; Dudley Seers, 'The Stages of Economic Development of a Primary Producer in the Middle of the Twentieth Century', *Economic Bulletin of Ghana*, 7 (1963), 57–69.

2. For background see Michael Crowder, *West Africa Under Colonial Rule* (London, 1968), 501–2.

3. G. K. Helleiner, *Peasant Agriculture, Government and Economic Growth in Nigeria* (Homewood, Ill., 1966), 107–18; Jan S. Hogendorn, 'The Origins of the Groundnut Trade in Northern Nigeria', Ph.D. dissertation, London School of Economics, 1966.

4. ADZ, Rapport commercial, 4e trimestre 1915; John D. Collins, 'Government and Groundnut Marketing in Rural Hausa Niger: The 1930s to the 1970s in Magaria', Ph.D. dissertation, The Johns Hopkins University, 1974, 29.

5. Collins, 'Groundnut Marketing', 37; ADZ, Économie Générale, Subdivision Magaria, Rapport économique, 3e trimestre 1928.

6. PRO CO/657/13, Report on the Groundnut Trade in Kano Province, 1924;

NNAK, SNP 9/12 635/1925, Kano Province Annual Report, 1924; NNAK, SNP 17/2 14686, Kano Province Annual Report, 1930; NNAK, SNP 17/3 21236, Kano Province Annual Report, 1933; Collins, 'Groundnut Marketing', 37–8 and 37n., 38n.

7. Collins, 'Groundnut Marketing', 38–40, Yves Péhaut, 'L'Arachide au Niger', in *Étude d'économie africaine*, ed. D.-G. Lavroff (Paris, 1970), 15–71.
8. Collins, 'Groundnut Marketing', 49.
9. Collins, 'Groundnut Marketing', 49–107.
10. Collins, 'Groundnut Marketing', 109–49.
11. Banque Centrale des États de l'Afrique de l'Ouest, 'Rapport d'activité, 1963'; Péhaut, 'L'Arachide au Niger', 73–4; International Monetary Fund, *Surveys of African Economies*, Vol. 3: *Benin, Ivory Coast, Mauritania, Niger, Senegal, Togo, Upper Volta* (Washington, 1970), 511–16, 438–40, 463–4; Collins, 'Groundnut Marketing', 176.
12. C. Raynaut, 'Le Cas de la région de Maradi, (Niger)', in *Sécheresses et famines du Sahel*, ed. J. Copans (Paris, 1975), II. 5–43.
13. Interview with Manzo Muhamman Abubakar, 5 June 1972 (tape 16), and 6 Dec. 1972 (tape 51); and Abdu 'dan Kalla, 15 Aug. 1972 (tape 27); Collins, 'Groundnut Marketing', 122–6.
14. Guy Nicolas, 'La Pratique traditionnelle du crédit au sein d'une société subsaharienne, vallée de Maradi, Niger', *Cultures et Développement*, 6 (1974), 737–73. For lending in Kano, see Ahmed Beita Yusuf, 'Capital Formation and Management among the Muslim Hausa Traders of Kano, Nigeria', *Africa*, 45 (1975), 167–82.
15. Guy Belloncle, 'Une expérience d'animation coopérative au Niger' (Centre de Recherches Coopératives No. 27, Paris, 1966); Guy Belloncle and Dominique Gentil, 'Pédagogie de l'implantation du mouvement coopératif au Niger' (Niamey, cyclostyled, 1968); and Stephen Baier, 'The Development of Agricultural Credit in French-Speaking West Africa with Special Reference to Niger', M.A. thesis, University of Wisconsin–Madison, 1969, 35–55.
16. ADZ, Rapport politique, 4ᵉ trimestre 1915; ANS, 2G 20–12, Niger, Rapport économique d'ensemble, 1920; ANS, 2G 23–8, Niger, Rapport agricole, 2ᵉ trimestre 1923; interview with Suley Sami, 30 Sept. 1972 (tape 35); and Abdu 'dan Dabba, 23 Oct. 1972 (tape 42).
17. ADZ, Économie générale, Commandant Zinder to Governor of Niger, 19 July 1940 (transmitting a report with information on artisans in 1921 and in 1940). See also Eric J. Arnould, 'Petty Craft Production and the Underdevelopment Process in Zinder, Republic of Niger', unpublished paper, 27 Apr. 1978. Arnould cites 1977 census data showing growth in a category defined as 'crafts population', presumably a broader group than the colonial craft census included; but this segment of the population failed to grow as quickly as the population at large.
18. ADZ, R. Mayo, 'Recensement des artisans et commerçants de la ville de Zinder', 3 Aug. to 23 Oct. 1971.
19. Interview with Alhaji Usman 'dan Haladu, 29 Nov. 1972 (tape 51).
20. Interview with Mato Sarki, 7 Dec. 1972 (tape 52).
21. Collins, 'Groundnut Marketing', 321–8; interview with Manzo Muhamman Abubakar, 5 June 1972 (tape 16), and 6 Dec. 1972 (tape 34); and Alhaji Jibaje Ali, 7 June 1972 (tape 17 and 19), and 7 Oct. 1972 (tape 34).
22. ANF-OM, Agence des Colonies, C141 Dr100, report dated 27 Nov. 1928, signature illegible; interview with Bernard Ruetsch, 11 Aug. 1972 (tape 25); and Abba Musa, 16 May 1972 (tape 6 and 9).
23. ADZ, Traite d'arachides, Issa Ibrahim, Secrétaire général, Syndicat des Acheteurs d'Arachides, to Governor of Niger, 4 Oct. 1955; ADZ, Traite

d'arachides, Association Professionnelle des Acheteurs d'Arachides to Commandant Zinder, 5 Oct. 1955; ADZ, Traite d'arachides, Association Professionalle des Acheteurs d'Arachides to the Governor of Niger, 29 Oct. 1955; Traite d'arachides, J. Dequecker to the Governor of Niger, 29 July 1955.

24. ADZ, Traite d'arachides, Djibo Bakary, Secrétaire U.D.N. to Governor of Niger, 20 May 1955; see also Finn Fuglestad, 'Djibo Bakary, the French, and the Referendum of 1958 in Niger', *Journal of African History*, 14 (1973), 313–30.
25. Collins, 'Groundnut Marketing', 138–9.
26. Fuglestad, 'Djibo Bakary', 319 ff.
27. Péhaut, 'L'Arachide', 66, 89.
28. J. Mars, 'Extra-Territorial Enterprises', in *Mining, Commerce and Finance in Nigeria*, ed. Margery Perham (London, 1947), 121; NNAK, SNP 17/3 27810, Kano Province Annual Report, 1936; NNAK, SNP 17/2 14686, Kano Province Annual Report, 1930.
29. Péhaut, 'L'Arachide', 57–61, 77–80; Jean Thrill, 'Étude sur l'opération hirondelle' (Niamey: cyclostyled, 1959).
30. ADZ, Traite d'arachides, Governor Bruin to Commandant at Zinder, 3 Nov. 1955; ADZ, Traite d'arachides, J. Dequecker to Governor of Niger, 16 Aug. 1955.
31. ADZ, Traite d'arachides, Djibo Bakary to Governor of Niger, 20 May 1955.
32. Mukhtar papers, Mukhtar to Governor of Niger, in care of Chef de la subdivision Travaux Publiques du Niger-Est, 12 Dec. 1948.
33. Denis Danset, 'La Commercialisation du bétail et de la viande au Niger' (Niamey: cyclostyled, 1964), 43; République du Niger, Ministère de l'Économie Rurale, Direction de Section de l'Élevage, 'Situation de l'élevage en République du Niger' (Paris, 1970), 51; République Française, Secrétariat d'État aux Affaires Étrangères, 'Approvisionnement en viandes de l'Afrique Centre Ouest' (Paris, 1969), I. 35, ·90. Derrick Thom, 'The Niger-Nigeria Borderlands: A Politico-Geographical Analysis of Boundary Influence upon the Hause', Ph.D. dissertation, Michigan State University, 1970, 193–6; interview with Malam Lawan Sidi, 12 May 1972 (tape 21 and 22); and Sarkin Kasuwa Garba Adabar, 4 Sept. 1972 (tape 30 and 31).
34. This information is from a survey conducted by the author in the Zinder cattle market between April and December 1972 (see appendix II); and from interviews with Usman 'dan Shaba, 9 June 1972 (tape 24); and Musa 'dan Maduga, 14 June 1972 (tape 24).
35. Interview with 'dan Ruga Awakas, 6 Sept. 1972 (tape 31); Sharubutu Isa, 6 Sept. 1972 (tape 31); Tahiru 'dan Maduka, 6 Sept. 1972 (tape 31); and Mani 'dan Tambai, 6 Sept. 1972 (tape 31).
36. For a contrasting case, see Sara S. Berry, *Cocoa, Custom, and Socio-Economic Change in Rural Western Nigeria* (Oxford, 1975), 83–5. During the depression cocoa farmers in western Nigeria continued to invest in cocoa by expanding the area of land devoted to the crop. Berry explains continued investment in cocoa by examining other sectors of the economy where opportunities for employment and investment declined more sharply than in cocoa farming.

CONCLUSION

1. For arguments about population pressure on land, see William W. Seifert and Nake Kamrany, *A Framework for Evaluating Strategies for the Development of the Sahel-Sudan Region: Vol. I, Project Objectives, Methodologies, and Major Findings*, Centre for Policy Alternatives, Report No. CPA-74-9 (Cambridge,

Mass.); for summaries of reports by all major donor agencies, see Jacques Giri, 'An Analysis and Synthesis of Long Term Development Strategies for the Sahel', Organization for Economic Co-operation and Development, mimeographed, 1976; for relations between human activities, the land, and the climate, see Derek Winstanley, 'Climatic Changes and the Future of the Sahel', in *The Politics of a Natural Disaster: The Case of the Sahel Drought*, ed. Michael Glantz (New York, 1976), 189–213; Norman H. MacLeod, 'Dust in the Sahel: Cause of Drought?' in *Politics of a Natural Disaster*, 214–31; H. N. LeHouerou, 'Ecological Management of Arid Grazing Lands Ecosystems', in *Politics of a Natural Disaster*, 267–81; and A. T. Grove, 'Desertification in the African Environment', *African Affairs*, 73 (1974), 137–51. See also David Dalby, R. J. Harrison Church, and Fatima Bezzaz, editors, *Drought in Africa* 2, International African Institute, Special Environmental Report No. 6 (London, 1977).

Bibliography

ARCHIVAL MATERIAL

I. France
    A. Archives Nationales de France, Ministère d'Outre-Mer.
        1. Afrique III, IV, XIII. Occupation of Bilma, caravan traffic in the desert.
        2. Afrique Occidentale Française I, II, VI, VII, XVI, XIV. Saharan policy, relations with foreign governments, reports of *chefs de poste*, caravan traffic.
        3. Niger VII, XVI. Administrative organization, political reports.
        4. Affaires Économiques. Agricultural reports, food supply, Sol mission to Niger in 1931–2, *Sociétés de prévoyance*, commerce among Saharan oases, statistics on agricultural production in AOF, export duties, motor transport, banking, currency, and exchange rates.
        5. Affaires Politiques. Situation of Bilma, resistance to French rule, periodic political reports.
        6. Agence des Colonies. Animal husbandry, veterinary reports, Agriculture reports, lists of merchants in Niger, commercial activity.
    B. Archives Nationales de France, Ministère des Affaires Étrangères. Afrique Occidentale. Commerce, Anglo-French relations, Saharan policy.
    C. Institut d'Élevage et de Médecine Vétérinaire des Pays Tropicaux. Unpublished reports on livestock trade.
II. Great Britain
    Public Record Office
        1. Foreign Office 101 series. Correspondence and reports from Tripoli consuls.
        2. Colonial Office 657 series. Northern Nigeria annual reports, annual veterinary reports, and annual agricultural reports.
        3. Colonial Office 465 series. Price series, commercial statistics.
III. Niger
    A. Archives Administratives du Niger, Niamey.
        1. Trésor des Chartes. Periodic administrative and political reports, correspondence from Agadez and Bilma, Tibesti

operations, monographs on Agadez and Zinder.

    2. Rapports de Tournée. Local economic conditions, settlement patterns, migrations, and price series.

B. Archives du Départment de Zinder.

    1. Correspondence. Registers of outgoing correspondence from the *cercle* of Zinder, 1902–6; 1908–10; 1916–19; 1923–4. Registers of outgoing correspondence from the headquarters of the Zinder region of Haut-Sénégal-Niger, 1909–10.

    2. Periodic Reports. Jan.–Dec. 1902; Jan. 1903–June 1904; July 1908–Aug. 1915; Dec. 1915–Feb. 1916.

    3. File marked 'Sultanat'. Historical and administrative information on the rulers of Zinder, records of the prosecution of the suspects in the plot of 1906, reorganizations of the administration.

    4. File marked 'Économie générale'. A few periodic economic reports, price fluctuations, and correspondence on economic conditions.

    5. File marked 'Traite d'arachides'. Correspondence on the problems of peanut weighers, problems associated with evacuating the peanut crop, and administrative regulation of peanut-marketing.

C. Archives Militaires de Zinder.
Report of Sergeant Bouthel, on conditions and administration in Zinder in late 1899.

D. Archives de la Subdivision de Tanout.
Correspondence with the *commandant* in Zinder, copies of a few periodic reports.

E. Archives de la subdivision de Tessaoua.
Correspondence.

IV. Nigeria
Nigerian National Archives, Kaduna.
    Secretariat, Northern Provinces. Kano Province Annual Reports, correspondence concerning the revolt of 1916, correspondence on trade with Niger, reports on the cattle trade and cattle traders of Kano.

V. Senegal
Archives Nationales du Sénégal, Dakar.
    1. 2G series. Annual economic, political, agricultural, and veterinary reports from Niger, *Rapports d'ensemble* from Niger, AOF annual economic reports, reports from the *Agence Économique* of the *Ministère des Colonies* in Paris.

    2. 1D series. Reports on the escort of salt caravans, reports on the Tibesti operations.

    3. 6F 4 series. Caravan traffic from Tripoli to the interior, 1908–14.

4. 11G series. Annual political reports from Niger, 1905–7, migrations, report of a *tournée* in 1904.
5. 21G series. Immigration to AOF, measures against the Lebanese.
6. 22G 33. General statistics for Niger, 1916.

VI. United States

National Archives of the United States of America, Washington, D.C.

Record Group 59, T 40. Correspondence from United States consuls in Tripoli.

ORAL SOURCES

The following is a catalogue of the Baier collection of the Archives of Traditional Music, Indiana University, Bloomington, Indiana, and the *Centre Régionale de Documentation pour la Tradition Orale* in Niamey, Niger.

Tape No.	Side	Interviews
1	1	Alhaji Amadu 'dan Ladi, Niamey, 8 Feb. 1972
		Alhaji Yahu Isa, Niamey, 10 Feb. 1972
	2	Alhaji Yahu Isa (continuation)
		Sarkin Dawaki Ibrahim Muhamman, Zinder, 31 Mar. 1972
2	1	Sarkin Dawaki Ibrahim Muhamman (continuation)
		Sarkin Dawaki Ibrahim Muhamman, Zinder, 8 Apr. 1972
	2	Sarkin Dawaki Ibrahim Muhamman (continuation)
		Sarkin Dawaki Ibrahim Muhamman, Zinder, 10 Apr. 1972
3	1	Dodo Mai Zaga, Zinder, 7 Apr. 1972
		Manzo Warzuga, Zinder, 13 Apr. 1972
	2	Manzo Warzuga (continuation)
		Dan Zara Muhamman, Zinder, 13 Apr. 1972
		Sarkin Dawaki Ibrahim Muhamman, Zinder, 21 Apr. 1972
4	1	Sami Sharubutu, Zinder, 11 May 1972
	2	Sami Sharubutu (continuation)
		Sarkin Dawaki Ibrahim Muhamman, Zinder, 22 Apr. 1972
		Sarkin Dawaki Ibrahim Muhamman, Zinder, 29 Apr. 1972
5	1	Sarkin Dawaki Ibrahim Muhamman (continuation)
		Usuman 'dan Haladou, Myrria, 30 Apr. 1972
		Suley Kakizaina, Myrria, 30 Apr. 1972

	2	Sarkin Dawaki Ibrahim Muhamman, Zinder, 8 May 1972
		Alhaji Katche Ango, Zinder, 6 May 1972
6	1	Abba Musa, Zinder, 8 May 1972
		Abba Musa, Zinder, 16 May 1972
	2	Abba Musa (continuation)
7	1	Abba Musa (continuation)
		Alhaji Adamu Abdumumuni, Zinder, 8 May 1972
	2	Alhaji Adamu Abdumumuni (continuation)
		Malam Cillo Alassan, Zinder, 9 May 1972
8	1	Malam Cillo Alassan (continuation)
		Musa Matam, Zinder, 16 Sept. 1972
		Ilia 'dan Madugu Ilias, 18 Sept. 1972
	2	Ilia 'dan Madugu Ilias (continuation)
9	1	Malam Mahamman 'dan Jawo, Zinder, 14 Sept. 1972
		Ilali Ali, Zinder, 15 Sept. 1972
	2	Ilali Ali (continuation)
10	1	Kelilan Gaja, Zinder, 18 Apr. 1972
	2	Kelilan Gaja (continuation)
11	1	Kelilan Gaja, Zinder, 19 Apr. 1972
	2	Kelilan Gaja (continuation)
12	1	Ahmadu Galdi, Zinder, 25 Apr. 1972
	2	Ahmadu Galdi (continuation)
13	1	Malam Hassan Modibo, Tanout, 23 May 1972
		Abdulhamit bin Muhammad, Tanout, 24 May 1972
	2	Abdulhamit bin Muhammad (continuation)
14	1	Isufu Muhamadu, Tanout, 24 May 1972
		Yacuba Sidi, Tanout, 24 May 1972
	2	Kasko Ahamat, Tanout, 25 May 1972
15	1	Muhamman Kane, Zinder, 20 May 1972
	2	Muhamman Kane (continuation)
		Muhamman Kane, Zinder, 21 May 1972
16	1	Kasko Ahamat, Tanout, 24 May 1972
		Muhamman Kane, Zinder, 21 May 1972
		Malam Almahadi Atalib, Zinder, 1 June 1972
		Muhamman Kelilan, Zinder, 1 June 1972
	2	Malam Almahadi Atalib (continuation)
		Muhamman Kelilan (continuation)
		Manzo Muhamman Abubaker, Zinder, 5 June 1972
		Mani Abdu, Zinder, 5 June 1972
17	1	Manzo Muhamman Abubakar (continuation)
		Mani Abdu (continuation)

		Alhaji Jibaje Ali, Zinder, 7 June 1972
	2	Alhaji Jibaje Ali (continuation)
18	1	Malam Ali Yaro, Zinder, 13 May 1972
	2	Malam Ali Yaro (continuation)
19	1	Malam Ali Yaro (continuation)
		Alhabi Jibaje Ali (continuation from tape 17)
	2	(blank)
20	1	Ilali Ali, Zinder, 17 May 1972
	2	Ilali Ali (continuation)
		Mato Sarki, Zinder, 20 May 1972
21	1	Malam Manzoza Almajiri, Zinder, 9 May 1972
		Malam Lawan Sidi, Zinder, 12 May 1972
	2	Malam Lawan Sidi (continuation)
22	1	Malam Lawan Sidi (continuation)
	2	Malam Lawan Sidi (continuation)
		Muhamman Kane (continuation of tape 15)
23	1	Gani Maburu, Zinder, 10 May 1972
	2	Hassan 'dan Uban Kassan, Zinder, 10 May 1972
		Muhamman Kane (continuation of tape 22)
24	1	Usman ('dan Shaba) 'dan Malam Shaibu, Zinder, 9 June 1972
		Musa 'dan Maduga, Zinder, 14 June 1972
	2	Musa 'dan Maduga (continuation)
		Alhaji Nahum Muhamman Balbaila, Zinder, 15 June 1972
		Umma Maina, Zinder, 8 Aug. 1972
25	1	Umma Maina (continuation)
		Bernard Ruetsch, Zinder, 11 Aug. 1972
	2	Bernard Ruetsch (continuation)
		Abba Musa, Zinder, 14 Aug. 1972
		Isufu Abande, Zinder, 14 Aug. 1972
26	1	Isufu Abande (continuation)
	2	Isufu Abande (continuation)
27	1	Abdu 'dan Kalla, Zinder, 15 Aug. 1972
	2	Abdu 'dan Kalla (continuation)
		Malam Almahadi Atalib, Zinder, 17 Aug. 1972
		Umbutu Gangan, Zinder, 18 Aug. 1972
		Malam Amadu Hassan, Zinder, 18 Aug. 1972
28	1	Malam Amadu Hassan (continuation)
		Isa(n) Talha 'dan Tambari Azowar, Zinder, 19 Aug. 1972

	2	Isa(n) Talha (continuation) Malam Almahadi Atalib, Zinder, 19 Aug. 1972
29	1	Malam Almahadi Atalib (continuation) Ma'azu Isa, Barbarkiya, 28 Aug. 1972
	2	Alhassan Muhamman, Barbarkiya, 28 Aug. 1972 Ibrahim Muhamman, Barbarkiya, 28 Aug. 1972 Hamza Isa, Barbarkiya, 28 Aug. 1972
30	1	Hamza Isa (continuation) Gani Maburu, Zinder, 2 Sept. 1972 Habou Abdullah, Zinder, 2 Sept. 1972
	2	Gani Maburu (continuation) Habou Abdallah (continuation) Sarkin Kasuwa Garba Adabar, Zinder, 4 Sept. 1972
31	1	Sarkin Kasuwa Garba Adabar (continuation) Saley Isufu, Dogo, 6 Sept. 1972 Tahiru 'dan Maduka, Dogo, 6 Sept. 1972
	2	Tahiru 'dan Maduka (continuation) Mani Tambai, Dogo, 6 Sept. 1972 'dan Ruga Awakas, Dogo, 6 Sept. 1972
32	1	Sharubutu Isa, Dogo, 6 Sept. 1972 Abdurahaman Bedari, Zinder, 7 Aug. 1972 Ma'azu Isa, Barbarkiya, 11 Sept. 1972
	2	Ma'azu Isa (continuation) Hamza Isa, Barbarkiya, 11 Sept. 1972
33	1	Hamza Isa (continuation) Isa Kadir, Barbarkiya, 11 Sept. 1972 Lushe Bukari, Barbarkiya, 11 Sept. 1972
	2	Lushe Bukari (continuation) Garba Surkule, Myrria, 29 Nov. 1972
34	1	Ilia Ilias, Zinder, 18 Sept. 1972 Malam Musa Sidi, Zinder, 21 Sept. 1972
	2	Malam Musa Sidi (continuation) Alhabi Jibaje, Zinder, 7 Oct. 1972 Abdu Agali, Zinder, 7 Oct. 1972
35	1	Mutari Nuhu, Tessaoua, 30 Sept. 1972 Malam Kulu Maila, Tessaoua, 30 Sept. 1972 Amurmur Yaro, Tessaoua, 30 Sept. 1972 Suley Sami, Tessaoua, 30 Sept. 1972
	2	Suley Sami (continuation) Muhamman Baban Gabas, Tessaoua, 30 Sept. 1972 Alhaji Sali Amadu, Tessaoua, 30 Sept. 1972

36   1   Alhaji Sali Amadu (continuation)
              Suley Sami (continuation)
              Sani Fari, Tessaoua, 30 Sept. 1972
              Suley Ekade, Tessaoua, 1 Oct. 1972

     2   Suley Ekade (continuation)
              Muhamman Baban Gabas, Tessaoua, 1 Oct. 1972
              Malam Cillo Alassan, Zinder, 6 Oct. 1972

37   1   Muhamman Kane, Zinder, 22 May 1972
              Muhamman Kane, Zinder, 30 May 1972
     2   Muhamman Kane (continuation)

38   1   Muhamman Kane (continuation)
              Mato Sarki, Zinder, 31 Aug. 1972
     2   Mato Sarki (continuation)

39   1   Mato Sarki (continuation)
              Muhamman Kane, Zinder, 8 Oct. 1972
              Wuru Tambari Mayaki, Gangara, 12 Oct. 1972
     2   Wuru Tambari Mayaki (continuation)
              Garba Idrisa, Gangara, 12 Oct. 1972
              Jibo Gaje, Gangara, 12 Oct. 1972

40   1   Fokondo Mala, Malam Tilum, 13 Oct. 1972
              Mai Gari Kanto Kolo, Malam Tilum, 13 Oct. 1972
     2   Fokondo Mala (continuation)
              Habu Taliya, Gangara, 13 Oct. 1972
              Guntu Nomo, Gangara, 13 Oct. 1972
              Usuman Saidu, Gangara, 13 Oct. 1972
              Atari Madiguburi, Malam Tilum, 14 Oct. 1972

41   1   Atari Madiguburi (continuation)
              Haruna Biriam, Malam Tilum, 14 Oct. 1972
              Amadu Mai, Malam Tilum, 14 Oct. 1972
     2   Atari Madiguburi (continuation of side 1)
              Haruna Biriam (continuation of side 1)
              Wuru Tambari Mayaki, Gangara, 14 Oct. 1972
              Musa Wantasa, Gangara, 14 Oct. 1972
              Sidian Igidan, Gangara, 14 Oct. 1972

42   1   Wuru Tambari Mayaki (continuation of tape 41)
              Mallam Cillo Alassan, Zinder, 20 Oct. 1972
              Abdu 'dan Daba, Zinder, 23 Oct. 1972
     2   Abdu 'dan Daba (continuation)

43   1   Abdurahaman Bedari, Zinder, 24 Oct. 1972
              Abdurahaman Idi Bagindi, Zinder, 27 Oct. 1972
              Hajiya 'yar Idi Bagindi, Zinder, 27 Oct. 1972
              Isa(n) Talha, Zinder, 27 Oct. 1972

	2	Isa(n) Talha (continuation)
		Malam Musa Gambo, Zinder, 31 Oct. 1972
		Sanda 'dan Gayi, Zinder, 31 Oct. 1972
44	1	Sanda 'dan Gayi (continuation)
		Haruna Muhamman, Zinder, 31 Oct. 1972
	2	Kasum Wurga, Zinder, 1 Nov. 1972
		Malam Ali Yaro, Zinder, 3 Nov. 1972
45	1	Malam Ali Yaro (continuation)
		Abdu 'dan Daba, Zinder, 9 Nov. 1972
		Malam Lawan Sidi, Zinder, 13 Nov. 1972
	2	Malam Lawan Sidi (continuation)
46	1	Malam Lawan Sidi, Zinder, 14 Nov. 1972
		Muhamman Kane, Zinder, 17 Nov. 1972
	2	Muhamman Kane (continuation)
		Muhamman Kane, Zinder, 18 Nov. 1972
47	1	Muhamman Kane (continuation)
		Usuman 'dan Shaba 'dan Malam Shaibu, 23 Nov. 1972
	2	Usuman 'dan Shaba 'dan Malam Shaibu (continuation)
		Muhamman Kane, Zinder, 24 Nov. 1972
48	1	Muhamman Kane (continuation)
		Sarkin Maka'da (praise songs), Zinder, 30 Nov. 1972
	2	Sarkin Maka'da (continuation)
		Sarkin Maka'da, Zinder, 1 Dec. 1972
49	1	Amadu Mai Gayya, Zinder, 2 Dec. 1972
		Muhamman Kane, Zinder, 3 Dec. 1972
	2	Muhamman Kane (continuation)
		Muhamman Kane, Zinder, 4 Dec. 1972
50	1	Muhamman Kane (continuation)
		Muhamman Kane, Zinder, 6 Dec. 1972
	2	Muhamman Kane (continuation)
51	1	Alhaji Usuman Haladu, Myrria, 29 Nov. 1972
		Sarkin Dogari Haruna Salau, Myrria, 29 Nov. 1972
		Sarkin Ma'kera Ali Abubakar, Myrria, 29 Nov. 1972
		Bashir Moctar, Zinder, 1 Dec. 1972
	2	Bashir Moctar (continuation)
		Manzo Muhamman Abubakar, Zinder, 6 Dec. 1972
52	1	Abdu 'dan Kalla, Zinder, 6 Dec. 1972
		Barma Usman Muhamman, Zinder, 6 Dec. 1972
		Mato Sarki, Zinder, 12 Dec. 1972
	2	Mato Sarki (continuation)

298

PUBLISHED MATERIAL

ABADIE, MAURICE. *La Colonie du Niger*. Paris: Éditions Géographiques, Maritimes et Coloniales, 1927.

AFRIQUE OCCIDENTALE FRANÇAISE. *L'Afrique Occidentale Française, 1931*. Vol. 1, *Colonies, Productions*. Paris: Agence Économique AOF, 1931.

——, *Problèmes de la viande en A.O.F.* 3 vols. Paris: Diloutremer, 1954–5.

——, Service de la Statistique. *Recensement de la population non-autochtone de l'Afrique Occidentale Française en juin 1951*. Dakar: AOF, 1951.

AMSELLE, JEAN-LOUP. 'Parenté et commerce chez les Kooroko', in *The development of Indigenous Trade and Markets in West Africa*, ed. Claude Meillassoux. London: Oxford University Press, 1971.

AMSELLE, J.-L. 'Les Réseaux marchands kooroko', *African Urban Notes*, 5, No. 2 (Summer 1970), pp. 143–58.

ANENE, J. C. 'Liaison and Competition between Sea and Land Routes in International Trade from the Fifteenth Century – the Central Sudan and North Africa', in *Les Grandes Voies maritimes dans le monde, xv–xix siècles*. Paris: SEVPEN, 1965.

ASHTOR, ELIAHU. 'Banking Instruments between the Muslim East and the Christian West', *The Journal of European Economic History*, 1, No. 3 (1972), 553–73.

AUSTEN, RALPH A. 'The Transsaharan Slave Trade: A Tentative Census', in *The Uncommon Market: Essays in the Economic History of the Atlantic Slave Trade*, ed. J. Hogendorn and H. Gemery. New York: Academic Press, 1979.

BAIER, STEPHEN B. 'Archives in Niger', *History in Africa*, 1 (1974), 155–8.

——, 'Economic History and Development: The Sahelian Economies of Niger', *African Economic History*, 1 (1976), 1–16.

——, 'Trans-Saharan Trade and the Sahel: Damergu, 1870–1930', *Journal of African History*, 18 (1977), 37–61.

——, and DAVID J. KING. 'Drought and the Development of Sahelian Economies: A Case Study of the Hausa and Tuareg', *Land Tenure Center Newsletter*, 54 (1974).

——, and PAUL E. LOVEJOY. 'The Tuareg of the Central Sudan: Gradations in Servility at the Desert Edge (Niger and Nigeria)', in *Slavery in Africa: Historical and Anthropological Perspectives*, ed. Suzanne Miers and Igor Kopytoff. Madison, Wisconsin: University of Wisconsin Press, 1977.

BAILLAUD, EMILE. 'La Question monétaire en Afrique occidentale', *Annales des Sciences Politiques*, 20 (Sept. 1905), 561–77.

——. *Sur les routes du Soudan*. Toulouse: Edouard Privat, 1902.

Banque Centrale des États de l'Afrique de l'Ouest. 'Rapport d'activité 1963'. Paris: BCEAO, 1964.

BARTH, FREDERIK. *Ethnic Groups and Boundaries*. Bergen: Universitets-Forlaget, 1969.

——. 'A General Perspective on Nomad-Sedentary Relations in the Middle East', in *The Desert and the Sown: Nomads in the Wider Society*, ed. Cynthia Nelson. Institute of International Studies, Research Series, No. 21. Berkeley: University of California Press, 1973.

BARTH, HEINRICH. *Travels and Discoveries in North and Central Africa*. 3 vols. 1857; rpt. London: Frank Cass, 1965.

BAUER, P. T. *West African Trade: A Study of Competition, Oligopoly and Monopoly in a Changing Economy*. 2nd ed. New York: Kelley, 1967.

BELLONCLE, GUY. 'Une expérience d'animation coopérative au Niger', Centre de recherches coopératives, No. 27. Paris, 1966.

BERNUS, E. 'Drought in the Niger Republic', *Savanna*, 2 (1973), 129–32.

——. 'Les Composantes géographiques et sociales des types d'élevage en milieu touareg', in *Pastoralism in Tropical Africa*, ed. Théodore Monod. London: Oxford University Press, 1975.

——. 'Les Touareg du sahel nigérien', *Cahiers d'Outre-Mer*, 19 (1966), 5–34.

——. 'Récits historiques de l'Azawagh: traditions des Iullemmeden Kel Dinnik', *Bull. IFAN*, 32 (B) (1970), 434–85.

——, and SUZANNE BERNUS. *Du sel et des dattes: introduction à l'étude de la communauté d'In Gall et de Tegidda-n-Tesemt*. Études Nigériennes No. 31. Niamey: CNRSH, 1972. ·

BERRY, SARA S. *Cocoa, Custom, and Socio-Economic Change in Rural Western Nigeria*. Oxford: Oxford University Press, 1975.

BÉTRIX, JEAN. *La Pénétration touareg*. Paris: Charles-Lavairelle, 1911.

BETTOLI, PARMENIO. 'Tripoli Commerciale', *L'Esploratore*, 6, No. 7 (1882), 265–73.

BISSINGER, ERHARD. 'Commerce of Tripoli', *U.S. Consular Reports*, 93 (May 1888), 231–2.

BISSON, J. 'Éleveurs caravaniers et vieux sédentaires de l'Aïr', *Travaux de l'Institut des Recherches Sahariennes*, 23 (1964), 95–110.

BOAHEN, A. ADU. *Britain, the Sahara and the Western Sudan*. London: Oxford University Press, 1964.

BONTE, PIERRE. *L'Élevage et le commerce du bétail dans l'Ader Doutchi-Majya*. Études Nigériennes No. 23. Niamey: CNRSH, 1967.

——. 'Esclavage et relations de dépendance chez les Touaregs Kel Gress', in *L'Esclavage en Afrique précoloniale*, ed. Claude Meillassoux. Paris: Maspero, 1975.

BOUBOU HAMA. *Contribution à la connaissance de l'histoire des Peul*. Paris: Présence Africaine, 1968.

——. *Histoire du Gobir et de Sokoto*. Paris: Présence Africaine, 1967.

——. *Recherches sur l'histoire des Touareg sahariens et soudanais*. Paris: Présence Africaine, 1967.

BOURGEOT, ANDRÉ. 'Idéologie et appelations ethniques: l'exemple Twareg', *Cahiers d'Études Africaines*, 48 (1972), 533–53.

BOVILL, E. W. *The Golden Trade of the moors.* 2nd ed. New York: Oxford University Press, 1968.

BRENNER, LOUIS. 'The North African Trading Community in the Nineteenth-Century Central Sudan', in *Aspects of West African Islam*, ed. D. F. McCall and N. R. Bennett. Boston University Papers on Africa, Vol. 5. Boston: Boston University, 1971.

——. *The Shehus of Kukawa: A History of the Al-Kanemi Dynasty of Bornu.* London: Oxford University Press, 1973.

BRÛLARD, M. 'Aperçu sur le commerce caravanier Tripolitaine-Ghat-Niger vers la fin du XIXe siècle', *Bulletin de Liaison Saharienne*, 9, No. 31 (1958), 202–15.

CALASSANTI-MOTYLINSKI, A. DE. *Le Dialecte berbère de R'edamès.* Paris: Leroux, 1904.

CAMPBELL, DUGALD. *On the Trail of the Veiled Tuareg.* London: Seeley, Service, 1928.

CAPOT-REY, ROBERT. *Le Sahara français.* Vol. 2 of *L'Afrique blanche française.* Paris: Presses Universitaires de France, 1953.

CAUNEILLE, A. 'Les Goueyda d'Ouenzerik: tribu du Fezzan', *Bulletin de Liaison Saharienne*, 11, No. 38 (1960), 161–73.

Chambre de Commerce d'Alger. *Missions économiques dans le Hoggar et au Niger (Mars-avril 1932).* Alger: Imprimerie Africa, 1932.

CHAPELLE, JEAN. *Nomades noirs du Sahara.* Paris: Plon, 1957.

CLAPPERTON, HUGH. *Journal of a Second Expedition into the Interior of Africa, from the Bight of Benin to Soccatoo.* 1929; rpt. London: Frank Cass, 1966.

CLAUZEL, J. 'Les Hiérarchies sociales en pays Touareg', *Travaux de l'Institut des Recherches Sahariennes*, 21 (1962), 120–75.

COFFIN, WILLIAM. 'Cotton-Goods Trade, Tripoli-in-Barbary', *Monthly Consular and Trade Reports*, 347 (Aug. 1909), 69–70.

——. 'Ostrich Feathers of Tripoli', *Monthly Consular and Trade Reports*, 347 (Aug. 1909), 55–6.

——. 'Sudan Tanned Skins', *Monthly Consular and Trade Reports*, 349 (Oct. 1909), 122–3.

——. 'Tripoli-in-Barbary, Review of Trade Conditions', in *Commercial Relations of the United States with Foreign Countries.* Washington, D.C.: Dept. of Commerce and Labor, 1911.

COHEN, ABNER. 'Cultural Strategies in the Organization of Trading Diasporas', in *The Development of Indigenous Trade and Markets in West Africa.* London: Oxford University Press, 1971.

——. *Custom and Politics in Urban Africa: A study of Hausa Migrants in Yoruba Towns.* London: Routledge and Kegan Paul, 1969.

——. 'Politics of the Kola Trade', *Africa*, 36, No. 1 (1966), 18–36.

——. 'The Social Organization of Credit in a West Africa Cattle Market', *Africa*, 35, No. 1 (1965), 8–20.

COHEN, RONALD. *Dominance and Defiance: A Study of Marital Instability in an Islamic African Society.* Washington: American Anthropological Association, 1971.

COLVIN, LUCIE G. 'The Commerce of Hausaland 1780–1833', in *Aspects of West African Islam*, ed. D. F. McCall and N. R. Bennett. Boston University Papers on Africa, Vol. 5. Boston: B.U., 1971.

CORDELL, DENNIS D. 'Eastern Libya, Wadai, and the Sanūsīyya: a *Tarīka* and a Trade Route', *Journal of African History*, 18 (1977), 21–36.

CROWTHER, SAMUEL and JOHN TAYLOR. *The Gospel on the Banks of the Niger.* 1859; reprint London: Dawsons, 1968.

CURTIN, PHILIP. *Economic Change in Precolonial Africa: Senegambia in the Era of the Slave Trade.* Madison, Wisconsin: University of Wisconsin Press, 1975.

DAHL, GUDRUN and ANDERS HJORT. *Having Herds: Pastoral Herd Growth and Household Economy.* Stockholm: Stockholm University, Department of Social Anthropology, 1976.

D'ATTONOUX, J. B. 'Tripoli et les voies commerciales du Soudan', *Annales de Géographie*, 5 (1895–6), 193–9.

DAVID, PHILIPPE. *Maradi: l'ancien état et l'ancienne ville: site, population, histoire.* Documents des Études Nigériennes, No. 18. Niamey: CNRSH, 1964.

DE BARY, ERWIN. *Le Dernier Rapport d'un Européen sur Ghat et les Touareg de l'Aïr (journal de voyage d'Erwin de Bary, 1876–77).* Transl. Henri Schirmer. Paris: Fischbacher, 1898.

DE ST. CROIX, F. W. *The Fulani of Northern Nigeria.* 1945; reprint Farnborough; Gregg, 1972.

DELAVIGNETTE, R. 'Souvenirs du Niger', *Revue Française d'Histoire d'Outre-Mer*, 54 (1967), 13–24.

DENHAM, D. and CLAPPERTON, H. *Narrative of Travels and Discoveries in Northern and Central Africa, in the years 1822, 1823, and 1824.* London: J. Murray, 1826.

DICKSON, C. H. 'Account of Ghadames', *Journal of the Royal Geographical Society*, 30 (1860), 255–60.

DICKSON, R. 'Report on the Trade and Commerce of Tripoli for the Year ending 1898', 'Great Britain, House of Commons, Sessional Papers, 1899, vol. 103.

DIGUEN, ABOU [pseud.]. *Mon voyage au Soudan tchadien.* Paris: Roger (1929?).

DOUTRESSOULE, GEORGES. *L'Élevage au Niger.* Mortain: Letellier, 1924.

——. *L'Élevage en l'Afrique Occidentale Française.* Paris: Larose, 1947.

DRUMMOND-HAY, F. R. 'Report on the Trade and Commerce of Tripoli for the Year 1879', Great Britain, House of Commons, Sessional Papers, 1880, vol. 74.

——. 'Report on the Trade and Commerce of Tripoli for the Year 1881',

Great Britain, House of Commons, Sessional Papers, 1883, vol. 72.

——. 'Report on the Trade and Commerce of Tripoli for the Year 1888', Great Britain, House of Commons, Sessional Papers, 1889, vol. 81.

DUNBAR, ROBERTA ANN. 'Slavery and the Evolution of Nineteenth-Century Damagaram (Zinder, Niger)', in *Slavery in Africa: Historical and Anthropological Perspectives*, ed. Suzanne Miers and Igor Kopytoff. Madison, Wisconsin: University of Wisconsin Press, 1977.

DUPIRE, MARGUERITE. 'Exploitation du sol, commaunautés résidentielles, et organisation lignagère des pasteurs woDaaBe (Niger), in *Pastoralism in Tropical Africa*, ed. Theodore Monod. London: Oxford University Press, 1975.

——. *Les Facteurs humaines de l'économie pastorale*. Études Nigériennes No. 6. Paris: CNRS, 1962.

——. *Organisation sociale des Peul: étude d'ethnographie comparée*. Paris: Plon, 1970.

——. *Peuls nomades: étude descriptive des Wodaabe du sahel nigérien*. Paris: Institut d'Ethnologie, 1962.

——. *La Place du commerce et des marchés dans l'économie des Bororo (Ful'be) nomades du Niger*. Études Nigériennes No. 3. Niamey: IFAN, 1961.

——. 'Trade and Markets in the Economy of the Nomadic Fulani of Niger (Bororo)', in *Markets in Africa*, ed. Paul Bohannan and George Dalton. Evanston: Northwestern University Press, 1962.

DUPRÉ, GEORGES and PIERRE-PHILIPPE REY. 'Reflections on the Pertinence of a Theory of the History of Exchange', transl. Elizabeth Hindress, *Economy and Society*, 2 (1973), 131–63.

DUVEYRIER, HENRI. *La Confrérie musulmane de Sidi Mohammed Ben Ali es Senousi*. Paris: Société de Géographie, 1884.

——. *Sahara algérien et tunisien: journal de route publié et annoté par C. Maunoir et H. Schirmer*. Paris: Challamel, 1905.

——. *Exploration du Sahara: Les Touaregs du nord*. Paris: Challamel, 1864.

EICHER, C. L. and C. LIEDHOLM. *Growth and Development of the Nigerian Economy*. East Lansing, Michigan: Michigan State University Press, 1970.

EKUNDARE, R. OLUFEMI. *An Economic History of Nigeria*. London: Methuen, 1973.

ELDBLOM, LARS. *Structure foncière, organisation et structure sociale: une étude comparative sur la vie socio-économique dans les trois oasis lybiennes de Ghat, Mourzouk, et particulièrement Ghadames*. Trans. Yvonne Richter and Marianne Melrad. Lund: Uniskol, 1968.

ETIÉVANT, LIEUT. 'Le Commerce tripolitain dans le centre africain', *Afrique Française*, 9 (Sept. 1910), 277–82.

FÉRAUD, L. CHARLES. *Annales tripolitaines*. Tunis: Tournier, 1927.

BIBLIOGRAPHY

FERGUSON, W. 'Nigerian Livestock Problems', in *Markets and Marketing in West Africa*, Proceedings of a Seminar held in the Centre of African Studies, University of Edinburgh, 29 and 30 Apr. 1966. Edinburgh: University of Edinburgh, 1966.

FISHER, HUMPHREY J. and VIRGINIA ROWLAND. 'Firearms in the Central Sudan', *Journal of African History*, 12 (1971), 215–39.

FONFERRIER, CAPITAINE. 'Études historiques sur le mouvement caravanier dans le cercle d'Agadez', *BCEHSAOF*, 7 (1923), 302–14.

FORD, JOHN. *The Role of Trypanosomiases in African Ecology: A Study of the Tsetse Fly Problem*. Oxford: Clarendon Press, 1971.

FOUREAU, FERNAND. *D'Alger au Congo par le Tchad: Mission saharienne Foureau-Lamy*. Paris: Masson, 1902.

——. *Documents scientifiques de la mission saharienne*. Paris: Masson, 1905.

France, Institut National de la Statistique et des Études Économiques. Service de la Coopération. *Étude démographique du Niger*. Paris: 1962–3.

France, Secrétaire d'État aux Affaires Étrangères, 'Approvisionnement en viandes de l'Afrique Centre Ouest: Analyse de la situation actuelle et projections'. Cyclostyled. Paris, 1969.

FUGLESTAD, FINN. 'Djibo Bakary, the French, and the referendum of 1958 in Niger', *Journal of African History*, 14, No. 2 (1973), 313–30.

——. 'La Grande Famine de 1931 dans l'Ouest nigérien: réflexions autour d'une catastrophé naturelle', *Revue Française d'Histoire d'Outre-Mer*, 61, No. 222 (1974), 18–33.

——. 'Les Révoltes des Touareg du Niger', *Cahier d'Études Africaines*, 49 (1973), 82–120.

FURLONG, CHARLES WELLINGTON. *The Gateway to the Sahara: Observations and Experiences in Tripoli*. New York: Schribners, 1909.

GADEL, CAPITAINE. 'Les Oasis de la région de Bilma', *Bulletin de la Société de Géographie de l'Afrique Occidentale Française*, 2, No. 30 (1907), 85–114.

GADEL, COMMANDANT. 'Notes sur Bilma et les oasis environnantes', *Revue coloniale*, 7, No. 51 (1907), 361–86.

GADEN, HENRI. 'Notice sur la résidence de Zinder', *Revue des Troupes Coloniales*, 2, No. 17 (1903), 608–56; 2, No. 18 (1903), 740–94.

GAMORY-DUBOURDEAU, P. 'Étude sur la création des cantons de sédentarisation dans le cercle de Zinder, et particulièrement dans la subdivision centrale (arrondissement de Mirria)', *BCEHSAOF*, 8 (1924), 239–58.

GAST, MARCEAU. 'Évolution de la vie économique et structures sociales en Ahaggar de 1860 à 1965', *Travaux de l'Institut des Recherches Sahariennes*, 24 (1965), 129–43.

GOODY, JACK. 'Adoption in Cross-Cultural Perspective', *Comparative*

Studies in Society and History, 11, No. 1 (1969), 55–78.

——. 'Strategies of Heirship', *Comparative Studies in Society and History*, 15, No. 1 (1973), 3–20.

—— and T. M. Mustafa. 'The Caravan Trade from Kano to Salaga', *Journal of the Historical Society of Nigeria*, 3, No. 4 (1967), 611–16.

Grall, Lieut. 'Le Secteur nord du cercle de Gouré', *Bull. IFAN*, 7 (1945), 1–46.

Grandin, Capitaine. 'Notes sur l'industrie et le commerce du sel au Kawar et en Agram', *Bull. IFAN*, 13 (1951), 488–533.

Great Britain, Colonial Office. *Report of the Nigerian Livestock Commission*. London: His Majesty's Stationery Office, 1950.

Grove, A. T. 'Desertification in the African Environment', *African Affairs*, 73 (1974), 137–51.

——. 'A Note on the remarkably Low Rainfall in the Sudan Zone in 1913', *Savanna*, 2 (1973), 133–8.

Hamani, Djibo. *Contribution à l'étude de l'histoire des états hausa: l'Adar précolonial (République du Niger)*. Études Nigériennes No. 38. Niamey: CNRSH, 1975.

Hancock, W. K. *Survey of British Commonwealth Affairs*. 2 vols. London: Oxford University Press, 1942.

Helleiner, Gerald K. *Peasant Agriculture, Government, and Economic Growth in Nigeria*. New York: Irwin, 1966.

Hill, Polly. 'Hidden Trade in Hausaland', *Man*, 4, No. 3 (1969), 392–409.

——. 'Landlords and Brokers: A West African Trading System', *Cahiers d'Études Africaines*, 6 (1966), 349–66.

——. 'A Plea for Indigenous Economics: The West African Example', *Economic Development and Cultural Change*, 15, No. 1 (Oct. 1966), pp. 10–20.

——. *Rural Hausa: a Village and a Setting*. Cambridge: Cambridge University Press, 1972.

——. *Studies in Rural Capitalism in West Africa*. Cambridge: Cambridge University Press, 1969.

——. 'Two Types of West African House Trade', in *The Development of Indigenous Trade and Markets in West Africa*, ed. Claude Meillassoux. London: Oxford University Press, 1971.

Hogendorn, Jan. S. 'The Origins of the Groundnut Trade in Northern Nigeria', in *Growth and Developmnent of the Nigerian Economy*, ed. C. Eicher and C. Liedholm. East Lansing, Michigan: Michigan State University Press, 1969.

——. *Nigerian Groundnut Exports: Origins and Early Development*. London and Zaria: Oxford University and Ahmadu Bello University Press, 1978.

Hopen, C. E. *The Pastoral Ful'be Family in Gwandu*. London: Oxford University Press, 1958.

HOPKINS, A. G. 'The Creation of a Colonial Monetary System: The Origins of the West African Currency Board', *African Historical Studies*, 3 (1970), 101–32.

——. *An Economic History of West Africa*. New York: Colombia University Press, 1973.

——. 'Economic Imperialism in West Africa: Lagos, 1880–1892', *Economic History Review*, 12 (1968), 580–606.

HOROWITZ, MICHAEL. 'Herdsman and Husbandman in Niger: Values and Strategies', in *Pastoralism in Tropical Africa*, ed. T. Theodore Monod. London: Oxford University Press, 1975.

IDIART, P. 'Métayage et régimes fonciers dans la région de Faguibine (Cercle de Goundam – Soudan)', *Études Rurales*, 2 (1961), 37–59; 3 (1961), 21–44.

Institut Fondamentale d'Afrique Noire. *Contribution à l'étude de l'Aïr*. Mémoires, No. 10. Paris: Larose, 1950.

JAGO, THOMAS S. 'Report on the Trade and Economy of the Vilayet of Tripoli in Northern Africa, during the Past Forty Years', Great Britain, House of Commons, Sessional Papers, 1902, vol. 103.

JEAN, CAMILLE-CHARLES. *Les Touareg du sud-est: leur rôle dans la politique saharienne*. Paris: Larose, 1909.

JOALLAND, JULES. *Le Drame de Dankori: Mission Voulet-Chanoine, Mission Joalland-Meynier*. Paris: Agro, 1930.

JOHNSON, MARION. 'Calico Caravans: The Tripoli-Kano Trade After 1880', *Journal of African History*, 17 (1976), 95–117.

——. 'Cloth on the Banks of the Niger', *Journal of the Historical Society of Nigeria*, 6 (1973), 353–64.

JONES, CUTHBERT B. 'Trade and Agricultural Prospects of Tripoli', *Consular Reports*, 8 (June 1881), 950.

JONES, G. I. 'The Beef Cattle Trade in Nigeria', *Africa*, 16, No. 1 (Jan. 1946).

KEENAN, JEREMY. *The Tuareg: People of Ahaggar*. London: Kane, 1977.

KUCZYNSKI, R. R. *Demographic Survey of the British Colonial Empire*. Vol. 1: *West Africa*. London: Oxford University Press, 1948.

LAIZÉ, M. 'L'Islam dans le territoire militaire du Niger', *BCEHSAOF*, 1919, 177–83.

LANDER, RICHARD L. *The Niger Journal of Richard and John Lander*. Ed. Robin Hallett. London: Routledge and Kegan Paul, 1965.

LANDER, R. L. *Records of Captain Clapperton's Last Expedition*. London: H. Colburn and R. Bentley, 1830.

LARRAT, R. *Problèmes de la viande en A.O.F.* 3 vols. Paris: Diloutremer, 1954–5.

LAST, MURRAY. *The Sokoto Caliphate*. New York: Humanities Press, 1967.

LAYA, DIOULDE. 'Interviews with Farmers and Livestock Owners in the Sahel', *African Environment*, 1 (1975), 49–93.

LHOTE, HENRI. *Les Touareg du Hoggar.* 2nd edn. Paris: Payot, 1955.

LE SOURD, M. 'Tarik el Kawar', *Bull. IFAN*, 8 (1946), 1–54.

LOVEJOY, PAUL E. *Caravans of Kola: Hausa Trade with Asante, 1700–1900.* Zaria: Oxford University Press, forthcoming.

——. 'Interregional Monetary Flows in the Pre-colonial Trade of Nigeria', *Journal of African History*, 15 (1974), 563–87.

——. 'The Kambarin Beriberi: The Formation of a Specialized Group of Hausa Kola Traders in the Nineteenth Century', *Journal of African History*, 14 (1973), 633–52.

——. 'Plantations in the Economy of the Sokoto Caliphate', *Journal of African History*, 19 (1978), 341–68.

——. 'The Wholesale Kola Trade of Kano', *African Urban Notes*, 5 (1970), 129–42.

——, and STEPHEN BAIER. 'The Desert-Side Economy of the Central Sudan', *International Journal of African Historical Studies*, 8 (1975), 553–83. Reprinted in *The Politics of a Natural Disaster: The Case of the Sahel Drought*, ed. Michael Glantz. New York: Praeger, 1976.

McPHEE, ALLAN. *The Economic Revolution in British West Africa.* London: Routledge, 1926.

MAINET, G. 'L'Élevage dans la région de Maradi', *Cahiers d'Outre-Mer*, 69 (1965), 32–72.

MALEY, JEAN. 'Mécanisme des changements climatiques aux basses latitudes', *Palaeogeography, Palaeoclimatology and Palaeoecology*, 14 (1973), 193–227.

MARS, J. 'Extra-Territorial Enterprises', in *Mining, Commerce, and Finance in Nigeria*, ed. Margery Perham. London: Faber and Faber, 1947.

MARTY, PAUL. 'L'Islam et les tribus dans la colonie du Niger', *Revue des Études Islamiques*, 1930, 333–432. Exerpt published Paris: Geuthner, 1930.

MAUROY, M. *Du commerce des peuples de l'Afrique septentrionale.* Paris: Imprimeurs Unis, 1845.

MÉHIER DE MATHUISIEULX, H. 'Une mission en Tripolitaine', *Renseignements Coloniaux*, Jan. 1904, 20–34.

——. *A travers la Tripolitaine.* Paris: Hachette, 1912.

——. *La Tripolitaine d'hier et de demain.* Paris: Hachette, 1912.

MEILLASSOUX, CLAUDE. 'Essai d'interprétation du phénomène économique dans les sociétés traditionnelles d'auto-subsistence', *Cahiers d'Études Africaines*, 4 (1960), 38–67.

MÉNIAUD, JACQUES. *Haut-Sénégal-Niger.* Vol. 2. Paris: Larose, 1912.

MÈRY, G. 'Renseignements commerciaux sur le mouvement des échanges entre la Tripolitaine et le Soudan central', *Bulletin du Comité de l'Afrique Française*, Sept. 1893, 2–4.

MEYNIER, OCTAVE. *La Mission Joalland-Meynier.* Paris: Éditions de l'Empire Français, 1947.

MIÉGE, J.-L. *Le Maroc et l'Europe.* 4 vols. Paris: Presses Universitaires de France, 1961–3.

MIGEOD, F. W. H. *Through Nigeria to Lake Chad.* London: Heath Cranton, 1924.

MIRCHER, H. *Mission de Gadamès (septembre, octobre, novembre, et décembre, 1862). Rapports officiels et documents à l'appui.* Alger: Duclaux, 1863.

MITTENDORF, H. J., and S. G. WILSON. *Livestock and Meat Marketing in Africa.* United Nations Food and Agriculture Organization publication No. 14235-R-1. Rome: F.A.O., 1961.

MOHAMMED EL-HACHAICHI. *Voyage au pays Senoussia.* Paris: Challamel, 1912.

MOLL, CAPT. 'La Situation économique de la région de Zinder', *Renseignements coloniaux*, 9 Dec. 1901, 197–9.

MONTEIL, P.-L. *De Saint-Louis à Tripoli par le Tchad.* Paris: Alcan, 1894.

MOORE, NOEL TEMPLE. 'Report on the Trade and Commerce of Tripoli for the Year 1891', Great Britain, House of Commons, Sessional Papers, 1892, vol. 84.

MOREL, E. D. *The Affairs of West Africa.* London, 1902; rpt. 1968, F. Cass, London.

MORGAN, W. B. and J. C. PUGH. *West Africa.* London: Methuen, 1969.

MORTIMORE, M. J. 'The Changing Resources of Sedentary Communities in Aïr, Southern Sahara', *Geographical Journal*, 31 (1972), 71–91.

——. 'Famine in Hausaland, 1973', *Savanna*, 2 (1973), 103–7.

——. 'Population Distribution, Settlement, and Soils in Kano Province, Northern Nigeria 1931–62', in *The Population of Tropical Africa*, ed. John C. Caldwell and Chukuba Okonjo. London: Longmans, 1968.

——, ed. *Zaria and its Region.* Ahmadu Bello University, Department of Geography, Occasional Paper No. 4 Zaria: Ahmadu Bello University, 1970.

—— and J. WILSON. *Land and People in the Kano Close-Settled Zone.* Zaria: Ahmadu Bello University, 1965.

MUHAMMAD UBA ADAMU. 'Some Notes on the Influence of North African Traders in Kano', *Kano Studies*, 1, No. 4 (1968), 43–9.

MURPHEY, ROBERT F. 'Tuareg Kinship', *American Anthropologist*, 69 (1967), 163–70.

NACHTIGAL, GUSTAV. *Sahara and Sudan: Ergebnisse Sechsjahriger Reisen in Afrika.* 3 vols. 1879–81; rpt. Graz: Akademische Druck- u. Verlagsanstalt, 1967.

NEWBURY, C. W. *British Policy Towards West Africa: Select Documents, 1875–1914.* London: Oxford University Press, 1971.

—— 'North African and Western Sudan Trade in the Nineteenth Century: A Reevaluation', *Journal of African History.* 7 (1966), 233–46.

NICHOLSON, SHARON. 'Saharan Climates in Historic Times', in *The Sahara and the Nile*, ed. H. Faure and M. E. J. Williams. Forthcoming.

NICOLAISEN, JOHANNES. *Ecology and Culture of the Pastoral Tuareg with Particular Reference to Aïr and Ahaggar*. Nationalmuseet, Ethnografisk raekke, Vol. 9. Copenhagen: National Museum, 1963.

——. *Structures politiques et sociales des Touaregs de l'Aïr et de l'Ahaggar*. Transl. Suzanne Bernus. Études Nigériennes No. 7. Paris: IFAN and CNRS, 1962.

NICOLAS, FRANCIS. 'Contribution à l'étude des Twareg de l'Aïr', in *Contribution à l'étude de l'Aïr*. Mémoires de l'Institut Fondamental de l'Afrique Noire No. 10. Paris: Larose, 1950.

——. 'Étude sur la coutume et la tradition: matriarcat et patriarcat', in *Contribution à l'étude de l'Aïr*. Mémoires de l'IFAN No. 10. Paris: Larose, 1950.

——. 'Étude sur l'Islam, les confréries et les centres maraboutiques chez les Twareg du Sud', in *Contribution à l'étude de l'Aïr*. Mémoires de l'Institut Fondamental de l'Afrique Noire, No. 10. Paris: Larose, 1950.

——. *Tamesna: les Ioullimmenden de l'Est*. Paris: Imprimerie Nationale, 1950.

——. 'La Transhumance chez les Iullemmeden de l'Est', *Travaux de l'Institut des Recherches Sahariennes*, 4 (1947), 111—24.

NICOLAS, GUY. 'Aspects de la vie économique dans un canton du Niger: Kantché', *Cahiers de l'Institut de Science Économique Appliquée*, série V, No. 5 (1962), 105–88.

——. 'Les Catégories d'ethnie et de fraction ethnique au sein du système social hausa', *Cahiers d'Études Africaines*, 15 (1975), 399–442.

——. 'Circulations des biens et échanges monétaires au nord Niger', *Cahiers de l'Institut de Science Économique Appliquée*, série V, No. 5 (1962).

——. 'Circulation des richesses et participation sociale dans une société Hausa du Niger;. Cyclostyled. Bordeaux: Centre Universitaire de Polycopiage de l'AEGB, 1964.

——. *Dynamique sociale et appréhension du monde au sein d'une société hausa*. Travaux et Mémoires, Institut d'Ethnologie No. 78. Paris: Institut d'Ethnologie, 1975.

——. 'Étude de marché en pays haoussa'. Cyclostyled. Bordeaux: Centre Universitaire de Polycopiage de l'AEGB, 1964.

——. 'Fondements magico-religieux de pouvoir politique au sein de la principauté Hausa du Gobir'. *Journal de la Société des Africanistes*, 39, No. 2 (1969), 199–231.

——. *Notes ethnographiques sur le terroir, l'agriculture et l'élevage dans la vallée de Maradi*. Études Nigériennes No. 8. Niamey: IFAN, 1963.

——. 'La Pratique traditionnelle du crédit au sein d'une société subsaharienne, vallée de Maradi, Niger', *Cultures et Développement*, 6

(1974), 737–73.

——. 'Un Village bouzou au Niger: étude d'un terroir', *Cahiers d'Outre-Mer*, 58 (1962), 138–65.

—— and GUY MAINET. *La Vallée du Gulbi du Maradi*. Documents des Études Nigériennes No. 16. Niamey: IFAN, 1964.

NORRIS, H. T. *The Tuaregs: Their Islamic Legacy and Its Diffusion in the Sahel*. Warminster, Wilts: Aris and Phillips, 1975.

OKIGBO, P. N. C. *Nigerian National Accounts 1950–1957*. Enugu: Government Printer, 1962.

——. *Nigerian Public Finance*. Evanston, Ill.: Northwestern University Press, 1965.

OLAYIDE, S. O. and S. A. ONI. 'Short-Run Demand for Beef in Western Nigeria', *Nigerian Journal of Social and Economic Studies*, 11, No. 2 (1969), 165–72.

OLUWASANMI, H. A. *Agriculture and Nigerian Economic Development*. London: Oxford University Press, 1966.

OSUNTOKUN, JIDE. 'Nigeria's Colonial Government and the Islamic Insurgency in French West Africa, 1914–1918', *Cahiers d'Études Africaines*, 15 (1975), 85–94.

PATAI, RAPHAEL. *The Tents of Jacob: The Diaspora Yesterday and Today*. Englewood Cliffs, N.J.: Prentice-Hall, 1971.

PÉHAUT, YVES. 'L'Arachide au Niger', in *Étude d'économie africaine*, ed. D.-G. Lavroff. Paris: Pedone, 1970.

PERHAM, MARGERY, ed. *The Economics of a Tropical Dependency*. 2 Vols. London: Faber and Faber, 1946.

PÉRIÉ, JEAN. 'Notes historiques sur la région de Maradi', *Bull. IFAN*, 1, Nos. 2–3 (1939), 377–401.

PIAULT, MARC-HENRI. *Histoire mawri: Introduction à l'étude des processus constitutifs d'un état*. Paris: CNRS, 1970.

PINEAU, GUY. 'La Guerre de Kaossen, 1916–1919', *Afrique Littéraire et Artistique*, 10 (1970), 50 5.

POLANYI, KARL. *Dahomey and the Slave Trade: An Analysis of an Archaic Economy*. Seattle: University of Washington Press, 1966.

RASH, YEHOSHUA. 'Des colonisateurs sans enthousiasme: les premières années françaises au Damerghou', *Revue Française d'Histoire d'Outre-Mer*, 59 (1972), 5–69, and 59 (1972), 240–308.

RAULIN, HENRI. 'Travail et régimes fonciers au Niger', *Cahiers de l'Institut de Science Économique Appliquée*, 166 (1965), 119–39.

RAYNAUT, C. 'Le Cas de la région de Maradi (Niger)', in *Sécheresses et famines du Sahel*, ed. J. Copans. Paris: Maspéro, 1975.

REIBELL, EMILE. *Carnet de route de la mission saharienne Foureau-Lamy, 1898–1900*. Paris: Plon, 1931.

RENARD, J. 'Étude sur l'évolution des Kel Gress vers la sédentarisation', *BCEHSAOF*, 2 (1922), 252–62.

RENNELL OF RODD, FRANCIS. *People of the Veil*. London: MacMillan, 1926.

RICHARDSON, JAMES. *Narrative of a Mission to Central Africa*. 2 vols. London: Chapman and Hale, 1853.

——. *Travels in the Great Desert of Sahara in the Years of 1845 and 1846*. London: R. Bently, 1848.

RICHER. A. *Les Touaregs du Niger (Région de Tombouctou-Gao): Les Oulliminden*. Paris: Larose, 1924.

RIOU, LIEUTENANT. 'L'Azalay d'automne 1928', *Renseignements Coloniaux*, May 1929, p. 281.

ROBINET, A. H. 'Cuirs et peaux au Niger: perspectives, production', *Revue de l'Élevage et de Médecine Vétérinaire des Pays Tropicaux*, 17, nouvelle série No. 1 (1964).

ROWLING, C. W. *Report on Land Tenure, Kano Province*. Kaduna: Government Printer, 1949.

ROYAL GEOGRAPHICAL SOCIETY. *Records of the African Association 1788–1831*. Ed. Robin Hallett. London: T. Nelson, 1964.

SALIFOU, ANDRÉ. *Le Damagaram ou sultanat de Zinder au XIXᵉ siècle*. *Études Nigériennes*, No. 27. Niamey: Centre Nigérien des Recherches en Sciences Humaines, 1971.

——. 'Kaocen et le siège d'Agades, 1916–1917', *Journal de la Société des Africanistes*, 42, No. 1 (1972), 193–195.

——. *Kaoussan ou la révolte senoussiste*. *Études Nigériennes* No. 33. Niamey: CNRSH, 1973.

——. 'Malan Yaroh, un grand négociant du Soudan central à la fin du XIXᵉ siècle', *Journal de la Société des Africanistes*, 42, No. 1 (1972), 7–27.

SCHIRMER, HENRI. *Le Sahara*. Paris: Hachette, 1893.

SEIFERT, WILLIAM W. and NAKE M. KAMRANY. *A Framework for Evaluating Strategies for development of the Sahel-Sudan Region: Vol. I; Summary Report: Project Objectives, Methodologies and Major Findings*. Center for Policy Alternatives, No. CPA-74-9. Cambridge, Mass.: CPA, Massachusetts Institute of Technology, 1974.

SÉRÉ DES RIVIÈRES, EDMUND. *Histoire du Niger*. Paris: Berger-Levrault, 1965.

SMALDONE, JOSEPH P. 'The Firearms Trade in the Central Sudan', in *Aspects of West African Islam*, ed. D. F. McCall and Boston: Boston University, 1971.

——. *Warfare in the Sokoto Caliphate: Historical and Sociological perspectives*. Cambridge: Cambridge University Press, 1977.

SMITH, MARY. *Baba of Karo: A Woman of the Moslem Hausa*. New York: Praeger, 1964.

SMITH, MICHAEL G. *The Economy of the Hausa Communities of Zaria*. London: HMSO, 1955.

——. 'Hausa Inheritance and Succession', in *Studies in the Laws of Succession in Nigeria*, ed. J. Derrett. London: Oxford University Press, 1965.

———. 'A Hausa Kingdom: Maradi under Dan Baskore, 1854–1875', in *West African Kingdoms in the Nineteenth Century*, ed. D. Forde and P. Kaberry. London: Oxford University Press, 1967.

———. 'The Hausa System of Social Status', *Africa*, 29 (1959), 239–51.

———. 'Introduction' to *Baba of Karo: A Woman of the Moslem Hausa*, by Mary Smith. New York: Praeger, 1964.

———. *Government in Zazau 1800–1950*. London: Oxford University Press, 1960.

STAUDINGER, PAUL. *Im Herzen des Hausalander*. Berlin: Lundsberger, 1889.

STENNING, DERRICK J. *Savannah Nomads: A Study of the Wodaabe Pastoral Fulani of Western Bornu Province, Northern Region, Nigeria*. London: Oxford University Press, 1959.

STEWART, C. C. 'Southern Saharan Scholarship and the *Bilad al-Sudan*', *Journal of African History*, 17 (1976), 73–94.

STRYKER, J. DIRCK. 'The Malian Cattle Industry', *Journal of Modern African Studies*, 12 (1974), 441–58.

SURET-CANALE, JEAN. *French Colonialism in Tropical Africa*. Transl. Till Gottheiner. London: Hurst, 1971.

TAMBO, DAVID C. 'The Sokoto Caliphate Slave Trade in the Nineteenth Century', *International Journal of African Historical Studies*, 9 (1976), 187–217.

TERRAY, EMMANUEL. *Marxism and 'Primitive' Societies*. Transl. Mary Klopper. New York: Monthly Review Press, 1972.

TERRIER, AUGUST. 'L'Oasis de Bilma et les oasis environnantes', *Bulletin du Comité de l'Afrique Française*, 1907, pp. 287–9.

THOM, DERRICK J. *The Niger-Nigeria Boundary 1890–1906: A Study of Ethnic Frontiers and a Colonial Boundary*. Ohio University Center for International Studies, Papers in International Studies No. 23. Athens, Ohio: CIS, 1975.

TILHO, GEN. AUGUST. *Documents scientifiques de la Mission Tilho*. 2 Vols. Paris: Imprimerie Nationale, 1910.

United States, Department of Commerce and Labor, Bureau of Statistics. *Analysis of the Foreign Commerce of the United States, 1895–1905*. Washington, D.C.: Government Printing Office, 1906.

United States, National Monetary Commission. *Statistics for Great Britain, Germany, and France, 1867–1909*. Washington: Government Printer, 1910.

URVOY, YVES. 'Chroniques d'Agades', *Journal de la Société des Africanistes*, 4 (1934), 145–77.

———. 'Histoire des Ioulleminden de l'est', *BCEHSAOF*, 16 (1933), 47–97.

———. *Histoire des populations du Soudan central*. Paris: Larose, 1936, 67–97.

VADALA, R. 'Une colonie tripolitaine à Paris dans le commerce des plumes d'autriche', *Renseignements Coloniaux*, Feb. 1924, p. 89.

——. 'L'Immigration maltaise en pays musulmans', *Revue du Monde Musulman*, 14 (1911), 41–3.

VENEL, LIEUTENANT-COLONEL. 'Le Territoire militaire du Niger au commencement de 1909', *Revue des Troupes Coloniales*, 1909, pp. 307–23.

VIEILLARD, GILBERT. 'Coutumiers du cercle de Zinder, 1932', in *Coutumier Juridique de l'Afrique Occidentale Française*, vol. 3. Paris: Larose, 1939.

VISCHER, HANS. *Across the Sahara from Tripoli to Bornu*. London: Edward Arnold, 1910.

WINSTANLEY, DEREK. 'Climatic Changes and the Future of the Sahel', in *The Politics of a Natural Disaster: The Case of the Sahel Drought,* ed. *Michael Glantz.* New York: Praeger, 1976.

WOOD, JOHN Q. 'Commerce and Industries of Tripoli-in-Barbary', *Daily Consular and Trade Reports*, 164 (13 July 1912), 226–35.

'Le Commerce tripolitain dans la région du Lac Tchad et le Sokoto', *Renseignements Coloniaux*, Aug. 1898, pp. 208–11.

'Élevage de l'autriche et le commerce de ses plumes au Soudan français', *Renseignements Coloniaux*, Jan. 1897, pp. 11–14.

'Étude sur l'approvisionnement en viande de l'Afrique du Centre Ouest', *Bulletin de l'Afrique Noire*, No. 506 (1969), 11284–93.

'Les Greniers de réserve dans le territoire du Niger – note faite d'après plusieurs rapports', *Agronomie Tropicale*, No. 56 (1949), 321–2.

'Zinder', *Bulletin du Comité de l'Afrique Française*, June 1901, pp. 203–4.

UNPUBLISHED PAPERS AND THESES

BABATUNDE AREMU AGIRI. 'Kola in Western Nigeria, 1850–1950: A History of the Cultivation of Cola Nitida in Egba-Owode, Ijebu-Remo, Iwo, and Ota Areas', Unpublished Ph.D. dissertation, University of Wisconsin, 1972.

BAIER, STEPHEN. 'The Development of Agricultural Credit in French-Speaking West Africa with Special Reference to Niger'. Unpublished M.A. thesis, University of Wisconsin, 1969.

——. 'Local Transport in the Economy of the Central Sudan, 1900–1930'. Paper presented at the Conference on the Economic History of the Central Savannah of West Africa, Kano, 10 Jan. 1976.

BELLONCLE, GUY and DOMINIQUE GENTIL. 'Pédagogie de l'implantation du mouvement coopératif au Niger', Cyclostyled. Niamey, 1968.

BOUBOU HAMA. 'Enquête sur le sel – situation du sel au Niger'. Niamey, mimeographed, 1954.

BRENNER, LOUIS. 'The Shehus of Kukawa: A History of the Al-Kanemi Dynasty of Bornu'. Unpublished Ph.D. dissertation, Columbia University, 1968.

BRYSON, REID A. 'Climatic Modification by Air Pollution, II: The Sahelian Effect'. Report 9 of the University of Wisconsin Institute for Environmental Studies, Aug. 1973.

CHEVRIER, S. and A. NIVOLLET. 'Compte-rendu de mission: organisation des relations du Niger avec le Nigéria', Paris, mimeographed, 1967.

Companie Général des Recherches pour l'Afrique. 'Analyse des courants d'échange', Paris: COGERAF, mimeographed, 1961.

COLLINS, JOHN DAVISON. 'Government and Groundnut Marketing in Rural Hausa Niger: The 1930s to the 1970s in Magaria'. Ph.D. dissertation, The Johns Hopkins University, 1974.

CORDELL, DENNIS D. 'The Awlad Sulayman of Chad and Libya: A Study of Raiding and Power in the Chad Basin in the Nineteenth Century'. Unpublished M.A. thesis, University of Wisconsin, 1972.

DANSET, DENIS. 'La Commercialisation du bétail et de la viande au Niger'. Niamey, mimeographed, 1964.

DUNBAR, ROBERTA ANN. 'Damagaran (Zinder, Niger), 1812–1906: The History of a Central Sudanic Kingdom'. Unpublished Ph.D. dissertation, U.C.L.A., 1970.

DURAND-GASSELIN, J. P. 'Échanges inter-Sahariens: mission SEDES-OCRS, 18 Oct.–10 Nov. 1961'. Paris, mimeographed, 1961.

France, Secrétariat d'État aux Affaires Étrangères. 'Approvisionnement en viandes de l'Afrique Centre Ouest'. 3 vols. Paris: SEDES, mimeographed, 1968–9.

——. 'Perspectives économiques et aménagement des voies de communication en Sahara'. Paris: SEDES, mimeographed, 1960.

HOGENDORN, J. S. 'The Origins of the Groundnut Trade in Northern Nigeria'. Unpublished Ph.D. dissertation, London School of Economics, 1966.

KOECHLIN, J. 'Les Problèmes pastoraux en zone sahélienne: programme d'étude des pâturages en République du Niger'. Paris, mimeographed, 1962.

LACROUTS, MARCEL and JEAN TYC. 'Les Ressources animales de la République du Niger: leur exploitation, perspectives de l'avenir'. Paris: Impr. Technography, 1960.

LEPISSIER, H. E., I. M. MACFARLANE, and S. J. HENSTRA. 'Rapport technique sur le déroulement de la compagne conjointe contre la peste bovine en Afrique Centrale et de l'Ouest'. Dakar: O.A.U., Commission Scientifique, Technique et de la Recherche, mimeographed, 1969.

LOVEJOY, PAUL. 'The Hausa Kola Trade (1700–1900): A Commercial System in the Continental Exchange of West Africa'. Unpublished Ph.D. dissertation, University of Wisconsin, 1973.

——. 'The Salt Industry of the Central Sudan: A Preliminary Survey'. Paper presented at the Conference on the Economic History of the Central Savannah of West Africa, Kano, 5–10 January 1976.

MARTY, J. P., J. GREIGERT, and B. PEYRE DE FABRÈGUES. 'Mise en valeur du complexe pastorale situé au nord de l'axe Filingué-Tahoua au Niger'. Paris, mimeographed, 1966.

MASON, MICHAEL. 'The Nupe Kingdom in the Nineteenth Century: A Political History'. Unpublished Ph.D. dissertation, University of Birmingham, 1970.

MAYO, ROBERT. 'Recensement deš artisans et commerçants de la ville de Zinder', 3 août au 23 octobre 1971. Zinder, mimeographed, 1971.

NICHOLSON, SHARON E. 'A Climatic Chronology for Africa: Synthesis of Geological, Historical, and Meteorological Information and Data'. Ph.D. dissertation, University of Wisconsin–Madison, 1976.

Niger, Ministère de l'Économie Rurale. 'Situation de l'élevage en République du Niger, 1968–1970'. Paris: SEDES, mimeographed, 1970.

——, Mission démographique du Niger, 1960. 'Étude démographique du Niger, 1ᵉ partie'. Paris, mimeographed, 1960.

——, Mission économique et pastorale, 1963. 'Étude démographique et économique en milieu nomade'. Paris: SEDES, 1966.

NIVERD, C. 'Étude des problèmes de l'exploitation et de la commercialisation du bétail au Niger'. Niamey: Ministère de la Coopération, mimeographed, 1964.

OKEDIJI, FLORENCE ADEBISI. 'An Economic History of the Hausa-Fulani Emirates of Northern Nigeria, 1900–1939'. Unpublished Ph.D. dissertation, Indiana University, 1970.

PADEN, JOHN N. 'The Influence of Religious Elites on Political Culture and Community Integration in Kano, Nigeria'. Unpublished Ph.D. dissertation, Harvard University, 1968.

QUESTIAUX, JEAN. 'Quelques aspects de l'économie salinière dans les territoires d'Afrique nord-occidentale et centrale'. Unpublished doctoral dissertation, Université d'Alger, 1957.

RENARD, P. and TOUPOU MFOUAPON. 'Étude sur l'évolution des circuits commerciaux de bétail sur pieds dans le périmètre du bassin conventionnel'. Fort Lamy, mimeographed, 1971.

ROBINET, M. A. 'Conditions de commercialisation des cuirs et peaux du Niger'. Paris, mimeographed, 1954 (?).

SALIFOU, ANDRÉ. 'Rivalités tribales et intervention française au Damerghou'. Unpublished paper, August 1971.

SHEA, PHILIP J. 'The Development of an Export Oriented Dyed Cloth Industry in Kano Emirate in the Nineteenth Century'. Ph.D. dissertation, University of Wisconsin–Madison, 1975.

THOM, DERRICK JAMES. 'The Niger-Nigeria Borderlands: A Politico-Geographical Analysis of Boundary Influence upon the Hausa'. Unpublished Ph.D. dissertation, Michigan State University, 1970.

United Nations Food and Agriculture Organization. 'Projet de développement de la production animale et des ressources en eaux dans l'est du Niger: étude agristologique des pâturages de la zone nomade de Zinder'. Rome: FAO, mimeographed, 1970.

——. 'Projet de développement de la production animale et des ressources en eaux dans l'est du Niger: le problème de la commercialisation du bétail sur pied et de la viande dans la région de Zinder, vu du Niger'. Rome: FAO, mimeographed, 1970.

United Nations International Labor Office. 'Rapport au gouvernement de la République du Niger sur l'artisanat rural'. Geneva, mimeographed, 1970.

USUFU BALA USMAN. 'The Transformation of Katsina, c.1796–1903: The Overthrow of the Sarauta System and the Establishment and Evolution of the Emirate'. Ph.D. dissertation, Ahmadu Bello University, 1974.

WORKS, JOHN ARTHUR. 'Pilgrims in a Strange Land: The Hausa Communities in Chad'. Unpublished Ph.D. dissertation, University of Wisconsin, 1972.

Index